Romance of American Petroleum and Gas

A. R. CRUM, Editor in Chief

A. S. DUNGAN, Associate Editor

Romance of American Petroleum and Gas Co.

(M. M. MARCY, General Manager)

PUBLISHERS

311-329 TRIBUNE BUILDING, NEW YORK, N. Y.

THE DERRICK PUBLISHING COMPANY
PRINTERS AND BINDERS
OIL CITY, PA.

TABLE OF CONTENTS.

PREFACE.

THE Petroleum and Natural Gas Industry is a mining business. Its development has been attended by all the excitement incident to mining camps and the usual camp followers. In every branch, production, transportation and manufacture, it has presented the great hazards that test brave hearts and mould strong characters. It has created a race of men capable of meeting any emergency and ready for any achievement. Inevitably the story of such an industry is romance. The term here does not denote fiction for the truth of petroleum and natural gas is more exciting than imaginary scenes. The aim in these pages has been to preserve the truth and to tell the tale without the intrusion of the dry detail of a statistical or technical work. There has been no attempt to paint the lily or to gild refined gold. There is so much rich material in the origin and growth of the petroleum industry that it is wholly unnecessary to draw on the imagination for color. This is not a history, because it omits minutiae inseparable from a continuous record. It is just the romance of petroleum and natural gas, and some account of the human factors who have made the history of the business. It trails no other book, nor does it bar the way of any that may follow. It takes its own path into a fascinating field of romance in human endeavor, namely, the supplying of light to a waiting world; the preparation of the way for aerial navigation and the conquests of distance by private carriages. The ordinary walks of this mining with the drill lead into wonderland. In the ages there has been nothing like it. Aladdin's lamp was no more marvellous than the kerosene torch, nor did it bring to its owner more of wealth and luxury. Human progress and popular education have been thrust forward by the discovery of this resource of nature and the world owes a debt of gratitude to the men who have made its development possible. No other industry in the history of the world grew up so fast, and now, after half a century, it is only in its infancy. It will be the sinews of war in the next great conflict of nations and the bulwark of strength of the mightiest. Already it has yielded chemical treasures by the score; revolutionized the arts; given new sources of power; modified medicine; added to domestic economy; multiplied machinery and illumined the earth. The author offers no apology for invading the literary field with a subject worthy of more attention than it has received, even if he shall need one for not doing justice to his theme.

A. R. Crum

OIL CITY, PENNSYLVANIA.   EDITOR.

Romance of
American Petroleum
and Gas

CHAPTER I.

A STUPENDOUS DEVELOPMENT.

From the Drake well on Oil Creek in Pennsylvania to the Lakeview well in California is the span of half a century. The first was a fifteen barrel pumper and the latter a fifty thousand barrel gusher. Between has been the development of the most remarkable industry in the world, an industry that in the United States sustains half a million families and represents the investment of billions of dollars. From a doubting mining enterprise in 1859 it has become a giant of the first magnitude. Spreading from Oil Creek in Pennsylvania, the petroleum industry has embraced the earth.

A waiting world was never better prepared for the commercial development of a new commodity than when Edwin L. Drake sent his iron drill into the rock and brought forth petroleum. Popular education had begun and was demanding better artificial light. It has been incalculably advanced by this discovery. Science and enterprise had paved the way by the manufacture of mineral oils from coal and shale, and the devising of methods for treating it. Special lamps had been designed for burning oil of a similar character. Men were prepared to accept the value of the novel means to make light and leaped to the opportunity to create a new resource.

Petroleum was not a new thing when Drake left his New England home to delve for it. It had been known for centuries in Burma; had been used by the aboriginal Seneca Indians near the site of the Drake well for ceremonial and medical purposes, as well as for mixing their hideous war paint before the white man trod that soil; had been utilized to light a town in Roumania ten years before; had found its way to the lubrication of machinery; had annoyed the salt manufacturers of four States. But the greatness of rock oil dawned with the Drake well. Edwin Laurentine Drake must go into history as a discoverer and receive the share of praise due a pioneer. He started to dig for oil, conceived the idea of drilling for it and invented the process of driving pipe August 27, 1859, is the date when the petroleum industry was born; the fifteen barrels a day from that well on Oil Creek was the beginning that has led to the 600,000 barrels daily production in the United States and the more than half that much from other countries. It was the first well drilled for oil.

To-day petroleum furnishes motive power for the highest class machinery and lubricates the engines of all continents. Its spirit drives the airship and its body propels the most effective fighting craft. Without it railroad train and automobile would languish. It has entered into medicine and the photographer's art has gained incalculably out of its by-products. It occupies an important place in domestic economy and in the color trades. It remains the cheapest light and is used by a larger part of humanity than any other substance for that purpose. It is carried to the utttermost ends of the earth and into the most inaccessible places. No article of American manufacture is as widely distributed nor is any other so systematically marketed. Special ships ply the oceans with cargoes of oil and camels carry it across the deserts. It is transported in Chinese junks and packed on the backs of natives in the fastnesses of the island of Celebes.

In its inception the oil business was a succession of emergencies and it has bred a race of men who hesitate at no obstacles. When no appliances were known to meet a special requirement new were created to do the work and it has been so from the beginning. The industry has devised its own means of transportation; has improved methods of manufacture and has given the world a widely adopted model of business organization. Unhampered by precedents it has blazed fresh trails best adapted to its own requirements until the "Oil Regions" have come to be synonymous with resourcefulness. Petroleum is inevitably associated with wonderland, a sort of genie of the lamp of Aladdin,

THE DRAKE WELL—PIONEER OF AN INDUSTRY.

summoning adventure, fabulous wealth, miracles and luxury. It is difficult for many to understand where truth ends and fiction begins in this wonderful conquest of earth, air, distance and darkness. And with all the practical operations of the industry there is a close relationship of the fire god, terrible in his rage, but benificent in his gentler moods. There is danger in every minute and destruction has been the frequent accompaniment. It is a hazardous business.

Natural gas, twin sister of petroleum, has not been less wonderful in its gigantic development in recent years. If the miner for petroleum was rejoiced to find a mineral commodity, deep in the rocks, that would flow itself to the surface, what shall be said of the discovery of a better fuel than coal that would not only bring itself to the surface but would transport itself to market? Science and art have been unable to manufacture a fuel as perfect as this hydrocarbon fluid gas, from the laboratory of nature, popularly known as natural gas. It is not strange that it has attracted conservative capital to a greater degree than any other enterprise so nearly affiliated with mining. Gas, not less than oil, has its spectacular features, such as the opening of wells with pressure five times greater than that required on the steam boiler that operates a railroad train running sixty miles an hour—wells that flow more millions of cubic feet of gas daily than are manufactured by large artificial gas plants.

The mode of drilling for gas does not differ from that of exploring the depths for oil. In fact wells drilled for oil often find gas and wells drilled for gas find oil instead. In this respect the two industries are so closely supplementary as to be virtually one, but in all else they differ quite as widely as the substances produced. In the two it is estimated that three of four billion dollars are invested in this country. Not less than half a million families are dependent upon them in their various ramifications and many more have interests small and large. Truly a marvellous growth to be made in a period approximating fifty years.

The first authenticated utilization of natural gas in the oil region was the lighting and heating of the residence of Dr. M. C. Egbert on Oil Creek about 1864. It had possibly been used earlier to illuminate a boiler house on some lease and it was soon afterward used for fuel under the boilers of drilling and pumping wells. The first commercial adaptation of which the writer knows was that of Knowles & Panton who sold gas from a very strong well near Foxburg, Pa., to twenty or thirty drilling wells in the Grass Flats oil district, early in 1871. This well was on the hill overlooking the Clarion river and had a rock pressure estimated at 500 pounds with a flow of probably ten million cubic feet. Accuracy is impossible because there were then no appliances for measuring wells of that kind. Fredonia, N. Y., was piped and used natural gas for lighting before the Drake well was drilled.

These twin industries have been noted for yielding sudden wealth, and, in the maelstrom of speculative uncertainty, they have converted wealth into as sudden poverty. This has given them a romantic attraction for the multitude, creating a popular misapprehension that oil and riches are synonymous terms. The early phrase of "struck oil" implied the impossibility of doing so without entrance into the millionaire class, but the practical producer, transporter and marketer of these commodities is well aware that as a business it is not all profit, yielding only a fair average return in any of its branches. The occasional great rewards are but the necessary compensation for the constant hazard and not infrequent losses. It is, on the whole, profitable, as such an industry should be.

Oil was found in the Drake well on Saturday evening, August 27, 1859. On Sunday "Uncle Billy" Smith, the driller, found the fluid within a few feet of the top of the hole, which was 69½ feet deep. With the aid of a tin pitcher pump he and his young son raised several barrels of oil that day. Although the first oil well was located in an inaccessible region, devoid of railroads, telegraphs or other modern means of quick communication, the news spread rapidly. On Monday, August 29, 1859, keen, enterprising men were riding up and down the eighteen miles of the Oil Creek valley, from Titusville to the

Allegheny river, leasing lands for the production of petroleum.   One farm, the Davidson, nearly midway between the points named was purchased outright by Drs. A. G. and M. C. Egbert on that day.   Within the week nearly every farm along Oil Creek had been bartered in some form and there was a lively demand for carpenters to get out timbers for derricks.   The same keen haste has been characteristic of the petroleum industry ever since.

A month after the Drake well was struck lands had been leased along the Allegheny river, above and below the mouth of Oil Creek for several miles, the news had spread to Erie, Cleveland, Pittsburg and the eastern cities. Adventuresome men from far and near were on their way to the "oil country" to try their fortunes.   The "rush" began that has never ceased.   The men who came in found ready employment at good wages, if willing to work and many were proffered interests in wells in lieu of wages by impecunious leaseholders, whose only capital was invested in acreage and scant facilities for the desired operations.   Times were "hard" and this extra employment was welcomed by the country.   Suitable machinery was scarce and expensive, so the popular method of drilling was by "spring pole" with two lusty men for motive power.   A spring pole, be it understood, was a flexible sapling, with the heavier end anchored outside the derrick and the smaller swinging free where the drilling was to be done.   From near this free end the drilling tools were suspended.   At the unanchored end the stirrup hung in which the two men each put a foot; when they put their weight on that foot the tools went down and struck a blow on the bottom of the hole, being lifted again by the "spring" in the pole.   It was hard work and slow progress, but scores of lucky fellows "kicked" themselves into fortune in that way.

Drake's first well was drilled with a steam engine, but the second oil well, drilled near the first, was put down with the spring pole.   It was completed in December, 1859.   The third well was drilled in the same way on the Archie Buchanan farm, fifteen miles below the Drake well along Oil Creek.   It, too, was finished in December, owned by Rouse, Mitchell & Brown.   Then followed the well of Watson, Brewer & Co., at the oil spring on the Hamilton McClintock farm, which was drilled in early in January, 1860.   This well was on an island in the middle of the creek about two miles above its mouth, where the Indians had dipped oil and their white successors had followed their example for many years.   This farm afterward became famous as McClintockville, and as the site of the oil refinery that was the first business venture of Henry Huddleston Rogers.   The same month a well was completed by James Evans, a blacksmith, on his lot at Franklin, the county seat of Venango county, that produced heavy, or lubricating oil.   On the first day of February the well of Barnsdall, Mead, Rouse, Abbott & Co. came in at Titusville.   In March there followed the first well of Jonathan Watson & Co. on the Widow McClintock farm, adjoining the Buchanan farm, and the second well of Rouse, Mitchell & Brown on the Buchanan.   The Widow McClintock farm yielded the wealth so spectacularly squandered, a few years later, by "Coal Oil Johnny" Steele.   The second well on the Buchanan farm was noted as the first oil well to make a spontaneous flow when drilled into the oil sand, which was afterward known as the "first sand."   It was 180 feet deep as compared with the 69½ feet of the original Drake well.   In June, 1860, the total production of all wells was 200 barrels a day and the first discussion arose as to whether there might be an over production.

In July, Watson, Tanner & Co. found oil at a depth of 143 feet a mile east of Titusville, the well making thirteen barrels a day. When it was drilled a few feet deeper it astonished the natives by flowing 480 barrels the first twenty-four hours. This was a new record and one that attracted much attention. The well broadened the producing territory and it was difficult to care for so much oil. The same month King, Ferris & Co. brought in a well at Tidioute on the Allegheny river, thirty-five miles above the mouth of Oil Creek, that pumped ten barrels a day. This well was 125 feet deep and was the sensation of the day on account of its distance from the original discovery. It was the first well to reach the famous "third sand," but the important fact was not

SHIPPING OIL, STORY FARM, OIL CREEK, 1863.

then recognized. The depth varied little from that of wells on Oil Creek and no one then had knowledge of the dip of the oil bearing rocks. A few days after the completion of the King, Ferris & Co. well there were sixty wells drilling at Tidioute, the second being completed in August with an output of 200 barrels daily. The Drake well, then one year old, was pumping eighteen barrels a day, slightly better than its start, and the opinion prevailed that the supply was as inexhaustible as that of water. The petroleum industry was established and wells were starting in every valley for miles around. No one dared to drill on the hills for it was believed the oil existed only in the valleys.

At the close of 1860 two oil refineries had been built at Erie and the daily production was fully 500 barrels along Oil Creek and at Tidioute. Oil was selling at the wells at twenty-five cents a gallon. In May, 1861, the first well on Oil Creek to be drilled to the "third sand" was brought in by Captain A. B. Funk and was named the "Fountain Well," on account of its character.   It found its oil at 460 feet and was then the deepest oil well.   It flowed about 300 barrels a day for six months and stopped suddenly, choked with paraffine, as was subsequently learned.   Just before this well was opened the production along the Creek had reached a total of 500 barrels a day and wells along the river were producing 700 barrels daily.   The French Creek valley had then about 100 barrels a day, all lubricating oil, making a grand total of 1,300 barrels.   When the 300 from the "Fountain well" was added there was an over production and depression of prices.   To make matters worse the Burning Springs district in West Virginia came into action and speedily reached several hundred barrels a day.

The Candian oil fields were heard of about the same time.   They were more isolated than the Pennsylvania fields and farther from transportation, which resulted in much of their flood of petroleum running into the streams

TARR FARM, 1862.

and being lost.   Oil buyers depressed the market on Oil Creek by telling that oil was selling at ten cents a gallon in West Virginia and at Burning Springs they told that oil was selling below ten cents a gallon on Oil Creek.   On Oil Creek more flowing wells were struck, that of Bradley & Co. making 800 barrels a day.   Heydrick & Co. struck one at Walnut Bend on the Allegheny river, almost as large.   Finally in September, 1861, the William Phillips No. 2 on the Tarr farm on Oil Creek came in with a production of 4,000 barrels the first day, accompanied by the Empire well at 2,500 barrels a day.   There was so much oil it was simply impossible to care for it or to provide barrels to put it in for shipment.   Oil ran in rivulets to the creek and on the creek to the Allegheny river, the surface of the river being covered down to Emlenton, a distance of nearly fifty miles.   The price of oil in January had been ten dollars a barrel.   The average for September was twenty cents a barrel.   This was the first great depression in the industry and losses were tremendous. There was no market for so much oil even if there had been facilities for getting the product out of the producing region. Many times since then the same conditions have been duplicated. Despite the fact that the consumption of petroleum has increased faster than that of any commodity, with the possible exception of Portland cement, the production has frequently outrun consumptive demand and caused serious depression in prices. By December the price had rallied to thirty-five cents a barrel at the wells, but in January, 1862. it fell to ten cents a barrel, the lowest in the history of the industry. There was little effort made to save it and thousands of barrels ran down the streams. The world had not been educated to consume so large a quantity and there were no strong interests to buy and hold the surplus.

Some of the results of this depression were the abandonment of many small wells and the wrecking of many small fortunes. Nothing short of a flowing well was worth looking after. Drilling ceased in large measure and many wells were shut in to keep the oil in the ground until conditions improved. The British government at this time levied a tariff of one cent a gallon on all petroleum imported from the United States as a measure of protection for the shale and coal oil industries of the United Kingdom. The consumer got little benefit from the low prices in the producing region. The cost of shipping a barrel of oil from Oil Creek to New York was $7.45 and the price of a gallon of lamp oil was thirty-five to forty-five cents. The price of a better grade of burning oil is now less than four cents a gallon on board vessel at New York. although the price of crude is ten times higher at the wells. By March, 1862, the market had improved to fifty cents a barrel for crude oil at the wells and the producers had a new misfortune to worry over. The Congress proposed a revenue tax on both crude and refined petroleum as a war measure. This tax was averted by protests from the producers until the year following. but was ultimately laid and collected.

Millions of dollars were paid directly by the petroleum industry, for the expenses for the war for the Union, in the form of a tax of twenty cents a gallon on refined oil, and, for a couple of years, one dollar a barrel on all crude petroleum produced. The tax on refined, levied in 1863, was not abated by Congress until 1868. In addition the men of the oil region contributed large sums individually for the comfort of the soldiers and the maintenance of hospitals for the wounded. Later the fighting men from the front flocked to the oil producing regions by hundreds at the close of the war and exerted a marked influence upon the further development. freed from the handicap of a great conflict.

During these early years of pathfinding in a new industry. discovery of flowing wells and the building of drilling rigs was not all of the story. There was a side of intense human interest. Owners of poor land were suddenly dragged from poverty and made immensely wealthy through no effort of their own. by the payment of "royalties." From simple farmers and lumbermen they were converted into capitalists and men of affairs. Lusty laborers, by "kicking" the springhole came into possession of valuable interests in producing wells. Be it said to their credit, the vast majority accepted their good fortune with grace and modesty. but a few lost their heads and made consummate spendthrift asses of themselves. It was these who gave to the petroleum region its notoriety, through exaggerated song and story of the time. The extravagances of "oil princes" were hardly worse than those of others made rich quick by different means, at earlier and later dates, but there were more of them at that period and they attracted undue notice.

The youthful and unsophisticated John Steele, "Coal Oil Johnny," who came into possession of several hundred thousand dollars by the sudden death of his foster mother, who tried to hurry the kitchen fire by pouring on petroleum, "cut a wide swath" while the money lasted, showering favors upon theatrical and other acquaintances. He obtained exceptional notoriety because his exploits coincided with a world-wide awakening of interest in petroleum

DINGLEY ACRE, NEAR TIDIOUTE, PA.

speculation, when every eye was turned upon the new source of wealth and every pocket bulged with certificates of stock in some one of the numerous joint stock companies, organized for the production of oil or the swindling of the public. Young Steele's folly did much to promote this stock gambling of the multitude, who never saw the color of dividends, being magnified and exploited by shrewd promoters for that purpose. Thousands proved themselves no wiser in the use of their money for investment in worthless oil company paper than the youth whose head was turned by too sudden affluence from genuine oil operations. At least Steele proved himself capable of returning to useful avocations and the earning of an honest livelihood after his wealth had disappeared, with no word of lamentation. He is living at a good, old age when these lines are being written, in comfortable circumstances, having been "delivered from the curse of great riches" and from extreme poverty.

It was not until 1864 and 1865 that the wild speculative furore in petroleum reached its height. Then everybody was "in oil." Thousands were "done" in oil who never sat to a painter. Promotions were floated by the hundreds, while wells were being drilled by tens. The tide of development left the valley of Oil Creek and swept up its picturesque tributary, Cherry Run. Then it leaped over the hills between Oil Creek and Tidioute, on the Allegheny River, producing the mad excitement on Pit Hole creek. There was built the famous Pithole City, created in six months and destroyed within three years. A city whose postoffice attained the dignity of ranking third among the post-offices of Pennsylvania in 1866 and on whose streets cattle now graze peacefully. Possibly a year before the first well was started on Pit Hole Creek, a prospectus was issued by an enterprising promoter, offering shares in an oil company operating on Dunham creek, near the "famous summer resort of Tyrrel's Corners." It included the picture of an imposing steamboat plying the waters of Dunham creek at Tyrrel's, represented to be a part of the company's property, and the company at once became popular in Philadelphia and Boston, where it secured hundreds of subscribers to its shares. The humor of this beautifully engraved circular was apparent only to the few who had traversed the highway between Oil Creek and Tidioute; who knew that Dunham run was a tributary of West Pit Hole Creek; that the latter stream was not navigable anywhere for canoes and who knew that at Tyrrel's Corners there was a solitary wayside inn, patronized by raftmen, primarily, and latterly by a few oil men passing that way.

It would be idle to enter upon the task of mentioning the many oil companies whose shares were floated at this period. There were some of sterling worth, and more that were organized in good faith, but on extravagant expectations, including those whose operations were along Cherry Run and later those at Pithole. There were many of the same class as that which embraced the joint oil prospects and "summer resort" beauties of Tyrrell's, where palatial steam passenger boats, in imagination and the printed circulars, ran on an inch of water in a stream not ten feet wide. Between the abrupt ending of the Pithole dream and the failure of the scores of fraudulent promotions to begin, petroleum stocks fell into disrepute. For years afterward the business of producing was carried on by individuals, partnerships and a few close corporations with no stock to sell. The general public was so severely "bitten" that oil was regarded as extra hazardous as an investment, as well as hazardous as a business. Even servant girls had been beguiled into buying "shares" that represented no property whatever, and others that covered a few acres of valueless land many miles removed from any petroleum producing area.

Amid the wilderness of bogus promotions bona fide oil corporations laid the foundations of many substantial fortunes. The Columbia Oil Co., organized in Pittsburgh, operated the Story farm on Oil Creek with great success. Among its stockholders was Andrew Carnegie, the Star Spangled Scotchman, and his longtime partner, Henry Phipps. It was from their small investment in Columbia stock that they obtained the funds for the later purchase of Andrew Kloman's forge, the foundation of the great steel business and the "swollen fortunes" that have yielded so abundantly in Carnegie free libraries, Phipps' popular conservatories, tuberculosis sanatoria, hospital endowments and sanitary tenements. Other Pittsburgh holders of Columbia stock have prospered amazingly from its early dividends. These include the great Hartje fortune, now invested in paper manufacture and recently given great notoriety in the Allegheny County, Pa., divorce courts. The Columbia was not alone in success among the early oil producing companies, but is used for illustration because no other was more competently managed throughout, much credit being due to D. B. Stewart, superintendent.

After the wild speculative bubble had burst the popular organization for oil operations returned to a basis of halves, quarters, eighths, and sixteenths. Occasionally partners were admitted for smaller shares, such as thirty-seconds

UPPER CHERRY RUN IN 1869.

and sixty-fourths. Usually one or two of the partners held a half or more and consequently controlled the policy of the concern. Sometimes these organizations adopted some fancy or descriptive name, as a company; sometimes they bore the name of the principal owner, or owners, probably followed by an inclusive "& Co." Not infrequently the "company" took the name of the first farm operated upon, but from 1866 to 1890 there were probably not more than two score incorporated joint stock companies with issues of negotiable stock certificates. From the "Hardly Able Oil Co." to the "Metropolitan Petroleum Co." the interests were as closely held by a few men as in the partnerships known by the names of one or two men. This method of organization was eminently satisfactory. The participants, generally, were persons fully conversant with the nature of the business, knew the risks of "spotted" territory, took their failures philosophically, and, in the event of conspicuous success had more than a moiety of the returns. There was no opportunity in an organization of that kind for a few designing men to fatten from the assessments levied upon an army of innocents who had no voice in the management and practically no chance to get any money back.

A new era of stock company promotions was inaugurated with the development in Northwestern Ohio, but on a very conservative basis. In fact, this proved the rule of all fields east of the Mississippi River after the "craze" that virtually ended with the collapse of Pithole in 1866. The fields of Texas, Kansas and California revived the era of joint stock promotions and speculation in "shares," the Sunflower State rivaling the Pithole era in the daring of its stock company swindles. Oklahoma has had a few companies of this character, but the greater part of that very remarkable development has been "on the square." Much of the drilling in the domain of the Indians has been done by oil operators migrating from the eastern fields, imbued with the principles of honor there taught by the masters, so the Oklahoma oil fields have been spared much of the disgrace attendant upon the operations of tricksters. The "old guard" in that region has been more sinned against than sinning, more "sharks" being found outside the oil and gas producing ranks.

SCHRUBGRASS FERRY
1872

SUMMIT CITY

ACROSS THE BELT AT
BARRINGER

THRUSH

TURKEY CITY
IN 1874

FIRST HOUSE AT TRIANGLE CITY

MAIN STREET ST PETERSBURG

VIEW IN EDENBURG

CHAPTER II.

THE LOWER REGIONS.

After the extremely exciting times in Venango County, Pa., petroleum developments were made down the Allegheny River, and the newer scenes of activity were termed the "Lower Oil Fields" and the "Lower Regions," the latter term being often facetiously construed as descriptive of a future state. Pithole's brilliant career and dismal collapse did not end the Venango development by any means, the region about Pithole creek having yielded several ephemeral towns, such as Red Hot and Cash Up, upper Cherry Run having the "excitement" at Shamburg, the old Oil Creek sections producing the McCray Hill boom at Petroleum Center. There was the Pleasantville development, southeast of Titusville; Cherrytree Run, west of Oil Creek, and a revival in Warren County, near Tidioute, that gave rise to Triumph Hill, New London and the wicked little town of Babylon. But the trend was down the Allegheny River. Angell and Prentice, following their "belt theory" of petroleum deposits, carried the work to Scrubgrass with great profit to themselves and others. Oil was found near Emlenton, and then at Parkers Landing, the latter in Armstrong County, Pa. A small well was completed at Brady's Bend, in Armstrong County, in April, 1869, and several of the same kind about Parkers Landing in May.

Operations in the "lower fields" were extended cautiously on both sides of the river near Parkers Landing. By the close of 1870 wells were drilling two miles up Bear Creek to the southwest and about the same distance to the northeast, around the mouth of the Clarion River. In 1871 the "Grass Flats" on this stream was the most important scene of new production until Marcus Hulings drilled in a well that produced 125 barrels a day, about four miles in advance of "Grass Flats" to the northeast. Intervening territory was eagerly sought. The town of St. Petersburg grew rapidly and the town of Antwerp was established near the Hulings well. These "cities" did not rival Pithole in size, but their creation was quite as sudden. Meantime Parkers Landing advanced rapidly in population and reached 7,000 souls in 1875, when it possessed the leading oil exchange in the world and was the scene of riotous speculation in petroleum certificates, or pipe line vouchers for oil in storage. In August, 1872, Marcus Hulings again struck the belt with a wildcat well on the Delo farm, nearly six miles northeast of his previous success at Antwerp. In this same year operations had been pressed nearly as far to the southwest, the active frontier in Butler County being at the thriving new town of Petrolia. Two or three pipe lines were operating on each side of the river. Production was increasing steadily and prices for oil were unsatisfactory.

Very early in 1872 the South Improvement Company was organized, the leading spirits being a number of railroad officials. It was designed to include all railroads that were carrying oil from the producing regions and as many refiners as would join. The Standard Oil Company, of Pittsburgh, was an active factor and the Standard Oil Company, of Cleveland, reluctantly joined the movement.   An advance in oil freights was a feature of the proposition, against which the oil producers rebelled vigorously.   The Standard

FOXBURG IN 1872.

Oil Company, of Cleveland, being the owner of a number of refineries and an advocate of combination, was accused of being the instigator of the South Improvement Company scheme, instead of its Pittsburgh competitor, and was roundly abused.   Meetings of producers were held in every important town in the producing regions, resolutions were adopted and an organization effected on a fighting basis.   These were stirring times and heated indignation was freely indulged.   A committee of producers and of refiners, located within the producing region, secured from the railroads an agreement to give them the same rates for transportation as those given the South Improvement Company; Congress was moved to appoint a committee to investigate the acts and franchises of the South Improvement: the State Legislature was appealed to.   Finally on March 29, 1872, the Pennsylvania Legislature passed a bill repealing the charter of the obnoxious company.   More pipe lines were organized and the search for oil continued aggressively.

After several good wells had been opened at Petrolia, in Butler County, and the Hulings well on the Delo farm had started a pandemonium of drilling in Clarion County, the producers started a movement to shut down all wells for thirty days.   Another series of meetings was held, eloquent orators told of the advantage of curtailing production and the agreement was generally signed.   Wells in the Clarion County district, drilling and pumping, were shut down on September 27th.   In the Petrolia district the shut down took effect at midnight of September 28th.   By October 1st nearly every well in Pennsylvania was stopped.   Prices advanced on the exchanges and feverish speculation in storage certificates engaged the attention of the almost idle populace.   The producers' organization planned a "Petroleum Producers' Agency," to market all crude oil, fixing the price nominally at five dollars a barrel, each producer to receive three dollars in cash and the remainder in "tankage receipts," the latter to be redeemed whenever oil sold at a sufficient price to realize the money. The daily production at this time was about 17,000 barrels and the demand for consumption was estimated at about 15,000 barrels daily. The Standard Oil Company, of Cleveland, favored the producers' organization and agreed to assist by paying $4.75 per barrel; to buy only from the Producers' Agency, the agency to sell to it alone. To make good its offer for 15,000 barrels a day the Standard Company, of Ohio, formed a Refiners' Association, admitting all who would conform to the rules. The price to producers was then fixed on a sliding scale in relation to the price of refined oil and later the agreement concerning the 15,000 barrels to be purchased daily was amended to "such quantities of crude oil as the markets of the world may take of them, the amount to be determined by the committees and representatives."

The first trouble under this agreement arose from complaints from producers in certain districts that their districts were discriminated against in the disposition of oil. Some asserted that none of their oil was taken, while all of the oil of others was sold. The Producers' Council—executive body of the Producers Protective Union—recommended at the close of December that no new wells be drilled for six months and that no torpedoes be used during that period to increase production of old wells. Oil was going to waste on account of insufficient tankage. Thus closed 1872, a year memorable for the extension of the limits of oil producing territory and for its many agitations in the supposed interest of oil producers. No attention was paid to the recommendation of the Council to suspend drilling, production increased, failure of the Refiners' Association to take all of the oil increased the

SCENE BELOW FRANKLIN IN 1875.

dissatisfaction, and in January, 1873, the combination of producers and refiners was declared a failure. The Petroleum Producers' Agency ceased to exist and every man went ahead on his own resources. Operations proceeded aggressively in both Clarion and Butler counties, the latter having the larger wells.

In June, 1873, the Refiners' Association disbanded. In July the daily production was estimated at 27,000 barrels, when the "fourth sand cross belt" was tapped at Karns City and Modoc City, in Butler County. Wells were reported every day flowing from 300 barrels to 1,000 barrels a day each. The "third sand belt" was developed simultaneously to Millerstown, proving almost as rich as the fourth sand in first returns, while the wells maintained their production better. In September the production of the Modoc district was estimated at 6,000 barrels daily, and that of the Millerstown district the same. To add to the market depression, the failure of Jay Cooke & Co., bankers, of Philadelphia, was reported on the 18th of this month and the

OPPOSITE THE DOUBLE WHISTLE WELL, RED HOT DISTRICT.

financial panic of 1873 followed. There were many failures of oil producing firms, but the mad rush to develop new territory and to obtain more production never slackened. The lure of big, flowing wells was too strong to be resisted.

The year 1874 opened with a perfect furore along the "fourth sand belt," which was yielding wells that started from 500 barrels to 2,500 barrels daily. Even at $1.10 a barrel, the lowest quotation for January on the exchanges, such wells were very profitable. Oil at the wells sold much lower, the range being from about 40 cents a barrel upward. Owners of small wells suffered, but their distress had no effect upon those who had a prospect of gushers. The total daily production at this time was above 37,000 barrels a day, while consumption had increased to probably 25,000 barrels daily. Surplus stocks at the close of December, 1873, amounted to 1,625,000 barrels, while at the close of January, 1874, they had mounted to nearly 1,950,000 barrels. There was a steady increase in this surplus until the Butler County field was defined and the scene of greatest activity had again shifted to Clarion County, higher prices having made the smaller wells of that district attractive.

The year 1875 was most notable for its pipe line movements. Producers were of opinion that more pipe lines would find more markets for their product. The Columbia conduit pipe line was completed from Butler County to Pittsburgh and the Atlantic pipe line built in Clarion County, with very little relief. The new lines advanced the price of oil at wells to almost the figures paid for oil on board cars, but surplus stocks continued to accumulate. In 1876 small wells were reported in McKean County, Pa., near the village of Bradford, in January, increasing in number as the year progressed. There was a new development about midsummer at Warren, in Warren County,

SHAMBURG FIELD IN 1870.

Pa. In July the Phillips Bros. brought in a good well on Bullion Run, in Venango County, Pa. In August the Bullion Run pool gave unmistakable evidence of being a gusher pool, but the market was boomed because surplus stocks in pipe line tanks were not increasing at the usual rate. In September the tanks of the pipe lines were gauged under supervision of a committee from the oil exchanges and stocks were returned as being 3,164,384 barrels. In October there were reports that the Pennsylvania Transportation Company had issued certificates for more oil than it had in tanks, and in November the failure of the company was reported. Several arrests were made, and the conclusion was that the pipe line stocks were not as large as reported by the gauge committee. The Bullion district was at high tide, but the crude market advanced, aided by a foreign corner in refined oil, to $4.16 a barrel on December 11. Since then petroleum has not sold as high as that. The influence of the Bradford field, in McKean County, Pa., began to be felt at about that time.

TARPORT, LOOKING UP THE TUNA VALLEY, IN 1881.

CHAPTER III.

THE BRADFORD FIELD.

After the war ended in 1865 an attempt was made to revive the oil wells at Burning Springs, on the Little Kanawha River, in West Virginia, without success. However, oil was found in the adjoining county, giving rise to the towns of Petroleum and Volcano, and among the successful prospectors there was Job Moses, who realized a comfortable fortune from his wells. Mr. Moses purchased a large tract of land near Limestone, N. Y., settled there and made a fine home. In 1874 he began testing his property for oil, the result being a couple of small wells, the oil being of somewhat inferior quality and found in a slate formation. The exciting developments at the front in Butler County, Pa., the production in excess of demand and the interesting transportation developments of the time prevented oil operators from paying much attention to this new discovery. The few who investigated returned south with the disparaging information that the "oil was produced from slate instead of a sand, was of low gravity, dark color and inferior quality." Three or four, however, thought there might be something better near by and sought lands in the vicinity. Among these was Frederick Crocker, who had drilled the famous "Empire Well" on Oil Creek, in 1861, and he soon had a well drilling near the village of Bradford, Pa., about eight miles from the Moses development. His efforts were rewarded with a well reported on the last day of July, 1875, to be flowing 100 barrels a day and in all there were twelve wells then drilling near the state line between Pennsylvania and New York.

When the Butler County field was waning, the northeast extension of the "belt" in Clarion County was attractive, the Clarion County "eastern belt" was found and then the Bullion pool sprang, like a meteor athwart the petroleum sky. Better prices stimulated drilling activity and but few would consider the "northern field," which was now producing oil from a "brown sand," a hundred feet below the shale where Moses found the first showing. The white sand was still the prime favorite. The few who went into the brown sand field had little competition in securing leases, but they had much trouble in disposing of their oil.

Marcus Hulings, who had attained fame as a successful "wildcatter" in Clarion County, had found a little oil in a white sand on Blue Jay Creek, in Forest County, Pa., northeast of the Clarion County field. He noted that McKean County, Pa., was "on his line" and pushed forward to the brown sand field. His theory led him a little east of operations and he arranged a partnership with Clark & Babcock, who owned a vast tract of timber land from which they were cutting giant white pine and leaving hemlocks. The firm, with the new partner, added petroleum exploration to the lumber business. Large wells were drilled in, the new industry made a home market for the lumber, it was discovered that hemlock planks were as good as pine for "rig building," so the timber more than doubled in value. By 1877 the white sand fields were being deserted for the brown sand area and the great Bradford oil field was under feverish development. Here there was no "spotted" territory, no dry holes among the producing wells. Drilling was easy and production increased as it never had before. The black oil was good, after all. Again the price of oil began to decline. The value of property in the Butler, Clarion, Venango and Warren County fields shrank in sympathy with the price of the product; formerly valuable leases, with their machinery, could not be sold for enough to pay their current liabilities. Men rated wealthy in the Centennial year found their fortunes had vanished. Without the loss of any tangible assets many were impoverished and not a few completely ruined, financially. But with characteristic pluck the majority gathered what capital they could realize and pressed forward to the new oildorado to try fortune again. Hundreds who had no capital remaining were soon at work in the new fields earning money to pay their debts and alert for an opportunity to get an "interest" that might recoup their losses.

In 1878 the prolific brown sand had yielded so generously that again the markets of the world could not absorb so much oil. Storage, which had been an incident, became a leading factor in the industry. Yet there was too much oil, tanks at wells overflowed and thousands of barrels of the precious fluid ran down the hillsides into Foster Brook, Kendall Creek and the Tununga-want, the latter shortened by the busy oil men to "Tuna." In January the Producers Union completed an organization for a pipe line to the seaboard, the Legislature was petitioned for an eminent domain bill and this was passed in April. Meantime the energetic wildcatter was busy and the Bradford territory was extended south up the East Branch of the Tuna, and northward over the state line and the dividing ridge between the waters of Foster Brook and Four Mile Creek. The Knapps Creek valley was proven and a new movement was inaugurated to "stop the drill." The shut down of drilling wells in McKean County was only partly successful and it only incited the operators, who still had some good territory in the older fields, to renewed activity. The flood of oil was too much for transporters and storers, and fully double the world's greatest demand up to that date. Pipe lines refused to receive from producers' tanks oil they had no means to dispose of.

Distress was manifest through the petroleum producing regions. Labor was unemployed to a greater extent than ever before in the "oil country." Many ills were laid at the door of the Standard Oil Company, then the largest refiner and marketer of petroleum and its affiliated United Pipe Lines. A fierce agitation was begun and feeling ran high. The Producers' Council petitioned the Pennsylvania Attorney General to prosecute several railroads and refining companies for being in an alleged illegal and unjust combination inimical to the producers of petroleum. Suits were entered in County and Supreme Courts and an injunction was asked to restrain the United Lines from refusing to accept any oil offered to them. This agitation continued into 1879, complicated in the early months of the year by the introduction of bills in the Pennsylvania Legislature to tax oil and to levy a license tax of $1,000 upon each drilling rig erected, to procure revenue to pay damages accruing from the railroad strike riots in Pittsburgh in 1877. There were demonstrations in Bradford verging upon riot and a few acts of vandalism directed to the injury of United Pipe Lines' property.   Unreasoning prejudice arose from the general distress.

Another shut down movement was inaugurated in the Bradford field this year, but it did not interfere with the steady extension of the limits of producing territory, particularly toward the east and southeast.   In June the United Pipe Lines gave notice that all tankage was full and that no oil would be run from producers' tanks unless cars or other means for immediate shipment were furnished for the same.   About the same time the development of the very rich Cole Creek territory began.   Then another producers' meet-

KERNOCHAN LEASE, NEAR TOWN OF RED HOT.

ing was called at Bradford to consider "stopping the drill," which ended in the adoption of the following resolution:

"Whereas, The shortest way to dollar oil is through 25 cent oil, therefore be it
"Resolved, That we favor pushing the drill as rapidly and diligently as possible, until the goal of 25 cent oil is reached."

The range of the petroleum market at that time was between 65 cents and 75 cents a barrel.   The humorous resolution relieved a tension that was near the breaking point, riotous demonstrations ceased and the overproduction continued without abatement.   The United Pipe Line built iron tankage as fast as it could, borrowing capital for the purpose, and some of the larger producers built iron storage tanks of their own.   The pipe line runs of oil from wells during 1879 aggregated more than 20,000,000 barrels and the surplus stocks mounted from 4,300,000 barrels at the close of 1878 to more than 8,000,000 barrels at the close of 1879.

At the close of 1879 the daily runs were the largest in the history of the industry up to that time. A rally in the market in November frightened European buyers, so that when the price fell again they came in for large quantities of cheap oil, believing they might never get another as good opportunity. This movement, together with the large amount of tankage built enabled the pipe lines to take all the oil offered. The result was that 1880 opened with the greatest activity in the Bradford field. A total of 216 wells were completed in January, with almost 900 under way at the close of the month. The tide swelled rapidly so that 1,054 wells were under way at the close of March, and in April 418 wells were completed in the Bradford field alone, having a combined production of 11,000 barrels on the last day of the month. That was the high mark of one of the most remarkable petroleum developments in the world, but by no means the end of it.

MAIN STREET, TITUSVILLE, 1861.

In 1880 attention began to be diverted to Allegany County, N. Y. The Bradford field had extended over the state line from McKean County, Pa., to Cattaraugus County, N. Y. O. P. Taylor began the search in Allegany County, adjoining Cattaraugus on the east, and was presently rewarded by some small wells in the town of Alma. Others followed, venturing westward, and they found the territory richer. The spring of 1881 found the center of excitement at Richburg, in the town of Wirt, and the scramble for leases sent the price of lands from $100 to $125 an acre and one-eighth of the oil, for farms that could have been bought in fee the year before for $25 or $30 an acre. Men slept "six tiers deep" on the village square about the school house, while the thermometer was below the freezing point, a bed being out of the question at any price. Richburg grew rapidly into a busy city and the little village of Bolivar became a town of 5,000 population. The Richburg field, annex to the great Bradford area, reached its zenith in the spring of 1882. Then things happened elsewhere. Cherry Grove rivaled Pithole, and one of the most exciting epochs in the history of petroleum began.

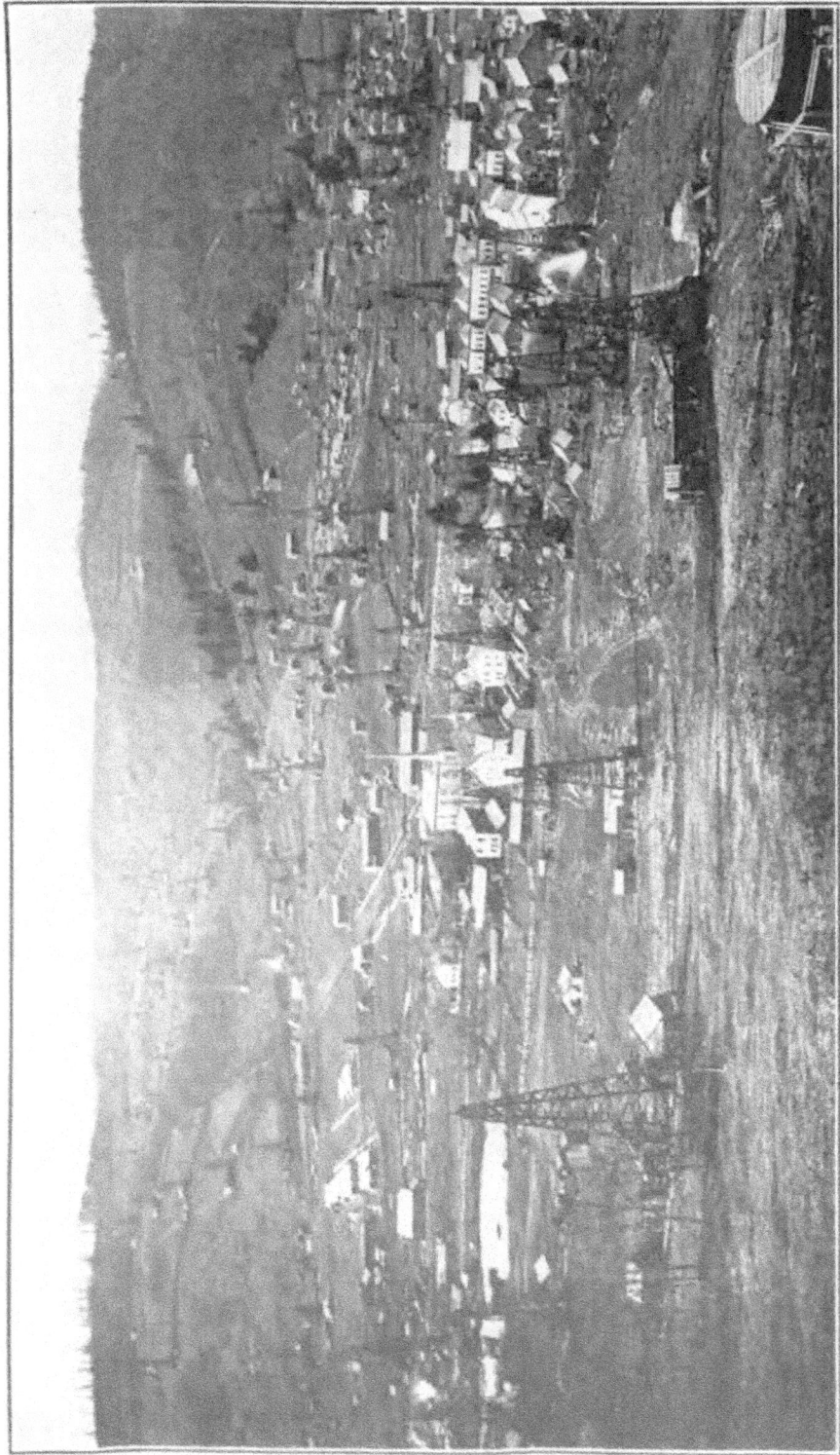

RICHBURG, N. Y., 1881, MOST NORTHERN OIL FIELD.

CHAPTER IV.

THE WHITE SAND POOLS.

While the brown sand field in Allegany County, N. Y., was being developed operators were not idle elsewhere. From Warren they had been feeling their way southward. They had found a profitable pool at Clarendon, on the headwaters of Tionesta Creek and another near Sheffield, farther down the winding stream, which cuts its way through the elevated plateau known as the "Big Level." Capt. Peter Grace and George Dimick, veterans of many oil campaigns, taking their way southwest from Clarendon, had located a well in the dense forest, on lot 646, Cherry Grove Township, Warren County, Pa. The spot was nine miles from Clarendon and an equal distance from Sheffield, sometimes visited by hunters of big game, but best known to the employes of Horton, Crary & Co., the Sheffield tanners, who were busy felling giant hemlock trees and peeling the bark for tanning extract. The lumber was not worth saving, so the huge trunks were left lying in the "slashings" to rot.

In this forest fastness was an excellent place to keep a secret. But on the 10th of March, 1882, the report spread over the oil producing regions, and to oil exchanges in distant cities, that the Grace & Dimick well on "646" was shut down, the derrick boarded up and guards stationed about it to warn and keep trespassers away. The well was made a "mystery," in the phrase of the day, as others had been. From the latter part of January of this year Elliot & Torrey had been manipulating a "mystery" well on lot 53, in the town of Alma, in the Richburg field, and new interest was aroused in it by reports from the well in the wilderness. At the close of March, however, the Alma well was not in need of additional tankage to hold its oil, but the "mystery" in Cherry Grove was building another tank. About this time a well was reported at Baldridge, in Butler County, Pa., several miles in advance of the old Butler field that had been the scene of so much excitement ten years earlier. Early in April the Baldridge well was making 125 barrels a day; Grace & Dimick were building another rig in Cherry Grove; the Elliot & Torrey "mystery" in the town of Alma was given up as a failure, and Baum & Parker were making a "mystery" of a well on lot 39, town of Bolivar, in Allegany County, N. Y. As this latter "mystery" lost prestige and gained reputation as a failure, interest grew in "646." The Anchor Oil Company was building a rig on the adjoining lot, No. 635; Michael Murphy had one under way on lot 619, and the Mehoopany Oil Company was busy on lot 611.

In May events were in rapid succession in Cherry Grove Township. On the tenth the Union Oil Company began stringing pipe for a pipe line; a few days later Murphy's rig was burned by a gas explosion, and on the 17th drilling was resumed on "646." Next day the well was reported good for 100 barrels a day, then 200 barrels, then 500 barrels. On the 19th it was known to be flowing 1,000 barrels a day, and the price of oil was going down on the speculative exchanges. Surplus stocks in pipe line tanks were now 28,000,000 barrels and the prospect was good for a large increase. At the close of May two more wells were in the sand in Cherry Grove and showing as large as the famous "mystery" on "646." In June more followed, and in July the field was known to be six miles long and of unknown width. The price of oil was forced down to 49¼ cents a barrel, the lowest for many years, for the high grade petroleum produced in the Pennsylvania fields, and it has not since been down to that point. The first ray of hope came in that month, when the Whale Oil Company's well on lot 648 was reported dry. By the close of the month a rapid decline in the big wells was noted, and in August some of the former gushers were down to small pumpers. In September they began to pump salt water. But in the meantime this white sand pool had developed a production of 40,000 barrels a day for two weeks in August.

UNION OIL COMPANY AND OTHER OIL COMPANY WELLS.

In August a well was drilled into the sand at Balltown by Grandin Bros. It was reliably reported good for 1,000 barrels, but was shut in and soon forgotten. This was nine miles south of Cherry Grove, in Forest County. In the same month a well was reported nine miles southeast of the Cherry Grove pool, also in Forest County, on the Cooper tract. This well was made a "mystery," but was generally supposed to be large. It was drilled in and opened to the public in September, producing 75 barrels a day. This well was owned by P. M. Shannon and others. In connection with the collapse of the Cherry Grove pool it led to the "boom" in the market of 1882 that carried the price up to $1.30 a barrel, accompanied by the wildest speculation in the oil exchanges ever seen. This was followed by the disastrous "panic" in November, after the Anchor Oil Company brought in the second well on the Cooper tract, good for 350 barrels a day. Another "panic" in December followed the opening of the Grandin well at Balltown, which produced 1,100 barrels the first twenty-four hours. There were now two pools under development in that section, Balltown and Cooper Hill. In the meantime, during that busy month of August, Andrew Shidemantle brought in a well at Baldridge, Butler County, Pa., that flowed 700 barrels in a day, and Wolfe & Kugler, in September, drilled one in Cranberry Township, Venango County, six miles south of Oil City, Pa., that produced 500 barrels in a day. The pendulum had swung back, the tide of excitement left the brown sands of the north and drifted south again. The steady production of the brown sands went on and the meteoric output of the white sand pools was added. The daily average production for July was 103,000 barrels, and for August it was 111,000 barrels. The year 1882 closed with more than 34,000,000 barrels of surplus oil in tanks of the pipe line companies. During all this time the pipe lines had refused no oil, but made almost superhuman efforts to save all and to store the surplus.

The next year was not without its sensations. Among them was the

OLINDA OIL DISTRICT, ORANGE COUNTY, CALIFORNIA.

opening of a white sand pool at Macksburg, Washington County, Ohio, in the southeastern portion of the State. This was the year of the market operations of the "Penn Bank syndicate" in Pittsburgh. It profited by an advance in prices when the Cooper Hill and Balltown pools began to weaken, only to lose all and wreck the bank later. During this year there was much drilling in the old fields and many alarms from wildcat wells, nearly all of them manipulated as "mysteries." The northern end of the Balltown pool furnished the famous "Good Friday" well, on Porcupine Run. It was so named because it was drilled into the sand, caught fire and burned on Good Friday, a market holiday. This was at the height of the speculative era and excitement "on the curb" was intense. The well was "mystified" and closely guarded while the rig was being rebuilt, and for some time afterward, during which time the production steadily increased owing to the gas pressure

blowing out the rock, a process termed "drilling itself in." It was finally
started at 1,100 barrels for the first day after it was opened.

This well was constantly surrounded by a small army of "oil scouts,"
each anxious to obtain and to transmit by telegraph the first authentic news.
For their accommodation a "shack" was built near the well, several miles of
wire was strung through the forest and two telegraph operators were constantly on duty in this emergency office. The greater number of the "scouts"

RUSHING UP RIGS IN THE NEW POOL.

rode horseback, daily, to and from Garfield, the distance to the Cherry Grove
town being about eight miles. On duty at the well they tramped about in
two feet of snow and made merry among the tall hemlocks. In a special
chapter the life of the "scouts" is more fully described.

But while the "excitement" during 1883 was in these white sand pools,
with their "gusher" wells of large initial production and their mysteries, the
old brown sand fields were completing more wells and adding more to the

stable production. The total pipe line runs of oil from wells was smaller than the year before, but the surplus in iron tankage rose above 36,000,000 barrels in July and August. The low prices of the year before had stimulated consumption, so that toward the close of the year deliveries from the pipe lines for consumption exceeded the receipts from wells. This was felt in the speculative market, despite the weight of the enormous surplus, represented by certificates.

The year 1884 opened auspiciously with everything hopeful. Soon, however, a white sand pool appeared at Wardwell, on the Allegheny River, a few miles from Warren, in Warren County, Pa. The "Grant & Ward" panic came on in Wall Street, the Penn Bank in Pittsburgh failed, and disaster was widespread in the petroleum exchanges and in the oil fields. The Wardwell pool was neither large nor long lived, but an agitation was again started to stop drilling. The Petroleum Producers' Association had effected a strong organization and its members were pledged to curtail their activities in the field. Everything promised well for the success of the shutting down movement, there being but little territory in sight. Only the few operators in the vicinity of Baldridge, in Butler County, were recalcitrant, and they were hunting for the pool they believed existed somewhere in that region. Thomas W. Phillips, head of the firm of Phillips Bros., was strongest in the faith, and on the last day of August had a well at Thorn Creek flowing 500 barrels. When tankage had been provided the well was drilled deeper on September 3rd and made 1,300 barrels in the next twenty-four hours. September 6th it was drilled again and increased to 80 barrels an hour. Mr. Phillips said that this was only the first "pay streak" and the well would be larger. Later, in the "second fourth sand pay," the well increased to 130 barrels an hour, and the wonderful Thorn Creek pool was the center of all interest.

On October 25th, Armstrong & Co. No. 2, on the Marshall farm, only 400 feet south of the Phillips well, was drilled through the sand and showed neither oil nor gas. It was considered a failure. On October 27th it was shot with forty quarts of nitro-glycerine, as a forlorn hope. Ten minutes after the torpedo was exploded Armstrong No. 2 was flowing as no American well had ever flowed before. It was four hours before the well could be controlled, several men were overcome by the gas, dragged out of the derrick and revived with difficulty, before the casing was capped and the stream turned into the tanks. The first production saved was 425 barrels in one hour, and the production for the first twenty-four hours after the shot was estimated at 10,000 barrels. A week later the well was making nearly 5,000 barrels a day. Then followed the rapid development of the pool, extending well into 1885. The next most sensational incident after the Phillips and Armstrong wells was the burning of one of the Fisher Bros'. wells, No. 7 on the Marshall farm, while flowing 7,000 barrels a day. It burned for a week, despite every effort, before the flame was controlled, meantime endangering thousands of dollars worth of other properties.

GREAT WESTERN RUN REFINERY IN 1864, NEAR OIL CREEK.

CHAPTER V.

THE TRENTON ROCK FIELDS.

Natural gas having been thoroughly harnessed during 1882, 1883 and 1884, a good many persons were drilling for it in regions somewhat remote from the oil fields. Gas was found near Findlay, Hancock County, in the northwestern portion of Ohio, in 1884. Early in 1885 B. C. Faurot, of Lima, Ohio, started drilling for gas at Lima, hoping to get an abundance of fuel for his strawboard factory. He struck oil, instead, in April. This was the beginning of general operations for oil, as distinguished from the rather localized developments in Pennsylvania. This Lima oil was found in the Trenton lime formation and is geologically the lowest of the oil bearing series. The first oil development in this horizon was near the top of the Cincinnati Arch, probably the oldest of the great upheavals of the cooling earth crust. The later "bucklings" have given us mountains by folding and mountains by fracture in various parts of the earth. The Cincinnati Arch is a plastic folding, its crests having been eroded away and its valleys completely filled, eons before Eric the Red touched the New England coast, or Columbus marked the path by which the white man came to the Continent.

The Lima oil was quite different from that found along the folds in the great subterranean valley lying between the Cincinnati Arch and the later folding of the Allegheny Mountains. It contained less of the ingredient known as paraffine and it was impregnated with sulphur, the Pennsylvania oil having none of the latter. The new oil had a vile odor and the gas of the Trenton rock was even more foul smelling. But the energetic oil man overlooked these faults and sought the fluid with as much ardor as in the older fields to the eastward. While refiners were spending money and exerting brains in experiments to devise a process that would eliminate the sulphur, the fields developed a production of thousands of barrels a day. Northwestern Ohio came to have its "tank farms," rivaling those of Pennsylvania and New York. This level country had its gushers, too, equal to those of the early days among the Pennsylvania hills, and these led to the first serious effort in the United States to build up a market for fuel oil.

It may be worthy of remark that the first discovery of oil in the Trenton rock occurred a little more than twenty-five years after the establishment of the petroleum industry on Oil Creek, and a little more than twenty-five years ago. It was the "half way point" from the beginning to the enormous petroleum industry of the present. It was also the means of preparing the trade for a wider field of activity and to deal with more diverse problems as well as different qualities of oil.

The Trenton rock development spread rapidly from its inception at Lima, in Allen County, into Hancock County to the north and into Auglaize County to the south. Then it spread farther north into Wood County, which proved the richest territory in Northwestern Ohio. The fields about Cygnet and

Bowling Green had many gushers and the trade was not long in discovering that the quality of the oil improved to the north. This in time gave rise to separate quotations for "North Lima" and "South Lima" oils, the former being a few cents higher than the other. Then came an expansion to the westward and the development of a new "belt" through the State of Indiana, where the oil was ranked as of "South Lima" grade. The Indiana fields never equaled their Ohio neighbors, but they had their flowing wells and made hundreds of farm owners rich from their royalties, while many small villages blossomed into towns of importance.

In both Northwestern Ohio and in Indiana natural gas became a feature of the developments, Indiana in particular enjoying a natural gas "boom."

STANDARD OIL COMPANY, SECTION 28, AND OTHER PROPERTIES.

Glass manufacturers removed their plants from eastern cities to the "gas towns" in Indiana on offers of very cheap fuel and thousands of workmen with their families removed to the new industrial centers. The gas was wasted prodigally. The people believed it was inexhaustible, but the boom was short lived. The gas pressure soon weakened. Prices were put up, meters were installed, saving devices were introduced and everything possible was done to conserve the remaining supply of the ideal fuel, but the fields were soon exhausted. The goose that laid the golden egg had been plucked too severely and laid no more eggs.

In Northwestern Ohio the natural gas boom led to an expensive experiment in municipal ownership in Toledo. After the city had been piped by the Northwestern Ohio Gas Company and the price of gas was advanced to twenty-five cents a thousand cubic feet through meters, an agitation sprang up to have the city supply fuel gas as it supplied water. Warning signals were displayed by many who had experience in gas and oil, but the agitators won the City Councils, a bond issue was ordered and a municipal gas plant became a reality. The City of Toledo bought and drilled gas wells in Lucas and Wood counties, laid pipe lines and began supplying natural gas to such citizens as were willing to abandon the private corporation then serving them. The outlook was rosy for a short time and then the gas supply began to fail. When new territory was opened, the private corporation bought the wells before the City Council could make up its mind, or could pass a resolution.

EAST SIDE COALINGA FIELD, FRESNO COUNTY, CALIFORNIA.

When the city decided to drill wildcat wells and develop new territories it was unfortunate enough to locate in "dry" territory where no gas was found. When it began investigating the compressing system, its competitor acted and put in gas pumps. The final blow came when the gas wells owned by the municipality began to produce salt water. At last the city councilmen adopted a resolution to sell the plant to the private corporation, which latter strained a point to make a bid that would cover the cost of the city's pipage system, there being practically no other property in the city gas concern of any value. The City of Toledo got out of its experiment in natural gas better than it had reason to expect, for it had nothing but junk to sell and nobody needed the junk. The Northwestern Ohio Gas Company was in a position to use some of the street mains, with the house connections, and was willing to pay the remainder for the "good will," so it made the price more than the stuff was worth.

In oil production the Lima and Indiana fields reached their zenith in 1896, when the daily average output reached over 69,000 barrels and the surplus oil in tankage reached more than 23,000,000 barrels. Nearly 6,000 wells were completed in those fields during that year and enormous benefits accrued to the towns and cities in the oil region. Many small pipe lines and refineries were established in Northwestern Ohio, but the bulk of the business was handled by the Buckeye and Indiana Pipe Line Companies, the Solar Refining Company at Lima, Ohio, and the Standard Oil Company of Indiana, at Whiting, Indiana, near Chicago, Ill. The oil producers' ranks, however, recruited many new men from these fields, and the aggregate of wealth derived from them was very great. The average depth of the wells in the Trenton rock fields was close to 1,300 feet and contractors were glad to drill them at about one dollar a foot, the formations being regular and the work quite uniformly successful. The wages averaged about five dollars a day for drillers and about four dollars a day for tool dressers, two of each constituting a drilling crew. With 500 or 600 wells under way at one time the amount distributed in wages was no mean item.

These fields were the scene of some remarkable feats in pipe line construction. Their development carried the source of production 300 miles farther from the Atlantic seaboard than the Pennsylvania fields. This distance had to be bridged and it was soon done, that the oil might reach the export markets. The fuel oil trade, however, was principally created in the region of the Great Lakes and the Northwest beyond. The production increased very rapidly, so that a pipe line to Lake Michigan became an early necessity, putting the marketers in closer touch with important consuming regions. A line of pipe, eight inches in diameter, was laid in record time, covering the 350 miles from Lima to Whiting, the work being completed in little more than three months. This included digging the ditch, laying the pipe and covering it. The cost was more than a million dollars, but it was lost sight of in the interest aroused by the rapid construction. The same pipe line has since been used in pumping oil in the opposite direction, on its way from Kansas and Oklahoma, west of the Mississippi River, to the Atlantic coast in the vicinity of New York and Philadelphia.

The Trenton rock fields not only proved the existence of oil elsewhere than near the western slope of the Alleghenies, and spread the producing area westward, but its low priced oil gave a new impetus to the consumption of petroleum in various parts of this country and abroad. It is true that oil had been found in California long before it had been found in Northwestern Ohio, but the Pacific coast fields had not, up to that time, attracted much attention. The oil of the coast contained asphalt and the territory was developed only in a desultory way, by spurts, between the discovery in 1862 and the arrival in California of Wallace K. Hardison and W. Lyman Stewart in 1887, two years after the discovery at Lima. Hardison and Stewart were Pennsylvania oil operators and they went at the California proposition in a way that produced results, and incited others to more successful effort. California, however, did not attain the pace or the place of the Trenton rock fields during the last two decades of the nineteenth century. Its product was essentially a fuel oil, and although the Standard Oil Company and others established refineries, the market was slow in growing. When the Kern River field was opened there was a serious overproduction and a decline in prices that bore heavily on those most successful in obtaining good wells. Yet the California development made the petroleum industry Continent wide in the United States and gave it a new importance. It was no longer an industry mainly confined to the State of Pennsylvania, although this State of its birth continued to hold first place in aggregate production, as well as in investment, up to the last decade of the nineteenth century. At about that time it began to lose its territorial identity, on account of the large and growing production of the same grade of oil in West Virginia and Southeastern Ohio. The petroleum of these areas is all classed as "Pennsylvania grade," yielding fully 99½ per cent of the crude oil in marketable products. There is no better petroleum produced anywhere in the world, and few other regions yield anything as good, although the "heavy," or natural lubricating oils are more valuable. These are produced mainly in limited areas, at Franklin, Pa.; at Mecca, Ohio, and at two places in the State of Wyoming, the total output being inconsiderable.

PETROLEUM CENTER ON OIL CREEK IN 1863.

CHAPTER VI.

SCIENCE TAKES A HAND.

Following the white sand pools of the "Middle Field," as we have seen, came the Thorn Creek gusher pool of 1884. Its development occupied the attention of the trade on into 1885. During this year the Cogley Run pool in Clarion County and the Rockland pool in Venango County made momentary diversions. But the real point of interest in Pennsylvania was now in Washington County. A well was drilled on the Gantz farm that produced a fine quality of oil and the rock from which it came was called the Gantz sand. A little later a test was drilled on the Gordon farm, which got oil in a lower sand. This was named by the drillers for the farm. Geologists soon identified the "Gantz" as the old "first sand" of Venango, Clarion and Butler County fields, and the "Gordon sand" as the "third sand" of those fields, but drillers clung tenaciously to the new nomenclature. These and other strange titles were carried through West Virginia and Southeastern Ohio as names of the many oil bearing sands of those regions, although the two mentioned presented all of the well known characteristics of the standard oil and gas rocks of the original producing fields.

The trade was a little slow in accepting the value of the Washington fields. John F. Carll, a well known geologist, at one time attached to the Pennsylvania Survey, declared his opinion that the development would not amount to much, because the oil bearing sands were more than 400 feet below sea level, and no previous field had been so deep. Other geologists did not agree with him and the practical drillers laughed at the idea. They just drilled wells, cautiously, as became a new territory, and they soon had the fact demonstrated that 500 or 1,000 feet below sea level was no bar to oil production. In 1886 they were opening gushers that rivaled those of the region farther north. This demonstration caused a rather profound depression of prices. Meantime Thomas W. Phillips had begun to develop the field around Reibold, southwest of Thorn Creek, in Butler County, the prolific horizon being known as the "hundred foot" sand. This was one of the richest and most profitable of pools and Mr. Phillips had the better part of it. Belief in the early exhaustion of petroleum resources, so often heralded by geologists, was by this time effectively destroyed.

About the time the Washington County development was at its height E. M. Hukill tried a test near Farmington, in Marion County, W. Va. He got a big gas well, but abandoned it. He next tried his luck near Mt. Morris, in Greene County, Pa., and got oil in good quantity. John Worthington, of the Nineveh Oil Company, had begun operations near Nineveh, in Greene County. He was one of the geologists who did not accept the sea level dictum, for he selected the lowest trough between the Alleghenies and the Cincinnati Arch for his field of activity, and drilled for the "third sand." He found oil in the third sand more than 2,000 feet below sea level. Later, as

Superintendent of the South Penn Oil Company, he had the satisfaction of bringing in gushers from the same level in Marion and Wetzel Counties in West Virginia. In 1888 Mt. Morris pool was attracting much attention and was developed across the state line into West Virginia, many others having joined in the search.

Professor Jackson, of the West Virginia State University, took his engineering class into the field and ran a line of levels from the Mt. Morris field in Monongalia County to the southern part of Marion County. Professor White, the geologist of the State University, then located the anticlinicals, corresponding to that at Mt. Morris. Associated with Clarence Smith, the Marion County Clerk of Courts, these gentlemen leased lands along their scientific lines and then sought the aid of operating companies to test their theory. One well was undertaken near Mannington by Montgomery and Co., and a few months later another was started on Mods Run by

ORIGINAL OIL POOL IN CITY LIMITS, MUSKOGEE, OKLAHOMA.

Dewitt & Co. to test the scientifically located leases. Other persons discovered something was going on. T. W. Fleming and others, of Fairmont, secured a lease on a farm near the village of Fairview and at once started a well. Another well was started on Cunningham Run, south of Mannington. This was the situation in the summer of 1889.

Meantime the South Penn Oil Company had entered the field at Mt. Morris and was reaching down into West Virginia. It soon secured large blocks of leases and prepared to test them. It sent F. H. Oliphant, a geologist of national reputation, into the field and he was joined by Mr. Worthington. As a result of these researches much leasing was done and many tests planned in Monongalia, Marion, Doddridge, Wetzel and Tyler Counties. The first well to be completed was that of Montgomery & Co., near Mannington, which proved good for about ten barrels a day. The next well was that of Fleming & Co., near Fairview, good for about fifteen barrels a day. By that time there was a rush to West Virginia by operators and leasers. The first well of the South Penn Oil Company was on State Fork, near Glovers Gap, which started at about 700 barrels, from the "Big Injun" sand. The development following these discoveries was the most rapid and on the largest scale of any witnessed up to that time in any oil region.

The line of pools, scientifically located, were opened in quick succession, with a smaller proportion of "dry holes" drilled than in previous history. Within a year the leaser and wildcatter had covered the whole area from the Pennsylvania State line to the old developments around Volcano and Burning Springs.

EFFECT OF EXPLOSION TESTING PIPE FOR 1.000 POUNDS PRESSURE OF NATURAL GAS.

The first efforts were made along lines extending from Mt. Morris and Nineveh. But soon there were ventures to the west in Marshall, Wetzel and Tyler Counties. The first great success on the western lines was at Sistersville, on the Ohio River, in Tyler County. This was followed by other ventures across the Ohio River, in Southeastern Ohio. There is yet much drilling in West Virginia and Southeastern Ohio, and the two sections have yielded an enormous amount of petroleum and fabulous wealth. Along with the oil field development there has been a gas development unprecedented. The gas from West Virginia has been piped to Pittsburgh, to Cleveland, to Columbus and to Cincinnati. This supply has been supplemented by the gas region of Central Ohio, drawn principally from a sand stratum in the Clinton lime formation, that has been fully equal in productiveness to the Trenton rock farther west. Oil has also been found in the Clinton, principally in Fairfield and Perry Counties, near the great Hocking Valley coal fields, and the end is not yet. Science has had a higher standing in connection with the location of oil and gas fields since the opening of the Virginia areas and no important region has been developed in recent years without preliminary geological examination.

Natural gas is more certainly located by the aid of scientific examination than oil and the gas companies all make use of such knowledge as is available. This does not mean that the element of chance is eliminated. It is simply that a competent geologist can determine where there is a probability of finding oil or gas by the general conformation and the character of the strata. It will never be possible for any one to tell from

HOPE NATURAL GAS CO., WELL AT LOST CREEK, W. VA., USED IN TEST. ROCK PRESSURE 1.025 POUNDS. NOTE FROST ON PIPE IN SUMMER.

the surface precisely what conditions will be disclosed by the drill hundreds of feet below. It is the province of the geologist to keep the prospector out of the salt water troughs and away from sections so obviously fractured that no volatile substance could be imprisoned within their strata. Whoever assumes functions much in excess of these is not a scientist, but a charlatan. Honest geology has reduced the hazard of exploration in all mining operations and is annually saving fortunes that might otherwise be squandered in places where mineral discovery would be impossible.

This recalls a story told me in West Virginia by a capable and conscientious civil engineer, who was also pretty well versed in geology. Some of his friends had secured leases on several farms in Allegheny County, Pa., not many miles from the City of Pittsburgh. They asked him to make an examination and to report on their chances of finding oil or gas in paying quantities, proposing to give him an interest if the prospects were favorable. He spent several days in obtaining levels and following the "dip" of the rocks, ascertaining that the territory leased was on the "wrong side of the anticlinal." He reported accordingly and advised against any expenditure in that locality. But some of his friends were obstinate, they had little confidence in geology and they drilled a well. It started at 300 barrels a day. As the engineer said feelingly: "I lost much of my reputation and an opportunity to get in on a good thing. I will be mighty careful in the future about condemning anything in oil territory." Yet in ninety-nine cases out of one hundred his advice would have been good. The pool he condemned was a "freak," it proved very small in area and short lived. It was not as profitable as the start of the first well indicated and its total production was not equal to the cost of the many dry holes drilled trying to find an extension in some direction from the wrong side of the anticlinal. Meantime the discredited engineer-geologist did better by locating an oil pool in West Virginia on the right side of the anticline, which "produced the goods."

No less than ten productive horizons have been found in West Virginia. Where conditions are right and one sand fails to yield either oil or gas, the operator usually goes deeper, until he has tried the ten. It is "hard luck" when not one out of so many rocks will yield any return for the outlay. The State has been very rich in its oil and gas deposits, from which many millions of dollars have been realized. Many more millions are yet to be earned from those fields. West Virginia is also extremely rich in coal and other bitumens, the oddest deposit being that in Ritchie County, where were located the Ritchie Mines. Before the industrial discovery of petroleum, when the manufacture of oil from coal was becoming an important process, this Ritchie Mine deposit was discovered, near the South Fork of Hughes River. It was supposed to be coal, but it had peculiar properties and, unlike coal, the "seam" was not horizontal, but perpendicular. The material was found to be highly inflammable, igniting readily when a lighted match was held to it, and it was rich in oil. Johnson Camden, afterwards United States Senator, and others, purchased the deposit, erected a large plant for extracting and refining the oil and started operations hopefully. It looked like a profitable enterprise until the discovery of petroleum and the simultaneous caving of the fifth level in the mine, which cost the lives of four men. The works were abandoned. The group of brick factory buildings, standing amid forest trees was one of the remarkable sights that met the gaze of the oil man when the immediate vicinity was tested for petroleum in 1890. In the light of knowledge gained from thirty years of oil development, the Ritchie Mine was no longer classed as coal, but was known to be solidified petroleum. There is a great "fault" in the geological formation in that region and the Ritchie Mine is a fissure, eight to twelve feet wide and of unknown length, filled with pure bitumen, solidified and compressed. The Ritchie Mine coal oil works were turning out real "kerosene" when petroleum was classed chiefly as a hindrance and a nuisance in the operation of salt wells, but the fact was not then known.

From the first assault on West Virginia in 1889 there was a return to Southwestern Pennsylvania. Many small pools were opened in Washington, Greene, Beaver and Allegheny Counties. In 1891 the McDonald pool was opened, partly in Allegheny and partly in Washington County. A new gusher record was established in this pool, the well of J. M. Guffey & Co., on the Matthews farm and also that of Greenlee & Frost on the Mevey farm, making 14,000 barrels in one day. This pool had the effect of greatly depressing the speculative market. In rapid increase of production this was one of the most spectacular of the white sand pools, but being near Pittsburgh, with a good train service, it was entirely lacking in the struggle to provide food and shelter that has marked so many oil developments. The city had accommodations and attractions for all. The McDonald oil was obtained from a sand below the "Gordon," or "third," and was classed as the "fifth" sand. The oil region of West Virginia transformed a hilly, poverty-stricken agricultural section to a wealthy country. Railroads were built among the monstrous hills, the county towns grew to cities, so that ten years after the discovery at Mannington the business of the entire State had increased more than three fold. The taxable valuation had mounted by millions and the population had almost doubled.

FIRST 36-INCH NATURAL GAS LINE LAID, 1890.

McELHANEY AND COLUMBIA FARMS, OIL CREEK.

CHAPTER VII.

WESTWARD HO, IN OIL.

While the West Virginia and Lima fields were engrossing public attention, J. M. Guffey and John Galey heard that natural gas had been found in Kansas. In 1894 they had investigated, verified the report, leased a great tract of land and drilled a well near Neodesha. It struck oil. At the best it was a ten barrel well and the product was inferior. In distillation it left a residue of asphalt instead of the paraffine of the Pennsylvania crude. Like the oil of California it was on the asphalt base. A second test gave similar results. But Guffey & Galey kept on drilling until they had a production of several hundred barrels daily. They also found gas in abundance. The mere discovery of oil and gas in a remote region does not constitute good fortune; it requires capital to get the stuff to market. Guffey & Galey soon decided they would be compelled to build a refinery, or a long pipe line, or both, if they were to utilize their new oil field. They had interests elsewhere that demanded the active employment of their capital, so they had not enough available to handle so large an enterprise. They appealed to the Standard Oil Company. The Standard investigated, became interested and finally purchased the whole property. This company realized that this new source of supply was 500 miles nearer to a large inland market than its nearest refinery at Whiting, Indiana. It could save the freight and sell the manufactured products that much cheaper.

The development of the Kansas oil field then began in earnest. First the Guffey & Galey property was transferred to the Forest Oil Company, and then two Kansas corporations were organized—The Prairie Oil and Gas Company, empowered to produce, purchase, transport, store and sell oil and gas; and the Standard Oil Company of Kansas, to refine crude petroleum and market its products. A refinery was built at Neodesha and a pipe line system installed for gathering the oil. Other producers soon entered the field, the producing territory was extended and the pipe line system enlarged. Another and larger refinery was erected near Kansas City and a trunk pipe line was laid to it from the producing region, 80 miles distant. Kansas was then ready for the boom. There was a "spot cash" market for oil as soon as produced.

In the meantime Guffey & Galey had gone southward to Corsicana, Texas. They drilled and found oil and gas; the wells were small, as they were in Kansas. But they found two productive sands, the one yielding a low gravity oil, and the other a much higher gravity. Again the Standard Oil Company followed the lead, built a refinery and began serving the Texas trade with cheaper products, because long transportation was eliminated. But the laws of Texas were hostile to "trusts" and the big company was soon under fire of prosecution, along with the partly owned marketing concern, the Waters-Pierce Oil Company. Colonel Guffey moved on to Beaumont, led thither by

Captain Lucas.   The first well was drilled on Spindle Top, and the American oil world was shocked by the report of a gusher doing 65,000 barrels a day. It was soon learned, however, that the oil was very heavy, on an asphalt base and distinctly of a fuel grade.   Yet it was the largest well ever struck, outside of the Baku district in Russia, and it created a sensation.   The Standard Oil Company was invited to Spindle Top, but it declined to go on the grounds that its business was primarily the refining of oil, while this was fuel, and that Texas was too unfriendly to risk large investments there.

The J. M. Guffey Petroleum Company, capitalized at $15,000,000, was organized to provide pipe and handling facilities, and a pipe line was started from Beaumont to Port Arthur, on the Gulf of Mexico.   Then followed the speculative furore in Texas that rivaled Pithole and the Pithole era.   Drilling was done again on acre and half acre leases and oil company stocks were sold by thousands of shares.   Much money was made, principally by those who organized the companies, and the fun was fast and furious while it lasted.

BARTLESVILLE, INDIAN TERRITORY, EAST SIDE, 1904.

After Spindle Top came Sour Lake, Batson Prairie and the other Texas and Southern Louisiana pools.   Of the many corporations organized in the flush time, few survive.   The J. M. Guffey Petroleum Company gave rise to the Gulf Refining Company, the Gulf Pipe Line Company and the Guffey Oil Company, W. L. Mellon being president of the group, J. M. Guffey having retired from them several years before.   The Texas Company, J. L. Cullinan, president, has also grown into an interstate and international producing, transporting and refining company, rivaling the Gulf Refining Company in the magnitude of its operations.

The Texas "excitement" had a profound influence upon the development in Kansas.   The latter soon had almost as many stock promotions as the Lone Star State, with the effect of stimulating operations and arousing an intense popular interest.   The producing fields were rapidly extended.   Under any circumstances stockholders in a majority of these Kansas companies must have suffered losses, but misfortunes do not come singly, and in 1904 the wild-catter had crossed the Kansas State line and begun a development in the Indian Territory and the Osage Indian Reservation, in Oklahoma Territory. On lands of the Cherokees a prolific shallow sand was found, and on the eastern edge of the Osage Reservation deeper drilling developed gushers. Above all it was soon learned this deep sand oil was of a much better refining grade than that in Kansas. The production rapidly mounted above any possible require-ments of the states between the Mississippi River and the Rocky Mountains. It became evident that the oil would have to be marketed at a distance and the price began to decline. The prospects of dividends from the Kansas com-panies vanished completely and the stockholders became clamorous. To di-vert wrath from themselves the promoters, many of them with too little ex-perience in the oil business to understand what was happening, laid the whole blame on the Standard Oil Company and the indignation grew intense.

Perplexed Americans turn inevitably to their popular legislative as-semblies for relief. It is the history of Congress and the legislatures. Kan-sans went to the Legislature at Topeka and the bills introduced and urged during the session of 1905 attracted the attention of the whole country. Among the measures proposed was an oil refinery to be operated by the State, employing convicts in the State penitentiary. This bill was passed, but was declared unconstitutional by the Supreme Court of Kansas. Had it been up-held as legal by the court it would have been impossible. Railroad rates on oil were limited by statute, pipe line regulations were adopted, and oil and gas inspection laws were enacted that have provided useless jobs for politicians ever since. However, no laws gave any assistance to oil producers. Prices fell more rapidly than before, pipe lines and refineries were hampered in their operations, railroads were rendered hostile to the industry and practical ruin fell upon the oil fields of Kansas. The oil star of the territories was in the ascendant. Sent there during the agitation to investigate conditions, the writer gave his opinion in March, 1905, that Kansas was simply being drowned in the flood of oil from the territories, which, if pipe line and storage facilities could be provided, would mount in six months to 120,000 barrels a day. This is history, long ago verified.

The last Territorial Assembly of Oklahoma adjourned in Guthrie a week after the adjournment of the Kansas Legislature at Topeka in 1905. It had before it bills similar to those adopted by Kansas, but rejected practically all of them, or adjourned before they were disposed of. However, the agitation had a profound effect upon the deliberations of the Constitutional Convention of Oklahoma—then admitted with Indian Territory as a State—and the Okla-homa Constitution was so drawn as to make legal what had been declared un-constitutional in Kansas. These provisions, and statutes afterwards enacted, have caused much trouble for oil producers, but more particularly for pipe lines and marketers in the new State, including interstate gas lines. Restric-tions of the Department of the Interior, affecting Indian lands and allotments in severalty have also been annoying. Despite all these Oklahoma made a world record in the development of production from its fields and in 1908, its total of 47,580,000 barrels was the largest among the States. It has since yielded first place to California, but its 1910 production has exceeded that of

1908. The rate of production of California indicates more than 77,000,000 barrels for 1910.

Local refineries sprang up in Kansas and Oklahoma, as they had in Texas. They absorbed much of the local and near markets for the products, the most profitable part of the business. The Standard Oil Company interests were compelled to seek an outlet for the oil in the export trade. Two eight-inch pipe lines were laid to connect in Indiana with the system extending to the Atlantic seaboard; these cost many millions of dollars. Prices of crude at the wells naturally fell, as the cost of transportation had to be deducted.

THE BEATTY WELL, BEAUMONT, FLOWING SIXTY THOUSAND BARRELS A DAY.

Production, however, exceeded the capacity of the pipe lines and storage tanks were erected at a rate not paralleled in the previous history of petroleum. The Prairie Oil and Gas Company now has more than 40,000,000 barrels of Oklahoma oil in iron tankage.

The Gulf Refining Company constructed an eight-inch pipe line into Oklahoma from its Texas terminal, 500 miles, and was immediately followed by the Texas Company. These found more oil than they could handle in the Glenn pool, south of the Arkansas River. The three great pipe lines were unable to cope with the flood of oil, aided by the many local refineries and others who shipped oil in tank cars. The situation was without precedent and naturally affected prices in other fields. The Standard interests have since established a modern refining plant at Baton Rouge, La., and constructed an eight-inch pipe line thence from Oklahoma, through Arkansas. The three big companies, in lively competition, have built up a large trade in fuel oil and put the products into the eastern domestic markets and the markets abroad, but the whole business has been on a scale of low prices, with much cost for transportation, converting plants and storage.

The latest American oil field of world importance is that in Caddo parish, Louisiana, extending over into the edge of Texas. Unlike the previous developments in that region, the Caddo field is yielding a high gravity oil on a paraffine base. The field was opened by the J. C. Trees Oil Company, the first well being drilled on the Stiles tract. It flowed at the rate of 2,500 barrels a day for many months. Other wells have been larger, one of the Producers Oil Company being credited with 25,000 barrels for one day, 10,000 barrels more than the Guffey well on the Matthews farm, at McDonald, Pa. Thus, the new field holds the single day's record for one well producing high gravity oil. The district has had a production of 53,000 barrels in one day, surpassing the record of Cherry Grove in 1882.

A CLUSTER OF GUSHERS AT SPINDLETOP, TEXAS.

Texas has the record of the largest production from one well for a single day, the Lucas & Guffey at Spindle Top. California has the largest production from a single well, the Lakeview, which started at fully 50,000 barrels a day and kept up that rate of production for several months. These records are American. The Baku district, in Russia, has produced larger wells than Spindle Top, but none that has continued gushing at a great rate as long as the Lakeview. What the future has in store none may prophesy, but this wonderful industry has not reached the limit of its expansion. It is in its infancy, although from the first production has been pushed more rapidly than genius and energy could create or cultivate a market for the output. Out of this fact have grown the many agitations, for which this industry has been noted, which have stirred the politics of States and the Nation, and extended to foreign lands.

PETROLEUM CENTER, 1864, WITH OIL BARGE LOADED WITH BARRELS IN FOREGROUND.

CHAPTER VIII.

PITHOLE CITY.

Wherever the English language is spoken the fame of Pithole has spread. It grew from an isolated farming community to a city with about 9,000 resident population, and a floating population of that many more, during 1865. This was the era of wildest speculation in oil company stocks, just after the close of the Civil War, when the currency was inflated and when the adventurous thousands of two great armies were seeking some excitement in peaceful avocations to compensate for the lack of that formerly found on fields of carnage. Hundreds of sutlers and camp followers in general, were also seeking other fields of conquest and the hurly burly of the oil region appealed to them. They aided materially in adding to the Pithole frenzy in all its features. Army officers and soldiers were conspicuous in the industrial and speculative affairs of the place; camp followers were among those who conducted gambling joints on the open streets and flaunted vice in the faces of the moving throng. ' Pithole was the one oil town where gamblers plied their trade by the wayside, crying their business to the multitude, after the manner of barkers at a county fair. It differed not greatly from others in its equipment of dram shops and more secret vice. But Pithole possessed the sterling virtues as well and was the alembic in which was tried out the metal of many good citizens, who have since made the world better for their living in it. It went under high pressure, as, indeed, does the serious business of the petroleum industry everywhere, so the moments of relaxation may have been rather more hilarious than the dictates of decorum sanction in older towns. Pithole differed from other oil towns, where excitement has been great, in the erection of costly hotels and other structures for the ephemeral purpose. The builders of Pithole did not know how evanescent an oil field might be. The collapse of Pithole was not more sudden than that of many successors on a slightly smaller scale. It was virtually built in six months and its glory had departed a year after it had reached the zenith of its greatness. Numerous fires assisted in removing the superfluous buildings. To-day, the site is occupied by half a dozen farms and their buildings, some of which betoken comfort and the prosperity that arises from a responsive soil. The one conspicuous survival of the boom time is the Methodist Episcopal church, endowed by the late Robert Duncan, which surmounts the highest hill and is ample for a congregation ten times larger than any that has gathered within its portals for more than thirty years. A part of the endowment of this church and the one at Plumer has been sequestered by appointed trustees.

A visit to the site of the vanished town is interesting and pathetic. Of the once busy and muddy streets, naught remains save the grass-grown grades, flanked on either side by depressions representing the cellars of huge hotels, fine residences, banks and other places of business. In these cellars may be noted an occasional seedling apple tree, full grown or a forest specimen twenty-five feet high, the squares near the elevated church maturing a goodly crop of buckwheat. These trees are mute reminders of the flight of time since Pithole was the most talked of city on the continent.

The following extracts from the "History of Pithole," by "Crocus," will give a more lifelike view than anything that might be written now. The author, whose nom de plume of "Crocus" was widely known, was the late Charles C. Leonard, a brave soldier and a newspaper writer of ability. He gathered news for the Pithole Record, the town's daily newspaper, and, after the bubble had burst drifted away. He attained considerable fame as a humorist while in Cleveland and died from the effects of wounds received in battle during the war of the Rebellion. No apology is offered for quoting so liberally from his pages, but due homage is tendered to his memory and his genius. The "History" was printed and published in Pithole, 1867, when the town was rapidly on the down grade:

INTRODUCTORY.

Two years ago the traveler passing through this part of the Township of Cornplanter would have found it a barren and almost uninhabited district. The few backwoodsmen it sustained depended more upon their rifles and the products of the forest for a living than their farms. Money existed as a general thing only in the imagination; greenbacks were unknown, and less than ten years since we feel safe in saying that not $100,000 was in circulation in the country contiguous to Oil Creek. The settlers who then inhabited this region little dreamed of the vast treasures lying beneath their farms, but in their peaceful homes cared not for the outside world, its cares or pleasures, and the idea of thriving and populous cities springing up on their farms never entered their minds. But upon the discovery of oil by the United States Petroleum Company, on the Thomas Holmden farm, an immense business sprang up as if by magic along the entire Pithole valley. The necessity of a business center soon became apparent. The Thomas Holmden farm, upon which was the famous U. S. well, being the point of production, naturally became the center of trade. Thither thousands daily rushed, bearing with them capital from every State. It was not an uncommon thing at this time for a million dollars to change hands in a single day. Fortune seekers from all parts of America and Europe were attracted to this quarter. The gold of California and Australia no longer tempted them with its glitter, and the "days of oil" usurped the days of "shoddy." On every train they came rushing to the "land of derricks." From the railway terminus they scattered on rickety horses or rickety coaches over rickety roads in search of some spot where the "grease" should shower upon them "untold millions."

Buildings were erected so rapidly as to extort expressions of surprise from every lip. Of course solidity and elegance were sacrificed to rapidity of construction—but a people who displayed such "goaheadativeness" in the beginning of an enterprise might safely be trusted with its completion, and the Pithole City of to-day is not the offspring of speculative excitement, but the result of real Anglo-Saxon energy.

The valley of Pithole Creek had attracted the attention of oil hunters for a number of years. Six or seven years since some "Bostonians" tried to develop the upper part of the valley about ten miles from the mouth of the creek, and not long after the residents of the valley followed the example. One party set about digging for oil with shovels. Others commenced sinking a well with horse power, and still another went to drilling with water power. All of these attempts were on the McKinney farm, where the holes in the neighborhood of the Homestead well, and the odd looking derrick near the burying ground, are still to be seen. The Boston parties struck heavy water veins, which they could not master, and turned their attention to the, at that time, more promising oil field on Oil Creek.

The history of Pithole commences properly with the first operations of the United States Petroleum Company. We next give the following sketch of the first developments made by that organization.

The United States Petroleum Company.

Was organized in the spring of 1864 by Frederick W. Jones, J. Nelson Tappan, of New York City; James Faulkner and J. N. Frazier, then connected with the Humboldt

Refining Company, of Plumer. J. N. Frazier afterwards became superintendent, and was considered one of the best oil operators in the country. From the date of this company's organization commenced the growth and prosperity of Pithole, although it was not until the succeeding year that the city was built. Leases were at once purchased upon the Thomas and Walter Holmden farms, also upon the Blackmer, Luther Woods, McKinney, Howard, Van Wyck, Tyrrell and Heckert farms, and wells were immediately started on each.

Too much credit cannot be rendered to the United States Petroleum Company for the energetic manner in which they proceeded to develop the apparently valueless lands upon the creek. Two or three wells had been sunk by other parties to the third sand, as in other localities, and when no oil was found it was deemed useless to go further. The officers of the United States Petroleum Company, however, from careful and shrewd

GENERAL VIEW OF PITHOLE AND BALLTOWN, 1865.

observations, felt certain that there was a fourth sand, and that oil would there be found. Subsequent developments confirmed this belief. Had less energetic parties been engaged in testing, and had the "Frazier" well proved a dry hole, Pithole City would never have been heard of, and the life and bustle of commercial activity since witnessed, would never have been seen in this vicinity.

The first well struck on Pithole Creek was the Frazier well, on lease No. 4, Thomas Holmden farm, which at this time was covered with a dense forest, with the exception of that portion of the farm where the city now stands, which was pasture land or meadow. That part of the farm along the creek that has since proved the most valuable, was then considered the poorest territory; and the Blackmer farm, from its location and basin-like appearance, was regarded by all interested as the most promising locality and the spot where oil would be found, if any where. But oil in paying quantities has never been produced on this farm.

The Frazier well was located by Thomas H. Brown, with the aid of the mysterious twig of witch hazel. A son of Thomas Holmden and William Lyons were the parties who put down the well which commenced flowing about the eighth day of January, 1865, at the rate of 250 barrels per day. The production of the well gradually fell off, but upon drawing the rods again flowed at the rate of 900 barrels per day. The finding of oil here was a matter of much surprise, and great excitement followed, which was shared by the owner of the farm when he found he had a fortune almost within his grasp.

Plumer was then the general rendezvous or headquarters of "oilists," who would ride over each morning and back at night. The forest which covered the flats was filled with innumerable swarms of insects and gnats which mercilessly preyed upon the unlucky individual who failed to cover his face and hands with handkerchief and gloves.

Mr. George D. Davis, Jr., sold oil at this well in January, 1865, for eight dollars per barrel. This is the largest price ever paid for oil on the creek. In comparison to the weather of later and muddier days, there was then sleighing for six consecutive weeks, and oil was hauled to Titusville on sleighs. The office of the United States Petroleum Company was originally at Plumer, but afterwards removed to this place. In all cases where leases were sold, the lessee was required to test the territory immediately or forfeit the lease. There were only three buildings in this vicinity at the time the Frazier well was struck; the Widow Lyons' house, a log structure now standing at the upper end of Holmden street, near the old machine shop of Leard & Wright; a plain and unpretentious frame building which stood about the center of Holmden street, near the United States Hotel, until destroyed by fire last winter, and which was known as the Thomas Holmden house, and a building at the foot of Main street, occupied at the time by Walter Holmden. At the time of writing, the following are the officers of the United States Petroleum Company:

Trustees—J. Nelson Tappan, S. Q. Brown, A. A. Sumner, John Burchill, Charles K. Randall and G. W. Smith; President, J. Nelson Tappan; Vice President, John Burchill; Treasurer, A. Somardindk; Secretary, F. G. Fenning; Cashier, Robert Leckey.

The Morey Farm.

This piece of land was for a long time after the discovery of oil on Pithole Creek considered of very little value; in fact, good for nothing except "buckwheat and speculation." Those who put down wells upon this territory were laughed at for their pains, and when a certain well (afterwards one of the best) was to be tested, it was done in the night and under the cover of darkness, so fearful were the owners of derision and a dry hole. But the striking of the Burtis and other wells upon the bluffs put an end to these troubles, and the farm speedily became an object of interest to all operating along the creek.

As an item of interest showing the shrewdness and speculation of the times, we give the following brief account of the purchasing of said farm, which was contracted for by A. G. Morey and D. Burtis, for the sum of $300,000, but was afterwards purchased for $100,000. While drawing up the papers necessary to transfer the right and title to the purchasers, A. G. Morey suggested that $300,000 (the price first contracted for), be inserted as the sum paid for the farm, instead of $100,000, the price actually paid. The object of this was to increase the apparent value of the land should a stock company be formed. Mr. Copeland, the owner of the farm, found no objection to this, and the documents were thus made out. So far everything was lovely, but when it came to "stamping" the deeds, as Uncle Sam requires, the owner of the land could hardly see "from where he stood" why he should furnish revenue stamps for a $300,000 bill of sale when he only received $100,000; but business was business, and after much exhortation and wire pulling, the stamps were plastered according to law and to the wishes of the purchasers. Everything now looked lovelier than ever; but a nephew of Marcus Copeland, who had seen more of the financial and speculative world than his ancient Pennsylvania relative, made a visit to his uncle, and after hearing and examining the facts of the case, thought he "perceived the odor of a small rat," or in other words, "smelt a mouse," and after consultation with prominent lawyers, suit was commenced by Marcus Copeland against Messrs. Morey and Burtis which resulted in the latter paying $300,000 for the farm. Moral: Expend your "stamps" and save your money.

Fifteen producing wells have been struck upon this farm, among which are the celebrated Burtis, Rice, Clara, Ellsworth and City of London wells.

An acre lease at one time sold for a bonus of $5,000 and half the oil. At one time, where four wells were going down on less than one-fourth of an acre of ground, three "thirty-seconds" of the land interests were sold at $7,000 each.

The Grant Well.

This was one of the finest of the large wells which at one time made Pithole famous. It was struck on the second day of August, 1865, at a depth of 604 feet.

There was not the slightest show of oil at first, and the parties who sunk the well put down the tubing merely as an experiment, but no sooner had they done so and pumped four hours, than it commenced flowing at the rate of 800 barrels per day, but finally decrased to a steady flow of 700 barrels.

This well has twice suffered severely by fire. It caught fire at the time it was struck and was burned again October 10, 1865. During the latter fire several thousand barrels of oil belonging to the well were destroyed; also the tanks and fine office belonging to the company. The well kept flowing during the fire, and it was several days before the flames could be extinguished. An account written at that time says: "A painter's skill could hardly portray the beautiful scene which this well presented while burning. The elevated pipe which had poured the oil over the tops of the tanks had fallen with its support and lay prostrate upon the ground, the oil pouring from it all the while and burning as rapidly as it flowed. Nothing could surpass the beauty of this jet of burning oil. Every imaginable color was presented momentarily to the observer, The oil from this well flows continuous but not steadily, about each successive five seconds it bursts forth, shooting at least thirty feet in a horizontal direction. The fire, of course, is all that is visible, darting rocket-like from the flame at the mouth of the pipe. The first burst is a ruddy blaze deeper in color than the deep red heat of the fire of the smith; then as it rises a whirl of mingled smoke and flame is seen, then the volume of black smoke, which again gives place to the secondary ruddy jet. * * * * Several workmen were badly burned at this fire, and one or two afterwards died.

The Grant well ceased flowing on the third of June, 1866, having flowed exactly ten months to an hour. It is now pumping 20 barrels per day. James Sheakley, Esq., of Greenville, Pa., is superintendent.

Thousands of strangers visited this well in 1865, and various descriptions were given of the same in many of the leading journals of the day.

But Pithole, renowned as it was for its monster wells, enterprise and the magnitude of its operations, with capitalists from every part of the Union developing its resources, was destined to receive still another attraction in the form of

Flowing Surface Wells

which astonished even the Pitholians, who had long since ceased to wonder at common miracles, but who were surprised at the new freak of nature.

The hillside, upon which the city is located, suddenly commenced yielding oil. The water springs and shafts sunk to obtain water, became flowing wells.

Many operators without the necessary means to purchase a set of drilling tools, or even a shovel, by the aid of a shingle or their hands, dug excavations in the soil that produced oil.

At first the story of these surface wells was not believed, and the leading journals of "America" refused to publish accounts of the same, believing it to be a hoax or story manufactured by our sensationalists. But when the truth became known, thousands visited these wells, including many of the leading journalists and "savants" of the country; and if possible the excitement was greater than that of earlier and oilier days.

Much speculation was indulged in at this time; building lots commanded high figures, and fabulous prices were offered for the "water wells" and "springs" that had previously been of little value. No one has ever offered a satisfactory explanation of this phenomenon, which to this day remains a mystery. The following is taken from the Pithole Record of February 5, 1866:

"As those who were engaged in putting out the fire yesterday were throwing water on it was discovered by so doing they were only adding fresh fuel to the flames; and on closer examination a quantity of our liquid greenbacks were floating on the water. A rush was made to the nearest pump from which water was taken, and there we found a lively 'negro' with his teeth chattering from fright at the flow of gas from the spout. He had pumped the well until all the water had been exhausted, then oil and gas flowed in liberal quantities.

"The pump was then handled very lively, the oil continued to come and the fire speedily lost all interest except to the losers. Many disbelieved the account and could hardly credit their own eyesight, thinking the oil was put there for a 'sell,' but before long it was found that two other water wells and some springs had commenced spouting oil, and incredulity gave way to belief.

"The news then spread through the town like wild fire, and every one left his work and went to the spot. We are all accustomed to visit the flats and see oil flow from deep wells, but it was something decidedly novel for the oil to return the compliment and bring its liquid treasures to our back doors from water wells only sixteen feet deep, to say nothing of the springs that were flowing fast.

"The wells so far are three in number, and there are some four or five flowing springs. They are situated on the west side of Holmden street, in the rear of John street. The oil is accompanied by some gas, although not so much as the wells on the flats show. It was tested yesterday and the specific gravity is 42 degrees, according to the United States Petroleum Company's standard. The water of these springs has been considered of very good quality until last Sunday, when a disagreeable taste was noticed, which has increased ever since. Not the least strange thing is that these new oil wells are all at least 150 feet above the flats. Perhaps the first discoverer of oil in Pithole City was Mr. J. L. Shelve, of the bath house, who discovered several inches of oil on the tank of the spring at six o'clock yesterday morning.

"The first well struck belonged to Mrs. Rickets, a widow, who has heretofore earned her living by washing. It is at a depth of sixteen feet, and was only pumped at intervals, yet the oil would come freely upon pumping, and fill a barrel in ten minutes. Mrs. Rickets was offered at first $1,000, then $2,000 for the well, until at last a gentleman secured the refusal at $5,000 until this morning.

"Mr. L. L. Hill's well was the favorite and was pumped very vigorously during the day, much to the amusement of an admiring crowd, who were more used to seeing a steam engine with its walking beam and other apparatus pumping oil, than witnessing a "one man" power at a pump handle. It filled a barrel in five minutes during the time it was pumped. This well is twenty-three feet deep. The owner refused an offer of $7,000 for it.

"Much amusement was caused by a discovery that the oil had created quite a rivalry among some three or four Irishmen for the hand of the fair widow, who had so suddenly ranked herself among oil princes.

"Many theories have been broached as to how the oil got there, and the most probable of them seems to be that the artesian well had exhausted large quantities of the water, allowing the oil to run out of the crevices and flow into the wells and springs. A few thought it might be caused by a leak in the Meredith pipes, but that is impossible, as the gravity is different and in that case there would be no gas. We shall be happy to hear from some of our practical oil men on the subject."

*   *   *   *   *   *   *   *

This excitement continued. The Record issued thousands of extras concerning the new discoveries, and they were gobbled up by the crowd as fast as printed. People from all parts of the oil country came flocking to see these curiosities. The ground seemed to be fairly saturated with oil, and was riddled with holes and shallow excavations from which the oil slowly oozed.

The scene resembled the gold diggings of Australia when the "yellow fever' was at its height. Barrels of oil were dipped from the springs with dippers, and the bottoms of a great many cellars were found covered with the oleaginous fluid.

Scientific men were puzzled as to the cause of this outpouring of nature's wealth, and their perplexity was added to by the flow of salt water and gas with the oil, which, according to their experience, was a most favorable sign.

Many ludicrous incidents relating to the excitement are narrated, but as the author of this work was carried away by the "fever," it will not be necessary to relate them. Suffice it to say that he was in Ohio at the time of the discoveries, but immediately telegraphed to his partner at this point to secure all the territory under the building in which he was clerking, and commence operations without delay; this was done, and upon the writer's arrival some days later he found a hole under the store big enough to bury an elephant in; but it proved to be "dry territory," and no pecuniary benefits ever resulted therefrom.

While the wells were thus giving oil instead of water, men and women, boys and girls, could be seen with tin pails, wooden pails, tea-kettles, etc., in their hands vainly searching for pure water. Oil might buy coffee or tea, but would not make it. Nor were the tea drinkers alone in their grief, for an ancient cow walked up to her accustomed water place, but one taste was enough, for she turned and left the spot, evidently thinking it might affect the price of her butter should she indulge.

An Irishman who had a small spring was highly elated at the turn fortune was taking; for said he "Yesterday I wasn't worth a cint; and be jabbers, to-day I'm worth me thousands upon thousands."

Oil continued to be found in the heart of the city. The streets and hotels were rapidly filled. Strangers who came, expecting it amounted to nothing, after an examination were convinced that the natural wealth of Pithole had not been developed.

For a month the yield of the wells and springs was immense, but they finally ceased to flow, and all interest in them was lost in the larger strikes daily occurring upon the flats.

The following theory is from the gifted pen of Professor Q. Reuskus, then engaged in dipping oil along the creek. We give the professor's letter in full:

On the Flats, January, 1867.

Mr. Crocus, Dear Sir:—You ask my opinion in regard to the flowing surface wells of Pithole that caused such an excitement a year ago. I claim that owing to the large amount of gas constantly arising from political circles throughout the land, the entire air is impregnated with benzine, which, when it rises to the ground below, becomes idealized or confused and percolates through the entire soil, into the solid cavities of the suburban rock.

From thence it meanders to the surface and is lost in oblivion or discovered by man and woman. To my mind it is very seldom where the source of this oil may be found. But, nevertheless, quite evident to the initiated. I analyzed specimens of this surface oil in 1866 and found it to be of moderate gravity, and the best oil for convivial purposes yet discovered.

Should the above be of any benefit to the public you are at liberty to publish this.

Q. Reuskus, Professor.

With this valuable document we close the history of the surface wells. The wells are also closed at the time of writing.

PITHOLE AS IT IS NOW.

Incidents.

The following is an extract from an article written in 1865. Some may consider the acccount exaggerated, or "high toned," but we assure the gentle reader that like other stories with a similar moral, this is "founded on fact." A pen and mind gifted with all the imagination of a divine novelist could not portray or do justice to the scenes of speculation and excitement of that time:

"All day, the several roads leading to this 'oily center' were traversed by pedestrians and horsemen (buggies are unknown here) whose faces point in but one direction—Pithole. In coming to this place the first object that attracts the attention of the stranger is the immense number of teams engaged in transporing oil to the nearest points on the railroad. These 'oil trains' very much resemble the wagon trains of a moving army, often forming a continuous line for miles. Here is seen the same old 'Army Mule' that toiled through days of war. It is doubtful whether he believes in the benefits resulting from a blessed peace. And we are sure that his sensitive nature is touched when he thinks of the days when 'government oats' were plentiful, and he was the proud mule that drew 'hard tack lobscouse' for 'Sherman's boys in blue,' instead of a degraded 'oil mule.' You can distinguish the ex-army mule at a glance, by his abject appearance and down cast eye. Now he never indulges in a 'kick up' or joyful whisks of tail, but with slow step performs his greasy work, and often dies the victim of a broken heart.

"Another feature of teaming, and one that reminds you of 'marching days,' is the prevalence of profanity among the teamsters. Seated on his mule—driving with one line—clothed in regulation hat, faded blouse and worn cavalry pants, you are almost willing to swear that he has tended mules for Uncle Sam in 'sunnier and rebellious' climes; but when his wagon gets stuck, as is frequently the case, in some bottomless pit of mud, then your doubts are all removed as to his previous occupation; for after trying a 'gee pull' and fetching them 'haw' without success, off goes our M. D. into the mud and amid kicks and blows indulges oaths and curses, accompanied by screeches and yells, which were never originated elsewhere than on a 'southern swamp road' and by a 'demoralized Yankee soldier.' During the early part of the day the moving throng of teams tends toward Pithole and in the afternoon in the direction of 'Titusville' or 'Miller Farm.'

"As you near the city you are surprised at the countless number of derricks going up and already erected along the creek. At first sight it seems that every available spot of ground is occupied by these lofty and skeleton-like structures, so near together that it appears impossible for a wagon to drive between them, while the walking-beams in motion seem in danger of colliding. But a near view shows that there is room enough and to spare; at least so think the owners of the land, who will sell you a lease, if it is only large enough to sink your drive-pipe upon; your derrick must be put up on your neighbor's territory.

"The manner of sinking a well may be of interest to those who never visited the oil country, or witnessed the method of procuring oil. And as many come to the place with the idea that all the tools necessary with which to strike oil were a pick and shovel, and that the 'grease' might be had by digging into the ground a few inches, the following description may afford some light upon the subject .   :

Putting Down a Well.

"First comes the derrick,—a lighthouse-looking structure, some forty-eight feet in height, and a temporary shed to cover it and to shelter the operators and afford them sleeping quarters, as it is not safe to leave the premises or machinery even for a night; if they did, they might return in the morning to find that every movable thing had disappeared. Even the derrick and engine have been stolen in a single night; and not long since an enterprising thief stole the tubing out of the bottom of a well as fast as the owner let it down from the top; in this manner he purloined nearly a thousand feet of tubing from a six hundred foot well; but the owner, suspecting something, set to work, and the thief was brought up in the sand pump. This is not a 'fish' nor an 'oil' story, therefore the writer is not a 'sardine.' But to return to the well and our subject.

"There is to be as many feet of cable or rope as will reach the intended depth. A rope socket connects the sinker-bar, of two inch round iron; below this comes the 'jars,' two pieces of iron five feet in length, working like two long links within each other, and designed, by the jar they cause in lifting, to more readily loose the drill should it become fastened. Below this comes the auger-stem, a round bar of two or two and a half inch iron fifteen or twenty feet in length which is attached to the center-bit, a blunt chisel-shaped instrument. The 'tools' when put together measure about forty feet in length, and weigh some 800 pounds, and when they fall a foot or two are calculated to make their mark. After drilling a few inches the tools are withdrawn, and the sand-pump is brought into requisition. This is a tube about eight feet long, made of sheet iron or zink, and with a valve in the bottom. This sinks of its gravity in the water or sediment at the bottom of the well, and when it starts upward the valve closes. It is drawn up by steam—all the work of boring, testing and pumping is done by steam. The pump is then emptied of its contents until the hole is cleaned. Then the 'reamer' takes the place of the centre-bit or drill, and is used to remove all inequalities in the sides of the well and give it a round and even form. These 'tools,' including engine, house, derrick, &c., are called a 'rig.' When all are in place and in working order, the first step towards boring is to put down the drive-pipe. This is generally a heavy cast-iron pipe six inches in diameter (although occasionally a smaller pipe is used); it is in sections eight feet in length and is secured at the joints by wrought-iron bands put on while heated. This pipe is driven down by a heavy descending weight, after the manner of 'pile driving.' It is put down to the first rock, or at least to where the earth is solid, and there is no danger of caving, say about twenty feet. It is important that it should go down straight, as it is to be the guide for the drill.

"Casing is now being universally adopted. It consists in putting down a three or three and a half inch wrought-iron pipe, and inside of this placing the tubing, which is a two inch wrought-iron pipe; both of these go together by a thread and screw. Casing is said to have many advantages, not only to the well using it, but to neighboring wells. It prevents 'flooding,' that is, waters rushing in and forcing the oil out; really facilitates the drawing of tubing for repairs; prevents injury to the seed-bag, &e."

Here operators count by "sands:" first, second, third and fourth sands. The third sand has some water and oil, but not in paying quantities. The fourth sand is the oil strata. The water which finds its way into the well from the third sand must of course be ejected, or it will eject the oil. This is accomplished by the "seed-bag." The height of the third sand from the bottom is ascertained, and around that portion of the pipe which will rest just below this sand, is wrapped a leather bag filled with flax seed. When dry, it is smaller than the hole and goes down readily; but when it becomes saturated with water, the seed swells and hermetically seals the aperture, and excludes the water from the lower part of the well.

Testing a Well.

When things have got to this stage all that remains to do is to "test" the well. This is done by pumping night and day until the water is exhausted. Sometimes it lasts for days. If the valves finally bring up oil you are a "rich man," and can board at a first-class hotel, wear white kids when at work on the flats, and move in the best society of Pithole, besides holding office in the "Swordsmen's Club." If your well is dry, the six or seven thousand dollars you have expended, is—to say nothing of the "bonus" money—gone up.

The City.

Like Rome, sits on seven hills and from its throne of beauty rules the world. This quotation and comparison is not correct but mistakes will happen in war times.

As you enter the upper strata of liquid mud, which distinguish the main streets of the town, a sight is presented which is not witnessed elsewhere on any discovered portion of the globe and the like will never be seen again.

It is a wooden town, not a brick or stone house in it. The streets are narrow, with but a single plank for a sidewalk, and in many instances the plank is so far beneath the surface that more than ordinary length of limb is required to reach it. The buildings on either side are of every size and shape imaginable, from a four story hotel to the diminutive stand of a ginger-bread or peanut merchant.

The smell of new lumber, fresh paint and the "crude," is everywhere evident. Here may be seen a building which is neither sided, floored nor finished, but the roof is up—from the peak of which swings a sign, informing the public that "Oil Leases" will there be bought and sold (if the building gets finished and the owner gets time).

The fronts of the buildings present a fine appearance, while many of the hotels and stores have a neat and substantial look not usually seen outside of "America's" more favored towns. But the mud in our streets.. Words cannot describe or poles fathom it. Empty wagons are frequently stuck fast in the center of our main streets, and a day or two since a lady accidentally stepped off from a crossing and became so hopelessly engulfed that it was only after the persevering and united efforts of three men that she was extricated from the mud and her dilemma.

But the "powers of mud" are only realized when a fire threatens to destroy the town. Then it is that our "native element" proves a blessing, for by its aid the flames are quickly smothered.

Pipe Companies.

Among the many enterprises originated for the purpose of transporting oil to places of shipment on the river or railroad were the following:

Pennsylvania Tubing Transportation Company.

From the first discovery of oil in this section, many inconveniences arose in regard to the transporting the oil to places of shipment. Teams were plenty, but the process of hauling oil to Titusville or the Allengheny was necessarily slow and costly.

The idea of transporting oil by a pipe to Oleopolis, on the Allegheny river, originated with Thomas C. Bates, of Syracuse. A company was then formed, with a capital of $100,000; Joseph Casey as President, and Thomas C. Bates as Vice-President. Col.

Brackett and S. M. Spencer completed the arrangements, and David Kirk was first appointed Superintendent.

The laying of the pipe was commenced in November, 1865, and oil was first shipped on the 10th of December following. The business for the fall closed on January 23d, 1866, the company having shipped during the meantime 20,000 barrels of oil.

The pipe is six inches in diameter, has a capacity of 7,000 barrels, and extends from Pithole to Oleopolis—a distance of seven miles. In this distance the pipe has a fall of 360 feet. From its continuous down grade it constantly drains itself. It follows Pithole Creek nearly to the river, and during this distance it crosses the creek twenty-one times.

Unlike the Miller Farm and other pipe lines, here no forcing power is required, and the oil is by its own gravity carried from the company's tanks at Pithole right through to Oleopolis and even to Pittsburg, without being touched by the hand of man.

The Pennsylvania Tubing Transportation Company has erected an iron tank at Oleopolis, capable of containing 16,000 barrels of oil.

In the spring of 1865 there was organized the Rochester & Oleopolis Petroleum Company, with a capital of $100,000, for the purpose of buying oil at Pithole, shipping to Oleopolis and there selling. During the summer this company shipped 120,000 barrels of oil.

As many suppose this company to be connected with the Pennsylvania Tubing Transportation Company, perhaps it would be well to state that it is a distinct and separate organization.

Miller Farm & Pithole Pipe.

The work of laying this pipe commenced in August, 1865, and was completed about the first of October the same year.

At first but one line of pipe was laid, but business increasing a second line was put down.

M. E. Van Syckel, of Jersey City, Henry C. Ohlen, of New York, Charles Hickox and Charles W. Noble, of Cleveland, Ohio, composed the original company. M. E. Van Syckle afterwards became the sole owner of the pipe.

The length of the pipe is five and one-quarter miles; diameter two inches. Four pumps were originally used in pumping oil, but only one is now in operation. The Surveyor of this line was J. P. Culver, of Titusville.

The pipe is now the property of the First National Bank of Titusville, and M. E. Bassett is agent at Pithole.

The Titusville Pipe Company.

Was organized by H. E. Picket and G. J. Sherman, of Titusville. The work of laying the pipe was commenced in January, 1866, and completed by the first of April. Two lines of two-inch wrought iron pipe extend from Pithole to Titusville, a distance of nine and one-quarter miles.

Five engines or steam pumps of twelve-horse power are used to force the oil through these pipes, which connect with the tanks of thirty-seven different wells at this place. The cost of the pipe was $120,000.

The office of the company at Pithole is on lease No. 50, McKinney farm. Charles P. Hatch is Superintendent, and E. O. Adams, General Agent.

Oil City & Pithole Branch Railroad.

This is decidedly one of the best enterprises with which our city has been blessed since its birth. Our citizens had long felt the want of proper communication with the outer world.

The process of getting freight from Miller Farm and Titusville was necessarily slow, and disastrous to the merchant doing business here. Oil could be pumped through pipes; but dry goods, vegetables and notions could not, and it was with feelings of joy that we heard the welcome news of the completion of the road. Extras were issued by the press bearing the glad tidings: "Pithole in America at last," and the event was the occasion of much rejoicing. The prospects of the town looked encouraging. Oil operators could now step from the derrick to their home circle in a few hours' time, and without being subjected to the torments and miseries of a ride over bottomless roads. Pittsburg, Cleveland and Buffalo dailies were received the day of publication, and the mails came to town hours earlier than usual.

The Oil City & Pithole Branch Railroad was built on a charter of the Clarion Land & Improvement Company, an act authorizing the company to build branch roads in either of the counties of Venango, Clarion, Mercer or Elk, the branch not to exceed twenty miles.

Work on the Pithole Branch was commenced about September 1st, 1865. The first trains of cars came through from Oeopolis to Pithole December 18th, 1865, and the first train from Oil City to Pithole March 10th, 1866. The length of the road is sixteen miles, and the cost of construction $800,000. Ten miles of the road, from Oleopolis to Oil City, was taken possession of by the Warren & Franklin Railway Company August 1st, 1866, through a decision of the Supreme Court of Pennsylvania, given in June, 1866

This road was constructed by Samuel J. Fox, and follows Pithole Creek nearly the whole distance from Pithole to Oleopolis. From the latter place to Oil City it follows the Allegheny River.

In the summer season the scenery and picturesque views which are seen in passing over the latter portion of the road cannot be surpassed for native beauty by any portion of this continent.

The officers of the road are as follows: Directors—Wm. Thorp, Wm. Reynolds, J. J. Shryock, T. B. Porteous, J. J. Vandergrift.

President—Wm. Thorp.
Vice-President—T. B. Porteous.
Superintendent—J. Shirk.
Secretary & Treasurer—J. T. Blair.

The Reno, Oil Creek & Pithole Railroaod.

We are sorry to inform the readers of the "History" that this railroad was never finished.

The road is graded and the ties laid through to this place, but as yet the ears of our citizens have never been regaled with the melodious shriek of the iron horse, as he comes in on this line. We will not give the reason for the non-completion of this enterprise. Perhaps it was due to the failure of Culver, Penn & Co., while some think it owing to the failure of Pithole.

For a while work was prosecuted with much energy upon this route, but it suddenly ceased and has never been resumed, although we are frequently promised that the cars will soon run between Reno and Pithole.

Some magnificent trestles are built on this route, and if the reports in circulation are true it should have been an excellent thing.

We were informed by a laborer who was engaged in cutting ties for the company that when the road was completed persons traveling on this line would be sure to arrive in Heaven or Pithole soon after they took seats. Each train was to be provided with surgeons, undertakers, amputating tables and other luxuries. The company furnished coffins, to all who desired them, free of charge. Hospitals were to be established along the entire route, and in cases of fatal accident the bodies of strangers should be immediately embalmed. It was thought the arrangements would be so perfect and accidents so sure on this road that many would have their limbs taken off and get embalmed, before starting, to avoid delay on the cars.

*   *   *   *   *   *   *

We cannot say that we believe the story of the "tie cutter," but as soon as the railroad is completed shall test the comforts and conveniences of this model route.

The Hotels of Pithole.

Have always possessed a reputation for elegance and style excelled by none in the oil region. Among the best are the following:

The Chase House

Is a fine four story building situated on Holmden street and has always been one of the finest and best regulated hotels in our city, and has a reputation throughout the oil country excelled by none.

This hotel was built in the summer of 1865, at a cost of $100,000, by H. Patchen and S. H. Allen. It was opened on the 11th of September, 1865, and known as the Patchen House, until purchased by George K. Chase, of New York City. From its central location and the convenience of its arrangements, this house has ever been the resort of oil operators, whose families were sojourning here, and is a universal favorite. Col. S. H. Allen is the present proprietor of this house.

The Bonta House

Was erected in the fall of 1865, by its present proprietor, James W. Bonta, at a cost of $60,000.

The architectural design, the manner in which it is furnished and its fine location —being situate on one of the high and healthy eminences which surround the town— render it one of the very best hotels in the oil region. This hotel was opened to the public January 1st, 1866, and although doing an immense business at one time, it has never proved a success, in a pecuniary point of view, to its owner.

The Danforth House

Corner of Holmden and First streets, is another of the large and elegant hotels which grace the town. It being conveniently located near the oil territory of Pithole—its magnificent arrangements for the accommodation of guests, together with excellent management—makes it decidedly popular with those doing business here; and there is no better kept hotel in the city. It was erected in the fall of 1865, by A. D. Danforth, at a cost of $40,000, and was opened on Christmas day, 1865. H. W. Mabb is the present manager.

The St. Nicholas Hotel,

Situated on Holmden Street, although more unpretending in size than its stylish kindred, has been kept up in a manner worthy of emulation, and it is an excellent hotel in every respect. Messrs. Wilson & Scofield are the present proprietors.

The Morey Farm Hotel.

This was another of the grand and imposing edifices which marked the days of "oil on the brain," and for which Pithole is so justly celebrated. It was erected in the summer of 1865, at a cost of $70,000, and was furnished regardless of expense.

This hotel was entirely destroyed by fire on the 1st of October, 1866, which was the work of an incendiary, who for some spite against the owners, thus sought revenge.

There were at one time no less than fifty hotels in the place, not including boarding houses and restaurants, and each one was doing a lively business. But the hopes of the landlords vanished with the departing strangers, and the number of public houses rapidly diminished.

The fires which so frequently desolated the place destroyed many of these structures, and many were never rebuilt.

The Post Office.

From the commencement of operations on Pithole Creek, the want of a proper mail communication with the outside world was felt by all. Oil City, Titusville and Plumer were at that time the nearest points reached by mail bags.

A postoffice was opened to the public by Captain S. S. Hill, on the 27th of July, 1865. The population at that time numbered about ten thousand. The work done by the office at this time was immense. The first mail dispatched contained over 1,000 letters, and the fourth mail over 4,000. When the post office was ten days old, upwards of 10,000 letters per day were handled by the postmaster and his assistants.

During the December following the opening of the office, it was entered by burglars and the mail bags stolen. Vigilant efforts were at once made to discover the thieves, but without success. A few days after the robbery the empty mail bags were found under the livery stable connected with the Hubbs House. The contents of the bags, or all that remained of them, were afterwards discovered behind a large rock on the highest point of the Walter Holmden farm, and near the reservoir of the Pithole Water Works.

The amount of business transacted proving too large for the then small office, it was removed in the fall to its present location in the Chase House building, and is now a model office as regards convenience. When business was at its height in 1865, it was often necessary to throw open every window of the office to accommodate the crowd; even then some hasty individual (on hand just in time to fall in behind a dozen others) would buy out the more lucky person nearest the delivery window, and thus get his mail a few moments sooner. This buying of positions was of frequent occurrence, and quite a "bonus" was often realized by the speculator.

Sunday was the day for everybody to go to the postoffice, and long before the appointed time for opening, a line of news-seeking individuals would be formed, extending for many rods down the street, each man clinging to his neighbor in front, the line wavering and sometimes half a dozen would go down, amid the laughter of those who quickly took the places of the "fallen ones," who were by this tumble compelled to go to the rear and work up gradually to their old position. And anything that had the least possible touch of the comic about it, would quickly excite the risibilities of the crowd, who would break out in vociferous cheering. To an attentive observer the day seemed any other than the quiet day of rest, known in "God's country" (as any place outside of Pithole was reverentially called) as the Sabbath.

Much more of interest might be written in regard to the postoffice, but we forbear.

A second attempt to rob the office resulted in the capture of the would-be thieves as they were about to enter.

For many months the Pithole postoffice was the third in size in the State—Philadelphia, Pittsburg and Pithole was the order of rank.

The Tented City.

The army was represented by many individuals, who, while in Uncle Sam's employ, drilled companies and regiments, but who now run another drill from that of Scott or Hardee; and with more money and less glory as a reward.

FAZIER WELL, PITHOLE, MAY, 1865.

Owing to the want of lumber, buildings could not be erected as rapidly as they were needed, and to furnish shelter for the hundreds of strangers daily arriving, canvas houses were erected. At one time the hill-side was fairly covered with these structures, from the size of a general's or sutler's "shebang" down to the diminutive "pup tent" of the high private. A few fortune seekers, too near dead broke to enjoy life in so expensive a dwelling as a tent, built themselves "local habitations" of logs, mud and stones, with barrel or stick chimneys, and almost any day when mule teams were plodding along the under-ground road, as it was termed, a scene was visible which brought forcibly to mind the days of war, and it only needed the presence of "army blue," the sound of the bugle, and the inevitable picket guard, to carry you back to the days of shoddy shoulder straps.

The hotels were doing a rushing business, especially about meal time, and long before the appointed time for dinner a steady tide of hungry and open mouths flowed in the direction of the boarding places, from whence through the open windows, came the clatter of plate and platter, as well as the savory odor of roast meats and "spoon vittels." Crowding around the entrance of the dining room, each one trying to get nearest the door by pushing his neighbor; small men crying to larger and luckier ones to get off from their corns; reverend and rogue, broadcloth and homespun, were here jammed together, often forming a line of battle which extended into the street; and presented a comical sight—if you were not very hungry and could afford to wait. The sound of the gong was the signal for a universal charge along the entire line, and happy the man who got a seat at the first table without being subjected to more than hydraulic pressure.

Where so many different characters and nations were represented much lawlessness necessarily prevailed; and although the stories of crime, so industriously circulated, were exaggerated, yet gambling, robbery and shooting were of frequent occurrence.

Before the organization of a police force, a self-appointed vigilance committee dealt justice to rogues in Texan or Californian frontier style.

Gambling was at one time carried on in the streets. We have seen a common dry goods box sold for $10, and ten minutes later it was doing duty as a faro table on Holmden street.

Street fights were a common occurrence. A humorous writer, in a letter from the "Pit" in 1865, says: "The greater portion of the population of Holmden street were engaged, at the time of our visit, in witnessing a fight between a colored man and one of the Caucasian race. The descendant of Ham proved the better man, and his antagonist made a hasty change of base. Business generally was suspended, and the folks seemed to enjoy the fun amazingly. There had only been thirteen fights that forenoon, and the weather was not considered very favorable for fighting either."

Theaters were established at an early date, and were filled nightly by appreciative audiences. Murphy's Theatre, on First street, was really a first class place of amusement and many of the leading theatrical stars of the country appeared upon its boards and played to crowded houses. Concert saloons, casinos or free and easys were plentiful, with all the usual concomitants of "pretty waiter girls," pimps and beer drinkers.

In addition to the foregoing "history" by "Crocus," it may be said Pithole had two famous organizations, the memory of which remains with all survivors. These were the Forty Thieves and the Swordsman's Club. The former was the outcome of the desperate speculation, failure of companies to pay dividends on grossly inflated capital being frequently charged to the alleged peculations of superintendents. This story was so frequently told to dissatisfied stockholders in the East that the maligned superintendents, in a jocular spirit associated themselves into the club known as the Forty Thieves and many were the humorous, but fictitious tales told of their depredations. As a matter of fact it would be hard for the world to produce a body of more honorable men than those who composed this club with the malodorous name, yet when a boiler was stolen, or an engine surreptitiously carted away, the crime was jocularly charged to this organization. The tenderfoot knew no better and went from the city believing all he heard about the Forty Thieves.

The Swordsman's Club was famed throughout the country for its banquets, balls and other entertainments. Its headquarters were in the basement of the Danforth House, but many of its social affairs were held in the banquet-hall of the Morey Farm Hotel. It is not necessary to recount the social triumphs of this club, but an incident of another nature in its history may be of interest. Some of the merrier members had a few bad hours over its outcome. There was in the city a young man whose mental faculties were not well developed. He was accused of spying upon the club in its executive sessions and of overhearing its "secret work." The victim was seized and taken to the club rooms, formally arraigned and convicted in spite of his protestations of innocence. The "Mogul" in command declared that he must be put to death; that blood alone would atone for such an outrage. The terrified victim pleaded for mercy. He was nearly frightened to death. Then a resourceful member suggested that it might be possible to save the life of the lad if he would procure a sheep for the sacrifice. After most serious discussion and argument, this plan was agreed to. Where the young fellow got the sheep is not known, but he produced the substitute in the Club room.

The members who could be reached were summoned in haste and as the hour of midnight approached the ceremonies were begun. They were impromptu, but none the less solemn and awful. The name of the victim of the lark was given to the sheep which had been substituted for the sacrifice, after which it was duly arraigned, tried, convicted and sentenced to death. The block was brought forth, the axman came forward with his shining blade, an incantation was chanted and the blow fell. The blood gushed upon the floor amid other incantations, the young man, as much dead as alive, was liberated and a group of members took the carcass out over the hills and buried it in the early hours of the morning. But this was not the end. It so happened the girls employed about the hotel had seen some of the mysterious movements, had secreted themselves in a room back of the club room, had overheard the arraignment and trial, and had heard the execution performed. When the torrent of blood gushed on the floor they rushed up the stairs from their concealment filled with terror over the murder they were sure had occurred and announced to the landlady they would not remain in her house where such frightful things happened. Thus the story began to be heard about the town, to the amusement of Swordsmen who heard it. But when the morning came and a search for the supposed victim began and resulted in the discovery that he had disappeared, the thing assumed a serious aspect. Several highly reputable members of the Club had important business elsewhere before warrants could be served. The grave in the woods was located and preparations for exhumation and legal inquiry were made. At this critical juncture a Swordsman on his way to more congenial quarters, accidentally met the victim of the hilarious joke in Titusville, whither he had fled as soon as liberated from what he supposed was a critical situation. He was induced to return to Pithole long enough to be seen by the authorities and when he departed again was as much richer as the Swordsman's Club was poorer. An interesting episode was at an end and the "secret work" of the order was abandoned for the future.

BONTA HOUSE.

TARR FARM, OIL CREEK, SCENE OF 3,000 AND 4,000 BARREL WELLS.

CHAPTER IX.

EARLY OIL REGION OIL TOWNS.

BY EDWIN C. BELL.

The industrial progression of a people evolves the romance of history. The commercial utility of petroleum, or "rock oil," marked the beginning of a new era of enterprise in the economic affairs of mankind. Much of the old ways of the plod of life came to an end with the discovery of petroleum—a product generated in the laboratory of nature. So great a revealment brought into requisition the building of hamlets, towns and cities. Consequently the assembling of thousands of "oil seekers" in the valleys of Oil Creek and Upper Allegheny river, Western Pennsylvania, in the first years of the industry, resulted in remarkable activity. Titusville, in 1859, whence first sprang commerce in petroleum, was a forest surrounded hamlet—a crossroads radiating in half a dozen directions. Settled in 1794-'95, by Jonathan Titus and Samuel Kerr the place had grown, in 1859, to but slightly over 400 inhabitants, thirty-five of whom were voters. At this time the village was of the primitive sort, hardly known forty miles beyond the limits of its defined boundaries. The nearest newspapers were printed at Meadville, Erie, Warren and Franklin, twenty to forty miles distant. An old-fashioned, lumbering stage-coach carried passengers and a daily mail to the hamlet from Erie City, which lay forty miles to the northwestward. Mail communication with Franklin and Meadville was had only twice a week. During many years, previous to the discovery of oil, the population of Titusville largely depended upon lumbering. This sturdy kind of employment was the leading factor, while a rude process of agriculture was an adjunct which helped press forward the ambition of the people in gaining a livelihood.

From 1795 to 1859, more than half a century had rolled into progressive American history. During that epoch-creating period, the hamlet of Titusville might well be termed a "back woods" settlement. The people were of the old time character—pioneers—busying themselves with hewing away the wilderness—engaging in primitive manufactures, such as would sustain home independence from importations—dealing in merchandise—giving some attention to religion—looking forward all the time, hoping that better conditions would come as the years trended toward the end of each decade. In their efforts they, seemingly, were blazing the pathway along which was destined to sweep a new era of enterprise.

One day, in the year 1858, a Yankee, possessing genius, and a persevering courage, rode into the hamlet. His mission was to demonstrate, not only to the doubting inhabitants of the little village borough, nestled amid the forest-clad hills of Oil Creek valley, but to the world at large, that crude petroleum, in vast quantities, was procurable by means of the derrick and drill. As a result of so extraordinary a discovery, a new commodity of commerce was rolled into the pathway of industrial evolution. So marked an announcement wrought a sudden change in the affairs of the less than half a thousand individuals, who lived in Titusville. On the morning after the 27th day of August, 1859, they awoke from the previous night's slumber, to learn that the very dwellings in which they lived, rested over subterranean reservoirs of wealth, computable beyond their comprehension. On that propitious occasion the place was composed of a cluster of residences, a leading hotel, a couple of country stores, a small tannery, shoemaker shop, harness shop, a small church, a schoolhouse, a mill for grinding grain, and two sawmills in the vicinity of the village. But, to achieve wealth from the production of petroleum, wells must be drilled, and, then, await the pouring forth of the dark green liquid. While this process of development was under way, news of the discovery was carried to other sections of Pennsylvania, to other States of the American Union, and to continents beyond oceans. In a few weeks and months thousands of wealth seekers, in "oil," invaded Titusville, and then moved down the valley of Oil Creek with the tide of the rise of the industry.

In five years, from August, 1859, Titusville was peopled by from seven to eight thousand permanent residents and two thousand floating speculators. The town also had daily and weekly newspapers, two national banks, three telegraph lines, twenty-five or thirty hotels, seven churches, central school, postoffice, ranking third in the state, and headquarters of many oil companies, some of which were bogus. It had a railroad, built from Corry, thirty miles distant, in the year 1862, which cost $800,000 to construct, and which paid for itself in six months. At that time $50,000 was not considered a very large price to pay for an acre of ground in the Oil Creek region, which, one year before, could not have been sold for ten shillings. All this change, for better financial conditions, in just five years after Col. Drake's pioneer oil well was completed a mile and a half below Titusville, Western Pennsylvania.

During this building up there were busy scenes in the original oil town. Hundreds of teams thronged the streets, drawing lumber, machinery and oil, carpenters were hammering from dawn to dark, stonemasons, bricklayers and other mechanics were at work. Well drillers, pumpers and teamsters, along with such others as came into town, kept things lively until after midnight, sometimes almost riotously boisterous. The new city had the life and amusements of a mining camp at high tide, with faro, roulette and keno on the side. Dram shops drove a harvest trade and even worse vice flourished on the outskirts. Good citizens were vastly in the majority but they were so engrossed with the production and marketing of petroleum they had little time to concern themselves with the morals of any but themselves and families. But now the Queen City is one of the most desirable as a place of residence, churches far outnumbering the combined resorts of evil.

OIL CITY'S FIRST DAYS.

The second town, in the oil region, to rise to importance, as a result of the discovery of petroleum, was located where Oil Creek debouches into the Allegheny river, seventeen miles due south from Titusville. For many years previous to the rise of the oil industry, the ground whereon was afterward built Oil City, had been principally used as a halting place for travelers, raftsmen and lumbermen, going up or down the Allegheny river. The town had its origin in 1860, and it grew, from two or three wayside taverns, or stopping places, a couple of small stores and a grist mill, to the magnificent Oil City of 17,000 inhabitants in 1910. The first real settler-pioneer—who felled the trees and built the first log cabin, was Francis Halliday. He there chose his land, some 500 acres, in 1803, which lay on the west side of Oil Creek and along the north bank of the Allegheny river. At this point the Allegheny river, in one of its bends, runs directly west. It was on a part of the Halliday land that the first portion of Oil City was built. In February, 1860, the Michigan Rock Oil Company, by purchase, came into possession of the larger part of the Halliday estate, and soon after laid out Main street, in what is now the Third ward of the city, and began selling lots. On the east side of the Creek and along the north shore of the Allegheny river, lay the Graff, Hasson & Company tract, once including a small iron furnace. Of this property, some 300 acres were sold, in 1864, to the United Petroleum Farms Association, upon which was built the larger and better business and residence end of the town, including Cottage Hill. That half of the town, which later became South Oil City, lies upon the opposite or southern shore of the Allegheny

MAIN STREET, EAST SIDE OF OIL CREEK, OIL CITY, IN 1861.

river, and comprises land originally known as the Bastian, Lee and other farms. In 1862, William L. Lay purchased the Bastian estate and founded the town of Latonia. In the spring of 1864, the Downing farm, adjoining the Bastian on the east, was bought and the town site of Imperial laid out. Albion, Downingtown Leetown, and Venango City were local names adopted by portions of this rapidly growing population. By order of the Venango county court, in 1866, several of these town sites were consolidated under the legal title of Venango City, which, as it grew in size, extended westward upon the lands of the Lee farm. In the course of years Venango City became an important residence locality for people engaged in business and other pursuits in Oil City. As a result, it was decided that the interests of both towns would be enhanced by coming under the government of one municipality. To effect so desirable an end, the union was accomplished on the 3d of March, 1871, by act of the State Legislature at Harrisburg. Hence, the origin of North and South Oil City, the latter for a long time having its own post office.

Early in the development of the petroleum industry, Oil City was designated the "Hub of the oil region," and it has maintained that euphonious name down to the present writing—1910. The cognomen was applied from the fact that, during the years of the great volume of oil produced along Oil Creek and the Allegheny river, the rich commercial commodity converged upon Oil City as the port through which the larger quantity was dispensed to market. The first transportation was by wagon and boat, the second by railroad, the third by pipe line.

In the first days of its rise with the tide of wealth that flowed from the oil wells, Oil City was considered a shanty town—built in a hurry with but slight regard for beauty or permanency. The people, there congregated, seemed, from observing the style of their buildings, to express the deduction that they were only sojourners to reap a harvest of fortune, then to flit away to other more genial habitations. Many however, remained as good and true citizens. Others did move away. During those early days the business of the place was wholly confined to speculation in oil and oil wells, and battling with knee-deep mud.

The ground, along the river bank, on the west side of Oil Creek, was the scene of the greater amount of business activity in the commerce of oil. The water of the river, in that vicinity, was fairly covered with oil barges and steamboats, while the wharves were piled high with empty oil barrels or covered with thousands more filled with petroleum. Amid this accumulation of commercial enterprise, men, by the thousand, rushed to and fro, each individual bent upon the pursuit of wealth by means of petroleum.

In those far away, historic times, the old Petroleum House, which had its beginning before the discovery of oil in the Drake well, and located upon the main street of the town, now defined as the Third ward of the city, was the leading rendezvous of the men engaged in producing and selling crude oil. This house had been re-named. Every morning, men by dozens, rode away on horseback from the famous "tavern," to visit their wells along Oil Creek, Cherry Run, and over the hills to the exciting scenes of Pithole. These cavalcades, oftentimes, presented the appearance of the advance of regiments of cavalry. At times it was difficult, in those days, to procure a bed in Oil City hotels, or even in boarding houses. Every room was provided with as many "hard" beds as it would accommodate, and each bed had two and, sometimes, three sleepers. Consequently rest, in those rushing times, was obtained under very great difficulties. In many instances men sat in the chairs or slept upon benches and floors all night. These scenes, in some of the hotels, had more the appearance of military camps than headquarters of those who peacefully engaged in the occupation of producing petroleum.

But the daily trend toward better conditions moved forward with improvement in the process of drilling, tanking and marketing the liquid commodity—oil. The city kept pace with these tendencies of the progressive period. Among the first was the newspaper—the Oil City Weekly Register founded January 14, 1862. There was also expansion in mercantile trade and more luxury in the comfort of home life. Then, in 1865, the first rail-road locomotive, on the newly constructed Atlantic & Great Western railroad, thundered into the place. One year later, 1866, the Farmers' railroad was built up the Creek, from Oil City to Petroleum Center, and, in the following year, the Allegheny Valley railroad was completed to South Oil City, from Pittsburg. A bridge, in the meantime, had been constructed over the Alle-gheny river, connecting Oil City with Venango City, and a new structure built over Oil Creek, to replace an old "swinging" bridge carried away by the flood of March, 1865. These were the beginnings of the new Oil City. The magnificent town, that has been built since those early days—paved streets, trolley railways, manufactories, mercantile pursuits, banking facilities, grand hotels, oil pipe line and gas interests, newspapers and editors, fine res-idences, schools, churches, parks and broad gauge citizenship—are subjects for chronicle by future historians.

At Oil City is located the National Transit Company's shops, where the largest oil pumping machinery and gas compressing engines in the world are built. The California type oil pumping engines are so large that a tall man may walk through one of the cylinders and five large railroad cars are re-quired to carry one away to its destination. The gas compressors are con-structed direct connected to internal combustion gas engines, in double and triplicate patterns. These shops also build internal combustion crude petro-leum engines for the driving of pumps and other uses of the pipe lines of the system. The huge factory has no goods for sale, its entire output being for the National Transit Company and companies affiliated, with the same own-ership.

PETROLEUM CENTER.

Titusville became an oil town in 1859. The nucleus of Oil City was laid in 1860. Lying nearly midway between these two towns was the oil field upon which Petroleum Center began its rise in 1861-'62, and which, at the zenith of prosperity in 1869, numbered fully 5,000 inhabitants. Three hun-dred, six hundred and one thousand barrel oil wells, were frequently struck in that vicinity; and, in some instances, two and three thousand barrel wells gladdened fortunate owners. The Maple Shade well, struck August 5, 1863, in a few months yielded 190,000 barrels of oil, which sold for $800,000. The Noble well, on the Farrel farm, a mile and a half above Petroleum Center, commenced flowing in May, 1863, and, in a few days more than a year, pro-duced 410,000 barrels of oil, which sold for $2,500,000. The Coquette, Jersey, Swamp Angel, Empire, Funk and Crocker wells, made Petroleum Center famous, as a producing section of the oil regions. To add to the great wells enumerated, was the prolific Benninghoff Run oil district, lying north of the Center, with Stevenson and Wood farms to the westward of the town, ending in the Pierson and Niagara tract, over the hill, in Cherrytree Run. All this territory proved to be very rich in the yield of wells. The McCray farm, which lay upon the hill, east of Oil Creek and north of the Egbert farm, helped give Petroleum Center additional history, as an oil town, in 1870. With all this vast and prolific territory, surrounding the place, it could well bear the title of "Center" of Oil Creek oildom. Three hundred barrel wells on the McCray farm gave the owner rich reward. At one time, during the period of the greatest excitement. James McCray was offered $1,000,000 for his property. So great a value placed upon his oil territory was refused. By this mistake of his life, McCray failed to make himself the richest man, at that time, in the oil region. He saw his wells dry up and his farm turned back to buckwheat crop and other slim agriculture. He died leaving but a small part of the wealth in "greenbacks" he once had under his control.

The valley site of Petroleum Center was settled early in the nineteenth century. At the time of the coming of the pioneer to the place, forest-clad hills and ridges hemmed it in on every side. Smoothly gliding Oil Creek swept into the plateau-like valley from a gorge in the hills at the north and out through another gorge southward. At the beginning of 1859, the settler, George Washington McClintock, owned 207 acres of this land. At one place in the Creek, oil bubbles had been seen to rise from the gravelly bottom to the surface of the water and float away with the current. No sooner had the Drake well, at Titusville, proved it possible to procure crude petroleum by process of steel drill, than Brewer, Watson & Company leased this McClintock

VIEW AT McCLINTOCKVILLE, 1861.

farm, as they also did other farms along the valley of Oil Creek. The royalty, which this firm agreed to pay McClintock, was one-quarter of the product. The first well was begun late in the fall of 1859, but it was never finished. About this time Kier, Mitchell & Company, of Pittsburg, sub-leased the property from Brewer, Watson & Company, and the first well was completed June 15, 1860. The head of this firm was S. M. Kier, who first sold petroleum from his salt wells at Tarentum. The next well commenced producing in July, 1861. It flowed at the rate of 800 barrels per day. Thus was begun the oil enterprise that resulted in the building of Petroleum Center, and the development of the surrounding territory. In 1863, the New Jersey Oil Company bought the leasehold of Kier, Mitchell & Company, and also secured the interest held by Brewer, Watson & Company. Then, purchasing the fee simple from McClintock, that organization became absolute owner of the whole 207 acres of oil land. After coming into complete possession of the property, the name of the corporation of buyers was changed to the Central Petroleum Company, and the holdings were stocked to the amount of $500,000. The next move was to lease some of the land to prospectors for oil. This was followed by adopting measures that would lead to enlarging and building up of the town. Leases were granted to residents, but no ground was sold. That kind of action, on the part of the company, retarded Petroleum Center from becoming a flourishing city—perhaps the largest, at that time, in the region. Nevertheless, it did assume the proportions of a very large business place, and gave to the world a remarkable record of wealth in petroleum. Not only was Petroleum Center remarkably prominent, as a yielder of great oil wells, but the town also had a reputation for marked integrity in business, and freedom of life among the people, who constituted the industrial and social community. No town upon the American continent was ever like it; no town upon the face of the globe will ever be its counterpart.

The most flourishing years of Petroleum Center were from 1863 to the close of 1870. The place was at the highest tide of oil prosperity, in the latter year. Then the gradual decline of the wells began, and, by 1873, the town was largely deserted. The great petroleum industry moved down the Allegheny River. But little of the Center remains to-day—1910.

Petroleum Center was famed, not only for its oil wells, but for its hotels, business houses, machine and blacksmith shops. During one period of its history, the most durable drilling tools were made in the Center of any in the oil region. The town had a bank, a newspaper—the Record—and it was there that the first 30,000 barrel oil tank was built. During much of the time of the town's greatest activity, they only had one policeman and no lockup in the place; and this lone policeman was able to maintain order. Sometimes he handcuffed his prisoners to telegraph poles, and sometimes he gave them a reprimand and paroled them on honor. The place had three churches—Presbyterian, Methodist and Catholic—a school and temperance society. It had two theatres—Soble's and Akin's—concert halls and whiskey mills. It had oil refineries, oil offices, oil pipe lines, and a horse railroad up Benninghoff Run, which was destroyed by fire in 1866. Petroleum Center supported petroleum proud aristocracy, as well as the poor plebeian. One lady—a leading oil man's wife—had a rich wardrobe of gowns, so it was said, and a handkerchief that cost $500, gold in Paris. A gentleman—an owner of an oil farm—sported a finger ring—diamond—that was said to be worth $4,000. He also wore diamond shirt bosom ornaments, which were reported to have cost $3,000. They had people at Petroleum Center, who, when they sold their land for $75,000, could not be sure of their count of $500 of the money.

There was a brief era during which Petroleum Center enjoyed unenviable notoriety among other oil towns as the wickedest among them. Those were the days when Gus Reil and Ben Hogan ran unsavory dance halls and the worst element in oildom sought the society to be found there. So long as this element did nothing to molest the good citizens little attention was given it and no effort made to restrain its vices. But when murder was committed in Gus Reil's place and he, himself, was charged with the crime, there was an outburst of indignation that led to a radical cleaning up. Ben Hogan and his ilk found the climate more salubrious in Babylon, Parkers Landing and other of the newer towns, many of them without municipal organization or police protection. But the fame of "The Center" will live as long as any of its denizens survive.

ROUSEVILLE.

Rouseville lies at the confluence of Cherry Run with Oil Creek, and, in its most flourishing days, was one of the important oil towns of the region. It had its commencement in 1860-'61, and, during all the years that have intervened in the measure of time to 1910, it has maintained some of the characteristics of nearly half a century ago, when its oil wells poured large amounts of treasure into the lap of wealth. It may truthfully be said that Rouseville began with an astounding oil fire and tragedy. On the 17th of April, 1861, Little & Merrick, sub-lessees of Henry R. Rouse, Mitchell and S. Q. Brown, drilled a well to the depth of 300 feet, and it broke forth flowing large volumes of oil and gas. The gas ignited at a neighboring boiler, a tremendous explosion followed, enveloping twenty-eight men in fire. Fifteen of these lost their lives, one of whom was Henry R. Rouse, and thirteen recovered, yet bore scars for life. Before he died, Rouse made a will bequeathing his property to various friends and objects. Among his gifts, he set apart a sum of money for the benefit of the poor of Warren County, the place of his home. He was a man of excellent qualities of citizenship, and the preservation of a history of his life is worthy of record.

Surrounding Rouseville were the lands of the John Buchanan and Archibald Buchanan farms. These lands yielded prolific oil wells, as did also other farms in that vicinity, up and down the Creek and for fully three miles up Cherry Run. The result was that, many people seeking wealth in petroleum, sought homes in the locality, and Rouseville grew. At the period of its greatest prosperity, the place numbered not far from 3,000 inhabitants. At that time it was provided with a theatre, a newspaper—Rouseville Bulletin—and famous Cherry Run Hotel. Many interesting incidents occurred at this hotel, during the early days, when the oil excitement was at the full tide of development One evening, in the summer of 1865, a party of oil seekers, from the west, arrived at Rouseville. They went down the Creek, from the terminus of the railroad at Shaffer farm, on a passenger flat boat. Seeking the hotel for lodgings, they were told that every sleeping place was more than full. But, if they chose, they could remain in the office room of the house. It was raining without, so the pilgrims, hunting for oil, concluded to camp as suggested. It was after midnight, and all the guests had retired but this party of genial new comers to the petroleum country. It was their first night in the region. Outside the office door lay a pile of green lumber—boards— 3,000 feet. The lumber had been hauled there to be used in a building. Time dragged upon the nerves of this "sit-up" party in the hotel office. So, to make the hours shorter, it was suggested that they bring the lumber into the office. Although rain was pouring down from the dark overhanging clouds, work was valiantly begun, and, just as the peep of day lit up the valley of oil, every board was nicely piled up in the office, completely filling the larger part of the room. By this time each man was soaking to the hide. But, nevertheless, there was hilarity at every step, each of the party feeling highly elated over the night's work. While thus at the full tide of their glee, the landlord appeared upon the scene. He became very wrathful, and inquired why they had labored so diligently to play such an unkind and unpalatable piece of knavery. "Sir," replied the leader, L. H. Smith, "it was raining, and we resolved to bring that lumber in out of the wet, that it might here be kept dry!" During the following forenoon they carried the boards out and piled them in the original place.

Traveling theatre companies visited Rouseville. The theatre was not of large proportions—would probably seat 400 persons. To give as many as desired an opportunity to see the play two performances in an evening were sometimes given. The first would begin about 7 o'clock and end at 10 o'clock. Immediately the house would re-fill with late comers, and the curtain ring down at midnight.

As the town grew in business supremacy, mercantile houses were established, a bank found remunerative patronage, a school was organized, a church found membership, and society diversions moved on in pace with the great outpouring stream of petroleum, that was transported to market down Cherry Run and from the farms along Oil Creek in that vicinity.

In 1865-'6, a railroad was projected from Reno, below Oil City, over the hills to Rouseville and up Cherry Run to Pithole. Just below Rouseville a 40 foot high, wooden trestle, bridge was built over Oil Creek, to bring the road down to the valley. Gen. A. E. Burnside, of Civil War fame, was civil engineer of the road. This road was never finished. The Farmers' Railroad reached the town a little later and, for a time, operated the other line to the Humboldt refinery and Plumer, half way on the road to Pithole. The Cherry Run excitement of 1864-'5 was merriest and maddest of them all, wells being drilled on half acres and less, while the offices of oil companies lined the road for two miles up from Rouseville. It was at the height of this crush that a lazy drilling crew slept from midnight to morning, the tool dresser turned cold water into his hot, dry boiler, the boiler blew up, killed the tool dresser, knocked down a tank filled with oil, the oil ran to the first boiler below, fifty feet, and in twenty minutes the whole valley was a seething cauldron of fire, a mile long. The alarm was spread ahead of the flames, men left their work and their beds and all fled to the hills with utmost haste, clothed or not, as they happened to be when the dread warning came to them. Providentially no lives were lost, except that of the man who caused the disaster.

McCLINTOCKVILLE.

A mile below Rouseville was located the oil village, or town, of McClintockville. It was situated upon the Hamilton McClintock farm. The first well below Titusville, after the Drake well was struck, was begun on this farm. The place, at one time—1865-'66—probably contained 500 population. It was an attractive town with its two-story hotel, bridge over Oil Creek and gushing oil wells. In those nineteenth century days, the intervening territory, between McClintockville and Oil City, was thickly dotted with oil wells.

RYND FARM.

A mile above Rouseville was Rynd Farm, another rich oil producing section of the valley. This was a scattering town, having, within its bounds, at one time, more derricks than houses. It lies where Cherrytree Run joins Oil

Creek, and has maintained existence although greatly diminished in production of oil and number of buildings, to the present time—the first decade of the twentieth century. Some of the old landmark buildings are to be seen, and when the pilgrim of the early days casts his eyes upon them, they bring to memory thoughts of the scenes of those stirring times amid oil and mud on Oil Creek, nearly fifty years ago. This farm was leased to Jonathan Watson and J. D. Angier, of Titusville, September 1, 1859, and from the first well put down to the present year, 1910, oil has been pumped from the ground.

Adjoining the Rynd farm, down the Creek, lies the Widow McClintock farm, from which the renowned Johnny Steel drew the fortune (it is said a million dollars, but more truthfully not to exceed $300,000), which he spent with such a liberal hand within the period of about two years, returning at that time to become a baggage master at the Farmer's Railroad depot at Rouseville.

PUMPING OIL WELLS AND EARTHEN RESERVOIR

TARR FARM.

Among the oil towns, of Oil Creek, Tarr Farm, for a period of ten years, held an even place with all the rest. During most of that period, it supported a population of fully 2,000 people, and was famed as the location of the Phillips and Woodford wells of 1861-'62. One-fourth interest in this farm of 198 acres was purchased in August, 1861, by Clark & Sumner for $30,000, and in September, following, the Phillips well burst forth, yielding 4,000 barrels of oil daily. As a result of so large an output, from so great a well, the town began to grow, and soon became one of the attractive oil fields on Oil Creek. During the best years of the oil production, the flats, along the bank of the creek, fronting the upper end of the town, were covered with wooden storage tanks. These were set deeply in the ground and they were covered with planking and dirt. This was done to protect the contents from fire. Two amply large hotels, stores, postoffice, boarding houses, comfortable residences, railroad station and livery stables, were the things that made Tarr

Farm attractive. While the town was in vogue, the population was dominated by excellent citizenship. Consequently the bad element, that usually congregated in some of the oil towns, failed to effect lodgment among those people.

COLUMBIA FARM OIL VILLAGE.

Next above Tarr Farm, and the first below Petroleum Center, was Columbia Farm Oil Village. This property was originally the Story farm. Late in the fall of 1859, the land was purchased for $30,000, by a company of Pittsburg capitalists which, later, was organized by act of the State Legislature under the name of Columia Oil Company. Here was one of the best managed and most remunerative oil properties in the valley of Oil Creek. It yielded fully $6,000,000 of profits to its stockholders, before its affairs were brought to a close. Among the things that made this village conspicuously

McKITTRICK DISTRICT, KERN COUNTY, CALIFORNIA.

attractive was a public library, a church, and the celebrated Columbia Cornet Band. These were the high-class social features of the village of 500 people. During the years of the existence of the band—1868 until 1873—it was considered the equal of any musical organization of the kind in the western part of the State. Some of the members of this band were afterwards connected with the Marine Band at Washington, D. C.

BOYD FARM.

To trace the oil towns north, which once had existence between Petroleum Center and Titusville, the first was Boyd farm. This small, yet, in the long ago, lively business place in oil, lay on the east side of Oil Creek, opposite the upper end of the Center. Its commodious hotel—the Oil Exchange—built in 1866, oil offices and coal sheds, several small oil wells, and, from 1866 until 1868, the terminus of the Oil Creek Railroad, were the enterprises that gave it stable business character.

FUNKVILLE.

Half a mile above Boyd Farm was the village of Funkville. The town lay at the upper end of what was known as the Lower McElhaney farm. The place was composed of a cluster of various kinds of buildings and residences, some of which seemed as though they were stuck against the steep side of the hill that rose to a high elevation, back from where the oil wells were located. On more level ground were a number of stores and warehouses. The wells were on the still more level flats, near the bank of the creek. Here were the great Funk or "Fountain" well, the first well on Oil Creek drilled to the third sand rock, 440 feet deep, June 1, 1861, the Empire, the Buckeye, and many other productive wells. The place supported a postoffice in 1864, and it was kept in a building on the flats, not far from where flows the waters of the Creek. A great pond of oil, formed by the flow from the Empire well, once covered considerable space on these flats. Many a boat was loaded from this pond. A wooden spout conveyed the oil from the pond to the boat. Funkville was one of the centres of operation, in the early days, and it was in the '70's before the oil was exhausted.

A number of men who afterward became prominent in the business of the petroleum world, had their first homes on Oil Creek, in Funkville. The town and oil territory lay, on the east side, in a half moon bend of Oil Creek, and the view of landscape, either up or down the valley, was attractive. In fact, there are but few points in the Oil Creek valley that are not full of nature's picturesue beauty.

PIONEER CITY.

Directly across, on the west side of Oil Creek from Funkville, the lively oil town of Pioneer was built in 1865-'66. Although this place was the scene of small operations in 1862, it was not until November, 1865, that extensive developments were begun. In that and the following year, as high as 500 and 700 barrel wells were drilled. These fortunate strikes brought many operators from declining Pithole, and other parts of the oil region, and, in the course of a year, a town, comprising not less than 2,000 enterprising inhabitants, was sustained by the oil industry. Two leading hotels, the Frost and Phillips, gave entertainment to the traveling public, while a machine shop, railroad station, pipe line oil shipping station, oil refineries, mercantile houses, oil offices, post office, news room, and boarding houses, were among the assets of the town.

The oil territory comprised the Upper McElhaney farm, Gregg farm, Foster farm and a corner of the celebrated John Benninghoff farm. Great Western Run, which debouches into Pioneer Run, begins and ends on the Benninghoff farm, and it was from the great volume of oil, there produced, with other wells lower down on Oil Creek flats, that gave the owner immense riches, which he stored in a sack in the farm house. Of his vast wealth, $300,000 were stolen in the winter of 1868, the robbers overpowering the household. Some of this money was recovered, and a number of the robbers sent to prison. But the greater bulk of the stolen treasure went to the benefit of the leader, James Saeger, who planned the robbery, who became a ranchman in the West, and who was never apprehended and punished.

SHERMAN FLATS.

Sherman Flats, just around a high point of hill from Pioneer, and which derived its name from the Sherman well, lay opposite Bull and Cow Runs, which join Oil Creek on the east side, nearly a mile above Pioneer. The town was built on the west side of the creek and, during its greatest period of prosperity, contained perhaps 300 residents. In 1864, it had a postoffice, and, later on, a number of small stores. The people who lived there depended upon the production of oil as a means of sustenance. The Sherman well, gushing forth 2,000 barrels of oil daily, was struck in 1862. Directly opposite, on the east side of the creek, a year later, the Noble well poured into great wooden tanks 3,000 barrels a day, and the Caldwell well, still later, 1,000 a day. At about that time Bull and Cow Runs proved good territory, and yielded large amounts of oil.

SHAFFER FARM.

Continuing up the Creek, two miles, was the town of Shaffer. This was a place, during the years 1865-'66, of fully 2,000 inhabitants. It was the terminus of the Oil Creek Railroad, built to the place in 1864, and it also became the terminus of the Harley pipe line, constructed over the hills from Benninghoff Run, in the winter of 1866. Here occurred one of the "teamster's pipe line wars" of 1866. An attempt to tear up the pipe line was made and a tank of oil burned. During the two years that the terminus of the railroad remained at Shaffer, it was a large oil shipping point. Much of the product of the wells, as far south as Tarr Farm, was hauled in wagons up the creek to Shaffer. But, after the railroad was extended to Petroleum Center and the introduction of the pipe line, hauling oil by team largely came to an end. The extension of the railroad to the Center doomed Shaffer and it decayed by the wayside. A fire burned some of its buildings, while others were torn down and moved to more prosperous localities in new oil fields. Two old shanties and a grass field now mark the site of once flourishing Shaffer City.

MILLER FARM.

A mile from Shaffer, farther up the creek, and upon the same west side of the stream, was Miller Farm. The Oil Creek Railroad was extended from Titusville to this place, in 1863. This facility for transporting oil, made Miller Farm a very large shipping point. In 1865, the land constituting the Miller farm was bought by the Indian Rock Oil Company. The new owners laid out building lots and tested the territory for oil. The wells proved unremunerative and were abandoned. As a residence location, Miller Farm never attracted more people than could there find employment. The Pithole oil excitement, of 1865, five miles distant, made Miller Farm a prominent depot whence were moved great quantities of supplies and thousands of travelers to that famous town. It also became the terminus of the Pithole plank road and of the Van Syckel pipe line in the fall of 1865. At this time and later, with the rise and fall of the Shamburg and Pleasantville oil districts—1867-1874—Miller Farm was a very large shipping point and storage tank station. During these times a number of refineries were built, and profitably run for some years. In those first days the Pierce and Alvord hotels entertained the public, but later, the Brown, built in the early part of 1870, and the Ingersol, took care of the public travel. There were also several boarding houses, oil offices, oil and coal warehouses, a railroad station and a number of residences. From Miller Farm to Titusville, four miles, the country, until the vicinity of the Drake well was reached, was barren of oil.

OUTLYING OIL TOWNS.

Pithole, Shamburg and Pleasantville were not considered oil towns and oil fields, as belonging to the basin valley of Oil Creek. Pithole City was located in the valley of Pithole Creek, seven miles from the confluence of that water course with the Allegheny river. Shamburg lay at the head of Upper Cherry Run, which had its outlet in Oil Creek at Rouseville. The Pleasantville oil field lay upon the headwaters of West Pithole Creek, a tributary of the main Pithole Creek. These two mountain streams mingled their waters at the lower end of the ridge upon which was built Pithole City.

SHAMBURG.

The first well, that brought the Shamburg field into active oil operation, was the Jack Brown, struck late in the fall of 1867. The William G. Fee well followed on January 1, 1868. The strikes resulted in flowing wells, which gave forth three and four hundred barrels daily, each. They were located upon the Atkinson farm, on which the village of "Atkinson" rose with the tide of oil production. Other large wells were completed on the adjoining Talman farm, in the early months of 1868, and from those first successful ventures the field spread out over a large area of territory. "Middletown" was built upon one end of the Talman farm, and "Old Shamburg" occupied the valley in Cherry Run, to the east of Atkinson and Middletown. "East Shamburg" was situated on ground a hundred rods still further east of Old Shamburg. East Shamburg became a producing centre in 1869, and in the fall of that year, Red Hot, half a mile to the eastward, was added to the, at that time, large and profitable scope of territory in that immediate vicinity.

PLEASANTVILLE.

What was termed the "Pleasantville oil field of 1868," was located south of that town, and largely east of upper West Pithole Creek. It was a productive field, during the days of its existence, but after two years of yield the decline set in. Many of its wells were abandoned in 1870, and by 1871, but little drilling was done in that territory.

During the excitement of 1868, Pleasantville grew from a scattering, old-time country village, to a rushing and rich oil town. Many of the best buildings in Pithole City were removed to Pleasantville. Among these was the Chase House, which originally cost $80,000 to build. Murphy's Theatre was also taken from Pithole to Pleasantville. The Chase House was finally destroyed in the Pleasantville fire of December, 1871.

PITHOLE CITY.

No town, in the Pennsylvania oil region, equaled Pithole City for rapidity of rise to the conspicuous eminence of giving shelter to 10,000 inhabitants, in the short space of less than three months time. Then its decline was almost as rapid. The history of the town extends over a period of not much beyond three years, although a small number of people lingered there after 1870. To-day—1910—there are hardly more than half a dozen families living upon the ground once occupied by the town and its surroundings. The valley, along the creek, where the great oil wells in the long ago, flowed thousands of barrels of petroleum daily, is largely grown to forest. The silence of nature reigns where the clang and roar of man's industry once held high carnival.

The "Frazier" well, which began flowing about January 8, 1865, introduced the Pithole field to the world of oil industry. The well was owned by the United States Petroleum Company, and produced as high as 900 and 1,000 barrels of oil daily. Oil was sold from this well, in January, 1865, for $8 per barrel. It was claimed that Pithole, late in 1865 and early in 1866, produced from 5,000 to 8,000 barrels of oil daily. The place had large numbers of great wooden and iron tanks, gave employment to thousands of oil teams, had telegraph lines, pipe lines, refineries and a railroad. It had a daily newspaper—the Pithole Record—the Swordsman's Club, Forty Thieves, banking houses, metropolitan hotels, churches, theatres, concert halls, gambling houses, the under world, highway robbers, police court and whiskey mills by the half mile. Pithole was a town, the records of which will enliven history down the ages of time.

THE UPPER ALLEGHENY RIVER.

The Upper Allegheny River Valley gave but few distinctive oil towns to the chronicle of history. The country villages of President, Tionesta and Tidioute were stopping places on the river, long before the discovery of oil on Oil Creek. Neither Tionesta or President yielded petroleum, but Tidioute did become a very large producing district. Oil wells were there struck in 1860, and for fully ten years, gave up prolific reward to operators. West Hickory, below Tidioute, yielded a few small wells, as did other localities between there and the mouth of Oil Creek at Oil City. Oleopolis was only an oil storage, refining and railroad station during the years of Pithole's yield of petroleum.

TRIUMPH HILL.

Triumph Hill, two miles from Tidioute, was first developed in 1866-'67. The second period in that field was in 1870-'71. The place had no particular town—only boarding houses and scattered dwellings.

FAGUNDUS CITY.

This town of a thousand inhabitants was ushered into existence from the striking of the 300 barrel "Venture" well, the first of May, 1870. The greatest period of yield of oil in this field was in 1870-'71. Then the wells began to decline and the place passed into history. The town was neatly built, comparing in its architectural outlines with the usually constructed oil town. A fire in May, 1871, consumed the larger portion of the place, and it was never re-built. The part burnt was constructed wholly on one side of the street. The opposite side of the street was given up to oil wells. The place was provided with a church, stores, news room and private post office.

POND FRESHET, MOUTH OF OIL CREEK, OIL CITY, PA., MARCH 14, 1863.

CHAPTER X.

A PROBLEM IN TRANSPORTATION.

When Drake drilled his well at the line of Venango County, Pennsylvania, near Titusville, there were but two means of transportation from that isolated region to the outer world. One was by wagon road and the other was by Oil Creek at flood periods, only. The nearest railroad point was Union City, on the newly constructed Atlantic & Great Western Railway and the next nearest was Corry, the crossing point of the Atlantic & Great Western and the Philadelphia & Erie Railroads. The road to Union City was the favorite for teams hauling oil and became a busy thoroughfare. The first oil sent from Oil Creek to Pittsburgh was by a man riding a horse, with a can swung on each side. The charge for draying a barrel of oil from Titusville to Union City was one dollar, when the road was in good condition, at other times two or three dollars. The railroad freight rate from Union City to New York was about six dollars and from Corry to Philadelphia the charge was about the same.

In 1860 steamboats were plying the Allegheny River from Pittsburgh to Franklin and Oil City. They could only run when the water was above normal and were compelled to tie up when the rise became a flood. Winter ice also stopped navigation. Oil could be rafted down the river in shallow draft, flat bottomed boats, but they waited at the Pittsburgh end of the line for steamboat navigation to get back. This was not so serious because the well timbered region adjacent to the upper Allegheny could furnish an endless supply of new boats. But sometimes the water in the river got too low to float a loaded barge, and in winter, when the stream was not frozen over navigation was rendered hazardous or impossible by floating slush ice. Oil was boated down Oil Creek, too, by means of natural and artificial floods, known as pond freshets, and the empty flat boats were towed up stream by horses, the latter wading in the stream. The "pond fresh" was made by building a series of temporary dams, so arranged that at a given signal supporting timber could be cut away, the dams collapsed and an artificial flood created to carry the loaded boats. It was sharp and dangerous work to navigate the temporary floods and more than one shipment came to disaster in the hurly burly of swirling water covered with crowding craft.

These expensive and wasteful methods of transportation prevailed, however, for the first half dozen years of the petroleum development. They began to be supplanted only when operations became active far from navigable, or partly navigable, streams. This was at Pithole where the difficulty of transporting thousands of barrels daily by teams became so impressive as to demand a better way. The preceding years did suggest other means and once a pipe line company was chartered by the Pennsylvania Legislature to lay a line of pipe from Tarr Farm to Oil City, and from Oil City to Kittanning, in 1862, but the project "died a bornin'." The trains of wagons hauling oil grew

longer and the mud they churned up in the highways annually grew deeper.
There were seasons when this was the most serious phase of the new industry.
The work was hard on horses and mules. Occasionally they fell and drowned
in the oily mud. The animals were driven to the utmost of their endurance
and it was not easy to recruit the ranks when they fell by the wayside. In
the absence of Boards of Health, vigilance committees of citizens were organized to have the decaying carcasses incinerated that pestilence might be
avoided. In the time when Cherry Run was at its height of development and
Pithole had come upon the scene it was not an infrequent spectacle to have
500 wagons in the trains on the roads to Oil City to Miller Farm and to
Titusville, with counter trains of as many going the opposite direction. Sometimes the greater number was on one road, sometimes on the other.

SHAFFER, END OF ABBOTT, HARLEY & CO. PIPE LINE, 1865.

With a train of 500 wagons and as many teams laboring through mud
two feet deep, an interruption to the steady but slow, progression was serious.
Did an unfortunate animal balk on too much work, or fall from fatigue and
bad treatment, the instant result was a blockade of the line, an inevitable in-
centive to voluble and picturesque profanity. Quick investigation would follow by the teamsters in the rear. If the aid of another team, or two, for a few
minutes, would suffice to clear the way, it was freely and promptly given. If
such means would not avail, the stalled vehicle would be promptly overturned
to the lower side of the road and permitted to roll as far down the hill as it
might. The first consideration was to clear the track. The tactics were those
of a modern railroad "wreck crew," to clear the road for traffic first and consider the damages afterward. If an owner protested too loudly over the sacrifice of his property, he quickly found the fight he was looking for and
usually had personal damages added to his property loss. It was an impa-

tient throng, most of the members as ready for fisticuffs as they were for a late supper after delays of the road. It was an impressive sight to see this oil wagon train wending its way down the hill on Plumer road into Oil City, stretching as far either way as the eye would reach.

Pithole will ever be memorable in petroleum annals, because from there the first pipe lines were built for the transportation of oil. Three projects were conceived and begun at about the same time. The first to be put into operation was the Miller Farm Pipe Line, the property of M. E. Van Syckel and others. It was six miles long, of two-inch iron pipe, with three pumping engines at intervals along the way. There was much leakage and trouble with joints that would not stay jointed, but it finally developed a capacity of nearly 2,000 barrels a day. The next to be completed was a six-inch line of the Pennsylvania Tubing Transportation Company, from Pithole to Oleopolis, on the Allegheny River. This was a gravity line and used no pumps. This line built an iron tank at Oleopolis, with a capacity of 7,000 barrels, another innovation of interest to the men engaged in the industry. The next was the Shaffer Farm pipe line, which would have been first but for the malicious interference of the teamsters, who feared the loss of their business. This line was cut on September 26, 1865. The Miller Farm pipe line, known as the Oil Transportation Association, began pumping October 10th. Another line, begun nearly at the same time as the three just mentioned, was the Titusville Pipe Line, but it was not completed until 1866. The method of all these companies was to have oil hauled, in barrels, from the wells to their receiving tanks and "dumped" into them. For this purpose an inclined way and elevated platform were constructed, so the barrels could be gotten to the top of the tank. The charge for piping oil from Pithole to Oil Creek, or to the Allegheny River, was one dollar a barrel.

At this time there was great rivalry among the railroads for the oil traffic. The Erie system, including the Atlantic & Great Western Railroad, was controlled by Jay Gould; the New York Central system was handled by Commodore Vanderbilt, himself, and the Pennsylvania Railroad was controlled by Colonel Thomas A. Scott. All were enterprising in the hunt for traffic and secret rates were then the commonest things in railroad practice. In fact railroad tonnage was bartered on the same basis as a wagon load of merchandise over the turnpike, the lowest bidder got the business and the best bargainer got the lowest rate. Colonel Scott and his associates of the Pennsylvania had organized the Empire Transportation Company a sort of car trust and "inside" corporation, designed to facilitate the getting of business, as well as the manipulation of freight rates for that purpose. But he discovered the Pennsylvania Railroad was not getting the share of oil to which he thought it was entitled. He suspected something was wrong and he dispatched Charles P. Hatch to the oil country to investigate. Mr. Hatch did not proclaim his identity or his mission on his arrival, but after he had satisfied himself that Gould and Vanderbilt were getting business by favoritism, on some basis, he was instructed to open an office at Shaffer Farm, as agent for the Empire Transportation Company. The Oil Creek Railroad had been built from Corry, through Titusville, to Shaffer Farm, which was then the terminus. All oil was then barreled and shipped in barrels on ordinary cars.

One day the attention of Mr. Hatch was called to a car that came in from the Erie Railroad, with some sort of tanks upon it. He at once requested tank cars. The first one sent had three small tanks enclosed in a box car. The tanks leaked and the car was somewhat damaged before the hoops were tightened and the cargo loaded by emptying barrels, through holes cut in the car roof, into the larger containers. But the experiment was a success. The tank car consisting of two small wood tanks set on a flat car, became common in the next two years. In 1866, Mr. Hatch was sent to Titusville to take charge of the Titusville Pipe Line, where he soon established the system of "run tickets" and of taking a percentage of the oil received to cover losses by leakage. His was then the only line that received oil for transportation, merely, the other lines having established the system of buying the oil delivered to them and selling it after shipment to the railroad. The tables of charges on a barrel of oil from Pithole to New York are given by the Derrick's Hand Book of Petroleum, as follows:

Transportation by pipe from Pithole to Miller Farm.....$1.00
Barreling, shipping etc., by Oil Creek R. R............... .25
Freight to Corry, by Oil Creek R. R................... .80
Freight from Corry to New York.................... 3.50

Total $5.55
Transportation by pipe line from Pithole to River.......$1.00
Freight on river to Pittsburgh...................... 1.50
Wharfage, loading, etc., at Pittsburgh................ .25
Freight from Pittsburgh to New York................ 2.24

Total $4.99

It will be seen the river route was slightly cheaper, but it was less regular or reliable. Time was a factor in many cases and rates were shaded on desirable shipments by both routes. Meantime the teamsters made an open attack on the Shaffer Farm pipe line of Harley & Co., burning a tank near the loading rack and doing other damage. The mob consisted of 200 or more men. The pipe line employes put up a brisk defense, including the use of guns, and several of the attacking party were wounded. Afterward teams were hitched to the lines, out in the open country, and the pipes dragged until broken. All of the companies were compelled to have their pipe lines patrolled by armed men. Gradually, however, the enmity of the teamsters died out and the pipe lines had peace. The opening of new fields furnished employment for the teams in drawing machinery and materials to the points of operation, a more profitable business than wagoning oil in barrels, and it was realized that the pipe lines were a benefit rather than an injury, even to the teamsters.

This stage brought into being numerous pipe lines. The Empire Transportation Company extended its activities to other fields; Vandergrift & Forman organized the East Sandy Pipe Line and others; the Mutual Pipe Line began business at Parkers and Foxburg; the Karns Pipe sprang up in Butler County; the Antwerp Pipe Line was promoted in Clarion County, a dozen small concerns operated in Venango County, and pipe line competition became of the fiercest character. Following the lead of the Empire Transportation Company, other railroad interests sought pipe line connections to get their share of the traffic and refiners were virtually forced to get pipe line affiliations to do business without a handicap. The several Vandergrift & Forman lines were consolidated into a compact system, capable of delivering to any of the railroads and these United Pipe Lines bade fair to dominate the situation. This organization absorbed the Antwerp Pipe Line and others. Because it would not favor the Pennsylvania Railroad with the greater part of its business, the Empire Transportation Company made war on the United Pipe Line. It extended its pipe system and absorbed some weak concerns. When both were on the verge of bankruptcy the Empire capitulated the United Lines took over the Empire pipe lines and the Empire retired to other transportation. There followed a reduction of pipe line charges for transportation and for storage. This entire end of the petroleum industry became more

FIRST PIPE LINE PUMP, USED ON PITHOLE & MILLER FARM, OCT. 1, 1865.

stable. The small pipe lines gradually went out of business, or were forced out by inability to meet the new conditions imposed by larger organization and business. Up to this time the pipe lines had been merely a means to reach railroad transportation, the principal mechanical improvements being the extension of pipes to tanks at wells, eliminating the waste of barreling oil at the beginning,and the delivery through pipes to the tank cars, making bulk shipments the standard.

However the trunk pipe line was attempted in 1875 to ship oil in competition with the railroads. This was the Columbia Conduit line from Butler County to Pittsburgh. The idea was developed quite rapidly. The development of the Bradford field led to the construction of two trunk systems toward the Atlantic seaboard, it having been realized that the export trade would have to be sedulously cultivated to find a market for the enormous production of oil. The National Transit Company, a growth out of and affiliated with the United Pipe Lines, was first to reach the goal, followed by the Tide Water Pipe Line Company. The cost of transporting a barrel of oil from the Pennsylvania producing fields to New York was reduced from the average of five dollars, at the close of 1865, to an average of less than one-fifth of that sum. It was accomplished with less leakage and other losses en route. The piping from field tanks to railroad points in the producing region had been reduced from one dollar a barrel to twenty cents, and the latter sum included the gathering of the oil from the wells. The problem of transportation had been solved and the cost reduced below that of most commodities.

TONGS GANG NO. 4, WORKING ON 6 LINE, APPROACHING KIAMICHI MOUNTAINS—OKLAHOMA PIPE LINE COMPANY.

The years since then, however have not been without improvement. The modern pipe line equipment is as far superior to that of 1880 as that was ahead of the primitive efforts to pipe oil from Pithole to the outer world. It has been systematized to one of the most efficient and cheapest methods of transportation known. Pipe line construction has been put on a scientific basis and is as carefully organized as railroad construction, though usually urged with more vigor. These operations require large capital and trained management, but they are essential to the development of modern oil fields. Storage has become an inseparable adjunct of oil transportation so that every pipe line must have steel tankage in proportion to the interest it serves. All pipe lines have adopted the early practice of purchasing all oil offered and the investment in crude oil is now not less than one hundred million dollars. The pipe lines are generally owned by the refining and marketing concerns, so that from the tanks of the producer to the consumer is a continuous process. This method has been developed in the petroleum industry but has been adopt-

MOVING CAMP OVER KIAMICHI MOUNTAINS, OKLAHOMA PIPE LINE COMPANY.

ed in many other lines of industry and commerce as the most economical procedure. It has been assailed in the courts as a form of organization that deprives the individual of opportunity, but it is not likely that its essential features will be destroyed by process of law. The newer large petroleum organizations aim to do their own producing of the crude, in addition to transportation, manufacturing and marketing, and they have been generally successful, including the Pure Oil Company, the Gulf Refining Company, The Texas Company and the Union and Associated oil companies of California.

The evolution of the transportation of natural gas has been more rapid than that of oil. In the earlier stages the gas was transported for comparatively short distances. Coming from the wells under extremely high pressures, it transported itself readily through pipes of a size commonly used for trunk oil lines. But it was soon learned the high pressure did not long continue and the supply of large communities became difficult. The problem presented itself acutely to the companies in Pittsburg in 1890. The Philadelphia Company tried to solve it by the use of very large pipe and laid a main three feet in diameter. The People's Natural Gas Company favored compression and began experiments along that line that resulted in a successful accomplishment in 1891. In 1890 there was general apprehension in Pittsburgh of exhaustion of the supply, the service for the preceding winter having been inadequate. The supply has been more ample ever since. The method of compression has been greatly improved and gas is now readily transported for 300 miles and more, after the flowing pressure of the wells has been greatly reduced. The writer was sent out in 1890 to investigate the prospect of a continued supply for Pittsburgh and reported that it would be ample for twenty years and more. There is less apprehension of gas exhaustion in Pittsburgh now than then. The business in 1890 was in its infancy. It has since developed across the Continent, in ever increasing proportions. The enormous supply derived from the fields of Kansas, Oklahoma and Louisiana, have given rise to the gigantic operations of the Kansas Natural Gas Company and the Arkansas Natural Gas Company, each involving transportation for several hundred miles and the investment of millions of dollars. There have been brilliant minds engaged in the development of this industry as well as in petroleum and its development has been hardly less romantic.

While pipe lines are the last word in land transportation, the tank steamer plays a conspicuous part in water transportation. The first of these is credited to Ludwig Nobel, of the Nobel Brothers, extensive operators in the Baku district of Russia. It was built in the Swedish shipbuilding yards "Motala" in 1877 and named "Zoroaster." It was 184 feet long, 27 feet beam, nine feet draft and loading capacity was about 1,600 barrels of oil. The latest vessels of the Nobel firm are the "Emanuel Nobel" and "Karl Hagelin," each with a loading capacity of about 35,000 barrels of petroleum. In 1883, W. A. Reidemann, who had built tank sailing vessels in 1874, devised and built a new type of tank steamer, the "Gluckauf." In the United States the Standard Oil Company was first to resort to the tank steamer for carrying oil in bulk and now has the largest fleet of "tankers" afloat, engaged in both the domestic and export trade.

The American "tanker" of to-day is a great advance over the original types, of great carrying capacity, equipped with wireless telegraph, burning oil fuel, divided into tight bulkheads and having every modern device. In addition to the fleet of the Standard Oil Company, large fleets are maintained by the Pure Oil Company, the Sun Oil Company, the Gulf Refining Company, the Texas Company, the Associated Oil Company and the Union Oil Company, the two last named of California. In addition to the foreign trade, these tankers ply between Atlantic and Pacific coast ports, distributing both crude and refined petroleum, greatly reducing the cost of transportation. Refined petroleum all along the coasts is distributed to the retail trade at a very small advance over the price at refineries The location of the producing regions, inland, enables a distribution to the interior territory of the United States at an average price not much greater than along the coasts, but the retail price is often at a wide advance over the price at refineries and other points of wholesale delivery, except where manufacturers maintain retail distributing systems. However, allowing for a profit of more than 50 per cent to the retailer, manufactured petroleum is much the cheapest commodity sold in this country, that is, there is the smallest percentage of margin for transportation, manufacture and distribution, between the price of the crude product and that to the ultimate consumer. This is one of the romantic achievements of the petroleum industry. Lamp oil is sent to the interior of China at a less price per gallon than that at which natural table waters are furnished within 100 miles of the spring, this price including the cost of the cases containing the oil. Petroleum transportation is not confined, however, to the

OLD HERO PUMP.

highly developed processes of pipe lines, tank cars, and tank steamers. In some of the far away corners of the earth, such as the interior of China and India, or the Island of Celebes, transport from depots to consumers is effected by such primitive means as the picturesque water buffalo and the human carrier but is always at the lowest possible cost. It is delivered much cheaper to the consumer in Mongolia, where the American distributors have access, than in Russian Siberia from which the American trade is excluded by the very high tariff maintained for the benefit of the Russian oil producers. It is the only commodity originated within little more than half a century that reaches those remote regions, indicating the superior energy of the men engaged in the oil business.

PARKER OIL EXCHANGE IN 1874.

CHAPTER XI.

CHERRY GROVE AND OTHERS.

In some respects Cherry Grove surpassed Pithole. It was not possessed of costly hotels and social clubs, but it grew with unexampled rapidity and faded away more suddenly than its predecessor, leaving many to mourn its untimely demise. The famous "mystery well" of Grace & Dimick on lot 646, Cherry Grove Township, Warren County, Pennsylvania, after some weeks of manipulation, was opened and turned into the newly constructed pipe line, May 19, 1882. Other wells came in quick succession, located by pure luck, along the "jugular," so that by the first of July there was a line of gushers, six miles long and no sign of approach to the producing limits in any direction. This line of wells was located in a dense forest, midway between the village of Clarendon on one side and the village of Sheffield on the other, the distance to either being about nine miles. From each of these villages a plank road had been built for about seven miles, to serve the tanneries in getting out hemlock bark, the oil field being between the ends of the two roads. Another road ran along the summit of the hill, pointing in one direction toward the village of Tiona, and at the other toward the small settlement of Balltown, each about as far as the two towns named previously. This was a dirt road, level on the summit, but descending with very heavy grades at either end. On the summit was a farm tilled by a retired Swedish bark peeler, named Peterson.

The rush began with the opening of the well on lot 646. Men poured in from the Bradford and Richburg oil fields, from the "Lower Fields," from Oil Creek and from all parts of the world. Two towns began growing, Garfield at the edge of the Peterson farm, near the end of the Clarendon plank road and Farnsworth to the eastward, near the end of the Sheffield plank road, the forest being cut to make room for it. At first more than a mile apart they grew until they met, along the dirt road on the summit. By the first of July this hilltop had a population of 5,000, and by the first of August it had increased to 10,000 or more. Business was transacted under canvas tents while slightly more substantial structures of wood were being erected. Men slept by hundreds in the open during June and July, despite the fact that night temperatures were very low, the altitude being nearly 2,000 feet above sea level. This flat topped hill was cut out of the Big Level, an elevated plateau, thousands of years ago, by the erosion of Tionesta Creek, which flows around it in an almost perfect circle. Thus Clarendon lies to the north of Garfield, on the Tionesta and the Philadelphia & Erie line of the Pennsylvania Railroad, Tiona is northeast, Sheffield is a little south of east, where the railroad reaches the stream from the mountainous region eastward, and Balltown is on the same stream to the southwest, farther from the railroad than Garfield. The circular course of the Tionesta was confusing to geographical conceptions of all save the oilman who always carries a map and usually a pocket compass.

The method of those compelled to sleep out of doors was to cut an abundance of hemlock boughs, large and small. These were arranged in a circle, the trunk ends of the larger boughs pointed toward the center, the branching ends outward. The finer boughs were distributed over this foundation to make the couch more downy. At best, some way short of curled hair or compressed felt matttreses, the hemlock boughs are superior to a rattlesnake infested section of Arizona desert with a dug out depression for the hips. Having completed the circle, the fifteen to twenty men, accidentally met for the night, gathered from the forest such tinder and firewood as might be available, built the fire in the center of the circle, told a few impromptu stories, or twice told tales, and retired, using overcoats or whatever best they had for blankets. Whoever was first awakened by the chill replen-

UNION OIL COMPANY PUMPING WELLS, SANTA MARIA

ished the fire from the store of gathered wood and wooed Morpheus again as he might. It was not luxury, one may well believe, but the writer having tried it, can testify that to thoroughly tired men it was not the worst possible substitute for a bed. During July there was a line of these brush camps between Garfield and Farnsworth, numbering more than a hundred, giving accommodations to 2,000 men, appropriated by whoever arrived first to occupy them. Men with hundreds of dollars in their pockets camped thus alongside men with only a dollar or two, total strangers who might never meet again. companions for a single night. But not one attempt at robbery was reported. There was a tacit understanding that honesty was the best policy among this throng, gathered outside the visible sphere of influence of the law. Rooms and beds were engaged before the first nail was driven in the plank buildings.

Breakfast, dinner and supper might be procured in some one of the numerous tents used as restaurants, at a price suited to the purse of the diner, if not of proportions adapted to his appetite. Hotels and restaurants were erected as rapidly as material could be procured and energetic carpenters could throw the rough lumber together. Boarding houses multiplied along

the highway and "speakeasy" shacks dispensed warm beer without the formality of obtaining a license, the hill top being devoid of any kind of water
supply.   Hotels and restaurants had water brought in by the barrel from
springs down the hillsides, while a few enterprising fellows sold spring water
by the glass at a price twenty times higher than producers could get for their
crude oil.   Literally, the woods were full of "bootleggers," who dispensed
ardent spirits from bottles and jugs surreptitiously brought in from some
mysterious source of supply.   In course of time a corps of constables and
deputy constables led a lively existence in pursuit of these illegal liquor
sellers, and the Court at Warren did a thriving business imposing fines upon
them.

In August a new well was reported at Balltown, eight miles southwest,
and soon afterwards another on Cooper Hill, eight miles south.   These attracted the "oil scouts" and a few of the curious, but were ignored by the

DISTRICT, SANTA BARBARA COUNTY, CALIFORNIA

mass of the busy population in Cherry Grove.   The daily production of the
pool had mounted to 40,000 barrels, which gave employment to many tank
builders.   The Union Pipe Line and the McCalmont Pipe Line were struggling to remove the oil from field tanks, but daily fell farther behind their
task.   Both were building iron storage along the banks of the Tionesta, to
which the oil would flow by gravity, but despite all efforts of the lines and
the multiplication of wooden tanks on the leases, some surplus oil found its
way to the ground.   The United Pipe Lines early decided upon a large trunk
line to the tank farm at Colegrove and Anson C. Miller, superintendent in
the Clarion division, was called to the work of construction.   He made a
record never surpassed.   This pipe line was rushed, day and night, regardless
of expense.   A great pump station named Vandergrift, in compliment to the
President of the United Pipe Lines, was installed a mile south of Garfield
and the huge pumps were working within an incredibly short period of time.
This enterprise cost considerably more than a million dollars, expended
within two months, but the production of the field was saved.   Two months
afterward one small pipe line was ample to move all of the production obtained from Cherry Grove Township; tank and rig builders were not needed.

drillers and tool dressers were moving to newer fields and the towns of Garfield and Farnsworth were deserted villages. The collapse was more sudden than the growth. The pipe lines, especially the United, were the heaviest losers, but producers, hotel men and householders were sufferers in proportion to their investment. Early in September a number of wells had stopped flowing.

By December, 1882, buildings were being torn down at Garfield and Farnsworth and removed to Gusher City on Cooper Hill and to Balltown. The population of the "Hill" was scattered to these new towns, to Clarendon, Sheffield and a hundred other points. Cherry Grove had passed into history before the narrow gauge railroad, begun in July, had commenced to run trains into Garfield, although its construction had been as rapid as possible. It arrived to serve a lingering remnant of the busy cities and survived to carry tan bark and hemlock lumber from the vanishing forest, supplanting the plank roads as a transportation route.

The Cherry Grove experience prevented the building of great towns on Cooper Hill and at Balltown. Of course lively villages sprang up at each, sufficient to care for a more conservative growth of population, but many operators and others rode daily to and from Garfield where the Jamestown House continued to offer better accommodations than could be had in Gusher City, Forest City or Balltown. The big Farnsworth Hotel had little vogue and it passed with the remainder of the town where it was located, into oblivion. The inevitable oil town fire put an end to Farnsworth, permitting the surviving population to move to Garfield, nearer the railroad terminus. A few farm houses now occupy the sites of these one time famous cities, whose daily telegraph business, during a few months of 1882, exceeded that of the ordinary city of 100,000 population. It was no longer necessary to prohibit smoking throughout the field on account of the dense accumulation of natural gas.

With the beginning of Cherry Grove came the "oil scouts." Prior to that time the newspapers of the region had been depended upon to furnish information concerning new wells and new fields. But the fever of speculation grew beyond bounds at that period, the market fluctuated in sympathy with news from the field and accurate information on the instant came to be of the first importance. While the "646 mystery" was maintained, Silas B. Hughes had "scouted" around the premises and obtained the secret. Before another well had been completed, Louis Beaumont was "scouting" for the Anchor Oil Company. James Tenant was in the field for the Bradford Oil Company and Owen Evans and Joe P. Cappeau represented the Forest Oil Company. Frank H. Taylor, oil editor of the Derrick, and the late Thomas P. Kern, of the Bradford Era, were in the field. Soon afterward the late Justus C. McMullen, a well known oil statistician and newspaper man, was on the ground representing Edward H. Jennings, Benjamin S. Tupper, Daniel Herring, J. H. Rathbun, James Emery and the writer followed, acting for traders in the exchanges. A. L. Snell, late managing editor of the Derrick, arrived from Bradford in July. Patrick C. Boyle, formerly publisher of the Richburg Echo, and since 1885, editor and publisher of the Oil City Derrick, came in as the representative of the Union Oil Company. "Jake" Bruner, represented the Millerstown Exchange, and "Billy"

Boyle was there. There were others. A good many producers took a hand in the game on their own account. It was the business of a "scout" to keep tab on the important wells drilling, on the total production and on the new wells starting, keeping his principal in oil company office or oil exchange well posted. The fact that many wells were guarded to keep strangers at some distance compelled the scouts to do a little work at night, when the guards could not see all over the ground, and the opening of a gusher was the signal for a mad race among them for the nearest telegraph office. The fleetest footed horse was a treasure.

All telegrams were cypher, for, while telegraph operators are generally honest, the extravagant rewards for quick information were tempting. "Open" messages were also subject to prying eyes of others, who hung about sending or receiving offices. So keen was the scent of news hunters that "codes" had to be changed occasionally, as they were spelled out by clever interceptors. When the scene of action shifted to the Shannon well

OIL SCOUTS AT THORN CREEK, 1884.

on Cooper Hill, all of the "scouts" named were on duty. The guards stationed about that "mystery" were woodsmen from the region of Williamsport, armed with rifles and quite reckless in their use of them. They were more familiar with the furred wildcats that roamed the adjacent woods than with the species of "wildcat" they were employed to guard, and apparently had little fear of the law in case some one should be hurt when they fired at random during the night. No one was shot during that siege, but "Jim" Tenant had his trousers cut by a rifle bullet, where they bagged at the knee, and promptly returned the fire with several shots from his revolver. Another "scout" was probably saved because he happened to be behind the trunk of a large tree when the bullet imbedded itself in the other side. There was less excitement of that sort about Balltown, but more fast riding to the telegraph office when there was news to report. The famous "Good Friday" well on Porcupine Run furnished exercise for the horses and put the wits of the scouts to the test for a couple of weeks in the spring of 1883. A little later that spring, the scouts succeeded in drilling in a well or two on Cooper Hill, before the owners were ready. In the fall of the next year the "scouts" had transferred themselves to Thorn Creek, their ranks recruited by the addition, in particular, of Hon. M. L. Lockwood, Charles E. Goodwin and Charles Newlon. A few had gone to Macksburg, Ohio, among them P. C. Boyle and James Tenant.

BURNED WELL ON LOT 647, CHERRY GROVE, 1882.

The Phillips Bros.' well at Thorn Creek came in without the "scouts" in attendance. The first news to the outer world was conveyed by a message from Superintendent Hardman to the writer of these lines, at Oil City, who was on the ground the next morning. But the further progress of the well was closely watched by the "squad," a telegraph office having been opened in the small school house near the well. The same office served for the great Armstrong No. 2, located but 400 feet west of Phillips No. 1. This well showed no oil until it was torpedoed with forty quarts of nitroglycerine. The market advanced one day on the report that it was dry and dropped the next on information that it was the largest flowing well ever opened in Pennsylvania. The following account of this event was written by Frank H. Taylor, then oil editor of the Oil City Derrick:

"On October 27, 1884, those who stood at the brick school house and telegraph offices in the Thorn Creek district and saw the Semple, Boyd & Armstrong well torpedoed gazed upon one of the grandest scenes ever witnessed in oildom. When the shot took effect and the barren rock, as if smitten by the rod of Moses, poured forth its torrent of oil, it was such a magnificent and awful spectacle that no painter's brush nor poet's pen could do it justice. Men familiar with the wonderful sights of the oil country were struck dumb with astonishment as they beheld the mighty display of Nature's forces.

"There was no sudden reaction after the torpedo was exploded. A column of water rose eight or ten feet and fell back again; some time elapsed before the force of the explosive emptied the hole and the burnt glycerine, mud and sand rushed up in the derrick in a black stream. The blackness gradually changed to yellow; then, with a mighty roar, the gas burst forth with a deafening noise like the thunder bolt set free. For a moment the cloud of gas hid the derrick from sight, and then, as this cleared away a solid golden column half a foot in diameter shot from the derrick floor eight feet through the air, till it broke in fragments on the crown pulley and fell in a shower of yellow rain for rods around.

"For over an hour that grand column of oil, rushing swifter than any torrent and straight as a mountain pine, united derrick floor and top. In a few moments the ground around the derrick was covered inches deep with petroleum. The branches of the oak trees were like huge yellow plumes and a stream as large as a man's body ran down the hill to the road. It filled the space beneath the small bridge and continuing down the hill through the woods beyond, spread out upon the flats where the Johnston well is. In two hours these flats were covered with a flood of oil. The hillside was as if a yellow freshet had passed over it. Heavy clouds of gas almost obscuring the derrick, hung low in the woods, and still that mighty rush continued. Some of those who witnessed it estimated the well to be flowing 500 barrels an hour. Dams were built across the stream, that its production might be estimated. The dams overflowed and were swept away before they could be completed. People living along Thorn Creek packed up their household goods and fled to the hillsides.

"The pump station, a mile and a half down the creek, had to extinguish its fire that night on account of the gas. All fires around the district were put out. It was literally a flood of oil. It was estimated that the production was 10,000 barrels the first twenty-four hours. The foreman, endeavoring to get the tools into the well, was overcome by the gas and fell under the bull wheels. He was rescued immediately and medical aid summoned. He remained unconscious for two hours, but subsequently recovered fully.

"Several men volunteered to undertake the job of shutting in the largest well ever struck in the oil region. The packer for the oil saver was tied on the bull wheel shaft, the tools were placed over the hole and run in. But the pressure of the solid stream of oil against it prevented its going

lower even with the suspended weight of 2,000-pound tools.   One thousand
pounds additional weight was added before the cap was fitted and the well
closed.   A casing connection and tubing lines connected the well with a tank."

Earlier in 1884 the "scouts" were busy in Warren County at Wardwell,
reinforced by "Jerry" Hefferman, who continued in that employment to the
last.   But in 1885, after the opening of the Trenton Rock fields, scouting
became the sober work of gathering information without spectacular accom-

THE "MYSTERY" IN THE WOODS.

paniments.   Few speculators continued to employ men in the fields, but the
larger producing companies kept men who could be sent on short notice wherever wildcat wells seemed likely to develop new territory, but the romantic
and undescriptive title of "scout" has passed out of use.   It lasted much
longer than Cherry Grove, but had a short life.

CHAPTER XII.

SPECULATION IN OIL.

Quite naturally there has always been speculation in the petroleum industry. There is an inevitable hazard in every operation from the drilling of wells, yea, from the taking of leases on which to drill, to the marketing of the product. Wherever there is a natural hazard there is a speculator to toy with the chances. In the beginning the chief speculation was in lands, where wells might be drilled. Later this took the form of speculating in stock certificates of the numerous oil corporations, the entire country and a part of Europe being involved at about the close of the Civil War in 1865. The wide fluctuation in prices, as production varied, made every buyer of crude oil a speculator. Thus the drop from twenty dollars a barrel, soon after the Drake well was completed, to the ten cents a barrel in January, 1862, and the re-. covery to eight dollars a barrel at Pithole, in January, 1865, represents a range on which fortunes could me made and lost, not to mention the rapid and violent fluctuations between the extremes. A buyer starting into the field from Oil City, with the latest Pittsburgh quotation on the morning of one day, might return on the evening of the next, to learn that the market had advanced a dollar or had declined even more. In the meantime he had bought five thousand barrels and paid cash for it. He had won or lost as the case might be, five thousand dollars. This was a sort of speculation to stir the blood and to sharpen the faculties.

The same buyer might make his calculations on having his barreled oil delivered by team at seventy-five cents a barrel and find that an unusual demand, or a sudden change to bad roads, made his transportation to the river cost him a dollar and a half a barrel. He might have his oil delivered along Oil Creek, instead of at the river, load it on boats for the pond freshet, get in the "jam" and lose the entire cargo. A thousand barrel shipment of oil at ten dollars a barrel was a tidy loss to suffer in the fifteen minutes of a pond-freshet jam, almost as exciting for the buyer as for the men on the breaking boats, who had their lives at stake. These risks were unavoidable. Every buyer, including the refiners who bought oil to manufacture, had to figure on these chances. After the oil was loaded on the river it was jeoparded by sand bars in summer and ice floes in winter. The item of leakage was a steady loss, but none could tell in advance whether it would be large or small. Each took the speculative chance. Then there was always the danger of fire, a hazard that persisted from the moment the oil was bought in the tank at the well until it had undergone the last process of manufacture and had been delivered to the consumer. This hazard has been reduced by thoughtful precautions, but in the smaller degree is present to-day.

Gradually there grew a speculation that was based upon the hazards of transportation on the one hand and upon the changes in supply and demand on the other. The industry was new, its possibilities were imperfectly understood, the production was in the hands of a thousand independent operators, the marketing was by a hundred independent refineries. It could not be otherwise than that fluctuations should be frequent and violent. As a gambling game, nothing could be more fascinating than betting upon the price of crude oil. The purchase and sale of oil for future delivery became a popular diversion in which men made and lost fortunes with great facility. A thirty-day option might witness a change of two or three dollars a barrel in either direction. A few thousand barrels of oil might make, or break, a man without his having seen the color of the grease. Yet these transactions came to be made on the word of honor, without any written record save the private memorandum of the buyer or seller. No papers were signed, no witnesses invoked. Settlements were made on the same basis, although it might happen that one or the other of the traders was unable to produce a sufficient sum to meet his entire loss. In that case he gave up all he had, without a whimper, and turned to some other part of the industry for a new start in life. Not infrequently a speculator who closed his deal several thousand dollars in debt, would struggle for years to get it paid in full, scorning to take his legal privilege to call it a gambling debt and thereby wipe it out. Much business is still done between the older men of the oil region on the same basis of honor, no articles of agreement being necessary. The first writing in many real estate deals is that of the final deed.

It is not difficult to imagine that pipe lines were welcomed for their elimination of the more serious hazards of transportation. No one thought to question their charge of one dollar a barrel for pumping oil a distance of six miles. The entire trade had been educated to the wide margin of profits necessary to cover the well recognized hazards. It was rather a surprise when the pipe lines began to consolidate into larger organizations that transportation charges were voluntarily reduced. All were glad when the pipe lines devised a scheme for covering the loss of oil in storage by a general average assessment on all holders, for this reduced the fire hazard materially, to the individual whose oil might be burned. But speculation was not killed. The buying and selling of futures continued and exchanges were organized in the principal towns to carry on the business. Refiners, however, were not usually compelled to use this means to secure their supply, and their organization had brought about a more stable market for the producer's crude. However, it soon became evident that a buyer at the pipe line office was a convenience and the system was evolved whereby the producer could sell his oil for cash at the pipe line office the day after it was run from the tank at his well, the price being that at which oil was selling, at the moment, on the principal public exchange. The lapse of time was that necessary to send the data of the "run ticket" to headquarters, to compute the amount from a "gauge table" representing the capacity of the particular tank for every fraction of an inch of its height, and the return of this information to the field office of the pipe line. This in turn gave rise to the plan of issuing a pipe line certificate for each thousand barrels of oil put into storage. The producer could take a certificate in lieu of the cash, if he had that much oil and could sell his certificate on the Exchange, or to the purchasing agency, whenever he chose. Oil was held in pipe line tanks for thirty days, storage free, after which time, whether represented by a certificate or a credit balance, it was subject to a storage fee of twenty-five one-thousandths of one cent a barrel each month. This amounted to twenty-five cents a month on a certificate for one thousand barrels.

These storage certificates became the medium of speculation. Deliveries of actual oil on Exchange contracts were superceded by delivery of the certificates representing the oil. Speculation in these tokens became rife. The Oil City Oil Exchange became the center of the speculative business because its quotations were accepted as official by the agents at the field pipe line offices, but very active exchanges grew up in Bradford, Pittsburgh and New York. In the era of buying and selling futures, the Oil Exchange at Parkers Landing had been the place where the market was made. The greater part of the traders there had removed to Oil City and Bradford, however, as the scene of operations drifted to the brown sand fields. Daily transactions on

OIL CITY "CURBSTONE EXCHANGE." 1870.

these boards mounted to hundreds of thousands of barrels. The unit of fluctuation was fixed at five-eighths of a cent when the Oil City Oil Exchange was formally opened, and a single unit was the broker's commission. Fluctuations, however, were frequently several cents in a day, but as the stock of surplus oil in storage grew, the fluctuations became narrower and the transactions larger. The Oil City Exchange amended its rule and permitted the use of one-eighth of a cent in lieu of five-eighths, the other exchanges following the lead.

Speculation in petroleum certificates reached its zenith in 1882 to 1884. Transactions on the floor of the Oil City Exchange amounted to millions of barrels daily and they were only slightly less in the Exchanges at Bradford, Pittsburgh and New York. Naturally these were the years of "oil scouting," as every large speculator, or broker with a large clientage, had to have instant information concerning conditions "at the front." Upon this information the market went up, or down, and promptness was of even greater importance than accuracy. Yet it was essential that the information be accurate, for the slower means were certain to bring the truth and the movement of prices would be in accord. Speculators, themselves, sometimes went afield to be sure of their information, but were usually beaten in quickness of estimation, accuracy and in the race to the telegraph office, by the scouts who made that sort of work their regular business. Ordinarily it was found to be economical to trust the "scouting" to the fellows trained in perception and inured to the hardships of crawling around in the snow or about the leafy summer forests at night.

With the rise of the Cherry Grove pool, the market went down to the lowest price for many years, less than 50 cents a barrel. With the announcement, three months later, that salt water had made its appearance in the wells, the market went on an unprecedented "boom." Thousands in all parts of the country were again "in oil." Profits came so quickly and regularly that the "craze" spread to thousands more. Galleries of the Exchanges were crowded with visitors, anxious to be near their brokers and to see the turmoil around the "bull ring" for themselves. Distant telegraph offices were crowded with other speculators who desired to be in quick communication with the Exchange. Men forgot their tame little business at home and women deserted their domestic duties to watch the fluctuations of the petroleum market and to make easy money in oil.

But one day in November the scene changed. The price fell. There was a rally and then the price went down again. All that day was a succession of weaknesses and rallies of strength, until at three o'clock in the afternoon, the Exchanges closed, leaving thousands nerve-racked and uncertain. Many spent the sleeping time taking stock of the situation. Many perceived for the first time that the collapse of Cherry Grove had not been accompanied by any immediate reduction in the stock of oil held by the pipe lines. Many hundreds decided that it was time to sell their oil and take their profits. In the early morning crowds were assembling about the Exchanges and the telegraph offices, long before ten o'clock, when the Exchanges opened for business. All tried to look cheerful and the majority succeeded in appearing miserably anxious. Nerves were strung tense and nerves were totally unstrung, before the gongs sounded at the stroke of ten. There was a rush to sell, and hardly anyone to buy. In five minutes there was a panic. Brokers went white in the face and speechless, other brokers went mad and vociferated with all the power of their lungs. If by chance one bid to buy he was seized by many hands and dragged until it could be decided who had been lucky enough to sell. Men's coats were torn from their backs, collars were thrown upon the floor, hands and limbs were bruised in the eager grasp to attract attention, but no one heeded. Men even spat in each other's faces in their haste and excitement and none had time to resent the indignity. Pandemonium had broken loose and continued until the gongs rang at three o'clock. So great was the tumult and so eager the throng that the familiar sound was not heard by many. Officers of the Exchanges had to exert themselves to stop the trading or efforts to trade, and secure order.

Brokers and clerks worked late into the night preparing their sheets for the clearing houses. Some failed to clear. Bank officers and clerks burned the midnight light casting up accounts to learn how far short their collateral had fallen. Men and women, far and near, mourned the disappearance of the apparent profits of their trading, as well as the wiping out of their real capital, deposited as margins. There was widespread disappointment, rage and sadness, according to the individual temperaments. Philosophers were not lacking who had invested on the principle that they had just so much that they could afford to lose. Ruin stared some in the face and there was gladness nowhere. It was another bad night. Strong capitalists mustered their resources and the next day there was some support for the market. The worst of the panic was over, and in a few days, the Exchanges were back to normal. A few days later, however, there was a repetition of the panic in even worse form. The first slump occurred November 10th, the second on November 14th. The first panic came on November 17th, while the second lasted from the 22nd to the 24th and was most disastrous. Despite this experience the craze for speculation gathered new force and the market advanced forty cents a barrel from the lowest on November 24th to the highest on December 8th. Another panic started with the opening of the Grandin well No. 3 at Balltown, causing a decline of twenty cents a barrel in three days from $1.15, and ultimately to seventy-five cents a barrel before the close of December. This caused more severe injury to the speculating public than the panics in November, because there were no longer any paper profits to lose. Much of the loss was paid out of resources acquired in business other than speculative, or by labor.

While the crashes of the closing months of 1882 drove out of the petroleum market a good many lambs that had been sheared just as winter came on, there were others to take their places. In 1883 the operations of the Penn Bank syndicate in Pittsburg gave the speculators a lively run. The market was again advanced considerably above a dollar a barrel. The collapse of this syndicate, the loss of the funds of the bank and its depositors, and the prosecution of the leaders, dampened the speculative ardor in Pittsburgh temporarily, but with the opening of the Thorn Creek pool, a few miles north of that city, and later the development of the Washington County field a few miles south of the city, Pittsburgh came near taking supremacy from Oil City in the speculation in petroleum certificates. This speculation continued until it reflected discredit upon the whole industry, but was finally suppressed when the Seep Purchasing Agency announced it would not be governed by the speculative quotations in buying credit balances from producers. This was more than ten years after the tremendous speculation era beginning in 1882, namely in 1895.

In California, since about 1889, there has been speculation in oil company stocks. These are listed on the San Francisco and Los Angeles Mining and Petroleum Exchanges. Within very recent times the dealings in California oil stocks have been quite extensive and highly speculative in character. The opening of the coast field in Texas, at Beaumont, led to a speculative craze in oil company stocks that paralleled that of the East in the days of Pithole and immediately preceding. This wave reached Kansas, which treasures its share of sorrow as a result of ill-advised speculation in oil company stocks. These stock speculations have been principally confined to persons distinguished for their previous lack of knowledge concerning the oil industry. The certificate speculation, on the contrary, impoverished the producers of oil. They were constantly tempted to try to advance the price of their commodity, by buying, on thin margins, large quantities of the oil which they sold actually and for cash in much smaller quantities as they produced it. Rarely did a producer "sell short" against his future production, on the chance that the market would be lower when he had the oil to deliver. In the wheat pit, every speculating farmer buys, even when he has wheat to sell and the planter who gets in the cotton market is sure to be on the "bull" side. The oil producers have been more prosperous since the speculation in certificates has ceased. They are not helping to pay storage on the surplus, or for other losses.

During the heyday of speculation on the Oil Exchanges, fortunes were made and lost quickly. It was no uncommon thing for a speculator to start

OHIO OIL COMPANY TANK FARM LOADING RACK, CASEY, ILL.

in the morning with a few hundred dollars and close the day's business with thousands in the bank. One member of the Parker Exchange, about the time of the development of the fourth sand "cross belt," began business in the morning with $75,000 in the bank and went home in the evening $50,000 in debt. In a few years he discharged that indebtedness through the gains of small trading as a broker's client. As a member of the Oil City Exchange he cleared $65,000 in the month following the first signs of collapse at Cherry Grove and doubled the amount from the violent fluctuations in November and December, acting on information of his "scout." Yet during those months he sometimes lost as high as a hundred thousand dollars in a day, to be regained the next. His case may be extreme, for he was a venturesome trader, but it is typical of the general experience in those days. Wall Street has occasional periods of great life; the oil market had them four or five times a year. It was the maddest game the speculator ever played.

Yet the producer of this commodity, who harvests his crop every day, can also sell it for cash any day he chooses. There is no other business organized on the same basis. The Seep Purchasing Agency at Oil City, Pa., pays out more than $3,000,000 a month to oil producers for their product. This is all for oil produced east of the Mississippi River and not including Illinois. Oil is purchased on daily runs in Illinois, Kansas, Oklahoma, Louisiana and Colorado, and the disbursements in those States exceed, in the aggregate, those of the Eastern fields. In Texas and California the greater part of the business is done on special contracts.

WELLS IN THE PLEASANTVILLE FIELD IN 1871.

CHAPTER XIII.

WAR AND WELLS.

In the early days on Oil Creek, the newcomers, travelers, and moving prospectors were denominated "The Carpet Bag Brigade." The leather suit case and Oxford bag had not been invented. The trunk was too cumbersome for light travel. Men carried bags made of carpet, Brussels or worse, queer shaped receptacles, with long carrying straps or handles, the carpet bag almost dragging on the ground. So to all who had been on "The Creek" for a year, the travelers and the fastidious who deemed a razor and an occasional change of linen necessities, were "The Carpet Bag Brigade." This honorable contingent swelled suddenly and prodigiously soon after the surrender of General Lee at Appomattox. The highways and the byways were thronged with men and vehicles, on horseback and afoot, accompanied by the inevitable "carpet sack," men intent upon investment, adventure and securing employment. A letter from David Lowry, himself a veteran of the war and an early arrival on Oil Creek, says among other things:

"Although Memorial Day dates back from 1867, if I was asked where the first Army reunion was held I would answer unhesitatingly, 'On Oil Creek.' With the salutes of last Memorial Day yet ringing in my ears, I would say, 'twas there the young veterans (you must not forget the large proportion of young men in the ranks) first reuned. They gathered on Oil Creek from the East to the far West; from every State in the Union and from the Territories as well. The greetings when they met were so unlike all other meetings I have witnessed that they were deeply impressed upon my memory. Men who fought side by side, men who fought against and captured each other, met with unmistakable friendship and recalled the past in tones so hearty that all listeners were interested; speculators intent upon their own exciting business were held in momentary rapt attention. 'Hello! Haven't seen you since we made Humphrey Marshall jump at Mill Springs.' 'Shake! Yes, you had it pretty well your own way there and all through East Tennessee, but we evened up when we got down in Mississippi in '62.' Another pair: 'Heavens, if it isn't Smith, shoot me!' 'Yours to command. And you're Wilson?' 'Yes, the same Wilson you captured and thought you'd clamped for the balance of the war. However, them two months was the best living I had while I was out. What doing?' 'Drilling a well. And you?' 'Same thing, that is, for another man.' And so on without end. Twenty times a day you might witness such meetings.

"I sat opposite General A. E. Burnside at the hotel table in Oil City without recognizing him until my memory was jogged, the surroundings were so unnatural. General Burnside was the chief engineer, constructing the ill-fated Reno and Pithole Railroad. Outside the hotel I pondered the strange freak of fortune, with Burnside the central figure in my thoughts, to be aroused by a mournful voice, saying: 'Can't get a horse for love or money, tried everywhere.' It was the muddiest road I ever looked upon, with one exception. That exception was the sea of mud, the Army of the Ohio, under Buell, Grant's Army and Pope's division were swimming in three days after the battle of Shiloh. Pope had joined us in the heart of the thick woods there; the land was flat as a pancake, the mud black and thin. We made more than twelve miles of corduroy road and even then it was difficult to get over the ground. I am within the truth when I say the road in front of that Oil City hotel was twelve to fifteen inches deep and mixed with oil. So I said to the man who had been musing aloud: 'Where do you wish to go, sir?' 'Up the Creek,' he replied. 'There's nothing for me to do here. I am a machinist, looking for work.' I promised him a seat in my brother's wagon to Petroleum Center. My brother ratified the proposition and refused the fare our chance passenger urged upon him. Years afterward a gentleman called to see me at the editorial rooms of the Pittsburgh Chronicle. I had no difficulty in recognizing in him the chance passenger, who navigated with me the sea of mud between Oil City and Petroleum Center. But I was astounded to learn that he was Captain Jones—the Captain Jones whose fame as a furnace master had already spread far and wide—the Captain Jones who was long the right hand man of Andrew Carnegie and Henry Phipps. who installed the Bessemer process for steel making in America and whose inventions and improvements helped to make Pittsburgh supreme as the steel manufacturing center of the world. He made no fortune in oil. but was a member of 'The Carpet Bag Brigade' after the war."

The men of the armies, North and South, flocked to the Oil Regions by thousands, seeking fortune and adventure. Thousands gripped by the wanderlust. later floated away to conquer the great West and filled the mining camps from the Rockies to the Pacific Coast. Hundreds remained and made their impress upon the youngest industry. Many of these were officers, accustomed to command. all were hardy soldiers with a heart for any fate. These men had been meeting the problems of transport for vast armies, they had been fighting valiant and stubborn foes. Withal they had discipline ingrained in their very being. They were a splendid acquisition to this new business that had everything to accomplish, and they were equipped to plunge into this commercial battle, as earnest and deadly as any they had fought. To this grand army the petroleum industry owes much for bringing order out of chaos and for carrying forward the development in the face of difficulties. The spirit of these men was communicated to all about them and obstacles assumed the aspect of things to be overcome without delay. Speed and energy had not been lacking. as we have seen, in the earliest times along Oil Creek, but they were heightened by the advent of men who had moved railroad trains by human hand power when victory depended upon getting supplies forward in quick order—men who had carried the works by storm.

There was ample exercise in this industrial battle for all the talents of engineers. commissary sergeants and corps commanders. When some venturesome wildcatter found oil in a remote locality there was an instant move on the works of the enemy. Trees must be felled. rocks blasted, heights surmounted. Machinery, tools, pipe and material must be sent to the front and urged with all speed. Men must be lodged and fed, storage must be provided for the oil, pipe lines must be laid over hill and valley to transport the

product. Here there was no steady grind of labor as in factories and work-
shops. Lines of adjoining leases were battle fronts, where the first well down
got the best of the production and time was all important. Drilling crews
were offered premiums for the fastest progress through the rocks, and teamsters got double pay who could negotiate the impossible path and deliver
material on the ground a day ahead. Diggers fared well who could make
grade fastest and rig builders risked their necks to make records in running
up derricks. Tank builders got up in the night to put wooden reservoirs to
the unexpected gusher and risked gas asphyxiation by permitting oil to be
turned in before the tank was finished. There was a keen commander on
every job and often rivalry for accomplishment overshadowed the profits
to be made.

BAD ROADS ON SHERMAN FLATS, OIL CREEK.

Commercial warfare exists in many industries but the battles are fought
mainly by the Captains of Industry with unappreciative soldiers. Not so in
oil. The interest extends to the ranks and high privates are as eager for the
fray as the commanding officer. The wheel of fortune here turns so rapidly
and so frequently that the private of to-day is the commander of to-morrow.
Often, alas, the commander of to-day is in the ranks of to-morrow, but ready
to win another promotion. It is a democratic society in which mere money is
less respected than skill, ability and energy. Pluck is a mainspring. Nowhere is competition so keen, for, unlike mining for the metals, the first discoverer of the lode has not a sure thing on the riches of his claim. Mineral
oil is fluid and to some extent may be drained away by the wells on adjoin-

ing property. Possibly the struggle is less feverish in these days of comparatively low priced oil and comparatively large holdings of land. But it has not lost much of the alertness that characterized the operation of half-acre leases for five-dollar oil when the armies came home from the war in 1865.

In another respect the soldiers of the war made an impress upon the oil region by their advent in great numbers. That was in courage. Men who had faced death a hundred times and become intimately acquainted with it were not afraid to face misfortune. Misfortune came to those engaged in drilling for oil, in transporting, in manufacturing, in storing and in marketing it in many ways. There was always a chance for a "dry hole" instead of the gusher sought; there was always the danger of fire; there was ever present the violent fluctuations of value that made and unmade fortunes in

STANDARD OIL TANKS, RESERVOIR AND

a day. It requires courage to face these possibilities and more courage to meet the worst without flinching. But it is characteristic of the petroleum industry that disaster is met with fortitude and that the individual renews the struggle with more determination to win. Thousands rendered homeless in a night by one of the sweeping town fires that are all too frequent, begin rebuilding before the embers of their destroyed homes have cooled. It is all "in the game" and they have the courage to meet fate with a smile.

In 1865 there was great danger that highwaymen and desperadoes would hamper the prosecution of a business which required men to travel lonely roads carrying large sums of money. The National banking system had not been developed; the certified check and New York exchange were in the future. But the development of this sort of lawlessness was sternly suppressed. The disciplined army men were conspicuous in the maintenance of law and order at that period and with their coming the cut-throat crowd made its escape to more promising fields. Life and property have ever been safer from premeditated attack in the oil regions than in the best policed districts of larger cities. Drafts and certified checks have rendered unnecessary the carrying of such large sums of money on the person as was common in the early days, but currency is freely handled in a new oil field, ordinarily with small risk of robbery. Where robberies occur the culprit is usually a "tenderfoot," one unfamiliar with the oil business and the ways of the men engaged in it. It appears to be deemed safer by thugs, generally, to try the hold up of a coal mine paymaster than a fast driving oil superintendent on a mission.

The War of the Rebellion has almost been forgotten and the ranks of the veterans are thinning rapidly, but their impress upon a young industry is lasting. The generation engaged chiefly in fighting the oil battles west of

CAMP, KERN RIVER FIELD, CALIFORNIA.

the Mississippi River has probably no knowledge of the influence upon their industry exerted by the great war 1861 to 1865, or by the men engaged in it, but they are unconsciously governed in a large measure by that influence. The methods, the courage, the discipline, the spirit are the same, transmitted from one generation to another, and from the old center to every land on earth where petroleum is produced in commercial quantities. Like knights of old the American oil well driller has fared forth to Russia, Roumania, the Orient and the South Sea Islands to carry the cult into foreign lands. He is the modern soldier of fortune in a cause of peaceful industrial conquest of earth's treasures. He is recruiting new armies in strange lands, imbuing them with as much of the old spirit and discipline as he may, considering the material with which he works.

Oil development from the Allegheny Mountains to the Pacific Coast has been warfare. War with the elements, battling with the eternal rocks, human striving with human opposition. Fortunes, not lives, have been the apparent stakes, but life itself has been sacrificed in the struggle. The battles of the anticlinals have been fought with all the determination and enthusiasm of battles with deadly weapons and there has grown up a new grand army of veterans in this pursuit. They are heroes of many campaigns, of victories and defeats innumerable, seasoned, disciplined, invincible. Thousands of recruits have fallen by the wayside, or deserted, but the army grows every year. It numbers well above one hundred thousand of able-bodied men, many of them born amid the strife, and in no other industry are the women so intimately acquainted with the hardships of the firing line at the front.

Hundreds of families move every year from the old oil fields to the new. When not actually living in tents they are sheltered often in structures hardly more substantial. Menaced almost every moment by the danger of fire they go on making homes, improving their temporary quarters, seeking such society and education as is available at the time or place. It is no pleasant task to leave a comfortable home to make a new one from the raw material, to part from good friends to go among strangers, but they do it cheerfully, without a murmur. It is a part of the discipline of the camp. It is their share in the battle for greasy treasure. It is not to be wondered at that they become cosmopolitan in their tastes, democratic in their manners, hospitable to their neighbors and helpful in their ways. It is to be expected that these children grow up sturdily, fit successors to their elders in carrying on the conquest, capable of any achievement. In a half century there has been time to observe causes and effects and such are the results. No class is more resourceful or independent.

In our late war with Spain no troops acquitted themselves more creditably than those from the oil region. When typhoid fever threatened to decimate the camp at Chattanooga, these troops drilled deep water wells, constructed sewers and made sanitary surroundings. In Porto Rico they were at the front, refused to wait for the slow moving commissary and subsisted on the country traversed. In the Philippines they defied the tropical climate, as well as the bolomen and came home healthy and triumphant. To them real war was so little different from their ordinary avocation that they readily adapted themselves to its conditions, winning applause from the troops of the regular army. Due more, probably, to their training and habits than to any other cause. Turning back to Lowry's letter, this is his view of the oil country life in which he participated:

"From every point of view the Oil Creek I recall, in the sixties and seventies, was variegated. Spirited always, humorous despite the tragic aspect extraordinary losses assumed; picturesque, unlike anything one bred in a city and living in a city all his life could imagine. It is a page of life such as is rarely seen in this work-a-day world, brimming with action and romance. It was a world of chance, where Dame Fortune picked her favorites in the most inexplicable fashion, favoring one at the expense of another, permitting one man to flatter himself that his future was assured, only to dash the chalice from his lips. His well had produced, now, ten days in succession, forty barrels a day and oil was selling at five dollars a barrel. A fountain of wealth! And then Smith's well, seventy feet distant, came in. It 'tapped' the other man's well. His fountain of wealth was dry in an instant. It was what General Sherman described war to be, and it was no uncommon experience in those times. I have seen a well yield seventy-five barrels one day and the next morning there was not oil enough in it to grease the sucker rods. The business of drilling oil wells in those days was the gamble of gambles. Men had it all to learn. It was like a battle, where strange Fate decreed that two should die and one, who stood between them, should live. Not always was the favored one apparently more fit for life—or for success."

This very chance of one well "tapping" another made the warfare between leases. It is the element that still makes of the lease line a battle front. It is not merely a gamble in these later days, but a competition along definite lines, guided by experience. Among veterans in the industry the fight is conducted under fair rules, and wells are drilled, by common consent, some distance from the boundaries. When the rules are violated by reason of greed or inexperience the contest is waged without mercy and with all the artifices that experience has taught to the heroes of other campaigns. It is a struggle in which experience counts for much. "Men had it all to learn," in 1865 and they have not learned it all yet. But the "battle is not to the strong alone, it is to the vigilant, the active and the brave," as it has ever been. Nor is the battle fought alone in the producing fields. The marketing of the product has been a conquest of foreign lands, gained by trained armies in constant action. The weapons have been improved appliances and superior morale of the men behind the guns. The petroleum marketers have carried into strange lands, not only their burning fluid, but the lamps and stoves in which it is burned. They are still on the receding frontier, winning their way to new territories, battling with other commercial armies for possession. They are blazing new trails through savage wildernesses to carry light to all of the sons of men. Their conquests are an interesting chapter in the history of human progress. They are approaching the "roof of the world" in Tibet and they have floated their product over Lake Victoria Nyanza in the heart of "Darkest Africa." Battleships are burning oil fuel and the swiftest torpedo boat destroyers use no other. Thus war and wells meet again in a new combination.

CLOSED DERRICKS OF PITTSBURG PETROLEUM COMPANY, SHAMBURG, 1869.

CHAPTER XIV.

EVOLUTION OF MACHINERY.

Well drilling tools had been devised many years before Drake drilled his oil well. They were used in drilling salt wells, a considerable industry in Southwestern Pennsylvania, Southeastern Ohio and West Virginia, from near the beginning of the Nineteenth Century until the discovery of oil. Many of these salt wells found oil and gas in small quantities. At least one, in Kentucky, found oil in large quantity, became a gusher and literally, "set the river on fire." The oil covered the surface of the river for thirty miles and when ignited made the grandest illumination ever seen in the Cumberland Valley. The Beatty well, put down in 1818, caused a great fire on the Big South Fork of the Cumberland, but it was not a gusher. The big well was drilled in 1829 and was known as the "American Well." Natural gas from some of the salt wells, particularly in Southeastern Ohio, was burned under the pans to evaporate the brine. It effected great economy in the manufacture of salt. The tools used in drilling these wells weighed from 100 to 200 pounds and the diameter of holes varied from two and one half inches to three inches. The "spring pole" was the favorite drilling machine, although an occasional horse power was used. It was with this sort of tools that the Drake well was drilled for oil. The tools were made by William Smith, a blacksmith and driller of salt wells at Tarentum, who undertook to drill the Drake well and did. For these tools Smith charged Drake $76.50. It is supposed that Drake bought the material from some one else as the Smith charge was for "making" the set, but there is no other record. The bit was flattened like a cold chisel and the hole was smoothed by use of a flat headed reamer. The boiler and engine used were of Pittsburgh manufacture, made by W. M. Faber & Co., and colloquially known as "Long John." It was an improvement over the "spring pole" but no oil well workers of to-day could be induced to toy with it. It was several years, however, before engines and boilers were designed especially for the severe strain of drilling and handling oil wells. This was done by the late C. M. Farrar of Buffalo, who designed first a boiler, and then an engine, both made famous by Samuel G. Bayne, now President of the Seaboard National Bank in New York, but for many years the general agent for boilers, engines, tubing, casing and other oil well supplies, the foundation of the present National Supply Company. The Wood & Mann portable outfit, in which the small engine was mounted upon the boiler, was the popular type for the shallow territory adjacent to Oil Creek. These manufacturers are believed to have made the first eccentric link reverse engine used in the oil country, but they did not keep pace with the demand for heavier machinery.

It was one of this type with engine mounted on light portable boiler, that was at the bottom of the great fire in Cherry Run Valley, above Rouseville, in 1866. Mr. Stroup, the driller on the next well above, told me the tale on the ground where it occurred, substantially as follows:

"I was running the morning tour and came to work at midnight. My tooldresser and I noted the men on the well below were not working. Apparently they sought the slumber that revelry had deprived them of before midnight. But at about five o'clock in the morning they began to stir. We had noted their boiler 'blowing off' during the night and had feared an explosion but we were safer where we were than farther down the hill. Daylight was coming rapidly when we saw the tooldresser below, start toward the boiler. His driller followed, stopped him and we could see there was a warm argument about something. The colloquy ended by the helper proceeding toward the boiler, while the driller speedily sought retreat behind the 'Sampson post' in his derrick. I told my partner I believed the fool below was about to turn cold water into his dry, hot boiler and we, too, sought safety behind the timbers. The driller below told me afterward that he had tried to dissuade the man, assuring him the boiler would burst, but the man's retort was that he didn't care what happened to the boiler. He did not seem to give a thought to what might happen to himself. A few minutes later we heard the explosion. A large part of the boiler soared across the valley and grazed the roof of the Smith Farm Oil Company office on the other side of Cherry Run. Fortunately it did not strike the office, where Mr. Beers and another man were sleeping. The tool dresser was killed instantly. The engine, perched at the top of the boiler, was hurled with tremendous force against the 1,200-barrel oil tank at the next well down the run, which contained 600 barrels of oil. The tank was crushed; the oil rushed in a flood down the valley. A boiler at another drilling well stood about 200 feet below; and there was no time to put out the fire. In a minute flames were leaping high; every steam whistle in the valley was tooting madly. Drillers, pumpers and the suddenly awakened sleepers along the valley, scrambled up the hillsides, some very thinly clad, but none too soon to escape the blistering heat of the fiery flood. That many lives were not sacrificed was remarkable. At that time the valley was a forest of derricks, the side of the road was lined with offices, eating houses and refineries; tanks of oil were everywhere. The flames leaped from one to another with almost incredible rapidity and in a quarter of an hour that valley was a seething cauldron of flame half a mile long. From the hilltops, the men who had escaped with their lives could hear the detonations when the furnace heat raised too much steam on their boilers and sent them to join the original cause of the trouble. It was lively while it lasted and it continued long into the day." This and the fire that later swept Benninghoff Run, a few miles farther up Oil Creek, will never be forgotten by those who looked upon them from the heights.

The evolution of the engine was very slow, but the problems of handling heavy tools and of instant reversal of motion were solved, William J. Innis and C. M. Farrar being conspicuous in the development of machinery especially adapted to the purpose. The Oil Well Supply Company annually exports hundreds of improved Innis engines to the foreign oil fields of the world. The final development in engines has been the internal combustion gas engine, adapted to oil well uses by Joseph Reid of Oil City, Pennsylvania, in 1895. Mr. Reid sold the first gas engine for pumping oil wells to John A. Kirkwood on the old Rynd Farm on Oil Creek, May 13, 1895, for pumping his wells. This machine has been greatly improved and thousands are in daily use for drilling as well as for pumping, the wells furnishing their own fuel. With a nicely balanced "power" one of these machines will pump twenty wells with a remarkably small consumption of gas, the expense, computing gas at the full market price, being only a few cents a day for each well. This method has made possible the profitable operation of very small wells, that under the old conditions, would have been abandoned. The internal combustion principle has been applied to the huge compressors on the mains of the natural gas companies and to the monstrous pumps of the oil pipe lines. The latest departure along this line is an internal combustion pumping engine that uses crude oil for fuel and is operated with success on the trunk line of the Tide Water Pipe Line Company to pump oil from Illinois to Pennsylvania. It is expected this fuel will soon have a much wider field of application.

Drilling tools have been improved quite as much as boilers and engines since the time of the Drake well. It required but few years to demonstrate the advantage of heavier tools than those used on the first well. But the greatest single step of progress was made when some one substituted the "club bit" for the original rock drill and reamer. George Koch, a practical driller, claimed the honor. It was not necessary to have a thin, flat drill at the bottom. It was subject to breakage in hard rock. So he combined the "center bit" and "reamer" in one thick, blunt edged implement called the club bit, which was found effective for the double purpose and saved one-half of the drilling time to sink a well. The first man to devote himself to "fishing" lost articles from oil wells, was J. H. Luther, a blacksmith who had located at Funkville, on Oil Creek, in the early days. He devised many ingenious implements for recovering lost "bits," "augur stems," in fact whole "strings of tools" and sand pumps. The Luther "socket" is still in general use. It consists of a hollow rim in which is inserted a pair of clamps that slip down readily over the tools at the bottom of the hole, but when pulled upward, the "lips" on the jaws catch the "shoulder" of stem, or bit, and hold it tightly. The heavier the traction, the more firmly the jaws hold, as they slip into the metal rim. Mr. Luther also invented the rope knife for cutting cable from drilling tools when stuck at the bottom, and many other "fishing" tools. He sometimes used "pole tools," a device of the Canadian driller, and he and his sons followed the business of extracting lost tools for many years. Victor Gretter was an inventor of fishing tools also, locating in the Clarion County field in 1872 and following the business until his death in Bradford. He was, however, chiefly noted for his invention of the "oil saver," a device for controlling wells and saving the oil, while they were being drilled in the sand. The invention consisted of a ring, clamped into the "casing head" through which passed a smooth metal tube, the latter fitting closely around the drilling cable. This prevented the oil flowing up into the derrick and enabled the saving of the fluid through lead lines connected to the casing head. It was valuable in addition by preventing fires that had frequently followed the unrestrained flow of new wells, when casing was generally adopted. Mr. Gretter also attained to some fame as the man who extinguished the fire of the Anchor Oil Company's well on lot No. 647, Cherry Grove Township, Warren County, while the well was flowing 3,000 barrels of oil a day. In this undertaking he had to use a small cannon to shoot off the casing head, in order to concentrate the flow into one stream. He then dropped over the mouth of the well a great sheet iron funnel, flowing the fresh oil out of range of the fire, depriving the flames of fuel.

All of the early oil wells were drilled "wet." That is, there was no attempt made to shut out the fresh water until the well was drilled as deep as necessary. The tubing was inserted with a "seed bag" tied on. The seed swelled on contact with the water, completely filling the cavity between the tubing and the wall of the drilled hole. Ordinarily these wells showed no oil until the accumulated water was pumped out through the tubing. This was called testing. Sometimes the "seed bag" failed in its office, when it had to be pulled out and renewed until it was tight. Of course, pulling the tubing to repair valves "burst the seed bag" and let the water into the well, and

OIL PUMPING WELLS IN THE PACIFIC OCEAN.

sometimes the "seed bag" burst, without adventitious aid, and flooded the well with water. Such accidents were annoying and occasionally resulted in the complete ruin of the oil well. This led to casing. Thus the hole was started two or three inches larger in diameter and drilled "wet" through the lowest appearance of fresh water. Then large pipe, "casing," was inserted, the driller stopping in rock of a character that would furnish a good "seat" for this pipe. The well was then drilled the remainder of the way to the oil sand of diameter corresponding with the inside of the casing. This shut out all fresh water. The first casing was provided with "seed bags" to insure a tight joint, but it was soon found that in suitable rock the weight of the pipe drove it far enough in to take care of that. Wells drilled in this manner had no column of water to restrain the oil and gas, so they frequently flowed as soon as the sand was penetrated. Many were burned by the gas coming in contact with the fire under the boiler and all were difficult to control until connected to tanks. Here was where the oil saver came in, being put on a day or two before the drillers expected to reach the sand. It was a life saver as well as an oil saver.

There has been quite an evolution in the matter of tubing, too. In the Drake well copper tube was used, after the manner of the salt wells; then cast iron pipe was tried; then ordinary steam pipe. The first specially prepared oil well tubing was made on the order of John Eaton at the Taunton (Mass.) Iron Works and was butt welded in long pieces with heavy screw couplings. It was sold at $1.25 per foot. Soon afterward came the lap welded tubing with sleeve couplings, which superceded all others and is now sold at about fifteen cents a foot. The manner of handling the tubing at the well and removing it when necessary, has made progress. The first device

SUMMERLAND, SANTA BARBARA COUNTY CALIFORNIA.

was a swivel ring, holding a short piece of pipe, which had to be screwed into the coupling and out again. This was soon superceded by a clamp thrown around the collar, which, in various forms, has been employed ever since. When it was found desirable to shut out salt water, as well as fresh water, the packer was invented to supplant the cumbersome and unreliable seed bag. It employed rubber under compression in lieu of the swelling flax seed, the weight of the pipe furnishing the compression. Robert R. Armor first put this device on the market.

In the Pennsylvania oil fields all wells, from the first, have been drilled with "cable tools." That is, the tools are suspended at the end of a rope. The first cables were made of "sea-grass." Drilling cables are now made of Manila hemp, or of steel wire. The wire cable is particularly popular in California, where the wells are deep and the drilling process slow. In the Canadian fields, round wooden poles joined together were used in the early developments and are still employed for shallow drilling. This pole system has been introduced by the Canadians in the oil fields of Roumania and Galicia. The soft formations in Texas compelled the introduction of a new system, the rotary hydraulic. The principle is the rotation of a drilling pipe, supplied with a steel shoe at the bottom, water being forced down the tube under sufficient pressure to drive up the detritus outside the pipe. This method has been introduced in California and many of the wells there are put through the softer strata near the surface with the rotary rig and drilled through the harder rocks below with the standard equipment of cable tools. The portable drilling machine has also been developed to a high efficiency and is largely used in shallow territories. These machines use cable tools, but include a pole derrick. The derricks on Oil Creek were thirty to forty feet high, the corners frequently being single timbers. Deeper drilling involved the plank derrick, that gradually crept up to eighty feet in height. In California it has attained 104 feet, with double corners, to accommodate extra heavy tools and strains. The modern "string" of drilling tools weighs about two tons, more than twenty times the weight of those used to drill the Drake well. In favorable formation a drilling crew sometimes makes nearly 200 feet of hole in a twelve-hour "tour." This, however, is above the average. Derricks made entirely of steel are now in common use, put together with bolts so that they may be conveniently taken down and moved to other locations. These are favored by natural gas companies operating in deep territory, one derrick sufficing for many wells. Where oil is the object, some sort of derrick must be maintained for renewal of valves and other repairs.

Drake invented the use of driving pipe with which to penetrate the alluvial soil to "bed rock." He used heavy, cast iron pipe which had loose wrought iron bands riveted on the ends. This style, with some modifications, prevailed for many years. The first wrought iron drive pipe was used by Frederick Crocker in the pioneer operations in the Bradford field. The order was placed with John Eaton, President of the Oil Well Supply Company, for seven-inch pipe. Mr. Crocker's next order was for eight-inch pipe. Drake might have made a fortune from the drive pipe idea, but he never took the trouble to apply for a patent. Many other improvements in oil well appliances were never patented. Frederick Crocker was a pioneer operator on Oil Creek and while there he invented and patented the famous Crocker check valve, indispensable in many oil well and pipe line operations. A part of the drilling tools is known as the "jars." These are a huge double link, working each within the other, serviceable in releasing the bit when it sticks in a soft formation at the bottom, or catches on a projection of the rock. These were used in the beginning, made of wrought iron. George Smith at Rouseville in 1866, forged the first "jars" with steel lining, for Leo H. Nelson, an obvious improvement.

The windlass used for raising and lowering the drilling tools is known as the bull wheel. Originally it was a very cumbersome thing, with arms mortised into the ends of the shaft. George Koch made an improved bull wheel about 1876, known as the skeleton wheel, in which the arms were spiked firmly across the facets of the octagonal shaft end. The new wheel is not one half as heavy as the old and is much stronger. The bull wheel has always been controlled by an iron band passed around the rim of one of the wheels and attached to a brake bar so that it may be made to bind tight at will. On deep wells this band occasionally breaks and the uncontrolled wheels, rotating under the traction of the tons of tools at the end of the uncoiling cable, whirl so fast that they fly to pieces, or the journals, leaving the boxes, the wheels race up the derrick with great damage to the structure. Quite a number of men have lost their lives in this style of accident, but more attention is paid to these brake bands than formerly. They are made of broader and heavier iron. This, of course, in rigs where cable tools are used. Pole tools and rotary rigs do not draw and run down their tools at a speed of a thousand feet to the minute.

In the beginning oil wells were pumped as single units. Each had to have a boiler and engine of its own, the boilers being fired with coal or wood. Each required two men, working "tours," from noon to midnight and from midnight to noon. Along about 1870 it was found that gas from the wells made good fuel for the boilers. With gas to burn the pumpers had little to do and many of them found leisure to supplement the scant education they had obtained in schools. Soon it was perceived that several engines could be run from one boiler, and by 1880 it was discovered that one man could care for a boiler and several engines, thus connected. The next step was to couple several wells to one engine by means of shacklerods and a "pumping power," the down stroke of one well coinciding with the upward stroke or lift of another. Then came the gas engine to supply the little momentum needed to overcome the friction, the wells "balancing" each other. One man may now pump thirty wells and get from them as much oil as a like number could be made to produce un-

AN ODD OIL CREEK DERRICK.

der the original system with thirty boilers, thirty engines and sixty men employed. It is not necessary to point out the economy that is effected by these changes. But it is probably greater than in any other branch of the industry, save that of transportation. .

Great progress has been made in the processes for the manufacture of petroleum products. In the beginning refineries were small affairs with one or two stills. These were charged and their contents distilled by increasing heat, giving off benzine, lamp oil, lubricating oil, a little paraffine and finally tar. A charge could be disposed of in half a week, with good luck, allowing the refinery a capacity per week of double its still capacity. Without good fortune the output was less. The modern refinery operates under the continuous process system. The most volatile products are distilled with gentle heat in the first huge retort and passed to another series for further refining and treatment. What remains of these is more perfectly eliminated by the higher temperature of the next still, which starts the less volatile product to vapor, and so on down the line, till the residue in the last still is a small quantity of coke. Meantime each of the products has passed through other processes of distillation, washing, separation and deodorizing, to the perfect product of commerce. The wax is sent to a separate factory for treatment and the lubricating and neutral oils are passed along for classification, separation, blending or whatever is needed. The coke is dealt with in the laboratory, where it yields its analine dyes, its photographic developers, its medical properties and its disinfectents. The total products derived from crude petroleum number more than 300. Great as is the wealth produced in the oil fields, humanity is enriched three hundred fold. The economies introduced in manufacture are equal to those in the pumping of wells and in the transportation of oil and the utilization of by-products has reduced the cost of making the main products to a minimum. Certain waste supplies the principal fuel consumed for distillation, especially where the cheaper oils are refined.

It is not within the province of a work of this kind to detail every improvement made in the machinery, appliances and processes of conducting this great industry. They are legion and would require an immense catalogue for their mention. It is enough to point out that inventive genius has been a constant attendant of the development. New trails have been blazed and old trails broadened to highways in the most romantic manner, while the main pursuit, the production and marketing of petroleum in ever increasing quantities has never been neglected. The future of this young industry is on quite a different basis than its beginnings, when "men had it all to learn." What giants have participated in the development of all its branches! What genius has been displayed in meeting its many problems!

CHAPTER XV.

OIL IN CANADA.

Soon after the completion of the Drake well in Pennsylvania, an oil spring on Black Creek, Enniskillen Township, Lambton County, Province of Ontario, Canada, attracted attention. As on Oil Creek, for many years petroleum had been observed floating on Black Creek, a dozen miles above its debouchment into the St. Clair River. It had been gathered from pits, after the Oil Creek method of long ago, by James Williams, and sold for the same medical uses as other Seneca oil, its more disagreeable odor adding to its curative repute. Mr. Williams was the first to begin drilling a well for a larger supply, which he located near the seepage. He was only moderately successful. But in the summer of 1861, John Shaw, a poor laborer, a Yankee who had migrated to Enniskillen from Maine about the year 1836, took a lease and began kicking down a well with a spring pole. Shaw was a man who dreamed daylight dreams and had previously tried to get his neighbors to dig for minerals with the result of being laughed at. He had also proposed drilling through the rock for oil and his neighbors suggested the insane asylum for his pains. Had they followed his advice, Black Creek might have antedated Oil Creek. He built a rude rig of the spring pole pattern and toiled alone until his money and credit were gone and his energy well nigh exhausted. He had been refused clothing and groceries at the village store because he could not pay. But hungry and barefooted as he was, he persisted in his weary task. One day when the prospect was almost hopeless, there came a rush of gas that threw the light drilling tools from the hole, followed by a column of oil that roared through the crown block at the top of his derrick and far above it, descending in a golden shower. This was the first flowing well in Canada.

Shaw had provided no tankage, but a depression in the swampy flat caught the fluid. The well continued to gush unchecked; the natural basin, an acre or more in extent, was filled; the oil ran over into Black Creek, covering it and the river down to Lake St. Clair and spreading rainbow hues over the surface of the lake. Little was done to control the gusher until the news had spread to the Pennsylvania oil region and a prospector from there had arrived who knew what to do. He assisted Shaw in providing a seed bag and tubing the well so the oil could be saved. Shaw's credit was good again and he was looked up to by the enterprising horde that was soon on the ground scrambling for leases. But there were no means of transportation and only a lean market, at the best. Shaw realized a great fortune, that is, it was a great fortune to him, but he was an easy victim for the sharpers who gathered and his riches "took unto themselves wings." His gusher, estimated at 5,000 barrels a day at the start, continued to flow for four months, and then, like Grandfather's clock, "stopped, never to go again." Shaw enjoyed his wealth while he had it, became an itinerant photographer as it vanished, and is reputed to have died in Petrolia in poverty, after trying his luck in the Pennsylvania oil fields and returning to the scene of his early triumph. His death is said to have occurred in 1872, and none of the many who had profited from his pioneering, extended to him any assistance in the hour of his need.

Shaw's gusher gave rise to operations of great magnitude in Enniskillen. Black Creek duplicated the busy scenes of Oil Creek in Pennsylvania, but the new region was more devoid of transportation than the old. The oil was transported in barrels on wagons to Mandaumin, Port Sarnia and Wyoming, until the swampy trails became canals of thin mud. Then some genius conceived the idea of floating a boat, similar to the "stoneboat" sled of the pioneers, with the aid of his poor horses. This method was adopted by all. The scene is indescribable and must be imagined, the hundreds of boats towed by horses, floundering belly deep in thin mud, the drivers walking on the firmer earth on each side of the "road." Naturally there was tremendous waste. Oil continually ran down the streams and spread over the flat country, permeating the water wells and driving the population to drink—any-

FULLERTON OIL CO., MENGES OIL CO. AND GRAHAM & LOFTUS

thing save the native water. When Oil Creek was flooded with the over production from the Phillips and the Woodford wells on the Tarr farm, forcing the price there down to ten cents a barrel, the Canadian field suffered more acutely. The price was not sufficient to pay the transportation by "boat" to the nearest "port." But the oil mad crowd went on drilling wells, apparently rejoiced merely to see the spouting fountains, without thought of other profit. Thus the original Canadian oil pool passed into history as a losing venture and a terrible waste of natural resources. But if Shaw's neighbors had taken his advice and drilled into the rock for oil when he advocated the process in 1856, they would have made the first discovery and robbed Edwin L. Drake of his fame.

While little was gained from the first oil development in Canada, there have been other and more profitable fields in the Dominion. When the business in the United States had become better established, the prospectors went northeast from Enniskillen and found more oil. The town of Petrolia grew from the second discovery and is a thriving and prosperous refining and pipe line center. Canada also has its Oil City, but it never attained to the proportions or importance of its Pennsylvania namesake, which preceded it. The Canadian petroleum industry has been encouraged by the Government in every possible way. It is protected by a tariff on foreign oil imported and more directly assisted by a bounty upon every barrel of crude produced, the bounty often being equal to the market price of crude petroleum in some of the American fields, with a higher tariff on the refined product. The only considerable developments, however, have been confined to the general region in which the first discovery was made and the product is all consumed within the Dominion. It is an importer besides. But the search for better fields has not been abandoned. New companies have been recently organized to make deep tests and to try out the Northwest territories, that, in John Shaw's time, constituted the almost trackless trapping region west of Hudson's Bay. Oil seepages have been located in the province of Athabasca and there has been some development by drilling in Alberta, near the American

PUMPING WELLS, BREA CANON, ORANGE COUNTY, CALIFORNIA.

border, as well as in the region immediately west of the Kootenai Mountains. The oils discovered are not of the highest grade. The Alberta oil is of higher grade than that in the Kootenai region.

Some day, when petroleum is needed, it will be produced up near the Arctic Circle. But it is not needed now. The industry has suffered, almost from the beginning, from frequently recurring periods of over production. As the producing fields have spread over the earth the periods of depression have been more persistent and lasting. A constant surplus in storage has eliminated the violent fluctuations in price that characterized the early days, and there is no such utter demoralization as followed the first gushers. But if oil is in brisk demand it will be sought up to the Arctic Circle in Canada and in Alaska. It will be produced under novel conditions requiring fresh inventions to keep it fluid in the presence of extreme low temperature and it will require extreme caution to avoid gas explosions in enclosed structures. A promising development is under way in New Brunswick, involving natural gas, principally, as well as oil, and desperate efforts are being made to squeeze petroleum from the rocks of Newfoundland. They have met with small success.

A feature of late petroleum developments in Canada has been the effort of the old Hudson Bay Company to claim the oil lands sold many years ago. The Company has reserved all minerals in its many deeds, made before petroleum was known as a mineral deposit. The effect has been to subject the owners of the surface to the annoyances of development work without compensation. This has aroused the Canadian Parliament to action and while it has been found no law can be enacted to impair the ancient contracts, it has been found to be feasible to divert the bounty paid upon the royalty oil to owners of the surface. This matter is in litigation at this writing but preliminary decisions are in favor of the tillers of the soil. It will become a question of great importance if the developments are extended upon the domain of the famous fur and trading company. It has already excited the interest of the whole Canadian public and is quite likely to lead to a new order in future transfers from the trading company to the agricultural settlers.

The original Canadian oil field at Oil Springs was the richest territory. Its wells flowed as much as four thousand barrels in a day for a single well, ranging down into the hundreds. The aggregate at one time in 1862 was more than ten thousand barrels a day, a large part of which found its way to Lake St. Clair by the surface of Black Creek and the St. Clair River. Professor Winchell said of this waste: "I have ascertained that, during the spring and summer of 1862, not less than five million barrels of oil floated off on the waters of Black Creek—a national fortune totally wasted." At the height of this prodigal waste, the oil in Black Creek once became ignited by some means and the flames raged down the St. Clair River, making a spectacle never to be forgotten. It was a combination of grandeur and horror rarely witnessed. This conflagration did more than all else to restrain the reckless development and waste of a valuable resource. The second development in Canada was at Bothwell, southeast from Oil Springs and nearer to Lake Erie. The wells were less prolific. The development at Petrolia, five miles to the northeast from Oil Springs, was more orderly and more profitable. The chief gains at Oil Springs were by speculation and from the sale of lands at two or three thousand dollars an acre, that would have been regarded high in price at thirty dollars an acre before the culmination of Shaw's luck.

Canada has participated in the natural gas development in America to an even larger degree than in oil. The principal gas fields of the Dominion lie north of the eastern end of Lake Erie, in easy piping distance from the city of Buffalo. Their development first brought up the question whether gas was a dutiable commodity. The courts answered it in the affirmative and natural gas is subject to the tariffs. It has found quite an extensive market, however, in the Canadian towns and cities, stimulating manufactures in the region, almost as much as they have been benefited by the development of the cheap power at Niagara Falls—the commercialism that threatenes the extinction of Nature's grandest spectacle. A part of the gas field extends to the shores of Lake Erie and the operators have pushed out into the water with their operations. The piers that have been built for this purpose, together with their breakwaters, when viewed from the water side, resemble nothing so much as a series of forts and defensive works, protecting the coast. To a foreigner not familiar with the peaceful relations that have been maintained for nearly a hundred years between the United States and Canada, the peaceful works would suggest precautions against a hostile neighbor.

Gas has been found in Canada as far west as Edmonton and in the region of Medicine Hat. None of the wells in that section have developed the enormous pressures of wells in the United States, nor such flows as 30,000,000 or 40,000,000 cubic feet a day, but they are sufficient to frunish fuiel and light for the towns that have sprung up there. They are assisting in attracting to the new Northwest the population that is rapidly gathering where, when the petroleum industry began, it was supposed that civilized man could not

DISPUTED LINE, OCTAVE OIL CO., PURTELL FARM, TITUSVILLE, PA.

subsist. The valley of the Saskatchewan, then supposed to be a region inhabitable by trappers only, is now the scene of vast lumbering operations and farming on a generous scale. That valley, too, has heard the screech of the walking beam and the clang of the tool dresser's hammer. The results have not been of a nature to attract the oil seeking throng but small gas wells have been opened and none can say what may follow by the time the virgin soil begins to show signs of exhaustion. The climate is such that natural gas fuel would be more appreciated than in the Philippines or Borneo. Be that as it may, the profitable oil fields of Canada, up to the present, have been located on that ancient upheaval known as the Cincinnati arch—an extension of the uplift on which the Trenton Rock fields of Northwestern Ohio and Eastern Indiana are located. The gas fields impinge upon the area that is known to geologists as the first land that appeared above the waters covering the face of the earth.

Canada's early oil fields duplicated the history of Oil Creek. They were operated with the same bustle and confusion; with the same lack of orderly methods and knowledge of the substance sought. The Canadian driller developed his own way of sinking holes and his own type of "rig" for handling the tools. These have become famous in Southern Europe and are largely used in the petroleum districts of Roumania and Galicia. The Canadian driller, like his brother from the United States, has gone abroad to teach his art to the world and to bring forth the liquid wealth of distant lands. But in his own land his devices are being displaced by the standard rig and cable tools of the United States, rendered necessary by the deeper drilling; his pipe lines are operated on the same system as those over the border; his natural gas is burned in the same sort of stoves, with the same appliances.

EMERY, PATTERSON & CALDWELL LEASE, UPPER CHURCH RUN, TITUSVILLE, PA.

The modern refineries are the same as those in the United States and many of the skilled workmen in them have emigrated thither for the purpose. The Canadian fields do not produce sufficient petroleum to supply Canadian demands, but the Canadian tariff is so adjusted that American refiners find it profitable to export their crude oil and refine it on Canadian soil. It does not seem probable that Eastern Canada can rival the United States in petroleum production, because it does not possess the great variety of oil bearing rocks above those geologically known as floor rocks. West Virginia and Southwestern Pennsylvania have excelled all other regions in the number of productive strata. But there are possibilities in Western Canada that will induce much prospecting when the time is ripe for the search and when transportation is a less serious problem for that part of the Continent. It may be expected that Canada will play a part in the future oil romance of America.

Come what may, the pathetic story of John Shaw will hardly be equaled. Threatened with incarceration in an insane asylum because he wanted to drill for petroleum three years before Drake began to do so; successful in getting one of the largest flowing wells in Canada when prices were highest; shorn of his fortunes by ill advised speculations and machinations of rogues; reduced to an itinerant existence and finally to death in extreme poverty; his life is typical of the vicissitudes of the fascinating industry he came near originating, if tradition may be depended upon. His rise and fall were symbolical of the sudden advent and subsequent decay of Oil Springs—a career duplicated by hundreds of other oil cities since that time. In 1864 the town of Oil Springs boasted of three thousand population, several well conducted hotels, and a busy telegraph office. Its glory has departed. It is a small railroad station where an incoming passenger is regarded with curious attention, where the freight receipts of a year are not equal to the out-going tonnage of oil in a single day in 1864. The beginning of Petrolia was the beginning of the end for Oil Springs and Port Sarnia has received the principal permanent benefits from both.

Canada is a pioneer in one department of the utilization of natural gas, and that is railroad train lighting. From the wells at Medicine Hat, gas is compressed into suitable tanks, for the use of the Canadian Pacific Railway, on passenger trains, running west to Vancouver and east as far as Winnipeg. It must be understood that coal is not common in that region. It is much cheaper to compress natural gas than to manufacture gas from coal, and, with the use of incandescent mantles, the light is superior. It is quite probable this business may be extended to lighting business places in distant towns, the nearest coal of commercial importance being in the vicinity of Oil City, province of Alberta, where the new high grade oil field is located.

SHIPS LIKE THESE BURN OIL FUEL.

E.A.L. ROBERTS

W.B. ROBERTS

CHAPTER XVI.

AN AGENT OF DEATH.

It is probable that the controversy over who exploded the first torpedo in an oil well will never be fully settled. A patent upon the process was issued to Colonel Edward A. L. Roberts in April, 1865. It was proven beyond peradventure of doubt that he had exploded six torpedoes in oil wells by percussion, in January, 1866, while it was held by the courts that the other applicants for letters patent claimed only to have devised torpedoes that were not successfully exploded. No patent in the United States was ever more vigorously contested after issue, than this and under no other were so many suits for infringement brought and successfully enforced. The patent was reissued in 1873, but was bitterly resisted and persistently evaded until it expired, a second reissue being defeated by the combined oil producers and the powerful presentation of the case by Attorney James H. Boyce. None but flowing wells are now put to producing without being first torpedoed except those in the fuel oil districts of Texas and California, where the formations are believed to be too soft to need, or to stand, heavy explosions. The first Roberts torpedoes were of powder and later consisted of one or two quarts of nitro-glycerine. Recent "shots" have been noted in the oil news, of 325 quarts of nitro-glycerine, enough to blast about 500,000 cubic yards of earth and rock from a hillside, in condition to be removed by a steam shovel.

It is contended that John F. Harper attempted to explode a black powder torpedo in the Raymond well at Franklin in 1860. The can containing the powder collapsed before the electric spark was delivered. Later, however, the Ford well, near Titusville, was successfully exploded with five pounds of powder in an earthen jar, the explosion being produced by dropping a live coal through a string of small gas pipe, inserted in the top of the jar. The production of the well was increased. Harper, Skinner and Potter formed a company to continue the business and put in several torpedoes, using glass and earthen jars as containers, but the low price of oil the next year killed the demand for any means to stimulate production. William Reed, who assisted in the futile attempt on the Raymond well at Franklin, invented a modified device, known as the Reed torpedo. He left the oil region a few years after the issue of the Roberts patent, and after his claims had been defeated in Court. Fredrick Crocker, the well known Oil Creek producer, and later pioneer in the Bradford field, devised a torpedo in 1864, which was to be exploded by a pistol cartridge inserted in the bottom. The necessary concussion was to be supplied by dropping the torpedo from the top of the hole. Several were used, but sometimes a large amount of fluid in the hole impeded the fall of the shell and there was no explosion. George Koch, inventor of the skeleton bull wheel, claimed he exploded a torpedo of his own construction in May, 1864. L. H. Smith, later an extensive producer and President the New York Petroleum Exchange, torpedoed a well of his own at Pithole in 1866. He had the torpedo, of rock powder, made up in New York State and carried it in his hands on railroad trains and stage coach, to Pithole, pretending that it was a roll of maps. It did not help his well much, although it proved his courage, and he left Pithole, $20,000 in debt. The greater part of this data was collected by Attorney Boyce for his presentation of the case against the Roberts patent.

After the Roberts patent had been isued and repeatedly upheld by the courts, various devices were invented to circumvent it. The Roberts torpedoes were exploded by dropping a weight on fulminating caps inserted in the top. W. H. Harper secured a patent on one to be exploded by caps placed at the bottom, whereas the Roberts type had the caps at the top. It was exploded by means of a plunger, passing through an inner tube which was jerked up forcibly by the line used to lower the shell. One day on Turkey Run in 1875, one of these torpedoes failed to explode. Harper pulled it up, emptied the shell, carried it far from the derrick, moved the plunger to see why it did not work and an explosion followed. Harper lived nine days with a hole entirely through his lungs, "big enough to insert two fingers in it," to quote Dr. France, the St. Petersburg surgeon who attended him. Another patent was taken out in 1874 by Edward E. Swett, then residing at Mehrtina, in the Clarion County field, but Roberts had him indicted for infringement. At about that time there were many "moonlighters" operating, so called because they frequently put in their torpedoes at night to evade the vigilance of the Roberts agents. This was extra hazardous work and resulted in several fatalities. The most uncompromising foe of the Roberts monopoly was Alexander Hamar, a native of Hungary, highly educated and a chemist of no mean attainments. Mr. Hamar devised a torpedo and used it in 1864 in the Oil Creek region. When the firm of Hamar & Guyer were operating the Jefferson Furnace tract of several hundred acres in Clarion County, Mr. Hamar maintained a nitro-glycerine factory on the premises. He prepared his own compound, torpedoed his own wells and promptly paid the costs of infringement, asserting that "no lard oil glycerine of Roberts" should go in any of his wells. Mr. Hamar was a chief promoter of the Atlantic Pipe Line in opposition to the consolidated United and Empire Pipe Lines, and it was his accented English that earned for the project the name of "The Dutch Pipe Line."

There were "moonlighters," however, who worked in broad daylight throughout the tenure of the Roberts patents. In June, 1882, one of these had a narrow escape from death while trying to torpedo a well in the village of Allentown, in Allegany County, New York. The well was separated from the town by a roadway and a small stream. The "shooter" had a large number of spectators from the village, who turned out for the spectacle, little dreaming what they would witness. In that field there were two productive strata in the oil sand, and the average shot consisted of two sections of about forty quarts of nitro-glycerine each. The "moonlighter" unloaded a sufficient number of cans from his light spring wagon on the roadway, between the derrick and the stream. I happened to be walking on the street with Robert W. Dennison, a veteran Roberts torpedo shooter, lately transferred from Edenburg in the Clarion County field. We passed where openings between buildings gave a good view, just as the shooter began lowering the first shell. Mr. Dennison criticised the shooter's carelessness in leaving the team and wagon, the latter still containing two hundred or three hundred pounds of the explosive, so close to the well, and he suggested getting farther away, without loss of time. But he did not move. Obviously the well was about to make a flow. The crowd gathered about it, rushed pell mell into the stream, each trying to outstrip the others in a race for safety. We, on the street, dropped prone on the sidewalk, but with faces turned to the scene of action. The moonlighter leaped from the derrick floor to the heads of his horses, seizing the bridles with no uncertain grip. He meant to have no runaway and no overturning of the deadly wagon, down the bank into the creek. There came a muffled report. A few moments later a column of six-inch casing rose from the well, with frightful rapidity, struck the crown block at the top of the derrick, hurled it aside and continued to rise, full two hundred and fifty feet. It went up as one solid string, but it came down in sections like a shower of pipe. One of these in its swift descent clipped a piece from the metal hub of the right hind wheel of the "moonlighter's" wagon and imbedded itself in the roadway to a depth of three feet; a few fell back upon the derrick; a majority drove themselves like piles into the earth back of the bull wheel and then the flow of oil hurled itself aloft. The shooter's horses, frightened by the noise, plunged and tried to run, but he held them secure. In three minutes it was all over and everybody safe. One who had fled across the creek through knee deep water, paused to praise the presence of mind of the plucky shooter, who still stood at his horses' heads, to Dennison, busy dusting sidewalk detritus from his clothes. The veteran shooter replied: "His presence of mind is admirable, indeed, but absence of body is preferable in a situation of that kind."

Among the men who followed this dangerous business exhibitions of rare nerve in the face of danger have not been uncommon. James Hardy Hanks, born near Buffalo in 1855, who died peaceably in Bartlesville, Oklahoma, on July 5, 1910, did a remarkably plucky thing in the Kane field in 1887. Like the moonlighter at Allentown, he was in the act of lowering the torpedo when the well started to flow. The shell was only a hundred feet or so below the mouth of the well when it started up, so the chances were about even whether or not it would be exploded by friction against the casing as oil and gas pushed it along. Hanks realized there was no chance to get away and that if the torpedo should be hurled out of the hole into the derrick or against the walking beam, it would explode, bringing certain death to himself and a number of others. He braced himself where he stood; the shell came up at lively speed; he threw his arms about it and held it firm and steady. The rush of oil followed, nearly drowned the plucky fellow, but he clung to his deadly burden and saved the day. When the flow of oil subsided, he again lowered the shell, reeled up his line, dropped the weight, known in the vernacular as the "go devil," and recorded a successful shot. Hanks followed the business of manufacturing nitro-glycerine afterward.

Joseph Bowers, of Rouseville, Pennsylvania, had one of the narrowest escapes from death on record. He was taking a load of glycerine in a sleigh, to a well near Oil City. On a bad piece of road the sleigh upset, dumping Mr. Bowers and his load at the horses' feet. He clung to the lines, preventing a runaway, but while he was scrambling to his feet he heard the iron shod hoofs of the horses striking the glycerine cans. But he soon had the team quieted and found the cans so dented that he could not get them back into the square safety box whence they came, in which they had fitted nicely before the overturn. Why the concussion did not cause an explosion no one can tell. Mr. Bowers, however, retired from the torpedo business after that trip. That was not his first narrow escape, miraculous, one night say, but he resolved it should be his last. He had been a "shooter" for a quarter of a century or more.

Very different was the experience and courage of the young man who engaged to take a load of glycerine from the factory to a magazine near the

EFFECTS OF EXPLOSION OF A NITRO-GLYCERINE MAGAZINE, RYND FARM, OIL CREEK.

Allegheny River. He drove half way to his destination, became panic stricken when passing through a piece of woodland, leaped from his seat, unhitched his horses, mounted one of them and rode away from his cargo at top speed, allowing the other horse to follow. Incidentally he left the roadway blocked with as dangerous an obstruction as could well be imagined, but nothing happened. The owner secured a more courageous driver to go out and deliver the stuff to its destination.

Many poor fellows have been less fortunate in their encounter with one of the most treacherous and destructive liquids ever compounded. The first fatal nitro-glycerine explosion in the oil regions resulted in the death of William Munson in the summer of 1867. He was blown up with his glycerine factory near Reno, Pennsylvania. The second accident was early in the following summer, when the Roberts' Company factory, near Titusville, blew up, killing Patrick Brophy. Only bits and shreds of human flesh and bone were found in the wreckage. Later in the same year, Colonel Davidson and two employes were blown up with Davidson's magazine. In 1869 Dr. Fowler met his fate at a magazine near Franklin. The seventh fatality was one of the oddest in the annals. R. Redfield, a torpedo agent at Scrubgrass, on the Allegheny River, below Franklin, hid a partly emptied can in the bushes along the river bank, for further use. The can was square, of one gallon capacity, similar to the containers used for lard oil, then largely used as a lubricant. The can was found by Mrs. George Fetterman, whose husband had an oil well in the vicinity. Supposing it to be lard oil, Mrs. Fetterman took it to her husband who used it to lubricate his engine for several weeks. One day, when the engine was in rapid motion, Mr. Fetterman applied a few drops to a heating journal from a common oiler. The resulting

EFFECTS OF EXPLOSION OF NITRO-GLYCERINE FACTORY, RYND FARM, OIL CREEK.

explosion blew off his arm, crushed his skull and otherwise mutilated him. This was in the summer of 1870.

In August of 1871, Charles Clarke was blown up while driving with a buggy load of nitro-glycerine, near Enterprise, Warren County. Horses, buggy and man were torn to bits. Very similar were two accidents in 1872. William Thompson, who had been torpedoing wells on Bully Hill, started for the magazine near Franklin with two unused torpedoes. Something caused an explosion while he was driving along the road. A little later, William Pine, driving between Shaw Farm and Rouseville, was blown to atoms by some mishap to his cargo. One of the first persons on the scene and one of the most active in helping to gather the fragments of the victim, was James Barnum. A couple of years later Barnum became a shooter in the Clarion County field for the Roberts Company. On February 23, 1876, a bitterly cold day, he transferred 300 pounds of nitro-glycerine from the factory near Edenburg to his magazine near St. Petersburg. It is supposed that, benumbed with cold, he let something drop when he went to open the magazine, which contained about 200 pounds of the stuff. Both the contents of the magazine and the cargo on the wagon exploded. The concussion was felt five miles from the scene. Others had to perform for poor Barnum the services he had rendered in collecting the remains of his friend Pine, less than four years before, one of his ears being found more than half a mile from the scene.

The third accident in 1872 was remarkable in its features. Charles Palmer went with Captain West, a Roberts shooter, to the magazine, about a mile and a half out of Titusville, to get a load of the explosive. Palmer was reckless and Captain West admonished him to be more careful in handling the stuff. Palmer laughed. As West was placing the thirteenth can in the wagon, Palmer being in the magazine to get more, a frightful explosion occurred. Palmer and the magazine were blown to bits. The frightened Captain West leaped on the wagon and rode at top speed to the residence of Colonel Roberts in Titusville, the nitro-glycerine packages bouncing about in the wagon box as he rattled over the streets of the town, to the utter demoralization of all whom he passed. Captain West decided to retire from so dangerous a business, but went to Reno shortly afterward, to "put in his last shot." It failed to explode when the weight was dropped, but did explode when Captain West drew it up for examination. He was killed. "Doc." Wright, torpedo agent, and Telegraph Operator Wolfe were killed when a magazine at Scrubgrass was blown up in 1873.

Andrew Dalrymple, a "moonlighter," resided at Dennis Run, near Tidioute, Warren County, Pennsylvania, in 1873. A terrific explosion, one evening, wrecked his house, killing Dalrymple and his wife. It was supposed he had been filling a shell at his dwelling for a midnight excursion to one of the wells in the vicinity. The two-year-old daughter of the Dalrymples was rescued from the ruins of the dwelling almost unhurt and was afterward adopted by a wealthy Tidioute family. The tot had been asleep until the house came tumbling about it. Little of Dalrymple could be found. John Osborne met death in 1874, while driving a torpedo "buckboard" along Bear Creek, near Parkers Landing. In 1875, Alonzo Taylor drew an unexploded torpedo from a well near Troutman, Butler County. To avoid danger to those gathered about the well, Taylor carried the shell far into the woods to examine the percussion cap. An explosion followed, killing Taylor instantly. August 1, 1876, William M. Clawson, a "moonlighter," popularly known as "Slim Jim," was killed on the Beck Farm, near Edenburg, in Clarion County. Clawson set out after noon with two torpedoes of six quarts each and a two-quart "squib." The two torpedoes were successfully exploded in wells on the Moyer Farm. The "squib" failed; Clawson began drawing it out and it exploded near the top of the hole. The shooter's skull was rent asunder, the front falling apart from the back of the head and body. The cleavage was sharp as if performed by a surgeon's knife, and the face was burned as black as coal, resembling a black mask. December 10th of the same year, Daniel Smith and William Humphreys were blown up with the Roberts magazine at Petrolia in Butler County, where they were unloading 600 pounds of the explosive from a wagon.

October 2, 1877, came near ending the career of Colonel Roberts, the torpedo patentee. He had gone, with his nephew, Owen Roberts, to inspect a new nitro-glycerine factory on Bolivar Run, near Bradford. When the first "run" of the fluid was being made there was an explosion and Josiah T. Smith, in charge of the operation, was killed and Colonel Roberts and his nephew were injured. Had the explosion occurred a minute sooner, both would have been killed for they had been in a position where they would have received the full force of the concussion. Ellery Bartlett, a Roberts agent, was killed while exploding empty cans at Red Rock, in the Bradford field, December 5, 1877. He had placed the cans on a pile of oil soaked wood and fired the pile. One can did not explode when the others did, which aroused Bartlett's curiosity. Despite his knowledge of the dangerous

SHOOTER'S OUTFIT, ILLINOIS FIELD.

stuff he picked up the can to investigate and it exploded in his hands, tearing off one arm and one leg, besides cutting him badly about the body. On April 19, 1878, while Joseph Etner was lowering an eight-quart McIntyre torpedo into a well near Gilmor City, Bradford field, it exploded, killing Etner and Frank Hill, who was assisting on the derrick floor. Hill was looking down the hole and his head was split open before he could draw back.

On September 5, 1878, an explosion occurred on the Curtis farm, two miles south of Bradford, that killed four men. The magazine was owned by W. O. Gotham, of Petrolia, Butler County, but was in charge of N. B. Pulver. Pulver went to the place with "Andy" P. Higgins and Charles S. Page, well known "moonlighters," and others. Attempts had been made to burglarize the safe, in which the explosive was stored, on the nights of August 8th and September 8th, by placing a small quantity of nitro-glycerine in the lock and firing it with a fuse. Both attempts failed. It is supposed, however, that another attempt of the same kind had been made on the night of the 14th and that nitro-glycerine left in the lock exploded when Pulver went to open it, and caused the explosion of the contents of the magazine. Pulver, Page and two companions were killed. On October 29th of the same year, the factory of S. O. Gotham, the owner of the ill-fated Bradford magazine, blew up. It was located on the Pew farm, north of Petrolia, on the bank of a small stream called Silver Creek. Gotham, with Harry French and John Fowler, had gone to the factory to manufacture 400 pounds on an order. After the explosion, Gotham was found near the stream, dead, with no marks, save slight cuts, on his person. French was picked up from the middle of the stream with both arms broken, each in two places, and his skull fractured, but living. He died in a few hours. Fowler, aged 19, was torn to shreds. It was supposed Gotham and French were eating supper, while Fowler stood on top of the tank, stirring the mixture, when the explosion occurred.

A marvelous escape from death was the fortune of one Feeny, February 9, 1880. In company with Howard Hackett, he was driving in a cutter from Corwin Center to Cole Creek, in the Bradford field. When half a mile from Sawyer City the cutter upset and exploded the five 20-pound cans they were carrying. Hackett was thrown fifty feet, his head smashed, right leg torn off and he was otherwise mutilated. Feeney was buried under a pile of fence rails and snow, but was rescued, not seriously injured. The horse and cutter were torn to pieces. Another remarkable escape was that of John T. McCleery, a shooter. He was in the act of filling a torpedo at a well of John L. McKinney at Meeks Creek, when the well flowed. The shell was thrown from the hole and exploded when it struck the derrick floor. McCleery had started to run and was stooping under the bull wheel shaft for a jump, when the shell exploded. He was thrown twenty feet into the bushes, but leaped to his feet, just as the four cans, standing on the derrick floor, exploded. By this concussion he was hurled nearly one hundred feet, but again leaped to his feet and ran until he was overcome by fright, fatigue and injury. His coat tails were cut off as straight as if it had been done by a tailor's shears, and his back was full of splinters and pieces of tin, but his injuries were more painful than dangerous. He recovered, but sought other employment for his remaining years.

There have been many other nitro-glycerine accidents in the oil regions, but they are not so frequent as formerly. The annual consumption of nitro-glycerine is now computed in tons, where it was formerly computed in pounds or quarts, but the enormous increase in its use has not been attended by a corresponding increase in fatalities. On the contrary the casualties were reduced. Much care is exercised in the manufacture, to remove impurities, better containers are used and experience has taught the least explosive temperatures. The stuff is safest to handle when below 60 degrees Fahrenheit, but above the freezing point. Better methods avoid putting in the torpedo when the well is likely to flow and throw it back. But no precautions can relieve the torpedo business of all danger, while raw nitro-glycerine is used. In the forms of gun cotton, dynamite and solidified nitro-glycerine, it is far less dangerous, requiring especial fulmination or percussion to release its

dynamic force, but in those forms it is less effective in producing desired results. There are plenty of men in the oil country, however, willing to take
the risk as long as the business pays well. In time they forget the danger,
or rather become inured to it, like men under fire in battle. The Mid-Con-
tinent and Illinois fields have been the scene of several fatal nitro-glycerine
explosions, as have all the fields, active after the Pennsylvania fields began
to wane. There was one explosion of a boat load of the stuff on the Ohio
River below Shousetown, at a time when much of the compound was floated
from the Shousetown factory to the West Virginia development about Sistersville and St. Marys. The total fatalities have been more than double
the number here enumerated.

FOSTER FARM ON OIL CREEK, PENNSYLVANIA, IN EARLY DAYS.

CHAPTER XVII.

AN INFLAMMABLE SUBJECT.

Petroleum and natural gas we have to burn. Aside from a few of the heavier residuals the products of petroleum are valuable for their combustible quality, and natural gas has no other useful characteristic. This being true it might naturally be expected that fire has been a regular accompaniment of the industry. So it has been, but in addition it has been the scourge of every town and village brought into being by this industry. The list of oil country fires would be tediously long and the detailed incidents would require two or three volumes to relate. Yet fire is a feature in the romance of petroleum and gas, not to be ignored. The first oil fire occurred at the first oil well and none may predict the last. Probably it would be better to say that the first oil fire is not of record, for there were oil fires prior to the birth of the petroleum industry. The fires of the Baku district in Russia extend back into tradition and the Indians are reputed to have burned the oil on Oil Creek hundreds of years ago. We have had some account of the huge fires in Kentucky during the first half of the Nineteenth Century, resulting from the oil that flowed from wells drilled for salt. But we are dealing with the fires attendant upon the industry, and the first occurred at the Drake well.

About two months after the Drake well had been put to pumping, "Uncle Billy" Smith, who had drilled it, fancied something had gone wrong late in the evening. He sallied forth with a lamp to find the trouble, but could not locate it. Finally he went into the shed that had been built over the tanks into which the oil was pumped. An explosion occurred that hurled the astonished Smith and his lamp out of the enclosure, a fortunate thing for him, for there was a lively conflagration almost instantly. Tanks, oil, derrick and Smith's dwelling were soon in flames, the Smith family escaping scantily clad, but wholly uninjured. Mr. Drake's only comment on the episode was to say to Smith: "You were fortunate to escape. I am glad no life was lost." One surviving witness of the first oil well fire is Bates Fink, who worked in the saw mill of Brewer, Watson & Co., a few rods from the scene, who had helped build the tanks and who resided on the opposite side of the mill race. Fink and his wife were both ill with typhoid fever, or rather in the first stage of convalescence, too weak to stand. They could see the flames and hear the shouts of members of the Smith family and they feared destruction of their own dwelling, themselves and their small children. Fortunately the quantity of oil at the well was small and it burned out without reaching the waters of the mill race. From that time to the present, oil fires have been a constant feature of the business.

The first fatal oil well fire occurred on April 17, 1861. A well owned by Little & Merrick, sub-lessees of Rouse, Mitchell & Brown, on the John Buchanan farm, Rouseville, Pennsylvania, came in flowing at the rate of fifty barrels an hour. The news spread rapidly, as this was the first big flowing well on Oil Creek. A crowd gathered as by magic, including Hon. Henry R. Rouse, one of the owners, and a partner in the second and third wells completed on Oil Creek. The gas hung like a cloud about the well and oil soon covered the swampy land. Mr. Rouse stood on a hummock near the well when the gas ignited at a neighboring boiler. There was a terrific explosion that shook the village and the oily swamp was all ablaze. Mr. Rouse started to run, drew from his breast pocket a wallet containing papers of value to his business associates and hurled it outside the belt of fire. He fell as he ran but protected his face in the mud, arose and ran again until he

OIL TANK BURNING AT OBLONG, ILLINOIS.

fell, exhausted, just outside the fire zone, where he lay until rescued. He lived a few hours in intense agony, but dictated a will, as clear in its terms as one in prime health might have prepared, making bequests to father, friends and acquaintances. The residuary estate abolished poor tax in Warren County, where he resided. Fourteen other persons died from their burns and thirteen more were disfigured for life. The details of this holocaust were recorded by George H. Dimick, the widely known oil producer and oil dealer, who was clerk in the office of Rouse, Mitchell & Brown. He, too, would have been burned but for the fact that before going to view the wonder of a flowing well, he had gone to arrange for a supply of barrels to save the oil. Returning from his errand he witnessed the awful spectacle from a safe distance.

While this accident at Rouseville served to warn against an assemblage of spectators about newly opened flowing wells, it did not prevent frequent similar fires in which the workmen on the wells perished. Reasonable safety was not attained until the invention of the "oil saver," by Victor Gretter, in 1872. Neither did this experience or that of "Uncle Billy" Smith at the Drake well suffice to warn the public, generally, not to take fire or open lights near fresh oil, or escaping gas. The history of Oil Creek was a succession of fires, many of them very serious. Tanks were buried in the ground

TANK STRUCK BY LIGHTNING, ACME REFINERY, TITUSVILLE, PENNSYLVANIA.

as one means of fire prevention, but this simply facilitated ignition when burning oil flowed over them from higher ground. Iron tankage was first devised, not on account of the strength that would permit of large storage, but for greater safety to the contents. The great fires on Benninghoff Run in 1865 and 1866, were among the most terrifying. Great quantities of blazing oil ran down the valley, adding to its volume as the flames seized oil wells and tanks along the way. Workmen, residents one and all who happened there, were compelled to climb the steep hillsides in extreme haste, to seek safety on the heights. The unique "Horse Railroad" was badly damaged, ties being burned and rails warped by the terrific heat. The "Horse Railroad" was one of the enterprises, to secure better and cheaper transportation, evolved in 1865, the birth year of successful pipe lines. It was con-

structed by J. V. Criswell & Co. at a cost of about $20,000. The modus oper-
andi was to drag a car up with the aid of four mules, load it with barreled
oil and run it down by gravity, in charge of a brakeman, to regulate the
speed. While one car was being loaded, the faithful mules were driven to
the bottom of the incline and returned, towing a second car. The enterprise
was not much of a success, while the pipe line of Harley, Abbot & Co., from
Benninghoff to Shaffer, was a winner. This line, however, had trials of its
own. The teamsters, who feared loss of their business, broke it several times
and, on the night of April 18, 1866, they introduced the great enemy of oil,
burning several of the pipe line tanks on Benninghoff Run. Two nights later
a mob attacked the guards, who had been placed at the Shaffer terminal,
firing upon and driving them back. The guards rallied, however, returned
the fire, wounded one man seriously and several others slightly, won the day
and saved the pipe line property.

The year 1866 had a fearful fire record. The devastation of Cherry
Run, resulting from a boiler explosion, has been referred to. The first great
town fire occurred at Oil City, May 26, destroying all that portion of the
city on the north side of the Allegheny River and the east side of Oil Creek,
save the heights, then known as Cottage Hill. The losses exceeded $1,000,-
000, despite the efforts of thousands of men to stay the flames. Twenty wells
and 13,000 barrels of oil burned at Pithole on August 6th, entailing a heavy
loss and several smaller fires visited that ephemeral city, consuming many
buildings and much oil. September 1st, twenty-five wells and 5,000 barrels
of oil burned on Dennis Run, near Tidioute, the loss being estimated at
$100,000. In addition to these large fires there were many of smaller pro-
portions, in towns and among the wells. It was a year of misfortunes, including the collapse of Pithole and the failure of the string of banks and other
enterprises headed by C. V. Culver. These disasters convinced thousands
that business in the oil regions was extra hazardous, and many retired to other
pursuits, not to be enticed back by the successes of friends who "stayed with
the game."

The success of pipe lines and iron storage tanks led to the erection of
many of the latter. It was not long until it was learned that these oil reservoirs had a special affinity for lightning. The conjunction of the two became so frequent that a system of mutual insurance was established by the
pipe lines, by which fire losses were assessed pro rata, or by "general average," upon all owners of oil held by the line whose tank was burned. The
pipe line, alone, bore the loss of the tank. Incidentally another peril was introduced to oil region dwellers, who were liable to be aroused during or after
any thunder storm with the warning to get out of the way of a flood of
burning oil. A large iron tank may be expected to "boil over" two or three
times before its contents are consumed. The pipe line companies soon learned
to surround their storage tanks with embankments to lessen the destruction.
Various contrivances were tried to conduct the lightning to earth outside of
the tanks. Next, small cannon were procured to perforate burning tanks,
that the oil might be wasted before the flames reached it. This was soon
improved upon by the installation of pumps to draw off and save the oil.
The most modern practice is to group storage tanks on "tank farms," which
are systematically ditched, to carry off burning oil, equipped with pumps to

transfer oil from the bottoms of burning tanks to others and with steam pipes leading into the tops of tanks to smother flames. These precautions have greatly reduced the percentage of losses from fires, so that now, with 100,000,000 barrels in storage, the actual losses are less than thirty years ago, when the surplus stocks did not exceed 16,000,000 barrels.

The affinity of lightning for fresh oil is easily explained in the fact that from an open tank a column of gas rises to a great height. This gas is an excellent conductor and the electrical charge simply follows it to its base. The same phenomenon is observed in connection with barns, where green hay is stored, and accounts for the frequent destruction of such buildings by lightning. A gas well, with free vent, is an even more inviting mark for lightning. The most spectacular instance of gas well and lightning was near Caney, Kansas, in the spring of 1905. The well was the property of the Kansas Natural Gas Company. It was being drilled in, having an enormous pressure and a flow of probably 25,000,000 cubic feet daily. A severe electrical storm came up, and on the advice of J. C. McDowell, Vice-President and General Manager of the company, the workmen left the well for safer quarters. They were not far away when lightning and gas met. Seemingly a great pillar of fire leaped from the earth to meet the descending bolt. There was a deafening crash, and then the pillar of fire, only, remained. For twenty feet above the earth there was no flame, the compact stream of gas excluding the oxygen; above that the pillar of fire broadened for fitfy feet and for the remaining fifty feet narrowed to the apex, irregularly. The roar was deafening. The conquest of this monster was accomplished after three weeks of arduous labor, the work being directed by Mr. McDowell on the most approved lines. Orders were given by signals, as words could not be heard above the din and the workmen stuffed their ears with cotton to avoid permanent injury to the auditory apparatus. The fire was finally extinguished by dropping over it a huge boiler plate funnel, with a valve, by means of which the flames and gas were separated until the former were dissipated.

On the night of February 21, 1873, fire broke out in the saloon of Fred Hepp, St. Petersburg, Clarion County, shortly after 10 o'clock. At three o'clock on the morning of Washington's Birthday the town was a mass of blazing and smoking ruins. More than 500 families were homeless on a bitterly cold winter day. Such is the summary of a typical oil town conflagration. The flames from the little groggery communicated to the big Cramer Opera House adjoining. There was no fire fighting apparatus in the town and no adequate water supply. There had been too much haste in building the town and developing the surrounding oil territory to give thought to protection from fire. The Opera House burned like tinder. A high wind from the west drove the flames up the main street and they traveled at amazing speed. Bucket brigades worked with frenzied energy; willing hands carried out household goods, merchandise, anything portable and worth while. But the fire increased in fury and spread in area. An attempt at midnight to make a gap by tearing down a corner building only resulted in strewing the debris across both streets for the flames to cross easily. Finally the destruction was arrested by tearing down two buildings, covering the roofs of the next with wet salt and curtaining the sides with quilts, kept saturated with brine. Three score of buildings in the town were saved,

but $200,000 worth of property had been destroyed in four hours. The men
from Antwerp, a mile away, were heroes in the battle against the flames,
and each of them took home with him some of the shivering, homeless sufferers. Rebuilding had been begun on the evening of the twenty-second.
September 3rd, less than seven months afterward, Antwerp burned, with
the exception of three buildings, and was never rebuilt. The men of St.
Petersburg returned the winter favor, with less success. The loss of the
smaller town was about $50,000. On December 12th, the town of Modoc,
in the Butler County field, was burned.

On March 16, 1874, Modoc was burned again, with a loss of $100,000,
the first of a series of bad fires in that county. Millerstown followed on April
1st. In addition to the great property loss, six persons were burned to death

FLOOD PRECEDING FIRE AT OIL CITY, JUNE 5, 1892.

in this fire. The loss was $200,000. There were many narrow escapes from
death, as the fire started after midnight, and hundreds failed to save even
necessary wearing apparel. The town was rebuilt on a larger scale, for the
petroleum development in the vicinity had but fairly begun, and it was
burned again on December 7, 1877, with smaller property loss and no lives
sacrificed. It had its third visitation a few years later when the oil excitement had subsided. December 2, 1874, Karns City, in the Butler field, was
burned, having no better protection against fire than Millerstown. The
buildings in these towns were entirely of wood, and for the greater part of
such flimsy construction as to feed the flames readily. Edenburg, in Clarion
County, was burned January 14, 1877, loss $65,000, but rebuilt larger and
better than before. October 12, 1878, it burned again, with a loss of $400,-
000. It burned during the night amid indescribable scenes of confusion, the
origin supposed to be incendiary. This town was again burned May 22,

1880, and then provided a water works and some hose. But little of the burnt district was rebuilt after this last fire, in which the loss was $87,000. Bradford had its first big fire the same year on April 2nd, loss $100,000. It suffered from several others of even greater proportions before acquiring a first class fire department.

The Bradford field suffered severe and frequent losses by lightning, and even more from bush fires, a large portion of that area being forested when the oil development began. Thus, on May 6, 1880, the burning of some brush near Rew City started a fire that resulted in the destruction of 300 well rigs and 40,000 barrels of oil. The fire swept over Rew Summit to Harrisburg Run, Foster Brook and down that Valley from Red Rock to the East and West Branches of the Tununguwant. On the ninth day of the

AFTER THE FIRE AND FLOOD, OIL CITY, JUNE 5, 1892.

same month the town of Rixford was burned, forty-three wells and 2,000 barrels of oil in tanks at the wells. On May 12th the bush fires were raging in Tram Hollow, Ohio Valley and along Kendall Creek, the destruction including 292 wells, 125,000 barrels of oil, including a 25,000-barrel iron tank in Tram Hollow, fifty buildings and the United Pipe Lines' pumping station. On July 15th, the same year, lightning struck thirteen well tanks in the Bradford field, one iron tank at Duke Center, on Kendall Creek, and two at Custer City, on the West Branch. But the Bradford field was not the only sufferer that year. On June 11th, lightning struck a tank of the Tidioute and Titusville Pipe Line at Titusville. The fire communicated to the Acme Refining Company's Works and destroyed them, involving a loss of $1,000,000, and endangering the entire city. At Turkey City two 35,000-barrel tanks were burned. This was a fiery year above the average, but not standing alone, by any means. Other years brought even greater losses. Bush fires raged frequently in the Bradford field and for at least one other year the losses from them exceeded those of 1880.

Better methods have limited the losses in the newer fields but Ohio, Indiana, Illinois and Oklahoma have all had their spectacular conflagrations in which lightning played its part. The big tank full of fresh oil is always a favorite mark, although the "skimming" of gasoline from the crude, lessens the danger. Fires at refineries have been frequent and disastrous. Gasoline and benzine are highly inflammable and they cannot be extracted from crude without heat. Fires are a natural consequence. These are often attended by explosions which throw the inflammable liquid about, not infrequently enveloping employes and bringing to them a fiery death. Refining companies are compelled to provide their own insurance funds, which is not a small item in their annual expense. One, at least, the Standard Oil Company, maintains a fund for the benefit of employes who may be killed or injured, the families of dependents being quite well cared for. All large refineries have their own fire fighting apparatus and are often of timely service to towns in their vicinity. Their fire fighters are well trained and their equipment is of the best. Fires have even broken out on oil carrying ships at sea, and no more thrilling experience can befall any man than this, of having fire in so inflammable a cargo in mid-ocean. Lightning has been the cause in several instances. But these vessels are divided into tight compartments, equipped with close fitting manhole covers and with all else that may serve to conquer an oil fire. Disasters are rare compared with the seeming dangers of navigation of this style of craft.

An oil fire is a spectacle that once seen is never forgotten. At night it is a scene of grandeur indescribable. When a large tank is struck by lightning there is a burst of flame, leaping fifty feet or more above the tank, followed almost instantly by a huge column of black smoke. Those who have seen a factory chimney, belching smoke from a green fire of bituminous coal, may conceive a chimney two hundred feet in diameter, pouring forth the blackest of smoke in vast rolls. As these inky waves roll over in their ascent they turn red hot as they reach more oxygen at the circumference of the column. These flashes of light continue to a height of more than a hundred feet, half way to the top of the full grown, churning pillar of smoke. This aspect continues for hours, until tank and oil become sufficiently heated to "boil over." This ebullition is appalling. The flames, previously half smothered in smoke, now leap high in the air, there is a terrible roar and then boiling, burning oil rushes out like molten lava from a volcano in eruption. The heat is intolerable at a distance of three hundred yards and the fiery flood races over the ground until it meets a barrier, or finds its way into stream or ravine, to flow onward until consumed. I have seen green leaves burned from the tops of tall trees a thousand feet from a burning tank, in an instant of time, when the wind turned in that direction and woe be to the man who gets in the path of the fiery flood from the overflow. Racing with a prairie fire is child's play compared with escape from the flaming torrent.

Fire is terrible and flood is irresistible. A combination of the two is the extreme of horrors. However, Oil City and Titusville were devastated by flood and fire on Sunday, June 5, 1892, in the most terrible manner. Heavy rains had swelled the Allegheny River and Oil Creek to ordinary flood stages on June 4th. Then came a "cloud burst" on the Oil Creek watershed above Titusville. The resulting flood in that valley was the highest in history. Both towns were inundated and people were rescued from their homes in boats rowed along the streets. While this work was in progress on upper Seneca Street in Oil City and other streets were crowded with sightseers, there came a terrible explosion. Flames leaped to the very sky. A few seconds later there was another explosion, and then a third. The entire region along Oil Creek, from the Allegheny River a mile up the swollen creek to the Independent Refinery, was a roaring furnace, in which flood sufferers and heroic rescuers were roasted to death, the corpses falling into the muddy flood. Panic reigned throughout the city, the inhabitants fleeing to the hills

RUINS OF ACME REFINERY, TITUSVILLE, AFTER THE FIRE.

in wild alarm. No more terrible spectacle than that which followed was ever witnessed by mortal eye. The flames leaped as high as the precipitous hills, where they gave off white smoke so hot that it scorched the faces of spectators at the top of the hill on the south side of the river, nearly a mile away. The wind that carried the sinister gray clouds was hot as the breath of a furnace and the horrified residents of the south hill fled in terror to the open country beyond. It seemed that the whole place was doomed to destruction. One man ran down Main Street, wheeling a baby carriage in the middle of the thoroughfare, shouting, "Track! track!" with all the strength of his lungs. Another rode horseback out the road over the South Side hill, warning the fleeing multitude to keep away from the roadway, because the natural gas main might explode where they were. These were absurdities born of unreasoning panic, but the pathos of the terrible destruction and loss of life prevented even a smile on the part of beholders and auditors. There were deeds of heroism innumerable in the work of rescue, and brave hearts were stilled by the calamity.

The cause of the holocaust was gasoline. The flood had washed out the foundation of a gasoline tank that stood on the bank of Oil Creek, at the Independent Refinery, permitting the contents to escape to the surface of the water. When this had spread, from the tank to the mouth of Oil Creek, the vapor was ignited by coming in contact with the fire in a shifting engine at the Pennsylvania Railroad bridge. With the succession of the explosions the flames had traversed the entire distance to the mouth of the Creek, including the streets that were under water, where the men in skiffs were rescuing women and children from second story windows. At Titusville similar scenes were enacted and similar destruction occurred from identical conditions. Both cities were practically cut off from communication with the world outside by destruction of the telegraph offices, until a daring telegrapher climbed a pole outside the fire zone at Oil City, cut in on the wires and flashed out the dread tidings. These two oldest cities in the original oil country rapidly recovered from the disaster and increased their population during the remainder of the decade. But the terrible experience of June 5, 1892, will never be forgotten. Hundreds thought at the time that the judgment day and the end of all things terrestrial had come. The people in the oil regions, generally, are not given to superstitions, but there have always been a few who have regarded the extraction of oil and natural gas from the earth, as a sort of sacrilege, believing that these inflammable substances were stored by the Creator for the express purpose of the final destruction of the earth by fire, as foretold in the Book of Revelations. Some others, in the earliest days, believed the enterprising oil men were robbing the globe of the lubricant provided that it might turn smoothly on its axis! But in these modern days, after years of the educational uplift of kerosene light, these absurdities have few advocates. Yet, the horror of that day in Oil City revived the forgotten superstition for the moment. Fire will continue to go with oil and gas to the end of the chapter, as it has from the first, but experience will lessen the destruction and hazard. Nothing can eliminate them. The burning "Dos Bocas" well in Mexico, in 1907, was the worst disaster of its kind, far exceeding that of the gusher on Lot 647, Cherry Grove, in 1882, or the burning of Fisher Oil Company No. 7, at Thorn Creek, in 1884.

OIL CITY AFTER THE GREAT FLOOD, MARCH 17, 1865.

CHAPTER XVIII.

EARLY MENTION OF AMERICAN PETROLEUM.

That petroleum was known to the ancients is indisputable. It is quite probable the "pitch" used by Noah to seal the seams of the Ark was a natural asphaltic bitumen and it is altogether certain that the dwellers about the Caspian Sea worshipped at oil and gas fires twenty-five centuries ago. It is equally certain that petroleum from the Dead Sea region was used by the Egyptians in their embalming processes. There are evidences that petroleum was gathered and used for some purposes on Oil Creek and Pit Hole Creek, in Venango County, Pennsylvania, long before the advent of the white man. While the widely circulated story of the religious ceremonies of the Seneca Indians, said to have been witnessed by a French lieutenant, has been disproven, it is none the less the fact that timbered pits of great antiquity were found in that region by the early settlers. That these pits were for the collection of oil is obvious from the fact that they were in the area of known petroleum seepages and nowhere else. Some writers have ascribed these works to a race antedating the Indians. No attempt will be made here to settle the controversy as to whether Western Pennsylvania was inhabited by a superior race, prior to the advent of the Indians found in the territory by the French and English explorers, or as to whether the Mound Builders did or did not belong to such a race. This is not a work on ethnology and it is sufficient to know that petroleum was gathered from the approximate site of the Drake well, before history in that region began. Some of the pits were from twelve to sixteen feet deep, and the timbering consisted of halved logs, with the bark removed. They were rudely constructed. Their age was attested by trees growing in them, upon the deposited sediment, and trees that grew near them, the evidence indicating the lapse of more than 300 years between the date of construction and their discovery by pioneer settlers and lumbermen.

The first authentic mention of petroleum in the United States was by Joseph De La Roche Dailon, a French missionary, who penetrated the wilderness adjacent to Lake Erie and eastward in 1627. He mentioned, in a letter under date of July 28th, of that year, that he found "a good kind of oil which the Indians called Antonontons." In 1642, some Jesuit missionaries penetrated the same region and in the old territory of the Erie tribe of Indians, "found a thick, oily, stagnant water, which would burn like brandy." The map made by the missionaries, Dollier and Gallinee, in 1670, has marked upon it the "Fonteane de bitume," which was located near the present village of Cuba, Allegany County, New York. It is believed that the "fountain" was the origin of the "good kind of oil" found by Dailon, and the water "which burned like brandy," of the Jesuit missionaries. Such was the conclusion of Mr. John F. Carll, the geologist, whose researches discovered these ancient records, and that conclusion is accepted by Mr. P. C. Boyle, in his "Hand Book of Petroleum." This same oil spring was a factor in the later and more practical development of petroleum, for it was visited in 1833 by Prof. Benjamin Silliman, Sr., who wrote a paper upon his observations and published it in the American Journal of Science. Prof. Benjamin Silliman, Jr., made the analyses of the petroleum from the oil spring near Titusville for George H. Bissell and J. G. Eveleth, that led to the formation of the first oil company, the "Pennsylvania Rock Oil Company." This concern acquired the land on which the Drake well was drilled by the "Seneca Oil Company," and Prof. Silliman, Jr., was the first president of the first oil company. The younger man's interest in the subject began with the elder's paper. The elder Silliman's paper on the New York oil spring said among other things:

"The oil spring, as it is called, is situated in the western part of the

LOADING CASES OF OIL INTO NATIVE LIGHTER AT MACASSAR (CELEBES).

county of Allegany, in the State of New York. This county is the third from Lake Erie on the south line of the State, the counties of Cattaraugus and Chautauqua lying west, and forming the southwestern termination of the State of New York. The spring is very near the line that divides Allegany and Cattaraugus. * * * The country is rather mountainous; but the road running between the ridges is very good and leads through a cultivated region rich in soil and picturesque scenery. Its geological character is the same with that which is known to prevail in the western region; a silicious sandstone with shale, and in some places limestone is the immediate basis of the country. The sandstone and shale lie in nearly horizontal strata. The sandstone is usually of a light gray color, and both it and the shale abound with entrocites, encrinites, coralines, terebratula and other reliquae, characteristic of the secondary, or transition formation. The Oil Spring, or fountain, rises in the midst of marshy ground. It is a muddy and dirty pool of about eighteen feet in diameter, and is nearly circular in form. There is no outlet above ground, no stream flowing from it, and it is, of course, stagnant water, with no other circulation than that which springs from the changes in temperature and from the gas and petroleum that are constantly rising from the pool. The water is covered with a thin layer of petroleum or mineral oil, giving it a foul appearance as if coated with dirty molasses, having a yellowish brown color. Every part of the water was covered by this film, but it had nowhere the irridescence which I recollect to have observed at St. Catherine's well, a petroleum fountain near Edinburgh in Scotland. There the water was pellucid, and the hues of the oil were bril-

LIGHTER DISCHARGING OIL FROM STEAMSHIP STOLSENFELS IN FRONT OF SVERABAIA, GODOWN.

liant, giving the whole a beautiful appearance. The difference is, however, easily accounted for. St. Catherine's well is a lively, flowing fountain, and the quantity of petroleum is only sufficient to cover it partly, while there is nothing to soil the stream. In the present instance, the stagnation of the water, the comparative abundance of the petroleum and the mixture of leaves, sticks and other productions of dense forests, preclude any beautiful features.

"They collect the petroleum by skimming it like cream from a milk-pan. For this purpose they use a broad, flat board, made thin on one edge like a knife. It is moved flat upon and just under the surface of the water, and is soon covered by a coating of petroleum, which is so thick and adhesive that it does not fall off, but is removed by scraping the instrument upon the lip of a cup. It has then a very foul appearance, like very dirty tar or molasses, but it is purified by heating and straining it while hot through flannel or other woolen stuff. It is used by the people of the vicinity for sprains and rheumatism, and for sores upon their horses. It is not monopolized by anyone, but is carried away freely by all who come to collect it, and for this purpose the spring is frequently visited. I could not ascertain how much is annually obtained, but the quantity is considerable.   *   *   *

"The history of this spring is not distinctly known. The Indians were well acquainted with it, and a square mile around it is still reserved for the Senecas. As to the geological origin of the spring, it can scarcely admit of a doubt that it rises from the beds of bituminous coal below. At what depth, we know not, but probably far down. The formation is doubtless connected with the bituminous coal of the neighboring counties of Pennsylvania and of the west rather than with the anthracite beds of the central parts of Pennsylvania.

"I cannot learn that any considerable part of the large quantity of petroleum used in the Eastern States under the name of Seneca oil comes from the spring now described. I am assured that its source is about 100 miles from Pittsburg, on the Oil Creek, which empties into the Allegheny River, in the township and county of Venango. It exists there in great abundance, and rises in purity to the surface of the water. By dams enclosing certain parts of the river and creek it is prevented from floating away, and is absorbed in blankets from which it is wrung."

Prof. Silliman refers a second time to coal as the probable origin of the oil and notes that a pit dug some distance from the spring discovered no coal, but did discover more of the petroleum. He also noted, with surprise, that cattle drank from the oil spring, although there was pure water nearby. This latter fact has been frequently observed since, and also that the milk of cows drinking petroleum has both the odor and flavor of the oil. But Prof. Silliman's reference to coal as the origin of petroleum grafted an error upon the subject that required years of experience and observation to remove. No coal has ever been found near the Cuba oil spring, but the great Allegany County, New York, oil field is but a few miles away.

In 1721, Charlevoix in his journal of travels refers to an oil spring somewhere near the headwaters of the Allegheny River, about which he had been told, the product of which was like oil and had the taste of iron, and yet another exactly like it, "and that the savages made use of it to assuage all manner of pains." These springs along the Allegheny River were near its nearest point to the Genesee River. The Cuba oil spring is mentioned by Sir William Johnson, who visited Niagara in 1767, who says the "oyl" was brought in by Acushan, an Indian. David Leisberger, a Moravian missionary, told of oil springs in the Allegheny River region, but did not definitely locate them. In his report he said: "I have seen three kinds of oil springs— such as have an outlet, such as have none and such as rise from the bottom of the creeks. From the first water and oil flow out together, the oil impregnating the grass and soil; in the second it gathers on the surface to the depth of the thickness of a finger; from the third it rises to the surface and flows with the current of the creek. The Indians prefer wells without an outlet. From such they dip the oil that has accumulated; then stir the well, and, when the water has settled, fill their kettles with fresh oil, which they purify by boiling. It is used medicinally as an ointment for toothache, headache, swellings, rheumatism and sprains. Sometimes it is taken internally. It is of a brown color, and can also be used in lamps. It burns well." This written account was in 1767. The first definite mention of the springs on Oil Creek was by General Benjamin Lincoln, in a letter to Rev. Joseph Willard of Cambridge University in 1783. He said the troops had collected the oil and bathed their joints with it and had drunk freely of the waters, which acted as a mild cathartic. From that time there were frequent references to Oil Creek and the peculiar product found floating on its waters. In 1807, F. Cuming mentions Oil Creek and the Seneca oil, "much used by the Indians." He also notes an oil spring on the Ohio River, just above the Little Beaver. In 1808 Ruffner Bros. drilled a salt water well in Kanawha County, Virginia—now West Virginia—on the Great Kanawha River. They got a good flow of salt water and some petroleum. Many other salt wells had the same trouble, some of them producing large quantities of oil, which was allowed to flow over the tops of the cisterns to find its way to the river. The prized salt water was drawn from the bottoms of the cisterns to the evaporating pans in a practically pure state free from the oil which rose to the top. But to the boatmen of the Great Kanawha, the river became the "Old Greasy" on account of the waste petroleum from the salt wells. The drilling for salt at Tarentum, on the Allegheny River, began about 1810 and petroleum was soon encountered. This was regarded as a misfortune. But Samuel M. Kier, some years later, began to bottle the oil and sell it for medical purposes. About 1849 he opened an establishment in Pittsburg for its sale. He was first to regard it seriously as a new source of light, had it refined, had lamps made, and was busy with experiments along that line when Drake visited him on his quest for drilling tools and driller. Mr. Kier was among the pioneer oil operators on Oil Creek after Drake had made his discovery. He was also a pioneer in marketing the product.

Inspired by the article of the elder Prof. Silliman in the American Journal of Science, quoted on a foregoing page, Dr. S. P. Hildreth, of Marietta, Ohio, communicated to the same Journal in July, 1833, a paper on "The Saliferous Rock Formation in the Valley of the Ohio." In the course of this paper Dr. Hildreth tells of a well on Duck Creek, about thirty miles north of Marietta, "dug in 1814, and is four hundred and seventy-five feet deep." It was owned by a Mr. McKee. Dr. Hildreth wrote: "Salt water was reached at one hundred and eighty-five feet but not in sufficient quantity. However, no more water was found below this depth. The rocks passed were similar to those on the Muskingum River, above the flint stratum, or like those between the flint and salt deposits at McConnellsburg. A bed of coal two yards in thickness was found at the depth of one hundred feet and gas at one hundred and forty-four feet, or forty-one feet above the salt rock. The hills are sandstone, based on lime, one hundred and fifty or two hundred feet in height, with abundant beds of stone coal near their feet. The oil from this well is discharged periodically, at intervals of from two to four days, and from three to six hours at each period. Great quantities of gas accompany the discharges of oil, which for the first few years amounted to from thirty to sixty gallons at each eruption. The discharges at this time are less frequent and diminished in amount, affording only about a barrel in a week, which is worth at the well from fifty to seventy-five cents a gallon. A few years ago when the oil was most abundant, a large quantity had been collected in a cistern holding thirty or forty barrels. At night someone engaged about the works approached the well head with a lighted candle. The gas instantly became ignited, and communicated the flames to the contents of the cistern, which, giving way, suffered the oil to be discharged down a short declivity into the creek, where the water passes with a swift current close to the well. The oil still continued to burn most furiously, and spreading itself along the surface of the stream for half a mile in extent, shot its flames to the tops of the highest trees, exhibiting the novel and perhaps never before witnessed spectacle of a river actually on fire." Dr. Hildreth, in the same article, said that Seneca oil was so named by reason of its having first been found at Seneca Lake in New York. As a medical man he admits that the oil had some medicinal virtue and says it was generally used by the inhabitants of his section for saddle bruises and the disease of horses known as scratches. He said it was also much used to "prevent the deposit of eggs by the 'blowing fly' in the wounds of domestic animals during the summer months. In neighborhoods where it is abundant it is burned in lamps in place of spermaceti oil, affording a brilliant light, but filling the room with its own peculiar odor. By filtering it through charcoal much of this empyreumatic smell is destroyed, and the oil greatly improved in quality and appearance. It is also well adapted to prevent friction in machinery; for, being free from gluten, so common to animal and vegetable oils, it preserves the parts to which it is applied for a long time in free motion." Dr. Hildreth, it will be seen, was a pioneer historian of petroleum, with scientific appreciation of its many valuable qualities, but he did not mention its usefulness in road making.

In the same unique paper, published twenty-six years before the beginning of the petroleum industry, Dr. Hildreth also treated of natural gas. He said: "All salt wells afford more of less of this interesting gas, an agent intimately concerned in the free rise of the water, and universally present where salt water is found. Indeed, so strong is the evidence afforded by rising of this gas to the surface of the existence of salt rocks below, that many wells are sunk on this evidence alone. * * * In many wells, salt water and inflammable gas rise in company with a steady, uniform flow. In others the gas rises at intervals of ten or twelve hours, or perhaps as many days, in vast quantity, and with overwhelming force, throwing the water from the well to the height of fifty or one hundred feet in the air. * * * This phenomenon is called 'blowing,' and is very troublesome and vexatious to the manufacturer. The explosion is sometimes so powerful as to cause the copper tube which lines the upper part of the well, to collapse and to entirely misplace and derange the fixtures about it. By constant use this difficulty is sometimes overcome by the exhaustion of the gas, and in others the wells have been abandoned as hopeless of amendment.

"A well on the Muskingum, ten miles above McConnellsburg, at six hundred feet in depth, afforded such an immense quantity of gas, and in such a constant stream, that, while they were boring, it several times took fire from the friction of the iron on the poles against the sides of the wall, or from the scintillations of the augur, driving the workmen away and communicating the flames to the shed which covered the works. It spread itself along the earth, and ignited several combustible bodies at the distance of several rods. It became so troublesome and so difficult to extinguish whenever ignited, being in this respect a little like the Greek fire so celebrated by Gibbon, that from this cause only, the well was abandoned. * * * At A. P. Stone's well, on the opposite side of the river, a little below McConnellsburg, the gas rises in small, irregular puffs, or discharges, averaging one for every minute or two, causing the water to flow in jets from the spouts into a large cistern below. The water rises in the head through a bored log to the height of twenty-five feet above the surface of the earth. Through a hole in the top of a small receiver, or cup, the gas rises in a constant stream, and when a candle or torch is applied, kindles into a beautiful flame, burning steadily until extinguished by closing the hole—affording in the stillness and darkness of midnight a striking and interesting phenomenon. It is supposed that this well alone furnishes sufficient gas, properly applied, to light the town very handsomely. No petroleum rises with it, and very little in any of the other wells of this locality. * * * A few miles above Charleston, on the Big Kanawha, great quantities of the carburetted hydrogen are slowly emitted through the earth. A tract of several rods in extent, near the river bank, is so charged with it that on making shallow cavities in the sand, and applying a firebrand, it immediately becomes ignited, and burns with a steady flame for an indefinite period, or until extinguished by covering it with sand. The boatmen, a rude but jolly race, often amuse themselves by tracing a circle in the sand around some one of the company not acquainted with the mystery, and applying fire, a flame immediately springs up, as if by magic around the astonished wight, which, being entirely confined to the circle traced, adds much to his terror and increases the delight of his boisterous companions. In a short time the sand beneath the burning gas becomes red hot. The neighboring women sometimes make use of it to boil their water when washing clothes on the banks of the river, and boatmen occasionally cook their food in the same easy and cheap manner."

It is not strange that these phenomena excited the wonder of the boatmen and lumbermen, but it is odd that with their frequency and the interest of such educated men as Dr. Hildreth, it was left for Edwin L. Drake to drill the first well for petroleum and for his successors to utilize natural gas for the fuel of towns and cities. There is a destiny, however, that awaits the conjunction of the coming of the man and the hour. Soon after the fame of the burning sands on the Great Kanawha had spread, the Burning Springs on the Little Kanawha, thirty miles above the mouth of the river, were discovered. These emitted petroleum as well as natural gas and, being ignited, continued to burn for months. After Drake's discovery, their vicinity was the scene of the first oil operations in West Virginia, the results being similar to those of the operations along Oil Creek. But the war put an untimely end to those operations, the raiders having burned everything in the district. Attempts to revive the wells after the close of the war were futile, the oil having wasted and the oil bearing sand being saturated with the water that had been allowed, for four years, to percolate into it. From Burning Springs to Ritchie Mine, the scene of the early activity in making oil from "coal." is about thirty miles, the course being northeast. Oil seepages were also found at Volcano and Petroleum, probably forty miles north of Burning Springs. All of these localities were tested in the deeper sands, during the great development in West Virginia that began in 1889, but they did not yield as well as localities somewhat removed from the surface indications.

In 1853, J. D. Angier entered into an agreement with Brewer, Watson & Co., owners of the land, to work the oil spring, near the Venango County line, below Titusville on Oil Creek. In the summer of 1854, Dr. F. B. Brewer, son of the head of the firm owning the land, carried a bottle of the oil to Prof. Crosby, of Dartmouth College, where he had graduated about ten years before. There, Geo. H. Bissell, a native of the town, who had been practicing law in New Orleans and New York, saw the petroleum and became much interested. It was then decided to organize a stock company with a capital of $250,000 to develop the petroleum springs, one-fifth of the shares and $5,000 to be paid to Brewer, Watson & Co. for the land, one-fifth to be sold as treasury stock, one-fifth to go to Professor Crosby for certain expenses and two-fifths to be retained by Mr. Bissell and his law partner, J. G. Eveleth, for the trouble of organizing. Professor Crosby's son was sent to Titusville to investigate and there followed proposals and counter-proposals, not highly creditable to any of the parties, but no deal was made until nearly November. Mr. Eveleth went to Titusville after the middle of November to conclude a deal on an honorable basis, the Pennsylvania Rock Oil Company having been chartered in the meantime, and Prof. B. Silliman, Jr., having been engaged to make a very thorough analysis of the oil sent forward by Brewer, Watson & Co.

The analysis made by the younger Silliman was the first really scientific contribution to petroleum literature. He distilled the petroleum by varying degrees of heat, obtaining many of the products now entering so largely into commerce, burned portions in several types of lamps, made photometric calculations and recommended the substance for the manufacture of illuminating oil, lubricating oil and paraffine. The report of Prof. Silliman, Jr., was made to Eveleth, Bissell and Reed and gave the results of fractional distillation beginning at the temperature of boiling water and ascending to 518 degrees, Fahrenheit; distillation by high steam; photometric experiments both with the distillate burned in lamps and of gas made from it. The professor recommended it as an illuminating oil, and enricher of gas and the heavier part of it as a lubricant. It was on this report that shares in the first oil company were floated, plus the representation that the production from pits, dug upon the lands of the company, was constant from year to year. The value was computed on a basis of about seventy-five cents a gallon for the crude oil, no one, apparently, having a thought that it might be found in such quantity as to glut the market. The shares did not sell, as New York corporations were not in favor. Reorganization under a Connecticut charter was then undertaken, but Mr. Bissell discovered the old English law of mortmain, reenacted upon the Pennsylvania statutes, rendering ownership of lands by a foreign corporation impossible. So the property was conveyed by deed to two Connecticut gentlemen, who executed to the Pennsylvania Rock Oil Company, a lease for ninety-nine years and the promotion went forward to success. That is, the stock was floated, but nothing came of it until President Townsend, of the company—he had succeeded Prof. Silliman, as a result of bickerings in the organization—sent Edwin L. Drake to Titusville to rectify an oversight in the legal conveyance. Drake visited the salt wells at Syracuse on his way to Titusville and he stopped at Tarentum to view the Kier wells when he went to Pittsburg to obtain the signatures of Mrs. Brewer and Mrs. Rynd to his papers. After his return to New Haven a lease was executed to Edwin E. Bowditch and E. L. Drake, by the terms of which they were to pay five cents a gallon royalty on all oil raised for fifteen years. George H. Bissell and Jonathan Watson, representing a majority of the stock, refused to concur in this action of a majority of the directors. The lease was changed to a royalty of one-eighth in kind of all the "oil, salt or paint" produced, and this was recorded at Franklin. Bissell and Watson threatened legal proceedings and a supplementary lease was made, fixing the royalty at twelve cents a gallon. On this lease the Seneca Oil Company was organized on March 23, 1858, and soon afterward Mr. Drake, with his family, started for Titusville.

How Drake managed to get down the first well has been often told. He first tried to dig a deep well, but was overwhelmed with water. Finally he went to Tarentum where he secured a set of drilling tools and a salt well driller. The derrick was raised in May, 1859. Water interfered again and Drake devised the means of driving heavy pipe to keep it out. He exhausted the funds furnished by the company, spent all the money he had and used his credit to the utmost before the well was drilled. Naturally, Brewer, Watson & Co. were not excessively friendly, but Ruel D. Fletcher, a young merchant, almost embarrassed his business extending credit to the stranger and Peter Wilson lent all the assistance he could. And so Drake's well was drilled and "struck oil," Saturday, August 27, 1859. S. M. Kier was prompt to make a contract for a part of the production at fifty-six cents a gallon, and the remainder was shipped to New York and marketed through Schieffelin & Co. This covers the history of petroleum in America from the earliest times to the actual birth of the industry.

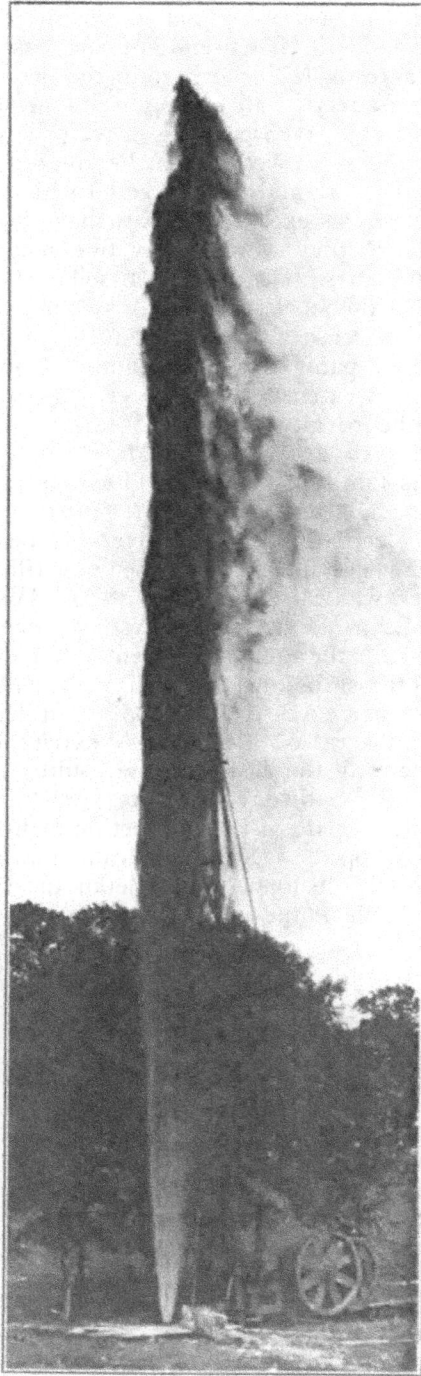

CUMBERLAND COUNTY, ILLINOIS—
PURE OIL CO. GUSHER

CHAPTER XIX.

GETTING OIL AND GAS LANDS.

What the right of way department is to a railroad, the land leasing branch is to the petroleum and natural gas industry. In California, Wyoming and Utah there has been no leasing, those fields being located upon the public domain and, therefore, the lands have been secured under the laws covering mineral claims. It appears probable, however, that future operations upon Government lands will be under a leasing system very similar to to that which has obtained where the lands have been in private ownership. In Oklahoma the lands of the Indian wards of the Government were leased upon terms very similar to those established by custom in the Eastern States, and much of the productive area in the Caddo field of Louisiana was leased by the operating companies from the Levee Board, a public committee charged with the duty of protecting arable lands from overflow. The parish has been the beneficiary of bonuses and royalties there paid for the privilege of extracting the oil and gas from the public lands. The Government cannot adopt a more equitable or just system.

In the beginning of the petroleum industry, the tract on which the first well was located was purchased from the owners, Brewer, Watson & Co., by the Pennsylvania Rock Oil Company. The actual operating company, however, entered upon the land by virtue of a leasehold. The proposition of that company to pay one-eighth in kind was eminently fair and proper, although the lessor forced an arbitrary contract for a fixed price per gallon. These terms proved so unreasonable, when the price of oil declined below the royalty price, that a new division had to be made—one that was not just to the lessees. They were compelled to take in fee a very small portion of the tract. After the first well was drilled in, the majority of transactions were leaseholds, reserving to the owner of the fee a fraction of the output in kind and this settled ultimately to the general practice of giving one-eighth of the oil. When natural gas became a factor, it was arranged for on the basis of a yearly rental, either fixed during the term of the lease, or graduated upon the production of the wells. Either of these forms is equitable, for while the fixed rental may seem inadequate for a very large well, it is quite certain to become excessive before the well, with declining production, is finally abandoned.

In general, the leasing of private lands for oil and gas purposes has been conducted honestly on fair terms. There were instances in the very early days, in which advantage was taken of unlettered land owners, usually by neighbors and acquaintances, rather than by capitalists attracted from outside the region. The Courts have frowned upon sharp practices, when given the opportunity by proceedings in equity, holding unfair contracts to be fraudulent in their nature and void. These decisions assisted in bringing the practice of leasers to practical uniformity, so that nearly all use regular blank forms providing for the payment of oil in kind and for gas by yearly rental. Even so, there are occasional instances in which shrewd but impecunious leasers have given the land owner a shade the worse of the bargain. On the other hand instances are not uncommon in which the landed proprietor has had all the better of it. In the nature of things he occupies the position of vantage and sometimes lies awake o'nights scheming to get the upper hand of the eager oilman.

One rather amusing case came under my observation in West Virginia. Before the development of 1889 had extended more than a few rods over the boundary from Pennsylvania, "Jim" Howard began leasing lands in Wetzel County, far in advance. His contract was fair, providing for one-eighth of the oil, for a well to be drilled within a year, or in default, a rental per acre until the well was drilled, and a rental of $300 per year for each commercial gas well. But when the energetic leaser had secured the desired "block" of land—a matter of a few thousand acres—his funds were completely exhausted. The laws of West Virginia were very strict on the point of having leases acknowledged before a Justice of the Peace, a Notary Public, or an officer of the Court, a fact that "Jim" learned at about the time that he discovered that he had no money with which to pay the fees. He was in a fair way to lose all the fruits of his months of toil and the amount of his expenses, but he was fertile in resources. He resolved to carry the day with a high hand. Accordingly he sent out notices to all lessors to appear on the following Saturday at the office of the nearest Justice of the Peace, to acknowledge the leases, to pay for the acknowledgments and to "save further trouble." The simple, honest folk were all there on Saturday, acknowledged the written instruments to "be their act and deed," paid the fee of twenty-five cents each, to the 'Squire, and returned home satisfied they had avoided a compulsory summons to the county seat. "Jim" sold and assigned the leases for a stake sufficient to pay for the next batch of acknowledgments and saved the "further trouble" of sending out notices. More often the leaser of a "block" is held up by a few of the landholders who will not lease on the terms their neighbors accept, and he is compelled to "come across" with a few hundred dollars in bonuses to the crafty minority. Many are the tales told among oil producers and leasers of the means used to circumvent the obstinate or crafty owner of a piece of desirable land. The late William Fleming was wont to relate an early experience of his own, in Butler County, Pennsylvania, where he competed with many others for a strip about five rods wide and eighty rods long that seemed to lie "on the belt" in its greatest dimension. The owner was one of those men that, when offered his own price, would immediately want more. He had worn out the patience of a dozen men eager to lease his land and willing to pay what it appeared to be worth. Mr. Fleming, on his second visit, renewed his offer made on the first, without success. At that moment he spied a calf in the barn-yard, a rather poor looking beast, worth possibly seven dollars. He offered the farmer eight dollars for it, provided he would lease the land at the previous offer. Of course, the owner wanted more. Mr. Fleming bid up the seven dollar calf to sixteen dollars, and the farmer, who had forgotten the lease in his keen desire to make a bargain on the calf, succumbed to his own stupidity. Mr. Fleming bought the calf and got the lease on the proffered terms. The farmer did not awaken from the trance induced by selling a seven dollar calf for sixteen dollars until the papers had been duly signed and acknowledged, when Mr. Fleming graciously presented the expensive calf to the farmer's wife as a bonus for her signature to the oil lease. The strip proved to be eighty rods along the prolific belt.

The early forms of oil lease were rather indefinite, if we except the lease of the Seneca Oil Company from the Pennsylvania Rock Oil Company. The lease granted by John Rynd to Jonathan Watson and Jacob D. Angier, dated September 1, 1859, recorded in Deed Book Q, page 538, at Franklin, county seat of Venango County, Pennsylvania, granted the "exclusive right of digging and boring for salt and oil," on the farm, the owner to receive one-twelfth of all the "oil collected or salt made, and other minerals found." This lease was dated but five days after the Drake well found oil. It was changed by agreement the following January to give Rynd one-fourth of the oil and his land proved one of the famous oil producing farms along Oil Creek. A lease bearing date of September 2, 1859, was granted by John McClintock to J. W. Hibbard and J. W. McIntyre granting an "oil spring" on the bank of Oil Creek, with 500 feet of land along the Creek, extending back to the hill road, with the privilege of digging and prospecting for oil for 999 years. The consideration was one-third of the oil and five dollars a month for one year. This was adjoining the Rynd Farm. The remainder of the John McClintock farm was leased—200 acres—to Bradford R. Alden and Cornelius Chase, on September 26, 1859, for one-third "of the salt, oil and mineral and $150 in hand." It was expressly agreed that the obligation of the parties of the second part would be fulfilled when they made "one boring of sufficient depth to be profitable to them for oil," or when they made a boring seventy feet deep, if practicable, and a payment of $75 and the same obligation to bore to be fulfilled by payment to the party of the first part of $100 in cash. This covered the site of the famous future operations of the Union Oil Company on Cherry Run. On September 27, 1859, Hamilton McClintock, Jr., leased to Eben Brewer, Jonathan Watson, G. E. Brewer, J. D. Angier and Rixford Pierce for one-fourth of the salt, oil and other minerals and it provided that upon demand McClintock should pay one-eighth of the operating expenses.

The next lease recorded at Franklin carried the business far afield. It was dated October 17, 1859, covering the farm of Robert Brandon in Sandycreek Township, Venango County, for a term of 50 years, for oil, salt and other minerals. There was no time limit set for the beginning of operations, but the consideration was to be five per cent of the net profits from sales of oil. The lessees were Vance Stewart & Co. This farm was below Franklin, more than twenty-five miles from the Drake well. Under date of November 14, 1859, James Nellis and William Bruner granted to J. M. Clapp the privilege to "dig or bore" for petroleum on their land in President Township, operations to begin within one year, and to have one well 60 feet deep within a year and a half, or the lease to be void. Consideration one-eighth of the oil. This land was eighteen miles up the Allegheny River from the mouth of Oil Creek. Mr. Clapp, and his brother, Edwin E. Clapp, both made fortunes from oil production. The seventh lease was dated November 19, 1859, and conveyed the farm of Henry Pope to U. A. Plumer and J. P. Park, to begin operations in one year and to hold for fifty years, for twelve and one-half per cent of the oil. This was the famous Pope oil farm three miles below Franklin on the Allegheny River. It produced many thousands of barrels of oil, but the owner, on account of failure of second parties to keep the foregoing agreement, derived little benefit from it. The next lease was given by Elizabeth and James Tarr to William Phillips. The royalty was one-fourth of the oil, salt or other minerals, with one year to commence work and two to find the product in paying quantities or forfeit the lease. It leased twenty-five acres in Cornplanter Township and bore date of November 19, 1859. On this lease was drilled the famous Phillips No. 2, which came in flowing 4,000 barrels a day in September, 1861, and found "the product in paying quantities." But the flood of oil from the gushers that followed put the price of oil so low that it did not pay to barrel

WEED HILL, UPPER CHURCH RUN, TITUSVILLE, PA.

it for some weeks. The principal owners in this lease were Charles Lockhart and William Frew.

Another form of oil lease executed on September 2, 1859, was virtually an article of partnership. This was between E. G. Stackpole and Ruel D. Fletcher, the friend of Drake. Stackpole "granted, bargained and sold" to Fletcher, for $100 and one-half of all the oil, salt or other minerals under his farm, retaining the other half and agreeing to pay one-half of the operating expenses. This was in the vicinity of Titusville. The lease of the site of the great Noble & Delamater well was granted by John Farel to Orange Noble, G. B. Delamater, L. L. Lamb, William Nason and G. F. Churchill, for $600 in hand and one-fourth of the oil or other minerals. This well produced oil that sold for a total of more than three million dollars and there were other good wells on the farm. The Archibald Buchanan farm was leased to Henry R. Rouse, John L. Mitchell and Samuel Q. Brown on the same terms. $600 in hand and one-fourth of the oil, the lease being dated July 2, 1860, although a well or two had been previously drilled under an agreement not of record.

The sub lease was early introduced, the first of record being a part of the Hamilton McClintock farm (McClintockville) from Brewer, Watson & Co. to Chas. Hyde, W. C. Hyde, Titus Ridgeway and E. B. Grandin. This reserved to the original lessees and the land owner, five-eights of all the oil and other minerals found. Some great wells were drilled on this lease and the sub-lessees were among the most active of early oil producers, Mr. Grandin continuing in the industry for many years. In 1865 the art of sub-leasing had progressed and was quite the thing. Those who had been fortunate enough to get whole farms in the earlier years found it profitable to subdivide them for the hungry operators who wanted a location on which

FOREMEN'S QUARTERS AT INSTALLATION, HANKOW.

to drill. Thus we find under date of February 3, 1865, from M. C. Egbert, et ux. to Thomas W. Phillips, a "conveyance of one-twelfth of the oil, salt or mineral in allotments 21 and 28 of the Egbert farm, in Cornplanter Township, Venango County, Pennsylvania, containing about one acre each. On No. 21 is the 'Jersey' and on No. 28 the 'Coquette' well." On September 25, 1865, T. W. Phillips bought from the Maple Shade Oil Company another one-twelfth of allotment No. 28, conveyed by deed. The wells mentioned in these papers were among the most famous on Oil Creek and the parties to the first transaction have been known throughout the oil regions. The Egbert farm yielded not less than three million dollars to the owners, who purchased it from Davidson, immediately after the Drake well was finished. The Buchanan farms at Rouseville were sub-divided among scores of companies and the Holmden and other farms at Pithole were similarly sub-divided into acre and half-acre leases. All of these included salt or other mineral, which had become the prescribed form, but nobody was looking for anything except oil. The price paid for these plots was fabulous in the aggregate. Choice locations sold for $50,000 and $75,000 an acre, and single farms brought from half a million to a million dollars. All of these lands could have been bought six years earlier for $20 an acre and less, their chief value being in the standing timber upon them.

The first lease to mention gas, specifically, was recorded in Warren County. It was from B. W. Lacy to the Warren Oil Company, and bore date of April 7, 1860. It conveyed a "corner of the farm" and contained the following clause: "And should no oil be found in profitable quantities, but other minerals or gas be found in such quantity as to justify production thereof, they are to have the corner designated for one-fourth of the gas or other mineral." It would be difficult to say why Mr. Lacy mentioned gas, but as he was a lumber man it was probable he was familiar with the salt well operations in West Virginia and Southeastern Ohio and had already conceived the possibility of using the natural gas for lighting. It is possible he derived the idea from the use made of such gas at Fredonia, New York, as early as 1828. Be that as it may, the inclusion of gas in the ordinary oil lease did not become general for a number of years after the execution of the Lacy lease. The majority of leases in the early days were for small pieces of land, but as the oil fields spread from the original areas the "wildcat" operators began trying to surround their pioneer wells with blocks of leases. This led to the introduction of a rental, in lieu of actual drilling, the sum varying according to circumstances and the character of the land owner. Phillips Bros. leased large acreage through Venango and Butler Counties in Pennsylvania, establishing the uniform price of one dollar per acre per annum for such time as actual operations were deferred. This became the ruling figure in Pennsylvania. In West Virginia, preceding the great development that began in 1889, the ruling rental was fifty cents an acre, principally on leases taken by residents, the operating companies generally adhering to the dollar per acre, established by Pennsylvania practice.

From giving one-fourth and one-half of the oil as royalty, the producers gradually settled to one-eighth of the oil. It was found that this proportion was more equitable. It paid the land owner well and left the producer some show to get out even with moderate wells. In the vicinity of large wells one-sixth or even one-fourth of the oil was sometimes offered for choice leases, but the favorite method for securing such leases, during the decades from 1870 to 1900, was to pay a cash bonus. This sometimes went as high as $5,000 per acre, but more frequently ranged below $1,000 an acre. The heavy losses suffered by producers in "gusher pools" have been due more frequently to enthusiasm leading to excessive cash bonus than to any other cause. Town lot excitements, of course, have inflicted losses on a good many operators, because the most thorough saturation of the oil sand could not yield sufficiently to pay for so many wells drilled on so small an area. These "town lot booms" have been a picturesque feature of the oil industry. With every chance to lose, men of experience, carried away by contagious excitement, have rushed in and invested in wells on plots thirty by one hundred feet. As the form of lease settled to one-eighth of the oil it dropped reference to "salt and other mineral," especially as the producing region extended to localities underlaid with coal. The oil men, themselves, had no desire to be under obligation to mine coal on a royalty of one-eighth or more. Natural gas stipulations became common during the decade, 1870 to 1880, and since the latter date the provision covering gas has been as carefully looked after as that covering oil.

It will be noted the early leases, which were indefinite as to the product to be sought, tended to long terms, such as fifty and ninety-nine years. Presently the term was shortened to fifteen and twenty years, with the addendum "and as much longer as oil or gas shall be produced in paying quantities." These are now the ordinary terms on leased lands. It was about the close of the decade 1880 to 1890 that a sleepless farmer in Allegheny County, Pennsylvania, discovered a flaw in the forfeiture clause, which provided that

UNION OIL COMPANY WELL IN WYOMING.

under certain conditions the lease should become null and void. His lease had not been formally cancelled and he made demand for his rental. It was refused on the ground that the lease had become void by simple neglect to meet its provisions. The court did not see it in that light and the operating company had to pay the rental. That decision led to a modification of the form of lease and to the adoption of careful measures to have leases surrendered and cancelled. The forfeiture clause is now the last thing on the printed forms and states specifically that a failure to pay rental shall work a forfeiture of all obligations. There was a temporary recurrence of the acre and half-acre sub-division of producing property in the development of the Spindletop pool in Texas, but it resulted disastrously to the sub-lessees and to the profit only of the sub-lessors, resembling, in that particular, the older experience of Pithole, as it did in the matter of stock company promotions to the detriment of the purchasers of the shares.

A new experience in leasing came to the petroleum pioneers when the oil development of Kansas crossed the southern border into Oklahoma and Indian Territories. There the leases had to be obtained from the Indians, who were wards of the Government. The Indian Territory Illuminating Oil Company preceded the development, obtaining a blanket lease for oil and gas purposes on the eastern half of the Osage reservation in Oklahoma. The lease was made by the President and members of the Council of the Osage Nation. It covered the largest acreage ever held under a leasehold in the United States. Until it became valuable it stood unquestioned, but when the sub-lessees of several generous tracts had begun development and brought in wells good for several hundred barrels a day, at the start, the Department of the Interior awakened suddenly and asserted the lease had been made without its sanction. It proposed to nullify the whole proceeding, but was confronted by the fact that such action would confiscate the property of innocent investors. The matter finally went to Congress and after much bucking and filling, that part of the lease that had been sub-let was ratified and has proven among the richest of the Oklahoma Territory. Meantime operators were leasing from individuals among the Cherokees and Creeks in the Indian Territory, east of the Osage reservation. They, too, were having troubles they had never experienced in the East. Beside making a bargain with the Indian, it was necessary to have it recorded with the Indian agent of the proper district and approved by the Secretary of the Department of the Interior. Frequently the delay gave opportunity for the Indian to repudiate the bargain. Much litigation and some losses were the result.

The Government, at that time, was busy with the task of allotting the lands of the Five Civilized Tribes in severalty. Thousands of allotments had been made, but the Government continued to direct their management and the act granting members of the Tribes citizenship, debarred sequestration of the allotted lands for a period of years. At about the same time Oklahoma was admitted to Statehood, the new Commonwealth, including both of the Territories, Indian and Oklahoma. This brought a fresh complication into the situation. Lessees under territorial law were left in doubt whether their rights would be sustained by the State. The Department at Washington undertook to change the royalty consideration agreed to by its Indian wards, and, as a final effort, made a ruling that royalties should be paid at a higher price than the open market. Of course, this absurd ruling had to be revoked and other conditions have been mitigated, but the lot of the Oklahoma lease-holder is not yet a happy one. The latest surprise sprung upon him is the contention that a lease made by a minor is not valid after such minor reaches his or her majority. While the State courts have shown a disposition to rule sensibly that such leases are valid, a State law is proposed to validate all minor leases and so clear away all doubt.

It may readily be gathered that the leasing of oil lands requires the qualities of diplomacy, great perseverance, some knowledge of the law and a high degree of alertness. The larger companies maintain leasing deepartments, and, of course, employ good legal talent for the inspection of papers and the searching of records. In spite of such precautions controversies occur and the courts are given considerable business in straightening out legal tangles over leasehold rights. Not infrequently cupidity leads a landholder to lease his premises a second time without the formality of having the first lease cancelled. Occasionally some slight technical defect in the prior lease affords the opportunity for such practice and occasionaly the litigation between the claimants to leasehold of the same property discloses fatal defects in the papers. This fact alone demands the exercise of great care and caution on the part of the leaser. Yet the most difficult part of his business is the judgment of varying types of human nature. No less than in medical practice is it necessary to study the idiosyncrasies of the subject. The offer of money to one man may be the means of getting a lease from him; the same offer to another may excite his cupidity and suspicion that the lease is more valuable. There are men who, like Oliver Twist, always cry for more even though the first offer be twice what they believed the concession to be worth. It is an old story about the farmer in the Pithole district who was offered $500,000 for his poor farm and refused, with the plaint: "I would have no place to live if I sold my farm." This story is apocryphal, but it has always been received with some degree of approval by those who have been engaged in taking oil leases. The average land owner desires abundant assurance that a plentiful number of wells will be drilled on his property, but many professional leasers have met the man, who, after listening to their enthusiastic promises on this score, says: "I think it is wicked to take the oil from the earth. The Good Lord put it there for his own purposes and we ought to lay it stay there." Usually when one of that kind is met it is good economy to let him alone until the prosperity of his neighbors, from their royalty, convinces him that no evil will befall him for sharing in the good fortune. There are many instances in the annals of petroleum where tidy fortunes have been founded upon obtaining a choice lease in unproven territory and the keen rivalry of leasers in the vicinity of a good well in new territory is one of the inspiring features of the business. The races of the "oil scouts" for the telegraph offices in Warren County were hardly more spirited than those of the leasers after land that has not been "tied up" before the gusher comes in. It is amazing what a keen scent these gentlemen have for "open" territory, and it is one of their methodical duties to canvass the neighborhood of a wildcat well to learn what farms or portions of farms have not been leased. These men often go about the country, riding on lonely roads, with enough currency in their pockets to make up a respectable factory pay roll, or to start a small bank. They are rarely molested and, if one should be, he would be likely to give an interesting exhibition of the art of self defense at a distance, or in close quarters.

Lease disputes have not always been taken to the courts at the first intimation of controversy. The resort to strategy and physical force are primitive traits too strong in their survival to give way readily to the orderly process of courts of law. The spectacle of two sets of men carrying material on and off a particular acre has been witnessed in many parts of the oil producing regions as a result of a dispute over the ownership of an oil lease. The two forces have been known to come to blows in more than one instance, and in a few cases there has been resort to firearms. In the village of Pickwick, in the Clarion oil field, in 1873, there was enacted a near tragedy that terminated farcically. A Mr. Shaffer, tall and slender, had obtained a lease of fifteen acres on the Henry Hummel farm. Subsequently Captain Wesley Chambers, short, but very broad, leased the same piece, the previous lease being held to be void on account of a non-fulfillment of provisions. Mr. Chambers promptly ordered lumber and machinery to begin operations. Shaffer then ordered some material and employed several men to remove the Chambers lumber, while his own was put upon the site. Mr. Chambers, being advised of the state of affairs, hastened to the front. When he arrived at the lease Mr. Shaffer ordered him off. When he refused to go the tall man drew a pistol and threatened instant death to Mr. Chambers if he did not surrender. The intrepid Chambers drew his own "hardware," as they call it in the West, and invited his antagonist to begin hostilities, or get off the premises. Spectators discreetly side-stepped the general range of fire, but a few remained close enough to offer counsels of peace. After ten minutes or so, Shaffer surrendered and the dispute was left to the arbitrament of the law, resulting in Capt. Chambers' favor, who magnanimously purchased the Shaffer material and gave the tall man the contract for building the rig, he being a well known rig builder.

Not all of the militant disputes have ended so happily. As indicated, many led to fisticuffs and a few to homicide. The most notable case in the latter category occurred in the Murraysville gas field in Westmoreland County, Pa. The Haymaker well was drilled there in 1878, but natural gas had not then attained to a high commercial position. About five years later several companies realized the value of the Murraysville gas to supply Pittsburgh. In the operations following, a dispute arose over title to a part of the property and Chicago parties undertook to enforce their claim by violence. Mr. Haymaker, in command of another squad, resisted their efforts. A melee ensued which resulted in serious injury to a score of belligerents, and Mr. Haymaker was killed. Arrests followed and one of the capitalists involved was convicted of manslaughter and sentenced to the penitentiary at Pittsburgh. The company represented by Haymaker retained the property and its claim was sustained by the courts after protracted litigation.

BENNINGHOFF RUN, PRIOR TO FIRE CAUSED BY LIGHTNING, JOHN BENNINGHOFF HOUSE ON HILL.

CHAPTER XX.

MEN GOOD AND BAD.

Some reference has been made to the seamy side of life in the oil regions. As in the mining camps of all parts of the world, all classes of adventurers have been in evidence and there have been many characters of whom the communities were not proud. Their evil repute has spread far and wide, while the better elements have been unheralded and unsung. Among those who achieved early success on Oil Creek, was Captain A. B. Funk, the first to drill a well to the "third sand" in that district. He was a native of Westmoreland County, but had been engaged for several years in the lumber trade in Warren County. One of the first uses of the great wealth he derived from the famous Fountain well, was to build a church in the village where he resided. He contributed very generously to another when he removed to Titusville. He gave much in charity.

The disposition of the wealth of Hon. Henry R. Rouse has been recounted. It rendered unnecessary the levy of any poor tax in Warren County, and enabled that county to construct exceptionally good roads and bridges. A monument to his memory has been erected at the Warren County home at Youngsville. Edwin E. Clapp, a successful pioneer, acquired a great tract of land in President Township, Venango County, constructed a handsome hotel in which to live, where he offered entertainment to all who passed that way. At his own expense he had many miles of public highway laid out and constructed on good grades through the rugged country. His benefactions in this manner cost him about $100,000, for which he expected no reward save the knowledge that he had benefited his neighbors.

Robert Duncan, one of the successful pioneers at Pithole, built two Methodist Episcopal Churches and endowed them—one at Pithole and the other at Plumer. The Pithole church stands in stately dignity without a congregation. That at Plumer has been torn down and a new structure made of it in a more accessible location. Nearly all of the endowment of the former and a part of that of the latter has been sequestered from the original purpose of the donor. But Mr. Duncan's name is borne in grateful remembrance by many of the survivors of the original congregations. James S. McCray was a large contributor to the church of his faith, the Presbyterian, in Petroleum Center, and treasurer of the fund of $6,500 contributed in two days. Dr. M. C. Egbert gave $1,000 of it. McCray took the money home and put it under the pillow of his brother-in-law for safe keeping over the night. Some of the Petroleum Center crooks evidently knew about it, for there was no money there in the morning. McCray paid for the church and the crooks spent the original fund among the resorts of contrary character in the town. Church and road building, however, were not all of the beneficences of the early and later oil producers. Marcus

Hulings, at the height of his success, donated a fund for the building of a dormitory at Allegheny College, Meadville, which is known as Hulings Hall. Captain William Hasson presented Oil City with a large park, and others have given of their means to the cause of education and the advance of civilization. Lewis Emery, Jr., has maintained for many years a private museum in Bradford for the use of the people of that city.

In emergency calls for assistance the oil region could always be relied upon for quick contributions. Thousands of dollars were subscribed for relief to the yellow fever districts in the South on several occasions. Other thousands were given for famine sufferers in India. The oil conribution to the Charleston earthquake sufferers was one of the first to reach them and again the oil region responded instantly to the cry of distress at Galveston when disaster overtook it. The great Chicago fire in 1871 was one of the first calamities to give the generous oil region spirit exercise and the contribution was such that it was remembered. When Oil City and Titusville were devastated by flood and fire in 1892, Chicago returned the kindness, accompanied by a message again expressing its gratitude for the relief extended by those cities in 1871. In the oil producing region cases of poverty have been rare, but when one has happened to be discovered relief has ever been prompt, and of the most generous character. The helping hand is ever ready. This is as true to-day as in the earlier years. Wages of labor in the oil fields have always been a little better than for similar services in other industries and the people have prospered. Comfortable homes are the rule. Of course, special cases of misfortune and poverty from dissolute habits have been known in this favored region. Labor strikes are unknown in the operation of wells, pipe lines or refineries, indicating the better than average compensation, conditions of toil, and character of employes. This is also due in part to the democratic relationship between employers and employes. Even in periods of serious depression in the industry there has been little actual suffering among workmen or their families. The benefactions of the leaders of the industry in the later years have been many and varied, aggregating untold millions of dollars.

There have been many odd characters among those drawn by the excitement of drilling for oil. One of these was Thomas Frothingham, who came to Oil Creek from Rochester, New York, in 1864, and built the Keystone House at Petroleum Center. In addition to keeping hotel he was an active seeker for oleaginous wealth and an open handed entertainer, a man with a voice easily heard a square away and one who had a remarkable command of a choice vocabulary of "cuss" words. He was known to everybody. But one day, riding over the ridge to Cherrytree with Col. Brady, he made a resolution in stentorian tones and with profane emphasis to stop "treating the Petroleum Center crowd to twenty-five cent whiskey and fifty cent cigars until he struck a hundred barrel well." He never had the fortune to get a big well, but he kept his word. He went back to Rochester and died many years ago.

Another loud voiced man, prolific in strong expletives, was Henry Verbeck, who was fortunate in getting big wells. In 1872 he was operating a lease on the Ashbaugh farm, on the hill opposite Antwerp. One summer day he was in St. Petersburg, little more than half a mile from his wells, when a thunder storm threatened. He started for the lease and was almost in sight of it when the sky was rent by a vivid flash of lightning, followed almost instantly by a terrific crash of thunder. Verbeck was so startled he actually jumped, but as he came down he roared, "By ——, I'll bet that hit my —— well." In a minute he had turned the bend in the road, running at the top of his speed. The flames and dense column of black smoke that met his gaze verified his emphatic prediction. His well had been "struck" by lightning and his derrick and tank were burning.

A peculiar genius arrived on Oil Creek from the indefinite West in 1865, who gave his name as Henry McKenty and announced himself as the owner of 20,000 acres of Western land. He carried a great number of testimonials from bankers, merchants, lawyers and others. He finally drifted to Tidioute, where he announced his greatest scheme under the title, "All the oil! No royalty." He said he had 10,000 acres of oil lands and he proposed to permit any person or company to drill on these lands. They could have wood for fuel, lumber for derricks and engine houses, all without cost. But if they found oil they were to pay him $100 per acre for the land in fee simple, one-half acre to the well. He failed to make anything out of the plan, returned to the West, and has been almost forgotten where he once flourished. It may be said, too, that his plan did not survive, the lease with a royalty remaining popular.

Of less desirable types there were many. The most notorious was "Ben" Hogan, a prize fighter, who made his advent at Petroleum Center. His principal business was operating "dance halls" of the lowest type. His principal ring battle was with "The" Allen in Iowa, but he gave some brutal exhibitions in the oil region with less famed pugilists. His conduct at Petroleum Center aroused so much indignant feeling that he removed to Babylon, a lawless oil village near Tidioute. Then he returned to Petroleum Center, but was soon made to understand that he would not be tolerated. With the drift of population to the oil fields down the Allegheny River, Hogan turned up in Parkers Landing, where he made a worse record. When the law was invoked, he had built a large house boat, named the "Floating Palace." The line dividing Armstrong and Clarion Counties was in the river, and when officers of the law in Parkers Landing went after Hogan, the "Palace" moved over to the Clarion County shore. When complaint was made in Clarion County, the "Palace" floated back to the Armstrong side. But eventually preparations for a concerted attack from both sides drove him out. He migrated to Petrolia, in Butler County, where he opened the "Seminary." In 1876 he located in Elk City, Clarion County, a considerable town with no organized government, or police, located only about a mile from Edenburg, the metropolis of the Clarion County field. The stories told of Hogan's "joint" in Elk City were thrilling, including riots and suspected murders, but none was proven. Hogan was finally compelled to move again and landed in Tarport, near Bradford. It was when the temperature of Tarport grew too warm for him that Hogan went to New York, intending to sail for his native Germany. Before embarking he procured the writing and publication of his book, "Ben Hogan, the Wickedest Man in the World." Attending a mission, he professed repentance, and has since posed as an apostle. He is now conducting a mission in Chicago.

Another undesirable character, whose career in Oildom began soon after that of "Ben" Hogan and ended some time earlier, was "Curly" Green, gambler. His real name may have been Black, or Brown, but he preferred to be known as Green. He practiced his "art" in Shamburg and Red Hot, drifted down the river and plied his trade in Antwerp, Pickwick and Elk City. He had all of the characteristics of the gamblers of the gold camps, made immortal by Bret Harte, from iron nerve in a tight situation to giving generously to the family in distress of one of his victims. Romance might be woven around "Curly," but a fair account between his "generosity" and his methods of capturing and "skinning" his prey, left a large balance on the ledger against him. After facing guns several times, without flinching,

A FAMOUS HOTEL OF PETROLEUM CENTER IN THE PALMY DAYS.

he disappeared from the oil region as mysteriously as he came, leaving no trail.

Street fighting was a common pastime at Pithole. It was the popular method of settling bar-room disputes. It continued more or less in vogue as other oil towns held the stage. But the first unconquerable "bully," who deserted industry for brawling, was George Kelly. He had been a driller, but in the Butler County field he became a fighter. For a long time he found no equal in rough and tumble struggles and no man was safe from his insults. He flourished about Petrolia and Millerstown from 1872 to 1875, invaded Clarion County in the latter year, returned to Butler County a little later, and finding little profit in being a fighting hero, resorted to theft and was sent to the penitentiary. "Tom" Cranston was another of similar sort, of less prowess, but he resorted to a knife when fists would not win, or when the liquor was unusually strong. His career was short.

The most remarkable "fighting man," however, was George Coyle, a giant from Canada. He came to the oil regions in 1872 and found employment at Antwerp, brawn being in good demand at tool dresser's wages. He was unsophisticated and peaceable. His splendid physique attracted attention and he was soon interviewed concerning his fighting ability. Coyle declared that he had never fought anybody and being challenged by some of the Antwerp bullies he declined to do battle. When attacked he made off as fast as possible untouched by the taunts of the idlers. But one evening he was surrounded by a cordon of toughs and literally compelled to do bat-

A TYPICAL "BOARING HOUSE" OF OIL CREEK DAYS.

tle with the biggest man among them. There was no escape from the cordon, except by fighting his way out and Coyle accepted the situation. He was more awkward than his antagonist, but his great strength compensated for his lack of fistic training. He knocked out his man. But when the onlookers started to congratulate him there was unexpected trouble. The first man forward received a blow that sent him sprawling and the one who stood next was knocked on top of the first. Coyle was angry and was ready to whip the crowd. When four or five were down the remainder fled, with the maddened Canadian in pursuit, across the common. When all had escaped his fury, the big fellow went back, picked up his dinner pail in one hand and his original antagonist in the other, and proceeded to his boarding house.

George Coyle was no longer a man of peace. He took to drinking and when he drank he wanted to fight. He became a terror of the town. Later he became a terror of the oil region. He was a good workman when sober and was always on the frontier in the newest town called into being by the onward march of oil developments. Every year he worked less, but drank and fought more. In every town of the great Bradford field, he cleaned up the fighting men singly and then contested with squads of them. Occasionally he was compelled to flee from half a dozen men armed with clubs, and wherever he was there were frequent disturbances of the nightly slumbers of the population, either by Coyle pursuing two or three through the streets, or by a half a dozen or a dozen pursuing Coyle. In the Richburg field he was a drunken brawler, at Cherry Grove he had sunk to a quarreler and in Gusher City he was killed in 1883. He went one night to the shanty of a man in charge of a lease and asked for admittance. The request was refused. Coyle began to kick the door. The frightened man inside fired his revolver at the door sill in the hope, as he testified, of driving the intruder away. The bullet stuck Coyle in the foot and his condition, resulting from dissipation and disease, was such that he died from the effects of the wound within a week.

Comparatively few murders have been committed in the oil towns, considering the number of brawls that have occurred. But few men in the oil regions were "gun toters." The fighting men depended upon their fists and guns were not needed for defence from highwaymen or burglars. After the first few years of the industry robbery became exceedingly rare, and men went about in lonely places day or night, without fear. In 1862, a man was murdered for his money on Oil Creek and one murdered near Titusville. In 1865 a gentleman from Jamestown was murderously assaulted, robbed, dumped into a hole, covered with rocks and brush, and left for dead, along the road between Pithole and Petroleum Center, but he crawled out and gave the alarm. The perpetrator was hunted so fiercely that he fled from the region. His victim recovered and devoted himself to search for the villain. He found him, had him brought back to Venango County, convicted and sentenced to the penitentiary.

The hunt for that miscreant had its effect in frightening others who might have followed his example, out of the region, or into good behavior.

Beside "Coal Oil Johnny" Steele, there were many young men, sons of oil farm owners, who obtained possession of more money than was good for them. Every new district developed one or more who took the high road to perdition, and, to adopt the phrase of an old Clarion County philosopher, they "went whooping." Liquor, cards, and evil women had attractions for these young fellows who had never learned the use of money and were overwhelmed by the flood of it when oil was found on the farm. Occasionally an older man went the same way with his royalty riches, for there were always plenty of camp followers who had no other business than to tempt and entice the ruralites who came suddenly into easy money and unaccustomed idleness. However, the majority survived the experience, parted from their unwonted wealth they took up some branch of the industry and traveled on to the newer development. Many of those made suddenly rich by the finding of oil on their lands kept their senses, invested in the industry and joined the army of oil producers. Very few saved their money for the improvement of their farms after the oil had been drained from them. More men dropped from the ranks of the invading hosts, took up the farms and settled down to till them.

An odd character who became a very wealthy and highly respected citizen of Pennsylvania, was the late John McKeown. He emigrated from Ireland and after a few years in New York, pushed on to the oil regions, arriving when Petroleum Center was near the zenith of its prosperity. He was a willing worker and rapidly mastered the art of dressing tools, drilling and pumping. He was careful of his money and when the development drifted to Parkers Landing he and another were in partnership as drilling contractors. The firm had plenty of work and McKeown was on the

BULLOCK CART (WATER BUFFALO) TRANSPORTING AMERICAN OIL IN THE ORIENT.

job, but somehow the bills were not paid. The partner kept the accounts as John's education had been neglected in his youth and he was not proficient with pen and paper. Presently, it became apparent that the sheriff would have to wind up the partnership, and in due time the blow fell. The partner disappeared, but McKeown stood his ground. When the sale was over he sought more contracts on his own account. When he got one he started the well without an augur stem, using four sinker bars in its stead. Rumor had it that he had sequestered those sinkers before the sheriff's levy, but in any event he got the well down in good time and had others to drill as fast as he could get them. There was no more popular contractor in Butler County and he prospered amazingly. Moreover, he paid the debts of the former firm that had been outlawed. Then he drilled some wells of his own and got a nice little production. When the Bradford field was young, John McKeown went there and secured choice bits of territory. He became one of the largest individual producers of oil in the region. He was early on the ground at Washington, Pa., and secured the best looking territory there, paying $60,000 cash, with an eighth of the oil. The territory proved better than it looked. But throughout his career, Mr. McKeown had no more partners and he had no debts. When others sought to induce him to share with them in ventures, his invariable reply was: "John has no partners. John pays cash for what he gets." He never made any charges against the partner he had in the contracting business, but he formed no more alliances with anyone and he bought nothing that was not paid for on the spot. He had no account save at the bank. When seeking a purchase he often garbed himself in dingy, old clothes and looked the part of a poor man. It is related of him that he went to Baltimore once to buy some real estate at a public sale, as an investment for idle capital. On the appointed day he rubbed elbows with elegant gentlemen, dressed in his oldest clothes. Nobody paid much attention to him until the bidding became spirited, represented six figures and was going upward $10,000 on each bid. The man in the old clothes was the most persistent bidder and a rival admonished him to be careful not to go too deep. "John pays cash for what he gets," was the reply. But the auctioneer became uneasy and requested information concerning the bidder's financial ability. "Telephone the ———— Bank; my name's John McKeown," was the terse answer. The auctioneer telephoned to know if McKeown's check was good for $200,000. The bank promptly replied, "It's good for a million," and the sale went on. Mr. McKeown bought the property and it was a bargain. He paid "cash for what he got."

John Benninghoff owned a farm along Oil Creek, mostly hill land, but it was the scene of very active operations from 1863 to 1869. During these years the farm produced about one million barrels of oil and the average price was four dollars a barrel. The leases were not uniform, but the average royalty was slightly more than one-fourth. The failure of the Culver, Penn & Co. banks in 1866, resulted in pulling down the bank at Petroleum Center. Benninghoff was a loser to the extent of some thousands of dollars, so he purchased a safe and kept his money in his house. On the night of January 16, 1868, a party of masked burglars entered the Benninghoff home, bound, gagged and maltreated the members of the family, and made off with the contents of the safe, variously estimated at from $200,000 to $500,000. The amount has never been officially proclaimed, but quite reliable private information is to the effect that the loot consisted of slightly more than $200,000 cash, $60,000 in Government bonds and approximately $30,000 of other securities, some not convertible. The robbery was the greatest ever perpetrated in the oil region and created a sensation. Rewards of $30,000 were offered for the arrest and conviction of the perpetrators. Thus stimulated the chase was a hot one. Detectives were not long in learning that the robbery had been planned by James Saeger, of Saegertown, Pennsylvania, an educated man who had descended from affluence to bankruptcy, and his accomplices were Eastern criminals employed for the purpose. These latter were apprehended and convicted, but Saeger disappeared, leaving no trail. It was not until 1874 that he was apprehended in Denver, Colorado, where he was arrested by local detectives, who thought the big reward was still in force. Capt. M. R. Rouse, chief of police at Titusville, was notified of the Saeger arrest and communicated with the Benninghoff family, then removed to a farm in Mercer County Pennsylvania. Capt. Rouse obtained a requisition from Governor John F. Hartranft and

NOTED OIL COMPANY OFFICE AT RED HOT.

Secretary of the Commonwealh Matthew Stanley Quay, and went to Denver. Later, Joseph Benninghoff, the eldest son of John, also went to Denver. The Denver authorities cooled perceptibly when they learned that all rewards had been withdrawn, but offered to deliver the prisoner in Venango County, Pennsylvania, for $2,000. Some days afterward they offered a settlement on behalf of Saeger, and after some persuasion, Benninghoff accepted it. The sum paid was small. Saeger was liberated and allowed to return to his ranch. Such is the testimony of Capt

Rouse, though many sensational and false stories were published asserting that Saeger was left in Denver because his hundred cowboys threatened vengeance. No Saeger cowpuncher was in Denver during the detention of that gentleman in the Arapahoe County jail.

C. V. Culver, mentioned in the foregoing item, was one of the most brilliant and talented men attracted by the early oil development. But he lacked caution. He plunged into the business, at first with great success, but his forward vision outran his judgment. The firm of Culver, Penn & Co. established a chain of State banks, the chief of them being in Oil City and Franklin, and, as was the custom of the time, issued circulating notes. Culver promoted the Reno Oil Company and then the Reno & Pithole Railroad, commonly known as the Pithole Road, with Gen. A. E. Burnside as chief engineer. In the meantime Culver had been elected to Congress and was quite the foremost citizen of the oil region. The crash came in 1866. The chain of banks went down, the wonderful railroad was never completed, but the Farmers Railroad operated the portion from Rouseville to Plumer for several years. Culver rallied and became an active man of affairs afterward, but was regarded as a visionary and was never again a leader. About a year before his death, in 1908, Mr. Culver told me in the new Capitol at Harrisburg, an incident of the boom times. The Senate wing of the new Capitol covers the site of the old State Treasury building, a brick edifice with brick floors. In 1865 Mr. Culver visited there for the purpose of depositing nearly a quarter of a million dollars worth of securities as a basis for new circulating notes of his banks. He found the only depository an old fashioned safe, locked with a key, and declined to entrust his securities to it. He went to Philadelphia, purchased a "burglar proof" safe, with combination lock, shipped it to the State Treasury, and later deposited his securities therein. That was the first modern safe owned by the State, and Mr. Culver waited two or three years before the Legislature made an appropriation to reimburse him for his outlay.

William H. Abbott, the first man to bring and invest outside capital in the oil region, after the Drake well was completed, also met with reverses in business and died poor. He arrived on Oil Creek in February, 1860, and paid William Barnsdall $10,000 for one-half of a quarter interest in the first well drilled in the region, after the Drake well began producing oil. From that time until 1877, Abbott was a conspicuous figure in the development of the petroleum industry. He was largely interested in the shipment of oil, and was one of the owners of a system of pipe lines that transported the greater bulk of crude petroleum from the wells in the Oil Creek and Upper Allegheny River region. During the best years of his business career, he bought large quantities of oil up and down Oil Creek. At one period in those transactions, no certificates of account were passed. The simple "promise" to pay was as sacredly kept by those parties to the deal as though they had been sealed under bond. On one occasion Mr. Abbott bought 10,000 barrels of oil at $4.00 a barrel, while sitting upon his horse midway in Oil Creek below Tarr Farm. This purchase was made by word of mouth and the contract was carefully liquidated. He also helped build the first oil refinery in the Oil Creek region. This structure was located on the Parker farm, a short distance below Titusville. It was built in 1860. Mr. Abbott also helped found a bank in Titus-

LOADING CASE OIL ON CAMELS IN EGYPT.

ville. While he was at the zenith of his business success, he helped others accumulate fortunes, yet, when he died, every dollar that he possessed had gone to the bankrupt's account. He was a good man in the community where he lived, and the maelstrom of business failure, which overtook him, was deeply regretted by all who knew him. It was with Mr. Abbott that John D. Archbold started in the business and but for the latter Mr. Abbott might have ended his days in extreme poverty.

Henry Harley was still another of the early oil region oil men, who became a leading factor in the transportation of petroleum from the wells to market. In 1866, he built a pipe line from the Benninghoff Run oil field to Shaffer, and from that time until the failure of the Pennsylvania Transportation Company in 1877, he moved upon the high crest of business success. In the early days he joined his Benninghoff pipe line with William H. Abbott's, which conveyed oil from Pithole to Miller Farm, and together they laid the foundation of the Pennsylvania Transportation Company. But the exhausting of the oil wells in the Oil Creek region, and the discovery of richer fields in the lower Allegheny River district, brought disaster to the transportation company, and Harley died poor.

Among the men of inventive talent who early became residents of the petroleum producing country, was Peter C. Heinz. His former place of abode was Buffalo, N. Y., whence he went to Pioneer, Pa., in April, 1863. He first found employment in the oil region as a master mechanic of oil well machinery belonging to the Hibbard Oil Company, then located on the Upper McElheny or Funk farm, upon which was built the village of Funkville. In the following September Mr. Heinz left the Hibbard company, and, joining partnership with Mark Sanborn, established a machine shop at Pioneer. A year later he purchased the interest owned by Sanborn and assumed full proprietorship of the business. He was a very useful man to the oil producers of those days. He mended their engines, drilling tools, boilers, cut and fitted pipe, and did many other useful things about oil wells. On one occasion he prevented a great conflagration on Pioneer Run. The moment he saw the fire start among the wells, and the oil on fire began running down stream, he, with the help of others, who were near by, began to throw a dam across the waterway. Near the bottom of this dam he inserted four lines of four and five inch casing, and when the blazing mass came against the obstruction, the fire on top was stopped, while the oil poured through the pipes and was caught below. This act saved 12,000 barrels of oil in tanks near where the run joins the creek. In consideration of this prompt act, one owner of the oil gave him $25. Mr. Heinz was the first to pump water through a pipe to the top of the hill at Pioneer. He did the work with a force pump which he bought from Samuel Van Syckel, who laid the pipe line from Pithole to Miller Farm. Mr. Heinz was also the first to put a rotary pump on a well in the region, for the purpose of increasing the oil and gas flow. This experiment was tried at the Dean well on Pioneer Run. He invented the first "water packer," used on casing, for shutting off the surface water in wells, and introduced it in the latter part of 1867 and early months of 1868. Later he invented a hydraulic steam gauge, which is a useful device. All old time oil drillers remember the sand pump invented by Bernard Morahan. The first one of these pumps was made by Mr. Heinz, in his shop at Pioneer. He also made the first Luther patent tool fishing socket, and the first Innis patented sucker-rod joints. From 1880 until August, 1891, he was master mechanic of the Tide-Water Pipe Company. He then accepted the position of master mechanic of the United States Pipe Line Company. He died at Bradford, Pa., about 1901.

Another of the useful men in the early days of the Oil Creek oil region was J. H. Luther, who had his machine shop, blacksmith shop, and residence at Funkville, which lay on the east side of the creek from Pioneer, and half a mile above Petroleum Center. He was the first man to devote his entire energy to fishing and removing drilling tools from wells where such things had become lost, broken or stuck. He also was the inventor of the first slip-socket for catching hold and jarring loose stuck tools in drilling wells. Along with this patented affair, which was known as the "Luther Socket," he designed a number of other useful devices for taking lost things out of oil wells. These were rope-knives, rope-sockets, horn sockets, grab sockets, and spears. In fact everything to clear wells from obstructions were in Mr. Luther's possession. If anything happened about a drilling well, in those early days, that could not be remedied by the drillers, Luther was sent for, and his knowledge was relied on. Sometimes he failed, but more often he succeeded in overcoming the difficulty, and work proceeded. Of course, since Luther's day, many improvements in well fishing tools have been made, yet the mechanical principle, upon which he labored, has been followed by all later inventors. In 1869-'70, James Hardison, then of Shamburg, began fishing with pole tools. He, however, used the Luther devices to accomplish the ends of extracting stuck and lost tools in wells. Hardison went to the California oil fields, and, from there to seek gold in an old Peruvian Inca mine in South America. Sometime later he returned East, and was engaged in developing oil interests in the Indiana field. Mr. Luther moved away from Funkville to the Bradford region about 1876, and died in Olean, N. Y. He was a genius worthy of memory in connection with the history of petroleum.

CHAPTER XXI.

RANDOM INCIDENTS OF INTEREST.

Without overdrawing the tale of history, tragedy, comedy and melodrama have been enacted in the oil fields of America. They have mingled, sometimes, in inextricable confusion, making a panorama of life unlike that of any other section and of infiinite variety of coloring. When Edwin L. Drake made his appearance in Titusville to drill for oil, he was quite generally shunned; by some as a visionary fanatic and by others as an adventurer not to be trusted. During his discouraging struggle to get the first well down none but R. D. Fletcher and Peter Wilson were really friendly and helpful. Without their aid it is doubtful if the project could have been carried through. But when he achieved success there were many to take advantage of his discovery. Drake, himself, profited little. As a justice of the peace and land agent he accumulated a few thousand dollars which he lost in speculation in New York a few years afterward. He was reduced to the direst poverty by illness in 1869 when his condition was accidentally discovered by Zebulon Martin, of Titusville, on a visit to New York. Mr. Martin gave him sufficient to relieve the immediate stress, and, returning home, called a public meeting to devise ways and means. As a result a fund of $4,833.50 was immediately subscribed by the oilmen of the region. Henry H. Rogers, of New York, contributed secretly to the maintenance of the family. In 1873, the Pennsylvania Legislature granted an annuity of $1,500 and as Mr. Rogers continued his giving, the discoverer of oil by drilling for it, passed the remainder of his days in financial security, dying on November 8, 1880.

David Yanney erected the first big steam boiler in the oil regions, and pumped wells at long distances, by means of pipes, through which steam was conveyed to engines that propelled walking-beams. The introduction of this economical change in the manner of pumping wells, was brought into practice in the summer of 1869. Although previously there had been a few instances where two engines had been supplied with steam from one boiler, yet the experiment of pumping six wells with one boiler had never been tried. Yanney was one of the pioneer operators at Petroleum Center. He made considerable money, but frequent losses in small wells, diminished his "pile," and he died comparatively poor, in Rochester, N. Y.

In 1866, they had a banking house at Petroleum Center. It was owned by A. D. Cotton & Co. Shortly after the failure of Culver, Penn & Co., which occurred March 27, 1866, the Cotton bank closed its doors. The afternoon on which this event took place, a man, by the name of Bernard Hughes, a Rochester, N. Y., citizen, was in the bank talking to the cashier. He had just deposited a draft for five thousand dollars. He was not aware that the bank was in financial trouble. Suddenly, an individual, who had a deposit in the bank, rushed in, revolver in hand, and demanded his money.

Pointing the weapon at Mr. Cotton, he exclaimed that he would shoot if the cash was not forthwith paid over. Mr. Hughes, observing the critical predicament of the banker, resolutely grabbed the intruder with the "gun," and hustled him into the street. The action was so quickly executed that the fellow with the revolver forgot all about using it. Mr. Hughes then turned and induced the cashier to disgorge $5,000, the amount called for by the draft, which he had deposited only a few minutes previously. He got his money and the bank passed out of existence. On the same afternoon that the Cotton bank failed, the telegraph operator at Petroleum Center played a winning deal. He received the dispatch ordering the bank to suspend business. Turning to the telegraph company's account with the bank, he made out the bill, presented it, got his money, then handed the cashier the telegram containing the order to close the bank.

The first oil exchange, or place for buying and selling crude petroleum, other than at the wells, was in a car set apart on the Farmers' Railroad, which ran between Oil City and Petroleum Center. This was in the year 1867. The railroad company attached a car to its trains, which was exclusively occupied by oil men going up or down the creek. Here, while the train rattled along over its new and rough roadbed, the oil producers busily engaged in disposing of their oil to buyers, who represented refining and speculating firms at a distance—Pittsburg, Cleveland, Philadelphia, New York and Boston. This mode of buying and selling oil continued for several years on the Oil Creek road. It was not eliminated even after the founding of the first oil exchange in Oil City, December, 1869. In those transactions there were no governing rules or certificates of sale. The word of a man was considered as binding, and the contracts were as faithfully carried out as though there were three witnesses called and a bond signed.

The story of William H. Reed is one of the most remarkable. He had been a young man of inventive turn in Pittsburg prior to Drake's discovery. He was early in the oil region and followed its fortunes with varying success. He drilled a dry hole in the corner of the Rynd farm, on Cherry Run in 1863. The following year a small well was opened down the run. Reed located a second well five rods from the first, and took as partners Robert Criswell, who owned three acres adjoining, and Frazier, of Pithole fame. The well came in at three hundred barrels a day. Reed sold his interest for $200,000 after he had taken a small fortune from the oil. Frazier drifted into the wilderness about six miles, organized the United States Oil Company, and discovered Pithole. Criswell was one of the best known oil producers in the region. Reed, however, had devised an instrument that was said by his friends to be sensitive to the presence of gold at several hundred feet. He went East and began cruising along the coast, principally about Long Island, supposed to be searching for lost treasure. One day he went out in a small dory, a gale came up and Reed was seen no more. He was an odd genius. A former Pittsburg friend says that when the latter came to the oil country after the close of the war, Reed studiously avoided him and gave no sign of recognition, why he never knew.

Many wells were located in the early days with the aid of the "divining rod," and the time-honored witch hazel twig. Some were located by the spirits of the departed. The most notable instance of "spiritism" was the location of the Harmonial well, near Pleasantville, by Abram James, a devout believer. He was driving from Pithole to Titusville with two friends when the "manifestation" was made. At a point about a mile from Pleasantville Mr. James leaped from the carriage and ran to a corner of a field on the Porter farm, where he fell in a sort of convulsion. He told his friends he had been told there were rivers of oil under the spot, which he marked. His companions were not impressed and hurried him back to the carriage, which proceeded on its way. Mr. James, however, had faith. He borrowed money and drilled a well on the indicated spot. It came in on February 12, 1868, at 130 barrels a day, and the Pleasantville pool followed. Later Mr. James located a well for Jonathan Watson, near Titusville, which was drilled to a record depth for that time without finding oil or gas. In fact the absence of promising sands in its 2,800 feet of hole discouraged prospecting to the north and west from that point.

One of the things that will never be forgotten by those who witnessed it, was the towing of oil barges prior to the introduction of pipe lines. The

STRANDED BARGE AND DEAD
HORSE ON OIL CREEK.

OIL CREEK AT LOW WATER AND
PITHOLE RAILROAD BRIDGE.

means of transportation were by wagon and by boat. The latter were run on Oil Creek and the Allegheny River. They were floated down the Creek by means of natural and pond freshets. They were towed up again by horses. At Tidioute boats were towed in shallow water in the river. The horses towing boats were not driven on a path alongside, as in the case of canal boats, but waded the stream. The cruelty of this traffic was awful but necessity knows no law. Frequently the poor animals, cut and bruised about the legs by sharp stones or thin ice, lay down and gave up the ghost in transit. More frequently they survived to get to the stable. In either case not much sympathy or ceremony was wasted on them. They were permitted to lie where they fell or were carted to some convenient resting place as near as possible. The result of this and other unsanitary practices caused an epidemic of typhoid and other maladies in Oil City and a sanitary brigade had to be formed to cremate carcasses. It also compelled a general cleaning of premises. Like other volunteer vigilance committees, this one was not gentle in enforcing its mandates, but it was energetic and put an end, once for all, to that sort of unsanitary practice. In winter the thin ice cut the horses horribly. It was not uncommon either between Tidioute and Irvineton, or along Oil Creek to see the water run red with their blood. Pipe lines were not only an economy and convenience, but they put an end to the most inhuman practices known in the history of oil. It was not because the drivers desired to be cruel, but because there was no choice in face of the demand for transport and speed. The cruelty was an incident, as the killing is in war, to greater things.

Samuel S. Fertig, one among the many pioneer oil well drillers of the Oil Creek region, helped develop some of the greater fields of the famous valley. In January, 1862, he began work on the Sherman Flats, seven miles below Titusville. Some of his first experience was with the "spring pole," known, in those early days, as the "Hickory or Hemlock Engine." This name was given the apparatus because the pole used was a small hickory or hemlock tree. He drilled the Sherman well, 1,000 barrels, on the Sherman Flats, in 1862, and the Caldwell well, 800 barrels, and Noble and Delamater well, Farel farm, 3,000 barrels, directly opposite, on the east side of Oil Creek, in 1863. In the beginning of his oil days, Mr. Fertig always took an eighth working interest in the well he drilled, and, in many instances, he was lucky in striking thousand barrel gushers. The great era of speculation in oil well shares, oil stocks and oil companies, took its rise in 1863, culminating two years later in the burst of the bubble.

One day, in the summer of 1863, a party of men, representing themselves as a Boston company, met Mr. Fertig on the street in Titusville, and said they desired to buy some oil production. They asked Mr. Fertig if he had any to sell. He answered, "Yes, an eighth in a well on the Story farm, which is producing." Asked how much he would take for it, he replied that he would sell the eighth for $16,000. The Boston parties said they would take it. Mr. Fertig then went to his office, in a building near the corner of Spring and Franklin Streets, and there wrote a bill of sale, using language something similar to the following:

"For, and in consideration of $16,000, in hand paid, I, the undersigned, do hereby sell to said Boston Oil Company, one-eighth interest in Well No. ——, Story, or Columbia farm, subject to the provisions of the lease governing operations at the well."

Having completed the bill of sale he went to the hotel where the parties had headquarters, and said:

"Gentlemen, here is your bill of sale."

They read the document over, then remarked:

"Our lawyer, here, has drawn a contract, which we desire you to sign."

Fertig, not being a lawyer, and not familiar with long drawn out Massachusetts legal documents, after listening to its reading, decided that the expressed terms of the agreement were so complicated and wordy in language, he could not sign it. So, having announced his decision, he, at the same time, presented his paper to the spokesman of the party, saying:

"This is my contract, or bill of sale. This is our way of transferring oil property here in the oil region. We have no other legal form. Do you want the well down at Story farm? If so, sign the agreement which I now present."

"No," they replied, "we do not want it."

"Very well," responded the oil man.

Going out upon the street, a stranger accosted him with the remark:

"Mr. Fertig, I am directed to see you on a matter of business. Have you any oil production that you will sell?"

"Yes," replied Mr. Fertig, "I have an eighth in a producing well on the Story farm."

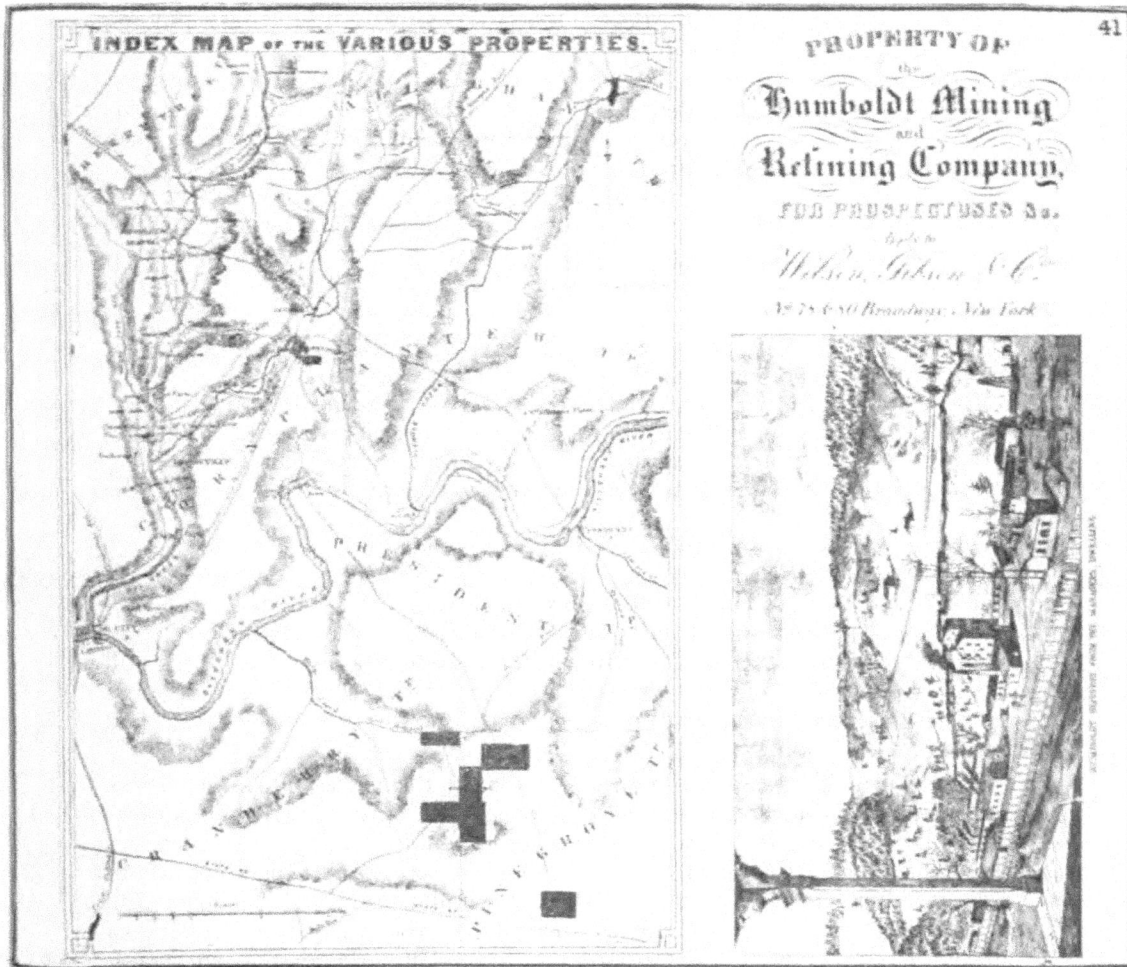

PROSPECTUS OF THE HUMBOLDT MINING AND REFINING COMPANY.

"How much do you want for it?" inquired the stranger.

"Twenty thousand dollars," said Fertig.

"I'll take it," was the quick response.

In not to exceed twenty minutes Fertig had a certified bank check for $20,000, and the purchaser of the well interest had the identical piece of paper, excepting the change of the name of buyer, that had been offered to the Boston company. Soon after consummating the deal with the stranger, Fertig met the spokesman of the Boston party, who said:

"Guess we will take that oil interest. After consultation, our party arrived at the conclusion that it would be the best move we could make."

"You can't have it now," replied Fertig. "I have just sold it for $20,000."

"But, Mr. Fertig, we want that interest," continued the Boston man. "Wonder if we can get it—buy it—from the man to whom you sold?"

"I do not know," said Fertig. "Perhaps you can. If I can find the party, I will see what can be done."

In the course of an hour, he met the man who had bought the interest. He seemed to be laboring under a heavy load of disappointment. This was manifest both in look of countenance and tone of voice. As soon as they began conversation, the man said:

"Mr. Fertig, I wish you would take that paper back! I will give you $1,000 if you will relieve me from a loss which I can ill afford at present. The party for whom I bought the interest refuses to take it off my hands."

"I don't know," replied Fertig, "what I can do. I'll see if I can help you."

Leaving the disappointed man in the street, Fertig went in search of the Boston party, whom he found at the hotel.

"I can secure, for you, that interest on the Story farm, if you want it," said Mr. Fertig, accosting his man. "The party to whom I sold is willing to part with the holding, providing there is a profit in the deal for him."

"How much does the gentleman want for the property?" queried the Boston party.

"Twenty-one thousand dollars," replied Fertig.

"We will take it," was the prompt answer.

In less than thirty minutes this last deal was consummated. During that short item of time, the property was transferred to the Boston Oil Company, Fertig paid $21,000, and the first purchaser had received back his full $20,000. The series of transactions had consumed less than three hours time. There were many other and larger deals put through in less time and with no more ceremony.

There were, thieves in those days. Toward the close of March, 1866, it was discovered that some scamps had stolen the entire drilling apparatus from the Burtis well, on Dawson Run, near Pithole. They had taken engine, tools, tubing, engine house, derrick, sampson post, and everything about the premises but the hole in the ground. A similar raid was made on Oil Creek at about the same time, but a quick alarm resulted in the recovery of the property, en route to the railroad at Union City. The innocent teamsters were turned back with their loads, but the rascals who had employed them were not caught.

In 1866, Oil City was the scene of a lively railroad riot. It occurred during the building of the Oil City & Pithole road. The Warren & Franklin Company was also projecting a road, from Irvineton to Oil City, covering along the river the route occupied by the Pithole grade. When, within the bounds of Oil City, the Warren & Franklin Company attempted to cover up the track of the Oil City & Pithole road as fast as the obstruction could be cleared away. Finally, Jacob Shirk, a director of the Pithole line, placed his foot upon a tie which one of the Warren workmen tried to pull off his roadbed. At the sametime Shirk drew a revolver. This action still further aroused the wrath of the opposing crew, and the whole gang made a rush at Shirk. One, White, the leader in the disturbance, led the crowd, shouting, "Kill him!" The assaulting aggregation was so great that Shirk was compelled to run to save his life. He sought refuge in his own residence. Previous to this outbreak, the man White had entered into a controversy with the burgess of the town, and had used insulting language, defying arrest. Upon getting tidings of the riot, the burgess, having an understand-

DELIVERING AMERICAN PETROLEUM TO CONSUMERS IN PARIS.

ing with the citizens of the town and the police, rang the police bell, calling them to assemble to quiet the disturbance. They went to the protection of Shirk, dispersing the mob. The burgess then issued a warrant for the arrest of White, whom he lodged in the lockup, and, later, sent to jail at Franklin. The Oil City & Pithole Company continued work and completed the road to the end of the line. But a decison of the State Supreme Court, afterwards, took the road and roadbed away from the Oil City & Pithole Company and awarded it to the Warren & Franklin Company. This decision was made because it was claimed that the Oil City & Pithole road had no legal right to occupy the route along which it was built. Its charter right was derived from an old Act of the Legislature, designated as the "Clarion

County Railroad Charter," granting privilege to build roads not to exceed twenty miles in length. This was not the famous Reno & Pithole railroad that went over the hills and up Cherry Run to the famous city.

Of the many who made great fortunes from oil in the early days, only a few retained their winnings. The majority let the money go as easily as it came, and some were extremely careless with it.

The Jack Brown & Ring well, at Shamburg, was struck November, 1867. It flowed 300 barrels a day and was the great leader that opened up the prolific Shamburg field. In the following year oil sold for from $3 to $5 a barrel. This well alone yielded fortunes to its owners. At the time the well was making its best production, Brown had a small shanty near the well, where he slept. As he was without a safe in which to keep his money he stored it in the loft of his shanty. In those days many oil buyers carried currency with them to pay for what petroleum they purchased. As fast as the money was received Brown pushed a board aside in the loft of his shanty and tossed up the packages of "greenbacks." He then replaced the board and proceeded to attend to affairs about the well. This carelessness went on until one day he had the sum of $40,000 lying loosely strewn about that shanty loft. Ring, the partner of Brown, spent his fortune and died in Denver, Colorado, while the last known of Jack Brown, it was said he was in the Far West running a threshing machine in wheat fields. William G. Fee struck the Fee flowing well, located but a few rods from the Jack Brown & Ring well, at Shamburg, January 1, 1868. The well flowed nearly 400 barrels a day. Later—in the early summer following—another newly drilled well, on the same lease, flowed a thousand barrels. Fortune by thousands of dollars a day, rolled under his grasp. The lucky owner was in high feather. He seemed to labor under the impression that there would be no end to his income. But the time came. His wells dried up, he moved on with the tide of oil men to newer fields. His fortune dwindled away and he finally became poor.

Many things, which did not occur in the early days of oil in the Oil Creek region, have crept into history branded as truth. One of these is the story that a well in the Pithole region, owned by J. Wilkes Booth, the assassin of President Lincoln, was struck by lightning on the night of April 14, 1865. It is a pretty tale, but it is not true.

J. Wilkes Booth did appear in the oil region in 1864, and become interested in some oil well property. His first ventures, it is related, were in the vicinity of Franklin, where he resided for several months, on the Allegheny River. The wells there drilled, although small in production, were profitable investments. When prospecting for oil began on Pithole Creek, in the latter part of 1864, or, rather, the location of leases, Booth became a partner in a piece of land on the Morey farm. This farm adjoined what afterwards became the celebrated Holmden farm, and proved to be one of the richer oil properties in the Pithole region. The first well in that vicinity, struck January 8, 1865, on the Thomas Holmden farm, was the "Frazier," owned by the United States Petroleum Company. The next wells to produce oil in that locality were the Twin wells, Nos. 1 and 2, completed on the 16th and 19th of June, following the "Frazier." Hence there was no well on the Booth lease on April 14th, date of the tragedy at Washington. However, a well was commenced on the lease in which Booth once held an interest, but it was never finished. A set of tools were lost in it, while drilling, and it was impossible to get them out. But another well was drilled near by, on the same lease, which proved a good producer. In the estimation of those people who were not acquainted with the facts in the matter it, without question, was this latter well that became connected with the Booth legend, but it was not there in April, 1865. The well or wells, whatever number were on the lease, were either owned, or else under control of one Mr. Hooper, whose home was in Erie City, Pa. During his absence William Harmon, a pumper, had charge of the wells, and he was familiar with all the changes upon the Booth lease. No well had been completed on that piece of ground until long after April 14th, 1865, and the death of Booth, as well as his victim.

In the early days of Pithole there was a movement for intellectual culture and amusement. A lecture course was decided on and the first selection was A. M. Griswold, known as the "Fat Contributor," and "Hunkidori." He was sent an offer and in due time he came. The sun obscured itself behind the Western hills—the evening set in. The hall or room in which he was to speak, was a hastily improvised affair—not yet finished by the carpenters. The seats were planks laid upon blocks, and the platform, upon which the orator was to stand, was likewise a hastily constructed affair. However, the place was packed with auditors. At the proper moment the speaker appeared and announced that his subject would be the "American Indian." Then he launched into the subject, filling every sentence with the keenest kind of humor. Of course the audience traversed the ground of his lecture with him, enjoying the satire in the happiest of moods. At short intervals, roars of laughter and loud applause echoed from the hall. It was an occasion to be remembered. At length the entertainer closed his address with words extolling the beauty of the town, the magnificence of her oil wells, and thanking the audience for the generous welcome extended him by Pitholeans in general. The people departed, and when Griswold went to look for his hat it was gone. The "Forty Thieves" were about. One of them had purloined the headgear, and it could not be found. The loss of the hat was no sooner discovered than somebody reported that the doorkeeper had decamped from the town, carrying away the receipts of the evening, amounting to several hundred dollars. The lecturer was indeed in a sore plight. Hat gone, and he had incurred an expense of $8. What further added to his embarrassment he had not a cent to settle the bill. At this moment of Griswold's unhappy state of mind, he was surrounded by a number of the committee, who had arranged the lecture, and for two days and nights he was kept in such a state of hilarity that his troubles were forgotten. At last his hat was found and returned. Then, in a sly manner, a great roll of "greenbacks" were slipped into his pocket. All the bills were settled by the committee and the famous "Fat Contributor" departed carrying away $250, the proceeds of the lecture. He never forgot Pithole City while he lived.

Patrick Tiernan was one who caught that "tide in the affairs of men, that, taken at its flood, leads on to fortune and to fame." He was a figure of some prominence in the second decade of the oil industry. His greatest triumph was in the "foreign refined corner," manipulated in Europe in 1876. The break that followed carried down George V. Forman and Major Henry Wetter, the latter being at that time the largest individual producer of petroleum in the world. Forman recouped his fortunes, but Major Wetter never did. Tiernan fell into dissolute and shiftless ways, became a "hanger on" around the Oil City Oil Exchange, and died about the middle of the eighties in extreme poverty. His story is one of the tragedies of the petroleum era. The reverse of this picture is the story of "Spotty" McBride, of Butler. For years he worked in the oil country, sometimes on the verge of poverty, taking interests in wells that always came in dry. He helped pay for nine of these in succession. Then in 1905 he leased a farm about a mile out of Butler in what was supposed to be dry territory. He succeeded in selling several interests to friends and got a well down to the fourth sand. It came in at 2,000 barrels a day. McBride sold his interest for a quarter of a million dollars. The company that bought him out and others drilled all around that well, but no more gushers were obtained. It was a one well pool, but a fortune for the plucky and lucky McBride.

Among the men, during the first two years—1860-1861—of wonderful discoveries of petroleum in the valley of Oil Creek, who amassed large wealth, was N. S. Woodford. In his early life he was a resident of East Randolph, N. Y., where he followed the pursuit of blacksmith. But sometime before the Drake well was drilled he removed to the borough of Titusville, where he became proprietor of the Eagle Hotel, and also opened and carried on the business of blacksmithing. In the summer of 1861 he became interested in an oil lease on the Tarr farm, and in December of that year, struck the Woodford well, which flowed 3,000 barrels of oil a day. The Woodford divided honors with the Phillips well, No. 2, which came in September of that year, 4,000 barrels a day, and the Empire at 2,500 barrels. These wells were the wonders of the day of that age. The flats, between where they stood and the sweep of Oil Creek, were covered with tanks, barrels and oil, in pools, upon the ground. It was a season of very great waste of a valuable commodity. While at Tarr farm, Woodford owned an interest in the Eagle well, and also had interests in the Conewango and Ram Cat wells on the Columbia farm which lay opposite the Tarr farm on the west side of the creek. Woodford made a fortune from his oil wells, but, like many other pioneers in the business, his easily acquired wealth passed between his fingers, leaving hardly the semblance of a rub against them, and he became a poor man. Then he returned to his old trade—blacksmithing—in the City of Jamestown, N. Y. There he remained during the declining years of his life, and there he found rest in the tomb.

One of the greatest oil concerns of the earliest years was the Humboldt Mining and Refining Company. Its refinery was located on Cherry Run about three miles above the confluence of that stream and Oil Creek at Rouseville. Among those interested were J. Nelson Tappan, of New York, and J. N. Frazier, of Reed well fame on Cherry Run in 1864, and the organizer of the United States Petroleum Company, that opened the Pithole field. The Humboldt had some producing property, but its great achievement was the refinery near Plumer. The manager's dwelling still stands and is a fine residence. It and the other buildings were erected regardless of expense, some distance from any oil production and three miles from even the unreliable water transportation of Oil Creek pond freshets. The first ambitions attempt at pipe line building was by the Humboldt, which constructed a two-inch line from Tarr farm to the refinery at Plumer, a distance of two and a half miles across the hills. The Barrows refinery then had a gravity line, about 800 feet long, on the Tarr farm. The Humbodlt line was not a success as the pipe would not hold at the joints under pressure of the pumps. However, despite the handicap of hauling crude oil in barrels for miles, and transporting the refined product in the same way four miles to the Allegheny River and the same distance to the railroad on Oil Creek, the Humboldt achieved success. Its output exceeded 100,000 gallons a month in 1863 and was greater than that of all the refineries of Cleveland, Ohio, combined. In 1865, when the Pithole furore brought the ill-fated Reno & Pithole railroad into being, the road passed the Humboldt refinery and gave it an outlet by rail. After the collapse of Culver, Penn & Co. the Farmers Railroad on Oil Creek obtained possession of and operated that part of the Pithole road between Rouseville and Plumer, serving the Humboldt and a number of smaller refineries along Cherry Run. The Humboldt finally succumbed to circumstances. Its uneconomical location told against it when the export business developed sharp competition and transportation became a cost factor of vital importance. It went down along with its smaller competitors along the Cherry Run valley, but its magnificence will not be forgotten by those who knew it in its glory. The old barrel house was torn down by the farm owner only a couple of years ago.

Dr. A. M. Crawford, who, besides being a physician, was a furnace master operating a charcoal furnace near Emlenton, Venango County, was chosen by President Lincoln to be the American consular representative in the Netherlands. He was much interested in the new industry that had been founded in his home county before he started for his foreign post and by correspondence he kept in touch with it. In Belgium he told of the new discovery and some merchants became interested. As a result the first order for refined petroleum to be exported was sent from Antwerp in October, 1861. That city became a great port of entry for American petroleum and is yet quoted as one of the world's markets. Dr. Crawford after his return home, had the pleasure of having an oil development on his furnace tract, in the southern end of Venango County, and so profited from the industry to which he rendered so great a service as to start its export trade. He lived the life of a cultured gentleman, at the site of the old furnace, a mile or so from the railroad and the village of Emlenton, until near the close of the Nineteenth Century.

CHAPTER XXII.

MEMORIALS PAST AND FUTURE.

On October 4, 1901, a beautiful memorial to Edwin Laurentine Drake was unveiled by the school children of Titusville, in Woodlawn Cemetery, of that city. There were present on that occasion men from all parts of the country, many of whom had traveled hundreds of miles to witness the ceremony. Mrs. Edwin L. Drake, widow of the discoverer of oil, was the guest of the city of Titusville to see the honor paid to the husband whom she supported in the poverty following his reverses of fortune and illness. But the donor of the monument was not there and his name was not disclosed to any. Mr. C. N. Payne, who acted for the donor in presenting the memorial to the city, simply announced that the giver was a gentleman who had arrived in Titusville by stage coach from Union City, precisely forty years previous to that day, who had ever since been identified with the petroleum industry, that he had also provided a trust fund of which the income would be paid annually for the care of the ground and the monument, a grateful remembrance from a great man. A blank on the last marble panel was left on which to engrave the name of the donor after his death. Those who now visit Woodlawn Cemetery will find graven there the name of Henry Huttleston Rogers.

The completed inscription upon the monument reads as follows:

Col. E. L. Drake, born at Greenville, N. Y., March 29,
MDCCCXIX; died at Bethlehem, Pa., Nov. 8,
MDCCCLXXX. Founder of the petro-
leum industry. Friend of man.

Called by circumstances to the solution of
A great mining problem.
He triumphantly vindicated American skill and
Near this spot laid the Founda-
tion of an industry

That has enriched the State,
Benefited mankind,
Stimulated the mechanic arts,
Enlarged the pharmacopia
And has attained world-wide proportions.

He sought for himself
Not wealth nor social distinction,
Content to let others follow where he led,
At the threshold of his fame he retired,
To end his days in quieter pursuits.

His highest ambition
The successful accomplishment of his task,
His noble victory the conquest of the rock,
Bequeathing to posterity the fruits of
His labor and his industry.

His last days oppressed by ills—
To want no stranger—
He died in comparative obscurity.
This monument is erected by
Henry Huttleston Rogers,
In grateful recognition and remembrance.

The Drake monument itself is a splendid work of art, allegorical in character, typifying the idea of primitive man wresting from the earth her secrets and gifts with all the energy, determination and vigor possible in a

AT THE MOMENT OF UNVEILING THE DRAKE MEMORIAL IN WOODLAWN CEMETERY.

representation of labor. It represents the principal characteristics which Colonel Drake exhibited in life—genius, power and skill. The selection of a proper design for the work was left in the hands of Architect Charles Brigham, of Boston.

The type of the monument is that of the "Exedra," so frequently found in Green and Roman architecture. This, in its simplest form, consisted of a stone enclosure with seat rectangular or oval in shape with high back or walls which were placed by the roadside, generally in close proximity to some monument or tomb. Many of the highways leading from the great cities of Greece and Rome were lined on either side with tombs and monuments and interspersed among them were resting places of this character for the weary traveler, as well as the devout mourner. Sometimes the monuments themselves were combined with this particular type, and this had led to a style of treatment which has been handed down to modern times. Well known examples of this interesting class of ornamental work have been executed in recent years in New York City, for instance, the Hunt Memorial on Fifth Avenue and Central Park and the Farragut Memorial in Madison Square.

In this particular case the architect has conceived the idea of a grand central architectural feature, a monument in itself of large and dignified proportions. This frontispiece being of considerably greater altitude than the rest and containing the great bronze figure, dominates emphatically the remainder of the structure. It is a complete classic motive in itself, consisting of Greek Ionic columns surmounted by a harmonious entablature and pediment with severely simple, but elegant decorations.

SCENE ON OIL CREEK WHERE DRAKE WELL WAS DRILLED.

Between the columns and forming the central figure, is a deeply recessed niche in which, upon an oval pedestal, stands an heroic allegorical figure in bronze, the focus of the entire design.

Upon the frieze of the entablature are engraved in simple letters, "DRAKE."

This monumental feature is flanked on either side by the exedra proper, that is, massive curved seats in stone with very high back surmounted by a balustrade perforated in Greek ornamentation and terminated at either end by piers on which have been sculptured in bas relief two allegorical figures. The pedestal and seats of the exedra are raised upon a broad granite platform, four steps in height, curved to graceful lines in the center, and the pedestal itself raised still futher by two more steps so that from any point of view in front the complete detail of all parts of the structure can readily be seen.

The total length of the monument is about 36 feet over all and the depth, 20 feet. The central figure is about 10 feet wide and 19 feet in height and the walls of the exedra and stelae at either end are about 10 feet in height.

It was only natural that the architect should seek to have allied with him the very best talent in the treatment of the sculptural work which has always been an important part of the conception of this memorial and in order to accomplish this end, with the consent of the then unknown donor of the monument, he instituted a friendly competition between two eminent sculptors, Mr. Charles Henry Niehaus and M. J. Massey Rhind, of New York, the result being the selection of the design of Mr. Niehaus for a central figure, as well as his suggestions for the bas reliefs upon the stelae at either end of the monument, which help so much to add dignity and balance to the whole.

Mr. Niehaus presented the idea of an athlete drilling the rock, which, to the eye of even the casual observer, is sure to typify energy, perseverance, power and which is so allegorically suggestive of the great event which this memorial seeks to perpetuate—the drilling of the first real oil well in the world.

This work, which is of heroic size, is executed in bronze and was the result of more than a year's constant thought and labor on the part of the sculptor.

HON. GEORGE S. CRISWELL.

The two figures on the piers at either end, representing grief and memory, have been sculptured in the solid stone from plaster models made by the artist, and are vigorous reproductions of the models.

Upon the platform at the time of the unveiling and dedication to the left of the speaker of the day were seated Mrs Colonel E. L. Drake and her friends, Mrs. Charles Kellogg, Mrs. Dr. George Moody and Mrs. R. D. Fletcher. Upon the right hand of the bronze statue were those who took an active part in the programme, Rev. Samuel Prather, pastor of the Titusville M. E. Church, who offered a suitable invocation. Hon. John Dalzell, of Pittsburg, the orator of the day, whose address, dealing as it does, with technical and historical subjects, ranks among the highest efforts of the kind, C. N. Payne, who represented Mr. Rogers, the then unknown donor of the memorial, R. D. Fletcher, perhaps Colonel Drake's most intimate friend at the time of the drilling of the Drake well, and who, as superintendent of the cemetery, presented to the City of Titusville the deed to the cemetery lot upon which the monument is located, Mayor J. J. McCrum, who, in behalf of the City of Titusville, accepted the deed and monument from Mr. Payne, and Hon. George S. Criswell, judge of the Court of Venango County, chairman of the exercises of the day. One of the most interesting things in connection with the dedication of the monument was the reading by Judge Criswell of a letter from Bishop Whitehead, of the Pittsburg Diocese of the Protestant Episcopal Church, expressing regret because of his inability to be present, owing to the fact that his duties required him to be in attendance upon the triennial convention of his denomination at San Francisco. Said Bishop Whitehead, writing of Colonel Drake:

"I have the record of well nigh fifty occasions when I administered to him holy communion in his sick chamber. In my mind his name was synonym for patience, resignation and trust in God, such as I have never seen excelled."

The inscription as it appears on the monument was adapted from a tablet prepared by Mr. P. C. Boyle, editor in chief of the Oil City Derrick, and selected by Mr. Rogers:

DRAKE.

Founder of the Oil Industry,
The Friend of Man.
History and Tradition are Explored in Vain For a
Parallel to His Genius.
In the Annals of Mining Discoveries He
Stands Alone.
A Leader in Industrial Invention His
Enterprise Knew no Bounds.
He United all the Qualities Necessary to Compel
Nature's Secrets and Drew from the Rock
"Rivers of Oil."
He Achieved for Himself Just Fame Without Added
Wealth or Reward.
Called by Circumstances to the Solution of a
Great Mining Problem
He Triumphantly Vindicated American Skill
And Near This Spot Laid the Foundation
Of an Industry that
Has Enriched the State,
Benefited Mankind,
Stimulated Mechanic Arts,
Enlarged the Pharmacopia
And Has Assumed World-Wide Proportions.
He Sought for Himself Not Wealth
Nor Social Distinction,
Content to Let Others Follow Where He Led.
At the Threshold of His Fame He Retired,
To End His Days in Quieter Pursuits.
A Spectacle so New and so Sublime
Was Contemplated with the
Profoundest Admiration.
And the name DRAKE
Adding New Lustre to American Achievement,
Resounded to the Remotest Regions
of the Earth.
His Highest Ambition
The Successful Accomplishment of his Task.
His Noblest Victory the Conquest of the
Rocks, Bequeathing to Posterity the
Fruits of His Labor and the
Results of His Ingenuity.
He Died as He Lived, in Obscurity.
His Last Days
Oppressed by Ills. To Want No Stranger.
This Monument is Erected
By
Henry Huttleston Rogers,
In Grateful Recognition of His Eminent
Services in Leading the Way to the
Economic Production of
PETROLEUM.
The World's Best and Cheapest Source of
LIGHT.

Another memorial has been proposed to commemorate the founding of the petroleum industry. It is to be erected upon the site of the Drake well, which, with five acres of ground, has been presented by Mrs. David Emery, of Titusville, to Canadohta Chapter, Daughters of the American Revolution, for that purpose. The ladies of the Chapter have been endeavoring for some time to raise a fund of $100,000 to build the monument,. and have secured more than one-tenth of the amount. It is a worthy project. This proposed Petroleum Memorial. designed by a well known architect of Boston. is officially described as follows:

"The monument is in the form of a monolithic Doric shaft bearing aloft a bronze lantern in the form of a globe. The shaft rests upon a single block of stone. upon the four faces of which are bas reliefs symbolical of the departments of human activity which have been most affected by the discovery of oil—heat. light, power and locomotion. The base rests upon a stylobate of three high steps. The stylobate is in the center of a paved area surrounded by a parapet having at the four corners salient masses, upon the outer surface of which are to be cut inscriptions telling of the history of the discovery of oil by Colonel Drake and of the evolution of the industry. The whole monument is to be raised upon a sodded plateau and is to be approached on all four sides by flights of thirteen steps.

"The dimensions of the monument are as follows: Plateau. 94 feet square; platform at parapet line, 52 feet square; diameter of shaft, 5 feet 6 inches; pedestal. 8 feet square: stylobate. 20 feet square; height of plateau. 8 feet; height of monument. 53 feet; total height of monument and plateau, 61 feet.

"The location of the old Drake well is on a sightly spot near the line of the Pennsylvania Railroad. so that the monument when completed can be viewed by all travelers between Pittsburg and Buffalo."

The memorial that I would like to see is a reproduction in imperishable material of the original Drake well and its buildings. the interior to be fitted as a library and museum and the top of the derrick bearing aloft a kerosene torch. which. hand in hand with Liberty. has been enlightening the world for more than half a century. There might be gathered the oils and sands of the many fields. the early tools used and many articles of interest that soon will otherwise perish and pass from the knowledge of men. There should be kept photographs of the characteristic scenes of the oil fields. the older views being already limited in number and hard to find. The history of the oil fields ought to be gathered in manuscripts. newspaper files. clippings—in whatever way the incidents can be found and preserved. The men who made history in the pioneer oil fields are rapidly passing to that bourne from which no traveler returns and unless the details of that time are soon gathered they will be beyond human ken. In another half century there will be few who will be familiar with the processes of to-day. But if a memorial in the form of a historical museum could be created and endowed the interesting record could be kept for future generations. It would become the mecca for petroleum pilgrims from every part of the earth, seeking information concerning the beginnings and progress of a tremendous industry. Only recently a gentleman from Japan called upon me to secure some information about oil in Pennsylvania. He had to have an interpreter along, for he spoke no English. He was a wealthy oil producer of Nippon who had come across seas to view the cradle of the industry in which he was so deeply interested. There was no place he could go to get the information he desired, save a busy newspaper office, where even courtesy is breathless and information is printed from day to day, not always with due regard for history. What a pleasure it would have been to that Japanese gentleman to have gone to a historical museum to see the relics of the olden time and the pictures of clustering derricks and tanks where there are none to be seen now. Truly this great industry that has done so much to make the world better and brighter is worthy of a memorial museum near the place where it was born. One hundred thousand might build it and provide an endowment sufficient to employ an intelligent caretaker.

CHAPTER XXIII.

SOME FACTS AND FIGURES.

During the past three years there has been a tremendous petroleum development in Mexico. The first successful concern in that Republic was the Mexican Petroleum Company, a California corporation. Its initial operations were at Ebano, where it found wells that produced as much as three thousand barrels daily. Following this success there sprang up a number of companies, notably the Oil Fields of Mexico Company, the Pennsylvania Oil Company, and the S. Pearsons Sons' Company. The first named developed a field at Furbero, the second started a well near Tampico, which was acquired by the Pearson concern just before completion. When brought in it "blew out," caught fire and terrorized the country. It probably produced more than a hundred thousand barrels a day of oil and the fire was absolutely beyond control. Not a barrel of the product was saved, the fire continued until the flow turned from oil to hot salt water, which continues at this writing. The Pearson Company established a refinery at Minatitlan and began a development in that region with indifferent success. Later it engaged in a war to control the market for refined oil and products in Mexico, converting its properties into the Mexican Aguila, or "Mexican Eagle" Oil Company. This company has found enormous crude production southwest of Tampico, having one well estimated to have made 100,000 barrels in a day.

Many other companies are now prospecting in the Mexican Gulf Coast region and the production is already more than the total consumption of that country. The oil is mainly of a low grade, on an asphalt base, but refiners have devised processes by which they extract a fair percentage of illuminating and lubricating oils, some gasoline and a good quality of paving asphaltum. For many years Mexico was a good market for American oil, despite a heavy duty on imports, but it now enters the list of petroleum exporting countries, with the United States as a probable market for a part of its surplus. Aside from the Pearson Company, the development is chiefly being made by American capital. The Mexican production already exceeds that of Canada, but the oil is not quite as good quality. Each of those two countries maintains a high tariff on petroleum, while the United States, by the action of the Sixty-first Congress, admits petroleum and its products absolutely free. Under these circumstances the Mexican oil industry is of peculiar interest to the oil producers of the United States. The total production of that country for 1910 was approximately 6,000,000 barrels.

There will be a good market in Mexico for fuel oil, as the coal of that country is inferior and the expense of importation is heavy. The residue, however, after taking off the gasoline and the best of the illuminating grade, will be better fuel than the crude. This will make the lighter derivatives practically by-products and all the more dangerous in competition in foreign markets. Several prominent and influential Mexican officials are connected with the Aguila Company.

In the United States the standard measure of crude oil is the barrel of forty-two gallons. In the early days of the industry there was controversy over the measure. This occurred when the production had increased so that sales in gallons were cumbersome. The barrel of forty-two gallons was adopted by mutual agreement. Refined oil is sold by the barrel and the standard is fifty gallons. When barrels are used as containers they vary in capacity, but the price is computed by the gallon for actual contents. In bulk oil the barrel is of fifty gallons. Crude oil sold in 1859 for 50 cents and refined for one dollar a gallon. At the close of 1910 refined lamp oil sold in bulk for export at 3.90 cents a gallon, crude varying from one cent to 3.10 cents a gallon at the wells. This, in one sense, measures the progress of the industry during little more than half a century. The barrel has been adopted as the unit of measure for crude in Canada and Mexico. In Russia the unit is the pood, but large quantities are measured in tons. In Roumania and in Galicia the unit of measurement is the metric ton. This latter measure is being quite generally adopted in other countries, being applied in Sumatra and Borneo by the companies operating there and in Burma by the Burma Oil Company.

RFINERY OF THE PURE OIL COMPANY, AT PHILADELPHIA.

For 1910 the total production of petroleum in the United States was approximately 214,000,000 barrels. To this total California contributed the vast amount of 77,697,568 barrels. The Mid Continent region, comprising Kansas, Oklahoma, Northern Texas and Northern Louisiana, produced a total of 59,032,333 barrels. The regions yielding Pennsylvania grade oil, the best quality, gave a total of 26,557,079 barrels. This division comprises Southern New York, Western Pennsylvania, West Virginia and Southeastern and Central Ohio. The Trenton Rock fields of Northwestern Ohio and Indiana produced 6,671,684 barrels. Kentucky yielded only 473,526 barrels. Illinois, the newest of the great divisions, had a total output of 32,984,736 barrels. The Gulf Coast Region, comprising the heavy oil districts of Southern Texas and Southern Louisiana, had a production of 10,823,440 barrels. Fields of less importance in Wyoming, Utah, Colorado and other States had a total of 347,000 barrels. These statistics are from the Oil City Derrick, an accepted authority. The petroleum production of the world in 1909, as estimated by Dr. David T. Day, of the United States Geological Survey, was slightly in excess of 297,000,000 barrels, and it is believed the production of the United States in 1910 was nearly two-thirds of the total produced by the world for that year.

The latest development of economic importance in the oil fields is the recovery of gasoline from casing head gas. In other words, the extraction of the volatile fluid from the natural gas as it comes from the wells. This is accomplished by compression and refrigeration and in territory where the wells are old has been found very profitable. Some gas has yielded as much as six gallons of gasoline to the thousand cubic feet of gas. The first intimation that this might be done came from the use of the vacuum gas pump on wells to secure a better supply of gas for the operation of the machinery. There was a residue of gasoline that had to be drained away. Gas companies operating compressors to facilitate transportation for long distances found it necessary to drain the lines where gasoline collected. The first attempt at commercial utilization was at Titusville about 1903. It proved successful on a very small scale. Next it was adopted by William Richards at Mayburg, in Forest County, Pennsylvania. This plant was followed by several in the Bradford field in the same year, 1906. Then a larger plant was established at Bolivar, in the Allegany field in New York. By 1909 the manufacturers of gas engines had their attention attracted and began to devise machinery for the purpose. As an industry this process practically dates from 1910, when several manufacturers had entered the field with machinery.

One popular type of compressor is direct connected to an internal combustion gas engine, the condensation of gasoline, after compression, being accomplished in a water cooled worm of pipe. Another is belt geared, gas engine to compressor, and utilizes for refrigeration the expansion of the gas. There are other types using ammonia for refrigeration in summer. All are fairly effective in getting the desired result. Experiment has proven that the gasoline is simply carried in solution by the natural gas, usually from having been in contact with crude petroleum, and the best results have been obtained at wells where the vacuum gas pump is used, the yield being larger to the thousand feet of gas. Dry gas yields very little gasoline and that little, secured by extreme pressure, is too volatile for practical purposes. In fact nearly all the casing head gasoline is improved by mixing with distilled benzine of a lower gravity. It is being largely used for propelling automobiles and may prove of superior value for aeroplanes, having little tendency to carbonize the cylinders. The investment in gasoline machinery, for the recovery of the fluid from natural gas, has reached a million dollars or more within a year. It will add materially to the profitable life of the old wells whose production of oil has fallen so low that it hardly pays to pump them.

For many years after the discovery of petroleum by Drake the series of naphthas were regarded as nearly worthless. Gasoline was permitted to waste on the ground. As much as possible of these lighter grades were run into the illuminating oil, making the fluid dangerous in the lamp. Explosions became so frequent that laws were passed prohibiting the sale of lamp oil having a lower flash test than 110 degrees Fahrenheit. Then some genius discovered that running a well full of benzine, or naphtha, would cut the paraffine that gathered on the producing sand and interfered with production. It was so cheap that it was largely employed for this purpose until the pipe lines refused to receive oil higher than 50 degrees gravity and the expiration of the torpedo patents made a "shot" of nitro glycerine cheaper than benzine as a stimulant. In the meantime it had been discovered that benzine was a good cleaner for fabrics and a trade was built up in that line. From the internal combusiton gas engine invented in Germany the transition was natural to the use of naphtha and the automobile made a vast market for the lightest products of petroleum. The former waste series has become the most valuable product of distillation and the illuminating oils are no longer in danger of being below legal standards in flash and burning tests. On the contrary it is profitable for the refiners to redistil to obtain every vestige of the volatile naphthas. The system of inspection is maintained simply because it affords lucrative places for political appointees. It is no longer of any value to the public, for the tests take no account of any quality save the temperature at which the fluid will flash and at which it will burn.

In recent years the demand for gasoline has been so urgent that cargoes have been imported from the East Indies, the first invasion of the American markets by foreign petroleum products. This competition will become increasingly irritating to the American producers of petroleum as the output of casing head gasoline grows and seeks a market. But there is no protection for the producer save that of price and ocean freights. It is believed the superior quality of the casing head gasoline will enable it to compete with that from abroad, but this is not certain. A part of the petroleum produced in Sumatra and a part of that from Roumania is very rich in naphthas, or, as it is called in Europe, "motor spirit." But in other qualities neither is quite equal to the oil from the original American fields known as Pennsylvania grade. Engines are being built that will run on refined or illuminating oil and even on crude petroleum, but for many purposes these cannot compete with the gasoline engine. Automobiles and aeroplanes in particular require the highest grade of gasoline.

Oil burning steamships are becoming common. The latest types of naval vessels are oil burners, as the lighter fuel gives them a larger steaming radius, with greater efficiency. Internal combustion oil burning engines are commanding attention and may speedily supercede the plan of raising steam with fuel oil. The efficiency is greater by twenty per cent. In former years it was said that naval supremacy would always be held by the nations having great supplies of coal. This may soon be changed to the nations having big supplies of petroleum. The same may be said of industrial supremacy, since petroleum and its products are becoming chief factors in the generation of energy. The United States is in a strong position in any case as it has now the largest supplies in the world of both coal and oil. It has no superior, either, in the possession of water powers that may be turned to account in the production of energy.

Petroleum has far outstripped gold in the value of its annual production in California, the Golden State. This has been within the years of the Twentieth Century. The following figures show approximately the production for the past thirty-six years. The total up to and including 1875 has been estimated at 175,000 barrels. Since then the estimated output is given by years:

Years.	Barrels.	Years.	Barrels.
1876	12,000	1894	783,078
1877	13,000	1895	1,245,333
1878	15,227	1896	1,257,780
1879	19,858	1897	1,911,569
1880	40,552	1898	2,249,088
1881	99,862	1899	2,677,875
1882	128,636	1900	4,329,950
1883	142,857	1901	7,710,315
1884	262,000	1902	14,356,910
1885	325,000	1903	24,340,839
1886	377,145	1904	29,736,003
1887	678,572	1905	34,275,701
1888	690,333	1906	32,624,000
1889	303,220	1907	40,311,171
1890	307,300	1908	48,306,910
1891	323,600	1909	58,191,723
1892	385,049	1910	77,697,568
1893	470,179	Total	386,775,269

This enormous quantity of oil has sold for a sum estimated at $175,000,-000, or more, at the wells. After transportation and, in some portion of refining, the value has been increased to a total of probably $250,000,000. As a fuel it has enriched the Pacific Coast, where coal is very expensive, by enabling the establishment of many industries, aside from the profits from production and manufacturing of the crude. Oil is burned in the locomotives of all railroads operating in California, adding inestimably to the pleasure of travel, free from smoke and cinders. Oil is sprinkled on the roadbeds of the railways, so there is no dust. Moreover, oil is used largely upon the ordinary highways in California, in Kansas and in other States, having the effect of preventing dust, more readily shedding water and preserving the pavements. For this purpose the heavier oils are superior to those of high specific gravity.

Since the beginning in 1859, the production of Pennsylvania grade petroleum and its value has been estimated by the Oil City Derrick as follows:

Year.	Wells Completed.	Total Production.	Total Value.
1859	2	8,500	$ 170,000
1860	150	650,000	6,240,000
1861	200	2,118,000	1,101,360
1862	300	3,056,000	3,208,800
1863	400	2,631,000	8,290,650
1864	500	2,116,200	17,247,030
1865	600	2,497,700	16,449,843
1866	400	3,597,500	13,490,625
1867	650	3,347,300	8,033,520
1868	780	3,715,800	13,469,775
1869	991	4,215,000	23,604,000
1870	1,007	5,659,000	22,070,100
1871	946	5,795,000	25,498,000
1872	1,032	6,539,100	14,521,625
1873	530	9,893,786	17,808,817
1874	433	10,926,945	12,565,987
1875	1,644	11,987,514	14,924,455
1876	2,319	9,120,669	23,497,123
1877	3,955	13,337,363	31,926,342
1878	2,988	15,381,641	18,016,747
1879	2,816	19,894,288	17,034,584
1880	4,213	26,245,571	24,703,644
1881	3,873	27,561,376	23,496,073
1882	3,268	21,528,621	16,899,967
1883	2,913	23,302,021	24,671,025
1884	2,300	23,952,290	20,030,102

1885....................	2,942	21,528,621	19,025,919
1886....................	3,670	26,603,945	19,988,566
1887....................	1,715	22,873,450	15,239,436
1888....................	1,557	16,905,890	14,708,124
1889....................	5,621	22,349,825	21,036,773
1890....................	6,573	30,067,307	26,045,804
1891....................	3,400	35,839,777	23,967,851
1892....................	1,980	33,425,877	18,551,362
1893....................	1,956	31,362,890	20,072,250
1894....................	3,756	30,781,924	25,779,861
1895....................	7,138	30,959,139	41,871,235
1896....................	7,811	33,970,222	40,424,564
1897....................	6,080	35,165,990	27,561,244
1898....................	4,796	31,647,860	28,839,112
1899....................	8,752	31,100,360	40,236,091
1900....................	8,845	36,152,937	48,896,847
1901....................	7,711	33,412,346	40,178,346
1902....................	7,723	31,766,906	39,311,547
1903....................	8,474	30,947,607	49,206,695
1904....................	8,859	30,351,816	49,321,701
1905....................	7,114	28,149,533	29,333,489
1906....................	7,568	26,627,744	42,604,190
1907....................	6,992	25,693,000	44,834,285
1908....................	10,027	24,871,993	44,272,147
1909....................	8,457	26,757,619	42,277,038
1910....................	5,284	26,557,079	35,659,905
Total............	194,038	1,014,949,842	1,338,214,576

The production of oil in California in 1910 was as follows by districts:

	Rigs Built.	Wells Completed.	Total Production.
Kern River........................	362	301	14,776,435
McKittrick	169	54	5,471,613
Midway	584	238	11,174,207
Sunset	180	79	9,218,904
Coalinga	278	218	18,651,470
Watsonville	1	...	36,660
Arroyo Grande	1	1	22,310
Lompoc ....'.	10	6	698,210
Santa Maria	33	20	6,909,620
Summerland	2	2	74,725
Santa Paula	56	19	492,147
Newhall	8	9	160,428
Salt Lake	33	37	3,263,104
Los Angeles	...	...	466,514
Whittier-Coyote	19	6	1,198,260
Puente	2	2	38,960
Fullerton-Brea Canon	41	23	5,044,001
Repetto	2	...	....
Total.......................1,781		1,015	77,697,568

The value of natural gas since its commercial adaptation in 1882 has been $703,036,343. The business has grown steadily, almost without interruption, since the beginning. In detail the value of gas consumed has been as follows by years:

Year.	Total Value.	Year.	Total Value.
1882	$ 215,000	1898	15,296,813
1883	475,000	1899	20,074,873
1884	1,460,000	1900	23,698,674
1885	14,857,200	1901	27,066,077
1886	10,012,000	1902	30,867,863
1887	15,817,500	1903	35,807,860
1888	22,629,875	1904	38,496,760
1889	21,107,099	1905	41,562,853
1890	18,792,725	1906	46,783,932
1891	15,500,084	1907	52,866,835
1892	14,870,714	1908	54,640,372
1893	14,346,250	1909	55,000,000
1894	13,954,400	1910	57,000,000
1895	13,006,650		
1896	13,002,512	Total	$703,036,343
1897	13,826,422		

In the beginning of the natural gas business on a commercial scale it was wasted prodigally on the supposition that wells might last forever. Contracts were made with factories at extremely low prices and domestic consumers were charged by the stove, at so much a month. Experience soon taught better economy and meters were installed everywhere. The invention of economical devices became an industry, while the price of gas gradually advanced as the production of old fields declined. Many towns have resisted the advancing rates and have endeavored to control them by ordinance. These efforts have resulted in some towns being cut off from any supply, for the companies engaged in this business have learned what it costs to keep up a sufficient production to meet demands. Hundreds of wells must be drilled each year, powerful compressors must be installed to get the gas to points of consumption after the pressure of the wells decreases and millions of dollars are tied up in pipe and machinery. Natural gas at any price up to fifty cents a thousand cubic feet is a cheap domestic fuel, when the convenience is considered. The limit to which gas can be piped to advantage has been put at two hundred and fifty miles. Exceptional lines are longer than that, but the service is not first class.

Geologists agree that gas bearing areas will be much greater than the total of oil bearing areas. Gas and oil come from the same source or sources but the conditions are often favorable for the accumulation of gas where petroleum would not collect. It is not within the province of a work of this kind to discuss the theories of the origin of natural gas and oil as there is controversy among the scientists upon the subject. It is sufficient to say that one school contends for an origin of organic matter, while the other believes in a chemical origin. Quite probably there may be some truth in the claims of each. The question of origin is of less practical importance than to learn where they may be found at least expense.

Another table of value compiled by the Oil City Derrick shows the daily average production and total stocks above ground of Pennsylvania grade oil at the end of each year, from 1870 to 1910, inclusive, together with the average price of crude petroleum at the wells and of refined lamp oil at New York.

Year.	Avg. daily	Avg. price bbls.	Ref. per bbl.	Crude per gal.	Total Stocks.
1870..........	15,350	$3.90	.26⅝	9½	544,626
1871..........	15,800	4.40	.24½	10½	532,000
1872..........	17,925	3.75	.23⅜	8⅞	1,084,423
1873..........	27,106	1.80	.18¼	4¼	1,625,157
1874..........	29,937	1.15	.13	2¾	3,705,639
1875..........	24,075	1.24¾	.13	2⅞	3,550,200
1876..........	24,505	2.57⅝	.19⅛	6⅛	2,824,739
1877..........	35,988	2.39⅜	.15¾	5⅝	3,127,837
1878..........	41,544	1.17⅛	.10¾	2¾	4,615,300
1879..........	54,206	0.85⅝	.08⅛	2	8,552,256
1880..........	71,114	0.94⅛	.09⅛	2¼	17,145,104
1881..........	75,004	0.85½	.08	2	25,761,051
1882..........	82,338	0.78½	.07⅜	1⅞	34,335,144
1883..........	63,365	1.05⅞	.08⅛	2½	35,715,565
1884..........	65,129	0.83⅝	.08¼	1⅞	36,872,892
1885..........	56,921	0.88⅜	.08⅛	2⅛	33,539,038
1886..........	70,679	0.71⅜	.07⅛	1⅝	33,367,898
1887..........	58,646	0.66⅝	.06¾	1½	28,357,112
1888..........	45,058	0.87	.07½	2	18,604,474
1889..........	58,869	0.94⅛	.07⅛	2¼	10,904,793
1890..........	82,376	0.86⅝	.07⅜	2	9,295,514
1891..........	98,191	0.66⅞	.06⅞	1⅝	15,343,233
1892..........	91,328	0.55½	.0607	1⅜	17,395,389
1893..........	85,926	0.64	.0524	1½	12,111,183
1894..........	84,334	0.83¾	.0519	1⅞	6,336,777
1895..........	84,820	1.35¼	.0736	3¼	5,161,905
1896..........	92,815	1.19	.0698	2⅞	9,550,583
1897..........	96,357	0.78⅜	.0591	1⅞	10,789,652
1898..........	86,706	0.91⅛	.0631	2⅛	11,541,753
1899..........	85,206	1.29⅜	.0798	3	13,163,819
1900..........	99,049	1.35¼	.0845	3¼	13,174,716
1901..........	91,541	1.20¾	.0748	2⅞	9,420,420
1902..........	87,032	1.23¾	.0733	2⅞	5,699,127
1903..........	84,788	1.59	.0863	3¾	4,823,199
1904..........	83,157	1.62½	.0820	3⅞	6,355,512
1905..........	77,122	1.39⅜	.0722	3¼	3,503,398
1906..........	72,953	1.59¾	.0761	3¾	4,937,392
1907..........	70,393	1.74½	.0830	4	5,951,784
1908..........	69,536	1.78	.0865	4¼	3,306,893
1909..........	63,366	1.60½	.0477	3¾	5,384,904
1910..........	72,952	1.37	.0414	3¼	4,541,385

The cost figures per gallon of crude and refined oil show the differential in value between the crude and manufactured products. In the one case it represents the value of the crude oil in the producers' tanks; in the other the price of refined oil in the open market. Before reaching that market the crude oil has these additional costs to meet: A gathering charge of 20 cents per barrel, or ½ cent a gallon; a trunk line charge of 50 cents a barrel, or 1⅛c per gallon to reach the seaboard; a manufacturing charge of ½ cent a gallon. The figures are of the average prices for each year. The present price of crude oil is $1.30 per barrel, and of refined 3.75 cents per gallon. Water white oil is 4.75 cents a gallon.

THE STANDARD OIL COMPANY.

BY J. I. C. CLARKE.

When the Standard Oil Company was formed on January 2, 1870, petroleum as it came from the ground had just passed the mark of 4,000,000 barrels of crude for the year, and there were perhaps 300 refineries competing for it. The yearly crude oil supply had barely doubled in the ten years from the discovery of oil. The Civil War, the Internal Revenue War Tax on oil, the uncertainty of the shallow wells of the period, a wild fever of speculation in prices and properties were influences that brought about many failures and worked against the orderly development of the petroleum business during its first decade.

Millions had been made by the lucky strikers of oil, and millions had been lost in wild-cat wells and companies. The refining of oil had not advanced as it should have done although refineries multiplied. In 1870 there was refining capacity for three times the supply of crude, yet illuminating oils of good quality were rare, and the by-products, whether those of the first naphtha condensings from the stills or the residue below the illuminating line, went practically to waste. Prices of crude oil soared with every big well that went out and slumped with every new well that came in. Crude oil might bring $10 a barrel to-day, but would not fetch more than 10 cents in a year to come. Devastating fires ruined costly properties. Transportation was primitive and uncertain. Associations of oil producers sought to impose rules on the supply in certain fields only to find that individual members violated them. One region fought for the supply or the trade against another region. In spite of all, however, there was progress. The richness of the petroleum flowings made many a handsome surplus over and above the economic disorder — almost mob law — that reigned. The great monied forces of the country gave petroleum

ANGLO-AMERICAN OIL COMPANY—
TYPICAL COUNTRY PEDDLER.

the cold shoulder because of its risks and its uncertainties, yet there seemed always to be money for new enterprises and new hope.

The time was ripe for strong, controlling hands to organize the splendid though all but frustrated promise into a solid and golden reality.

How the undertaking took shape, was in fact forced upon those who afterwards took it so masterfully in hand, is an interesting history in itself.

When John D. Rockefeller was 23 years old, he had been seven years in the commission business in Cleveland, and, looking about for further opportunity, his firm of Clark and Rockefeller joined with Samuel Andrews to organize a firm to refine and deal in oil.   Andrews was the manufacturing man of the concern.   And he had learned the process of cleansing the crude oil by the use of sulphuric acid.   They started business—the Excelsior refinery—and did well.   In 1865 the three years' partnership was dissolved. Mr. Rockefeller bought the business, and again cleaving to Andrews, organized the firm of Rockefeller and Andrews, giving up his commission business.   "It was really," he says, "my start in the oil business."   Meanwhile another Rockefeller, William, younger brother of John D., had entered the oil business in co-partnership with John D. and Samuel Andrews.   They proceeded to build and equip the Standard Oil works—note the name—in Cleveland.   Here then was the output of two considerable refineries to be taken care of.   It is not generally known that the progress of the use of illuminating oil was comparatively slow in this country.   The home market was limited, and the competition great for it.   The foreign trade invited the enterprising, and the Rockefellers grasped that fact early.   New York was the gate of the export trade and thither in 1865 went William, founding the marketing firm of Rockefeller & Co., and setting vigorously to work.   The export trade up to that time was carried on through jobbers almost entirely. It was William Rockefeller's task to do it direct.   And he did it.   In 1867 Henry M. Flagler entered the original Cleveland firm which was thereafter Rockefeller, Andrews and Flagler.   His coming was notable, for formidable qualities came with him—"a bright and active young fellow full of vim and push," says the senior partner forty years later.   Here, then, were the personal forces centered which were to tell so wonderfully in the conflict, which, all unknown to them, was coming up in a storm-cloud from the little strip of Pennsylvania territory known as "The Oil Region."   The fruits of combination were showing in the three inter-related firms, while in the general oil business uncertainty, loss, conflict were tending to chaos.   Having found the secret of success in large dealings and economical processes, the need of still larger and more powerful aggregation of capital was felt.   The actual situation, as will be shown, made such combination imperative.

A glimpse of the general oil situation and particularly its relation to Cleveland should here be given.   Oil production—that is actual drilling for oil—had taken care of itself from the beginning.   Capital and labor for that always came in plenty.   But the oil once out of the ground the trouble began.   Along Oil Creek flatboats were used to float the barrelled crude oil toward Pittsburg—when there was water enough.   For the rest it was hauling by team and wagon.   By and by a spur of the Pennsylvania Railroad furnished transit.   All of it was done at immense cost and with great waste.   The facilities for refining could not at first be provided in the oil region.   The first idea of the producers was naturally that by refining the oil as close to the wells as possible freight charges would be lessened, since the refined oil—kerosene—was only 40 per cent. of the crude, all the rest— since proved so valuable—being thrown away as waste.   Transportation as one can see, came to be largely the determining factor.   At first the chief refining point seemed to be at Erie, the nearest accessible point on the lake. Naturally a large part of the business gathered at Pittsburg, which was more distant, but was down stream for barges.   Notwithstanding the long and costly haul by rail for the crude material, important refineries were soon started in the great seaboard cities, Philadelphia and New York. For the export trade the seaboard refineries had obvious advantages. Cleveland, on Lake Erie, had, in the beginning, small facilities for the transportation of crude oil from the wells, but vast advantages for putting its refined on the market. Beside two competing lines of railroad and the Erie canal connecting with New York, it had the magnificent waterway of the great lakes. Cleveland, therefore, threatened early to become one of the chief refining centers of the continent. In 1865 there were thirty refineries in the town with a capital of $1,500,000 and a daily capacity of some 2,000 barrels. In 1866 there were fifty. Suddenly, in 1868, this splendidly growing industry seemed threatened with extinction.

With the coming of the railroads into the oil region refineries began to be established there. In 1865 twenty refineries were counted between Titusville and Oil City. By 1868 the Oil Region had become arrogant on the question and was boasting its purpose to take exclusive possession of the business of refining oil. Cleveland, Pittsburg, Philadelphia, New York must surrender their stills. "The business belonged to the oil regions, and the oil men meant to have it." And to the casual observer it looked that way. Refineries at the mouths of the wells were multiplying, and the Pennsylvania Railroad, eager to get the traffic in refined, was willing to make great concessions in freight—to the detriment of others not so comfortably situated.

Neither rail nor pipe communication had yet been completed between Cleveland and the wells. The crude oil had to be gotten by some means or other, upwards of sixty miles to the west, and when distilled had to double upon its tracks, and then, by lines less direct than the Pennsylvania, had to seek its principal markets in the East. At this time it was that General J. H. Devereux came to Cleveland as Vice President of the Lake Shore Railroad. Presently the entire body of oil refiners of the town came to him in despair of the continuance of their business at that point. They feared they would either have to abandon their business or move it to the oil region— all but one of their number. The longer haul, the higher rates were nearly prohibitive. Could not some compromise be arranged. It was the time of such compromises, but the conference resulted in a deadlock. The Pennsylvania road had made it understood that it "held a patent on the transportation of oil." Would not the Lake Shore stretch a point to gather in some potent fraction of that great carrying trade? Much discussion, but no result. The apparent deadlock brought great glee to the newspapers of the oil regions. Cleveland was doomed. Cleveland was "to be wiped out as a refining center as with a sponge." The body of Cleveland refiners saw no way out. One of them thought a way might be found. "Rockefeller, Andrews and Flagler," testified General Devereux later, formed "the only exception" to the general despair of the Cleveland refiners.

It was not the affair of an hour or even of a few days to prepare a solution for the difficult problem. Could any terms be proposed which should safeguard the refiners—with their sixty mile haul for crude—and yet—with the longer haul over the tracks—not bankrupt the railroad? Not until 1870 was a final adjustment reached. Rockefeller, Andrews & Flagler found the key to the situation, and it was Henry M. Flagler who handed it to the Lake Shore and its connecting line, the New York Central. It was briefly this:—

that the crude oil for their Cleveland refineries be carried from the oil regions to Cleveland and the refined oil to New York at a total rate of $1.75 a barrel—the contracting party guaranteeing a trainload of 60 carloads daily to New York—equivalent to 3,500 barrels. How to fill this large order? The capacity of the two Rockefeller refineries was only 1,500 barrels a day.

The incorporation of the Standard Oil Company of Ohio with a capital of $1,000,000 was the answer. The Rockefeller firms, two manufacturing and one marketing, were merged into it with John D. Rockefeller, President; William Rockefeller, Vice President; Henry M. Flagler, Secretary and Treasurer. The directors were John D. Rockefeller, Henry M. Flagler, Samuel Andrews and Stephen Harkness, Samuel Andrews taking charge as before of the manufacturing end. It was a combination of means and personalities to inspire confidence and guarantee progress. Here was the vehicle of salvation for the tottering oil refining business of Cleveland.

BENZINE FACTORY AND FORWARDING STATION, DUSSELDORF.

The refiners saw the strength and potentiality of the Company. Business instinct had already suggested it; the desperate situation had compelled it. Into it accordingly came the most clear-sighted of the Cleveland refiners. Most of them took Standard Oil stock in exchange for their refineries; many demanded cash. The master-stroke had been delivered and it was a question of joining the new force, of organizing a second group to meet the Lake Shore Railroad's conditions or seeing their concerns die on their hands. No threats were used; none were needed. The proposition accepted by the railroad was open to duplication by anyone. By having one such trainload a day guaranteed the railroad found that it could carry the amount of refined oil at one-third the cost in carriage and rolling stock, while the Cleveland refiners at a stroke were made secure in their supply of crude oil and put on a level as to rates to the seaboard with the refiners of the oil region. Cleveland's oil industry was saved, and the Standard Oil recruited from the best Cleveland oil men, and greater and closer organization with manifold economies of operation was possible.

The conception and execution of this brilliant, daring plan proved the right of the organizers of the Standard Oil Company to leadership in its locality. Wisely and boldly administered it never paused in its growth. By 1872 its capitalization had reached $2,500,000, and its tale thereafter was but a continuation of the progress already made. Nothing in the earlier business of the Rockefellers had been left to chance. Samuel Andrews, the practiced refiner, was one of the few men capable of making good illuminating oil, and his skill made possible that standardization of product which came by and by to mark every article of output from the Standard Oil Company, and which is its stronghold the world over to-day. Prior to 1867 they had bought their barrels, often of inferior quality, causing loss by leakage, and of which the supply was often inadequate. In 1867 they set up

TANK LIGHTER IN HARBOR OF STETTIN.

their own factory to make barrels by machinery, getting sound containers at half the previous cost. They established their own warehouses in New York and purchased their own lighters to transport the oil about New York harbor. "Provide our own facilities," was now the Company's motto. Its lines were drawn true from the very start. Various large capitalists subscribed largely to the stock and their connection enabled the Company to borrow the capital necessary for the desired expansion. The refineries of the new company were already not only much the largest in Cleveland but the largest in the entire country. Their business was probably fully 10 per cent. of the entire petroleum business of the country. The various economies they had introduced enabled the new Company to save much of the expense which their competitors had to bear. In fine, cheaper methods, and ample capital were their actual implements in the process of upbuilding. The old refineries were generally not incorporated, so the properties were bought outright. Among the prominent firms that were thus purchased were Clark, Payne & Co. and Alexander Scofield & Co. The refineries were utilized, and the best of them kept in operation, being connected by systems of pipes, the entire capacity being consolidated so that it could be most advantageously and economically operated.

With the new purchases came widened possibilities of exporting oil from the port of New York. To aid in this work, the Long Island Oil Company at Long Island City, with warehouses and extensive dock property on deep water accessible to ocean-going ships, was bought. The refinery was a large one. The Devoe Manufacturing Company, on Newtown Creek, where it had shipping facilities, was purchased. The Devoe business had largely operated for refining and canning oil for the European and Oriental trade wherein it had high reputation, obtaining high prices for its distinct brands of oil. It manufactured at minimum cost its cans which were especially adapted to the Orient. The oil regions were considered. Jacob J. Vandergrift and John Pitcairn, two enterprising oil men, had erected the large, modern Imperial refinery at Oil City, Pa., with good shipping facilities. This was purchased and furnished additional export oil. A still more important purchase was that of the Charles Pratt Co., whose refinery was in Brooklyn, on the East River. The high reputation of Pratt's Astral Oil was known throughout the Far East through the case-oil trade. It had dock property, warehouses and much cash capital. The acquirement of the Warden, Frew and Lockhart properties was another far-reaching stroke. It included the Atlantic Refining Co. of Philadelphia and four Pittsburg refineries. A purchase of note in 1875 was the Porter, Moreland & Co. property at Titusville with four refineries. The outspread of the Company cannot be followed here in detail. Refineries at Bayonne, N. J., at Baltimore in 1877, with scattering purchases at points already reached, marked the first great period of illuminating oil.

For the first years the main office of the Standard Oil Company was in Cleveland, Ohio, with a branch office in New York. The first modest New York quarters at 2 Cedar Street occupied by William Rockefeller in 1868, before the organization of the Standard Oil Company—were exchanged for larger offices at 140 Pearl Street in 1872, where the organization remained until May 1, 1882, when it moved to 44 Broadway. In February, 1884, the erection of the present Standard Oil Building, No. 26 Broadway, was begun. It was first occupied in July, 1885. An addition of six stories was completed in February, 1898.

Side by side with the control and operation of refineries marched the Standard's marketing companies. The tank-wagon, the tank car, the tank barge and the tank ocean steamships were far in the distance, but all that foresight and skill could then accomplish were at the service of Standard Oil.

The era of development of petroleum by-products was at hand. First came the lubricating oils, and in these the Standard began operation in 1877-8. The American Lubricating Oil Co. and the Mica Axle Grease Co., both at Cleveland, were merged under the name of the former. The Eclipse Works at Franklin, Pa., followed in 1878 and the Galena Signal Oil Co. was acquired in 1879 from a consolidation of two lubricating refineries. Three-fourths interest in the Vacuum Oil Co. at Rochester was acquired.

The paraffine wax, the vaseline and the naphthas were all in turn looked after.

But the flowing of the oil increased. Some other means of oil transportation was needed and the pipe-line was answering the question. It began at the mushroom town of Pithole, Pa., in September, 1865, when, to the fury of the arrogant teamsters, M. E. Vansickle laid the first five miles of two-inch pipe, to the railroad. Notwithstanding the success of the project, the extension of the pipe-line system worked slowly until the needs of the Standard Oil Company in its now outspread consumption of crude oil, made itself felt. It was in 1873 that these needs became pressing. The Company proceeded to meet the situation, partly by construction and partly by purchase. Nearly all the early pipe-lines were mere gathering lines, poorly constructed, under different owners and loosely managed. Of those acquired between 1874 and 1877 only one, the Columbia Conduit Co., forty-

VACUUM OIL COMPANY'S (LISBON) TANK AT OPORTO.

eight miles long, running from the wells to Pittsburg, was in the nature of a trunk line. A group of the purchased properties was made the nucleus of the United Pipe Lines, organized by the Standard. By the end of 1877 an efficient pipe-line system had been created. By the year 1882, the forty-eight miles of the Columbia Conduit Co. had grown, solely by construction from Standard Oil funds, to 1,062 miles of trunk line, with gathering lines reaching nearly 2,500 miles. The flow of crude oil which had risen from the 4,200,000 barrels of 1869 to 13,300,000 barrels in 1877, had brought new problems. Usually it was above the refining capacity of the country, and called for the construction of tankage on an enormous scale. A standard tank of 35,000 barrels was made, and these tanks were grouped in "farms," sometimes 100 to a "farm." It called for immense sums of money, and only the Standard Oil Company could find the funds. Thus the oil in storage in 1875 amounted to almost 4,000,000 barrels, but by 1886 it amounted to 32,-

000,000 barrels, representing, with the tanks, a sleeping investment of $32,-000,000. In this work of tank construction the Company's officers exhibited skill and force that called forth plaudits on every side.

Equipped, therefore, in every direction with all the elements of substantiality and progress the Standard Oil interest approached its first great aggregation in 1879 by the "Vilas, Keith & Chester Agreement," as it has come to be known, a tentative forerunner of the Trust of 1882, whose object was simply the gathering into the same hands of the various stocks and other interests, which, while they belonged in equity to a definite group of persons—the stockholders of the Standard Oil Company—were standing in the names of various different individuals, and subject to the embarrassments that such an arrangement might at any time create.

It is not to be thought that all this physical improvement and progress in Standard Oil fortunes had been achieved without opposition. From the very beginning of the Company's life, the Oil Region interests had made a frantic outcry against the Company. The chaotic condition at the wells produced an almost anarchical hatred against a force organized with the scientific precision of the Standard. The fact that the Company had succeeded in rescuing the Cleveland interests from the destruction which the Oil Region so whole-heartedly hoped for, nay, had made Cleveland for a time the leader in refining oil, was enough to account for the Oil Region's attitude. When, however, the Standard, as we have seen, began adding Oil Region establishments to its muster roll, the hostile feelings knew no bounds. When, in 1872, the South Improvement Co. excitement broke out, it was against the Standard Oil Company that the Region's orators fulminated. The Standard Oil Company did not invent that scheme for unifying the oil refining interests, and securing lower freight rates. It had, indeed, on the part of a couple of its officers, subscribed reluctantly for some of the stock rather than disoblige certain refiners of Philadelphia and Pittsburg. The best proof of the reluctance is that the Standard Oil did not need any better freight arrangement than it had with Lake Shore Railroad. Since the South Improvement Co. was stillborn and never did any business, it does not call for extended comment here, beyond noting the uproar its appearance caused in 1872. Differing from this and on a more formidable scale was the series of trouble that accompanied the growth of the Standard Oil Company's pipe-lines, culminating in the open breach between the Pennsylvania Railroad and the Company, over the Empire Transportation Co. which the railroad backed, and had put into the field of refining as well as transporting oil. Bitter, long and involved in all manner of complications had been the "war," but its most spectacular feature was the sudden transfer from the Pennsylvania Railroad to the Erie Railroad of all the Standard Oil petroleum and freight. The accomplishment fell to the lot of Daniel O'Day, a young traffic manager of positive genius and ferocious energy, and the swift and complete way he did it is a legend of wonder to this day in the Oil Region. For the moment the "war" became more desperate. Price-cutting in freight and refined oil, angry demonstrations, almost riots and impassioned oratory were its features; but in seven months, on October 17, 1877, the Pennsylvania surrendered. The Standard Oil Company bought the Empire Transportation Co.—refineries, pipe-lines and all, for $3,000,000.

and peace reigned, as the railroads retired from the oil business. All the Standard asked in settlement was a freight rate equivalent to its arrangements with the Central and Erie Railroads. It was also chosen to act as "evener" between the railroads and the refineries, and did so act for a couple of years. But the fruits of the victory were greater, and in 1879 the Standard Oil Company owned or controlled by contract the oil transportation facilities throughout the oil regions.

It is time to recognize that no matter what the success, it was one of men; that the same group of men in any business capable of development would have gone the limit of endeavor and achievement with a similar system. It is not only that John D. Rockefeller, William Rockefeller and Henry M. Flagler possessed acumen in a wonderful degree, but vigor, persistence and outreach beyond any trio that had ever taken up the burden of business on the North American Continent. Yet these qualities might not have sufficed if they had not been balanced by those superior qualities which ordinarily are the badge of conservative minds. To consolidate as they advanced; to keep up enterprise unremittingly but never to let it run to rashness; to keep their business word though the heavens fall; to make for permanence; to maintain credit; to standardize conduct and method as well as material output. And in the course of their triumphant march, the certainty with which the best men were always picked to extend the Company's lines was remarkable. When the Standard acquired the Porter, Moreland Company properties if it did no more than secure John D. Archbold it would have made no bad bargain. Here was an engine of energy with a nature of cheer and a vision that looked far indeed, while not missing a particle of the task in hand. Among the greatest assets that the Chas. Pratt Co. brought to the Standard was Henry H. Rogers, a paladin of commerce, and an inventor of genius, although the latter gift disappeared from use as his business undertakings increased, an inspiring leader, a lion in the path of opposition but who was ordinarily the gentlest and most courteous of men. To his bravery and watchfulness the great strides of the foreign trade in oil were largely due; his conduct of the great campaigns for the western extension of the pipe-line system were masterly. With unerring judgment the best men in all lines were made one with the Standard. Was it Oliver H. Payne, or Charles Pratt or William G. Warden; was it O. B. Jennings or Benjamin Brewster or Jabez Bostwick or Wesley H. Tilford or James McGee or Dan O'Day, the able and the capable were sought out and put in the seats of command.

The Standard Oil's victory in its first decade was complete, no less because of the methods it pursued than the men it chose, leaving the inefficient, the neglectful, the lax, and the hare-brained, to stand precariously with their primitive weapons against the onrush of the superbly officered and iron-disciplined phalanx of Standard Oil.

But there was, and there is, more of excellence than all that in the intimate conduct of Standard Oil—a mutual feeling of respect, the practice of unfailing courtesy, the finding of a way by peaceable examination and a resolve as apparent as if put in words that the Standard Oil service shall, man for man, be as profitable to the employee as any other like service in the land. This impress it has borne in all the forty-one years of its life;

and the explanation is simple. It was all in the impressive personality of John D. Rockefeller, enforced with a persistent gentleness on all with whom he came in contact. A forehanded consideration has marked all its dealings with labor, so it has never suffered from labor trouble.

With 1882 came the organization of the Standard Oil Trust. Like the agreement of 1879 it was simply a device to hold before the law in common what the stockholders owned in common. Nine trustees were elected for the Standard Oil properties to carry on Standard Oil business, with a capitalization of $70,000,000, afterwards increased to $95,000,000. The business went forward with increasing energy. To perfect its organization and meet the growing supply and increasing demand as new oil fields or new marketing territories were opened a number of subsidiary Standard Oil Companies were organized, as for instance the Standard Oil Companies of New York, New Jersey, Kentucky, etc.

The discovery of oil in the Lima (Ohio) fields in 1885 brought a fresh problem. So impregnated was its crude with sulphur that for a long time

STANDARD OIL COMPANY'S PRODUCING CAMP, MIDWAY FIELD, KERN COUNTY, CALIFORNIA.

there seemed no way of refining it. Some 23,000,000 barrels of it had, indeed, been placed in storage by the Standard Oil Company before Professor Frasch devised a method of purifying it. The courage to hold so much oil, founded on a belief in the skill of the American chemist, is one of the instances of the supreme business sense of John D. Rockefeller, as well as a test of the financial stability of the Company he had founded.

The ten years succeeding the formation of the Trust were a period of increasing work and prosperity for the Company, its marketing lines at home and abroad extending vigorously. Opposition to the Company was promoted by its competitors in the field of politics and the regions of public clamor rather than in the fields of petroleum itself. To the aid of this warfare came a feeling of public distrust of all corporations of size and vigor. The word "Trust" became a public bugbear fraught with mysterious and evil qualities. Pessimists and publicists alike told the country that it was in danger of becoming the farm of a few with enslaved millions doing the work at starvation wages. A Congressional Investigation of Trusts was held in 1888, and the leading officials of Standard Oil were examined at great length. Agitation through the press for the "curbing" or "busting" of the "trusts"—a term which became ever vaguer and more mysteriously terrible in the public mind—was conducted with great vehemence. This finally took form in the Sherman anti-trust law which was enacted by Congress in 1890, taking its name from John Sherman, then Senator from Ohio, and proclaiming that every combination in "restraint of trade" or tending to monopoly was criminal. Without any modifying clause this was equivalent to proclaiming every commercial concern which united with another illegal. The Interstate Commerce Law, abolishing railroad rebates, was passed in 1887 and although the Standard Oil Company had, like its competitors and all other business concerns of the period, taken what advantage it could of the custom, it now recognized that railroad rates were no longer to be regarded as merchandise, and bid for according to quantity used. It at once fell in with the new state of things. "Sauce for the goose was to be sauce for the gander." At no time thereafter did it seek or accept railroad rebates anywhere.

TRAIN OF CARS PHOTOGRAPHED AT ATLAS WORKS, BUFFALO, N. Y.

The trust form of the Standard Oil business was soon to be attacked from other than a Federal quarter. In 1890 the Attorney General of the State of Ohio entered a law suit challenging the right of the Standard Oil Company of Ohio to delegate its powers to a body of trustees outside its own organization. In 1892 the State Courts decided that such a delegation of powers was illegal, calling on the Ohio Company to withdraw from the trust, but not, as has so often been alleged, ordering the dissolution of the trust itself. The State Court had no control over that. Considering, however, the likelihood of other Attorneys General, in other States, setting out to score in like manner off the trust, the latter decided to dissolve. This proved no easy task with its meticulous complexities of fractional ownership in so many corporations, and was not completed until 1899, when a reorganization was effected under the New Jersey law which expressly legalized "holding companies," that is, companies owning and holding stock in other companies in whole or in part. The already existing Standard Oil Company of New Jersey, with $10,000,000 capital, was at hand for the purpose. Its capital was increased to $100,000,000, and it purchased the stock of other companies. Since November, 1906, it has been in the United States Courts in defense of its right to hold the stock of these corporations. Under the judgment of the United States Supreme Court delivered May 15, 1911, it is declared not to have that right, and is ordered to distribute *pro rata* among its own stockholders, the shares of the subsidiary corporations. This will be done, and those corporations will be operated by their own officers and through their own corporate organizations. The Company has been given six months to comply with the decree.

The story of the Standard Oil Company in its third period, from 1899 to the present, has been one of continuous prosperity on one hand, and (certainly in the last five years) of governmental litigation and harassment on the other.

Succeeding the Lima (Ohio) and Indiana discoveries the next great development had been in California. Oil had been known to exist under its surface for many years, but it was in 1895-6 that the drill found oil in the Golden State in quantities, calling into sudden existence an oil boom recalling the early days in Pennsylvania. The new century, however, was to see the phenomenal growth which gives promise of indefinite continuance. In 1901 the "strike" at Spindle Top, Texas, startled the world of petroleum, and led to an even fiercer rush to the land of oil geysers. The boom did not last. Its sensational features subsided with the falling off in the great wells. Kansas, however, now came to the front for a while, and Illinois advanced with a bound in 1903 to the rank of the great and steady producers. While in Kansas proper the boom did not last, dying down indeed amid a wide scandal of bogus and fraudulent producing companies—the developments in the neighboring Indian Territory, now the State of Oklahoma, surpassed all belief and records. California meanwhile continued increasing its output and to-day leads the country in production. Later the Caddo field in Louisiana has come into prominence and promise.

It had been the policy of the Standard Oil Company from the beginning to leave the work of drilling for and producing oil to the body of producers, its practice being to follow the drill wherever it struck oil, and, as effectively and quickly as possible, take care of the product, bringing its gathering pipes to the wells, and connecting them with the trunk lines. Not always, however, were the individual producers equal to the task of supplying the crude as needed, and in such and other cases related, the Standard became a producer itself. At the present writing the Standard owns or controls 11 per cent. of the entire production of the country. To meet the calls upon it for transportation, pipe-line construction and storage tank erection has formed in the past twelve years a large part of its care and expenditure. To-day oil can be pumped through its systems from Oklahoma or Louisiana to Bayonne, N. J., 1,500 or 2,000 miles. Its trunk lines are over 8,000 miles long, and its gathering pipes 75,000 miles. Incidentally, it has taken care of supplies of natural gas in various fields. The Company's crude oil storage capacity, and nearly all or more or less in use is nearly 100,000,000 barrels.

For the refining of oil of all kinds it operates twenty-two refineries, several of which, such as those in Whiting, Ind., Bayonne, N. J., and Bayway, N. J., can handle 30,000 barrels of crude oil a day, with an output from each of 15,000 to 20,000 barrels of illuminating oil, according to the quality of the crude, with proportionate quantities of gasoline, benzine, lubricating oils in endless varieties, gas oil, fuel oil, road oil, paraffine wax, candles and the highest grade of coke. Some of those refineries cover as much as 200 acres of land with their stills, agitators, pans, and so forth. To some of them are attached barrel making, boxing, tinning plants, sulphuric acid works and so on ad infinitum. They handle 70 per cent. of the refining of the entire country.

On its marketing side the Standard Oil Company has erected and maintains the supply of oils in over 3,900 stations throughout the United States. It has in storage over 80,000,000 barrels of oil. It keeps in motion 9,000 tank cars on the railroads. It delivers in its local trade with 5,000 tank wagons. But more than half of the oil it refines and the gasoline is produces it sends abroad. For this purpose it mans and runs over 200 vessels, including sixty ocean tank steamships, twelve tank steamships for coast trade, and five cargo steamers for case-oil shipments. An oil steamship fully laden leaves New York harbor every day in the year for European ports. Chartered steamers outside of the above carry different petroleum products all over the world. It has in this trade brought back to the United States over $1,000,000 of foreign gold to push along the cause of commercial and manufacturing industrialism in our great country. It is developing a great business in road oil and another in fuel oil. It makes over 300,000,000 candles a year from its own paraffine. It makes lamps, stoves, heaters, and oil-wicks. It develops over two hundred products of petroleum.

The story of its struggles for the foreign trade comes truly under the head of the Romance of Petroleum, for in the teeth of foreign opposition and foreign oil it has pushed and sold American oil everywhere between the two poles. Not only Europe, but Asia, Africa, Oceanica and South America have burned and paid for Standard Oil. The great foreign trade calls for much tankage, warehousing and many tank cars and tank wagons. It has withstood the competition of the most powerfully backed oil-combinations in Europe, sometimes supported by their governments; it faces import duties in almost every foreign state while no duties whatever face the foreigner sending his oil or his gasoline hither.

PORTUGUESE OIL PEDDLER.

The Standard Oil Company has never indeed been without competition at home and abroad. Four years ago the capitalization of the 125 refineries not connected with Standard Oil in the United States was $110,000,000; to-day, with many large plants added, it is over $200,000,000, and very active.

Its legal troubles growing out of the Interstate Commerce law can be briefly dismissed. The character of the Illinois suit concerning the rate on oil between Whiting, Ind., and East St. Louis is typical of all—a straining of hair-line technicalities to make a case that could not be demonstrated to a sane mind when fairly tried. The fine of $29,000,000 imposed by Judge Landis proved a folly that reacted on its applauders when the actual facts were forced to the light. So with the $30,000,000 suit in Tennessee. Of the prolonged case under the Sherman Act, the evidence in which fills twenty-two volumes, it would not be profitable to write here at length. The suit was carried to the highest court in the land, resulting in the judgment and decree previously indicated. What the Court in its opinion has to say concerning "reasonable" or "unreasonable" restraint of trade has already started a warm controversy, but it now concerns more closely than it does the Standard Oil Company nearly 1,200 other great business concerns in the United States, from the Steel Corporation down, and holding the enormous capital of ten billion dollars.

The Standard Oil Company employs over 71,000 men. Taking the four great divisions of effort, production employs over 9,300 men at the wells; the pipe-lines employ nearly 11,600 men; the refineries and factories give work to 24,000 men; the marketing in the domestic branch employs 13,200 men, and in the export trade, 13,100 men. As has been said, in its forty-one years of corporate existence it has been without labor troubles. It has never had a strike or a lockout, and this is an extraordinary record when one considers how many boom periods, severe panics, and slow-recovery interludes have marked the last four decades in the business world, not to speak of the increasing tendency to strike, fostered often by professed friends and organizers of labor. And its plan in this has been without mystery; the Standard Oil has held no patent upon it. First, the Company has always paid wages a little better than those paid, grade for grade, in similar businesses; second, it has worked on a practical civil-service basis, recognizing superior qualities by advances and promotion; third, it has a pension system for long service which secures the faithful employee against the terrors of old age. All this is administered in a frank, democratic spirit which seeks to forestall complaint.

When the malevolent or the thoughtless inveigh against the Company, they ignore this wonderful record of amity and co-operation, which is not at all the sign of the tyrant and oppressor. Likewise they ignore the merits of the business system which has carried the company along the commercial path. This system has made its credit the best in the world, for it includes not only the prompt and regular settlement of its obligations, but has fortified it in the good graces of its over a million customers, great and small, to the ends of the earth. As an instance it may be cited that during the stress of the Roosevelt panic of 1907 when the banks refused to cash private drafts in Pennsylvania, the Standard Oil Company's checks were honored as freely as if they were the paper issues of the Federal government.

To its customers it has supplied standard articles of uniform quality with unfailing regularity and in whatever quantity trade, its fluctuations and expansions demanded. In all the storm of comment upon the Company, none of it came from the customers or consumers. Surely this fact should not be overlooked by the diminishing number who unthinkingly follow the lead of the demagogues. Then as to prices—which, after all, are the true touchstone of merit of a business in its relations to the community. In January, 1870, when the Standard Oil Company was organized, the wholesale market-price of refined oil or kerosene—an unsafe, smoking, ill-smelling product—was $31\frac{3}{8}$ cents. In 1911—a safe, pure, pellucid oil burning with a brilliant flame—is sold wholesale at 7 cents or less. Nowhere has the Standard Oil price been unfair, and always the tendency has been downward. That is something of a record, and answers in bulk a vast number of accusations, for this downward scale runs through all the ramifications of the business—gasoline, benzine, lubricating oils, paraffine, and coke, as well as kerosene. One of its subsidiary companies, the Galena-Signal Oil Company, lubricates 97 per cent. of the railroad wheels that turn in the United States and a growing percentage of the wheels of the trolley systems. No complaint of price or quality from them; the Galena system and oils are used because they give better service than any other and at a 10 per cent. reduction in cost. Vainly did the counsel for the government in the late prolonged trial seek to find other influence than the merit of the Galena oils in the securing of these contracts from the railroads. He found none, because there was none. Just as vainly did he try to wring from the officials on the stand the compounding of the wonderful oils for the benefit of the Company's competitors.

How much the Standard Oil Company owed to forceful and prudent unity of direction from the beginning can scarcely be estimated, but that the plan and system of the great founders were sound is magnificently proved by the history of the Company to the present day. The first and foremost condition established was continuous attention to business in its smallest details as well as in its largest undertakings. The Company's ruling spirits met and passed judgment on the Company's affairs every working day in the year. This has never been deviated from. Wherever possible it abolished the middleman; wherever practicable it manufactured the accessories of its own business. It never put in operation an advance in construction without providing the means. To buy economically and get all the advantage of selling promptly, it neither asked nor gave extended credits. But the care with which men to carry out the new or carry on the old were selected has been one strong cause of its commercial and industrial progress. For, after all, it is the man that counts, and his function in the great machine is incomparably the crucial one.

It is remarkable that the three founders who still happily survive have been able practically to withdraw from the direct conduct of the business, and yet see it go on strengthening and broadening. Mr. John D. Rockefeller retired from active participation some sixteen years ago, to devote himself to gentler things and to the maturing and carrying out of his philanthropy. Mr. Henry M. Flagler had slackened his directing energies for Standard Oil nearly ten years earlier, and had undertaken his wonder-working efforts in Eastern Florida, beginning when nearing his sixtieth year a task that might have appalled a man of thirty, a task which after a quarter of a century is now all but crowned with the nearing completion of its ocean-traversing railroad through to Key West. Mr. William Rockefeller, still a great advisory force in Standard Oil, has for twenty years figured as one of the great individual factors in the railroad and banking world quite outside of Standard Oil. Henry H. Rogers has passed over to the majority. But through such broad and active men as John D. Archbold, C. M. Pratt, James A. Moffett—three of the Vice Presidents—the great traditions of the Company find able application in a constantly widening field. In their hands and those of their brother directors the future conduct of the company is safe.

The Directors for 1911 are John D. Rockefeller, Wm. Rockefeller, Henry M. Flagler, John D. Archbold, Oliver H. Payne, C. M. Pratt, C. W. Harkness, James A. Moffett, E. T. Bedford, Walter Jennings, A. C. Bedford. H. C. Folger, Jr., Walter C. Teagle, O. T. Waring, Lauren J. Drake. They stand supported by the loyalty and esprit de corps of the entire organization—and never were fellowship and comradeship more heartily the badge of a great and living industry than in the ranks of the 71,000 employes of Standard Oil. With assets of probably $700,000,000 behind its $100,000,000 of stock, untainted of stock-market manipulation or stock watering, it goes on its way, dealing with its business problems as effectively to-day when the oil wells of the United States are pouring forth the flood of 214,000,000 barrels in a year as when at the close of 1869 the year's output was 4,200,000 barrels.

No matter how the recent judgment of the United States Supreme Court may modify the precise form in which the Standard Oil properties may be legally held, it can be certified that the various activities which the Standard Oil Company has promoted, organized and advanced will continue to operate along the lines laid down by the Court and with the same material success as ever.

May 20, 1911.

THE TIDEWATER COMPANIES.

The use of pipes for transporting oil began early in the history of oil production, but, for a long time, was limited to small pipe, usually two inches in diameter, for moving oil from one part of a lease to another or to loading racks located on railroads near the oil production. About 1876, Messrs. Byron D. Benson, David McKelvy and Robert E. Hopkins, constituting the firm of D. McKelvy & Company, conceived the idea of transporting oil by pipe line across the Allegheny Mountains to the Seaboard. They organized a company, known as the Seaboard Pipe Company, and projected a pipe line intended to pump oil from the Butler field in Pennsylvania to Baltimore, Maryland. A survey was made and a right of way obtained from Brady's Bend in Armstrong County, Pennsylvania, across Pennsylvania and Maryland to Baltimore, and preparations were begun to build the line.

Such an innovation in transportation naturally met with violent opposition from the railroads carrying oil, as it was a menace to the very lucrative traffic in that commodity. Early in 1878, before actual work of construction of this pipe line began, the Butler field showed signs of exhaustion, while the production from the Bradford field was increasing rapidly and was becoming a large factor in the oil industry. It, therefore, seemed necessary to change the location of the line and build from the northern field instead of from the southern field.

At this time, the Philadelphia and Reading Railroad, which ran no nearer to the oil regions than Williamsport, Pennsylvania, was, by reason of its location, getting no part of the oil traffic. Mr. B. D. Benson, after many consultations with Mr. F. B. Gowan, then President of that Company, made a contract by which the Reading Railroad agreed to receive oil at any point on its system and transport it to New York or Philadelphia at a price so much below the then open rate charged by other railroads that it left the pipe line a large price for its work. After this contract was made, all work on the Seaboard line was suspended and finally abandoned. A survey was made and a right of way obtained from the Bradford field to Williamsport. In 1878, The Tide-Water Pipe Company, Limited, was organized to build this line. It first purchased from the Equitable Pipe Line Company a small line extending from Rixford, Pennsylvania, a few miles over the hill to Corryville, where the oil was loaded on the cars of the Buffalo and McKean Railroad, and it made preparation to extend this line at once to Williamsport, Pennsylvania.

The organizers of the Tide-Water Pipe Company, Limited, were Messrs. Byron D. Benson, David McKelvy, Robert E. Hopkins, Alanson A. Sumner, Samuel Q. Brown and Josiah G. Benton, and among its stockholders were such well-known oil producers as John Fertig, John L. McKinney, John Satterfield, H. L. Taylor, Benjamin Campbell and Andrew N. Perrin.

It was freely prophesied by those who watched this project that the construction of a line over the Allegheny Mountains would prove a colossal failure, as it was thought that pipe could not be obtained to stand the necessary pressure and that oil could not be made to flow over so great an elevation. Work of construction began in the early winter of 1878 and was pushed energetically under great difficulties. Much of the distance from Rixford to Williamsport, about one hundred miles, was through unbroken forests and over high and precipitous mountains. To construct a line through such a country under such conditions would have discouraged any men less determined than the men behind this pioneer enterprise. In the mountainous regions through which the line passed, there were then no railroads for nearly the whole distance and, for many miles, there was not even a public highway. No one unfamiliar with the character of the country as it existed at that time can have an adequate idea of the difficulties encountered. Experience has made pipe line construction an easy matter but the Tide Water line which blazed the way was a great undertaking, for it was largely an experiment, built when the physical laws covering the transportation of oil in pipes were not known and the pumps, engines and pipe itself had largely to be designed to meet new and unknown conditions. Great credit is due to Mr. J. G. Benton, who acted as General Superintendent of the Company from the beginning of the enterprise until his death in 1908 for the engineering plans and scientific construction of the line. and also to Mr. B. F. Warren, who was at that time and still continues the Chief Engineer of the Company and had supervision of the survey and Right of Way Department.

Added to the physical difficulties which the new project had to face, it met with the violent and active opposition of the railroads, which obstructed its course in every possible manner. The Northern Central Railroad, a branch of the Pennsylvania, went so far in its opposition as to send an engine and a force of men to tear out the pipe which had been laid under and across its roadbed. The matter was thrown into court and decided in favor of the pipe line. This decision made it possible for other pipe lines to cross railroads under certain conditions and subsequently a free pipe line bill was passed by the Pennsylvania Legislature giving pipe lines the right of eminent domain in that State and doing away with all fractious opposition from interested parties.

The line was completed and oil pumped through to Williamsport in May, 1879. Prior to its completion, the open rate for the transportation of oil from the oil region to the seaboard was $1.50 per barrel. The day the Tide-Water Pipe Company, Limited, began pumping oil the rate was reduced to 50 cents and has remained low ever since.

For a time, the line terminated at Williamsport and the oil was hauled from there to seaboard by the Reading Railroad. In 1881, the line was extended to Tamanend, Scuylkill County, Pennsylvania, where connection was made with the Central Railroad Company of New Jersey as well as the Reading. Finally, in 1885, it was completed to New York Harbor, making a continuous line from Rixford, Pennsylvania, to Bayonne, New Jersey, a distance of 286.17 miles. The powerful pumps to force the six-inch stream of oil are located from thirty to forty miles apart, according to intervening elevations, and worked at a pressure of about eight hundred pounds per square inch. Seven sets of pumps are required to put through the line its daily average capacity of four hundred and twenty thousand gallons.

Before the line was completed to Williamsport, contracts had been made with Eastern refineries to receive the oil, but, when the Company was ready to deliver it, several refineries had changed ownership and the new owners refused to carry out the agreements made with their predecessors. The only New York refiners who adhered to their contract were Messrs. Lombard and Ayres, operating what was known as the "Seaboard Refinery," under the firm name of Lombard, Ayres and Company. Some of the people interested in the Tide-Water Company built a refinery at Williamsport, Pennsylvania, known as the Solar Oil Company, which was the first company to take oil through the new line. This refinery, after being operated for a number of years, was finally abandoned.

It early became evident to the organizers of The Tide-Water Pipe Company, Limited, that, if they were to secure an outlet for their oil, they must own refineries, and, to this end, the Chester Oil Company was organized in 1880 and a large refinery constructed at Thurlow on the Delaware River below Philadelphia. Another refining company, known as the Ocean Oil Company, was organized a little later which constructed a plant at Bayonne, New Jersey, where The Tide-Water Pipe Company, Limited, had been foresighted enough to secure a large area of land. Messrs. Lombard Ayres and Company also secured land adjoining and moved their refinery from 64th Street, New York City, to Bayonne, New Jersey. In 1884, the Polar Oil Company was organized by the Tide-Water people to make paraffine oil and conduct a general lubricating oil business. In 1888, a consolidation of the refining interests took place. A new company to engage in the general refining business was organized, known as the Tide Water Oil Company, which purchased the Chester Oil Company, the Ocean Oil Company, the Polar Oil Company and the Seaboard Refinery belonging to Messrs. Lombard, Ayres and Company, and this Company has since continued in active operation. Its plant at Bayonne, New Jersey, covers more than eighty-four acres and is complete in every detail. It has capacity sufficient to refine all the crude oil which the pipe line can deliver.

The present authorized capital stock of The Tide Water Oil Company is $25,000,000, of which $24,000,000 has been issued. The officers are R. D. Benson, President; W. S. Benson, Vice President and Treasurer, and Dickson Q. Brown, Second Vice President, who have all been schooled from boyhood in every branch of the business, the Messrs. Benson being sons of the first President of the Company, and Mr. D. Q. Brown being the son of the late executive, Mr. Samuel Q. Brown. Mr. H. C. Folger, Jr., who has been engaged in the refining business since 1879, is one of the directors and other directors are Messrs. Francis L. Hine, President, and George F. Baker, Jr., Vice President of the First National Bank of New York, among whose clientele are many large stockholders of the Company.

In 1908, the partial exhaustion of the Allegany and Bradford fields, from which The Tide-Water Pipe Company, Limited, had theretofore drawn its supply of crude, made it necessary that a new pipe line should be constructed to a fresh field, and the line was therefore extended from Rixford, Pennsylvania, to Stoy, Crawford County, Illinois, a distance of about five hundred and fifty miles. The line runs in an almost straight line through the Western counties of Pennsylvania and across the entire states of Ohio and Indiana. The survey was made, right of way obtained and line put in operation in a period of a little over fifteen months, and oil was delivered through the new pipe line to Rixford in July, 1909.

The producing interests controlled by the Tide Water Oil Company, which is now the parent company of the Tide Water organization, are the Okla Oil Company, operating in Oklahoma, and the Associated Producers Company, operating in Illinois, West Virginia, Ohio and Pennsylvania.

The Tide Water Oil Company is perhaps better known in foreign countries than at home, as a large proportion of its products is exported. A great part of the burning oil which it ships is the grade known as case oil, so-called because it is packed in five gallon cans, two cans being shipped in one square wooden box or case. In this compact form, it is transported to the remotest districts of South America and Asia. A missionary from Philadelphia some years ago sent the Company a tag from an oil can which he had picked up in a remote valley of the Himalaya Mountains, and, more recently, another traveller sent a photograph which he snapped of a caravan carrying the Company's brand of case oil through the Khyber Pass between India and Afghanistan.

In addition to manufacturing burning oil, the Tide Water Oil Company manufactures high grade lubricating oils and paraffine wax, for which it has a large and steady trade. The Company does not advertise its products and has never been exploited in the newspapers, but it has a large and profitable business. The stock seldom changes hands, as the great majority of the stockholders are either original subscribers to the Company or their legal representatives.

JOHN DAVISON ROCKEFELLER.

John D. Rockefeller needs no introduction to the reading public, for his name is known everywhere. He is the man whose constructive genius is responsible for the most effective commercial organization in the world. His achievement is no accident. The foundations of his success were laid in his early youth on a New York State farm and the superstructure was begun in Cleveland, Ohio, before the petroleum industry had been started by Edwin L. Drake. Mr. Rockefeller has been accused of crushing competition ruthlessly by employment of unfair devices, but the truth of history will record that his most aggressive and able competitors have become his business associates and fast personal friends. His wonderful success has been attained by the application to his business of the science of economical process and the organization of his forces as perfectly as an army, but with a discipline never savoring of compulsion. The Standard Oil Company represents at once the highest type of loyalty and the largest degree of individual initiative. Its commercial triumphs have been accomplished by the efforts of scores of business giants, working each in his own way, but all co-ordinated to a single end—the production of the best possible commodity at the least possible cost.

John D. Rockefeller was born in Richford, Tioga County, New York, on a farm. His parents were William Avery and Eliza Davison Rockefeller, of good American stock, and they early inculcated in him the lessons of the dignity of labor, the value of money and the essential of Christianity. At nine years of age he showed his business instinct by saving his earnings and investing them at interest. When fourteen years of age his parents removed to Cleveland, Ohio, and he entered the High School there. At fifteen he joined the Euclid Avenue Baptist Church and was soon one of the most enthusiastic workers in the congregation. He personally solicited the funds to pay the debt then resting on the church. At sixteen he left school and sought employment, and after some discouraging experiences he succeeded in obtaining a position as assistant bookkeeper in the forwarding and commission house of Hewitt & Tuttle, at a salary of four dollars a week. He remained with the firm for several years, his salary advancing to $700 a year when he became cashier and bookkeeper. Before he was nineteen years old he had been elected a trustee of the Euclid Avenue Baptist Church, and soon thereafter he resolved to embark in a business of his own. With a thousand dollars he had managed to save and another thousand borrowed from his father, he formed a partnership with Maurice B. Clark, as Clark & Rockefeller, and set up in the forwarding and commission business, with which he was familiar. Close application to business brought success, but it did not prevent him giving a share of time to the church and to charities. Mr. Rockefeller had not reached his majority when the wonderful well of Drake was drilled in on Oil Creek and a new industry came into being. The following year, when he was twenty-one, his firm took an interest in a refinery, his start in the business of refining oil.

In 1865 Mr. Rockefeller sold out his interest in the commission business and, with a partner, Mr. Samuel Andrews, purchased the interests of his associates in the oil refining business. The firm of Rockefeller & Andrews rapidly enlarged their oil manufacturing. Mr. Rockefeller, with rare foresight, saw in the new industry the opportunity of a life time and Mr. Andrews was a practical refiner, capable of turning out a better product than was generally on the market. The firm had an excellent field in the lake region and Mr. Rockefeller's business acquaintance and knowledge were equal to its cultivation. As the business expanded William Rockefeller was taken into the partnership and another firm of William Rockefeller & Co. was organized. John D. Rockefeller was quick to see that the business was to be largely one of export to foreign lands and soon William Rockefeller was transferred to New York to handle the products at that end, while Mr. Henry Flagler was taken into the firm at Cleveland. In 1870 the business had grown to proportions that demanded further expansion and the Standard Oil Company of Ohio was incorporated, John D. Rockefeller being made President. At about the same time the National Refiners' Association was formed and he was chosen as its President. Mr. Rockefeller was then thirty-one years old, success had attended his efforts, his character was formed and he bent his remarkable intellectual and physical powers to the task of supplying to the world an artificial light that should give the maximum service at the least possible cost.

It was plain to Mr. Rockefeller that diffusive effort was not economical and he counseled a combination of resources to secure greater efficiency. Two years after the organization of the Standard Oil Company of Ohio, or in 1872, nearly the entire refining interest of Cleveland and a large portion of that at New York and in the oil producing region were combined in that Company and the capital stock was increased to $2,500,000. Its business in one year reached over twenty-five million dollars, the largest company of the kind in the world. In order that there should be no unnecessary expense and to assure a regular supply of crude, the Company bought interests in pipe lines, had iron cars built and systematized its transportation and marketing. Mr. Rockefeller noting the high cost of barrels arranged for the purchase of timber lands, the erection of saw mills and the addition of barrel works, thereby reducing the cost of packages more than one-third. Other leading refineries in Ohio, Pennsylvania and New York were impressed by the efficiency of the Standard system and associated themselves with it from time to time. For the better handling of the business in 1882 the Standard Oil Trust was formed with a capital of $70,000,000, which was later increased to $95,000,000. Through all these changes Mr. Rockefeller was the guiding spirit and directing head. His genius challenged the attention of the business world and his well known probity enabled the Company to finance its early necessities.

Mr. Rockefeller was married on September 8, 1864, to Miss Laura C. Spielman, a classmate in the Cleveland High School, the daughter of a Representative in the State Legislature, who was eminently fitted to be his companion and helpmeet, as their tastes were much in common, both being devoted to church work and charities. To this union five children have been born: Bessie, who is the wife of Charles A. Strong, associate professor of psychology in Chicago University; Alice, who died early; Alta, who is Mrs. Prentice; Edith, the wife of Harold F. McCormick, of Chicago, and John D. Rockefeller, Jr., a graduate of Brown University, who has his father's business talent and all his love for church and benevolent work. The Rockefeller children have all been reared with good sense and Christian teaching, they dress simply, live without display and are active in hospital, Sunday School and other good works, toward which their sympathies naturally tend.

Mr. Rockefeller retired from active business about sixteen years ago and has devoted much of his time since then to works of benevolence, disbursing from his large fortune with the same acumen and care that he exercised in its accumulation. His benefactions are too many to enumerate, aggregating more than a hundred million dollars, but the chief of them are the Rockefeller Institute for Medical Research in New York and the Chicago University. He has been a liberal giver to other educational institutions, but these two are his own creations, the Institute wholly so and the University practically so. No restrictions have been placed upon either and the only injunction from the donor of their splendid endowments is that they shall do their utmost to benefit mankind. Mr. Rockefeller has recently endeavored to incorporate the Rockefeller Foundation to administer his large wealth, but factious opposition has prevented action by Congress.

In the petroleum world Mr. Rockefeller has occupied the premier position and has devoted his energies to advancing the interests of his business associates and to giving the world good and cheap light. In the business world at large he has discouraged speculation and has used his power to minimize violent and injurious fluctuations. His success has been due to fidelity to his ideals and the extreme of integrity in his dealings. He has been grossly misrepresented, because in his consciousness of probity he has declined to reply to criticism. He has deprecated a defense at the hands of his friends on the ground that the record will show the truth in the final analysis. For the remainder his works speak for themselves. He has been a benefactor to his race on the same principle as he who makes two blades of grass grow where but one grew before. He has made good artificial light cheap and has given an impulse to general education without precedent.

Mr. Rockefeller has lived the simple life, ostentation and display being distasteful to his very nature. He is devoted to golf as a recreation and spends much time on the links in all weather. His visits to the South in winter have enabled him to observe the ravages of the hookworm disease and, with ready sympathy for human suffering, he has donated a fund for the eradication of the pest. This beneficence is one of the greatest he has undertaken and is fully appreciated in regions rendered miserable by the malady, but not so well understood at the North, where the disease is not common. This work and that of the Rockefeller Institute for Medical Research are designed to lessen suffering and to benefit all mankind. They have already fully justified themselves, in their very infancy.

JOHN DUSTIN ARCHBOLD.

No unimportant place in the commercial history of America in the nineteenth century can be assigned to the development of the great petroleum industry of Pennsylvania. Comparatively few years ago the product was a luxury; to-day it is a necessity, which all can afford. Its marvelous history is unparalleled in the annals of the mineral products of the United States. The first Pennsylvania oil derrick was erected in the year 1859. In that year the product reached 2,000 barrels of oil and in the following year it reached 500,000. In the year 1909 the production of petroleum in the United States alone, reached the enormous total of 186,739,569 barrels of forty-two gallons each.

John Dustin Archbold, equally with anyone in America, has seen the many phases of this development from its inception, through the exciting periods of its early history to its present great proportions.

Mr. Archbold was born on the 26th of July, 1848, at Leesburg, Ohio, a State famed for the business and political successes of her sons, who are scattered throughout the Union. His father was Israel Archbold, a native of Virginia. He was the descendant of an ancient Protestant Irish family, who settled in this country in 1786 and who had their origin more than a century before in the large immigration of Scottish and English settlers, who, in the reign of James the First, introduced Presbyterianism in the Irish province of Ulster The Archbolds sought America at a time when anarchy prevailed in their native land as a result of the deplorable warfare between Catholics and Protestants.

Israel Archbold married the daughter of Colonel William Dana, one of the pioneers of the then Far Western State of Ohio, having brought his family to Marietta by wagon from Massachusetts. John D. Archbold was given the best education obtainable in the primitive schools of that out of the way region, and at the age of thirteen became a clerk in the country store located in the village of Salem, Columbiana County, Ohio. There he remained for a little more than two years, but his later life has proven that his duties did not command all his time, or that at least his leisure hours were devoted to study and to the preparation for the more important labors in which he was so soon to become so prominent a figure.

Although the first discoveries had been made five years previous, the real tidal wave of the excitement came in the latter part of 1864 and early in 1865. A host of men of brains and energy at once gathered in the region, and in the former year Mr. Archbold was among the earliest in the field. During the ensuing eleven years he witnessed and took part in all the wonderful evolutionary process of development, saw fortunes made and lost in a day, and saw ephemeral towns, which now have absolutely no existence, receiving a greater volume of mail than even the city of Pittsburg. During these years he attained prominence, gaining experience in almost every branch of the petroleum business and being given rapid promotion, amassed a moderate capital and became a large owner of the Acme Oil Company. Of this company he was made President in 1875. In the fall of 1875 Mr. Archbold became identified with the so-called Standard Oil interests and very soon after became a Director of the Standard Oil Company. In this corporation his practical knowledge of the industry, his clear judgment and general ability have made him a prominent figure.

There is no detail of the vast petroleum industry, from the production of the oil at the well, namely, the refining of the crude, the transportation, distribution and merchandising of the refined product as well as by-products, which he does not thoroughly understand and of which he is not a past-master. In nothing has the vast organization with which he has so long and so prominently been identified been more noted the world over than for the remarkable ability displayed by its management and in nothing has the management been more successful than in the wise selection of men having special fitness and training for the peculiar duties that they are called upon to perform. Mr. Archbold, therefore, having this general mastery of all departments alike, is regarded by everybody familiar with the industry, as an "all-rounder," and his judgment is as ready and unerring as it is sought for whenever new or important questions press for solution.

A well-known business man, long an associate of the subject of this sketch, speaking of his peculiar mental characteristics, once said to the writer that "He reminded him of an elephant's trunk in that he could, with equal facility, pick a cambric needle from a pin cushion or throw an anvil across the street!"

The comprehensive scope of his mind is perhaps no better illustrated than by his testimony given at great length before the Industrial Commission in 1899, extracts from which are now being quoted broadcast by the press of the country: "If you should ask me, gentlemen, what legislation can be imposed to improve the present condition, I answer that the next great, and to my mind, inevitable step of progress in the direction of our commercial development, lies in the direction of National or Federal corporations. If such corporations should be made possible, under such fair restrictions and provisions as should rightfully attach to them, any branch of business could be freely entered upon by all comers and the talk of monopoly would be forever done away with. Our present system of State corporations, almost as varied in their provisions as the number of States, is vexatious alike to the business community and to the authorities of the various States. Such Federal action need not take away from these States their right to taxation or police regulation, but would make it possible for business organizations to know the general terms on which they could conduct their business in the country at large. Lack of uniformity in the laws of the various States as affecting business corporations is one of the vexatious features attending the business life of any great corporation to-day and I suggest for your most careful consideration the thought of a Federal corporation law."

Mr. Madison, afterwards President, one of the foremost members of the convention which formed the Constitution, offered an amendment while the provision was pending, defining the powers of Congress, authorizing that body "to grant charters of incorporation in cases where the publick good may require them, and the authority of a single State may be incompetent." This action of Mr. Madison is known to a comparatively few persons—those alone who have made themselves close students of the detailed proceedings of the convention, involving provisions which were defeated as well as adopted. It is unfortunate that the sagacious Madison made no argument and offered no reasons in support of Federal charters for corporations, this, possibly, because he regarded the propriety of so providing as manifest and self-evident. It remained for Mr. Archbold, therefore, nearly a century and a quarter thereafter, to assign these reasons and in a manner, we submit, that would have reflected high credit on the distinguished author himself. We recall no instance where this has been done in a more convincing form than in the words of Mr. Archbold above quoted. It is no longer doubtful that many of our foremost statesmen and publicists have reached the conclusion that the granting of acts of incorporations by the Federal Government, rather than by the States, will afford the best, if not the only, solution of this difficult economic problem. Whether this be so or not, we shall go far to find an authority more competent than Mr. Archbold to pass an intelligent judgment upon it from a business standpoint and also one who has presented the case in so small a compass or with more convincing logic.

Mr. Archbold was married in 1870 to Miss Annie Mills, the daughter of S. M. Mills, of Titusville, Pennsylvania, her brother being Colonel S. M. Mills, of the United States Army, recently Superintendent of the United States Military Academy at West Point.

The Archbolds have a beautiful summer home at Cedar Cliff, Tarrytown-on-Hudson, N. Y. Their children are Mary L (now Mrs. M. M. Van Beuren), Anne M. (now Mrs. Armar D. Saunderson), and John F. Archbold. A daughter, Mrs. F. C. Walcott, died a few years ago.

No sketch, however extended, would be symmetrical without a word concerning the personality of the man and of the many qualities possessed by him which endear him to the chosen circle of his friendship beyond most men. A man who never had a mood or humor in his life; one from whom an overflow of sparkling wit and pleasantry is always coming and never found to be commonplace or disappointing; one fond of a good story and always ready with a still better one of his own; one whose success in life does not lead him to assume superiority over others, but one who through it all remains unaffected, sincere and approachable, and showing a respectful and considerate regard for the opinions and feelings of other people, such are the traits most prominent on the social side of the man who, it would be superfluous to add, commands and deserves to command the confidence and esteem of a wide circle; one whose friends are limited only to acquaintanceship itself and all of whom are attached to him in no common degree of fidelity and devotion.

For many years Mr. Archbold has been able to devote much time and attention to educational and philanthropic affairs. He is a member of the Board of the St. Christopher's Home and Orphanage, of New York. He has also for some time been a Trustee of the Syracuse University at Syracuse, New York, and he is President of the Board of Trustees. During his incumbency of this important office, the University, which was organized in the year of Mr. Archbold's marriage, has more than regained its former prestige and has been more prosperous than ever in the forty years of its history, more than three thousand students now being in attendance. Mr. Archbold is also a patron of the Metropolitan Museum of Arts, and of the American Museum of Natural History, a member of the Union League, Racquet and Riding Clubs, of the Ohio Society and of the Ardsley Casino.

To have taken an active part in the development of the great industry with which, almost from its inception, Mr. Archbold has been intimately associated, is to have borne a part in a notable phase of our national history.

HENRY HUTTLESTON ROGERS.

A genuine American by ancestral lineage and typically American in intellectual and physical attributes, Henry H. Rogers was one of whom it might have been said, "There were giants in those days." He came to the oil region in 1861 and took a prominent part in shaping and developing the petroleum industry from that time to the day of his death. He was a man of keen vision and great breadth of perception, intolerant of nothing save cant and hypocrisy. Of remarkable energy and tenacity of purpose he surmounted obstacles at which another might have been dismayed. Wealth and position made no difference in his attitude toward others and while he compelled exactitude and the proper amenities he was a most companionable man in his hours of leisure. His grasp of finance and industrial problems made him a leader in the highest circles.

Mr. Rogers was born at Fairhaven, Massachusetts, in 1840, and died in New York in 1909. He graduated from the Fairhaven High School in 1856 and for a time was clerk in his father's store. Then he started to learn the railroad business but found the way to promotion slow and uncertain. After the discovery of petroleum he determined to go into that business. He traveled to Union City, Pennsylvania, by train and went by stage coach from there to Titusville, arriving on the evening of October 4, 1861. Joining with Charles P. Ellis, also of Fairhaven, he soon established a small refinery at McClintocks, on Oil Creek between Oil City and Rouseville. He remained there for six years, then going to the Pennsylvania Salt Works at Natrona, near Pittsburgh, which concern had, in addition to its chemical plant, one of the largest oil refineries in the country. In 1868 Mr. Rogers went to New York and associated himself with Charles Pratt, a leading oil refiner there. When in 1874, the leading refineries of Cleveland, Pittsburgh, Philadelphia, the oil region and New York were allied under the name of the Standard Oil Company, the famous Pratt works were included. When the Standard Oil Trust was formed, on account of his large practical experience, Mr. Rogers was made chairman of its manufacturing committee. In a short time he became one of the trustees and upon the organization of the Standard Oil Company of New Jersey he became First Vice President. He was President of the pipe line system to which he gave particular attention. About 1895 he became chairman of the Executive Committee, relieving Mr. John D. Rockefeller of the active direction of the big company. He continued in this position until his death.

Aside from the petroleum business, Mr. Rogers was widely connected in financial and industrial affairs. He engineered the consolidation of copper companies into the Amalgamated Copper Company, saving the next older industry than petroleum from serious embarrassment, if not from ruin, through gross overproduction. He was connected with many financial institutions and was on the boards of several of the leading railroads. His greatest single achievement was the construction of the Virginian Railroad, without an issue of bonds. This work was completed only a short time before his death. The railroad thus constructed will play an important part in the transportation business of the country in the course of time.

Mr. Rogers was a generous giver, as has been learned since his death, but during life he was very averse to having his benefactions known. He gave with the stipulation that no mention of the fact should be made public. To Fairhaven, the place of his birth and the location of his summer home, he gave a free library, a Masonic Temple, a High School building, a public park, a system of paved streets and many other things. He provided for the erection of a memorial church in memory of his mother. At Titusville he caused to be erected a memorial to Edwin Laurentine Drake, the discoverer of petroleum. At Oil City he assisted greatly in establishing the general hospital and the Grandview Sanitorium, one of the first refuges for sufferers from tuberculosis. He built the training school for nurses, in connection with the Oil City Hospital. To many other worthy objects he gave generously, his charities being on the same broad scale as his business affairs. He was a patron of art and literature, principally through agents who were bound to secresy, his contributions not being known individually even at this time. His success he personally attributed to good fortune and circumstance, but his business associates and friends well know that his industry, keen application, sound judgment and persistency were large factors in turning circumstances to account. He was a daring operator, but his ventures were made with just appreciation of the chances.

A few days after the death of Mr. Rogers, the following tribute from the pen of his personal friend, Mr. W. H. Libby, was spread upon the records of the Company:

The death of Henry H. Rogers an esteemed and highly valued Director of this Company, came as a shock and a sorrow to his family, friends and business associates.

In the early days of petroleum adventure Mr. Rogers went to the oil regions to seek his fortune and soon developed the forceful qualities which foreshadowed future achievement and human leadership.

He was a cormorant wherever hard work was visible and rapidly familiarized himself with the primitive methods of production, manufacture, transportation and distribution then in vogue. For nearly half a century thereafter he was destined to be conspicuously identified with the wonderful development of the petroleum industry at home and abroad, and in the solution of the varied problems daily confronting the world-wide commerce of this Company.

His well trained mind and memory inspired the value and variety of his counsel, which included in its equipment a comprehensive knowledge of the petroleum business from producing to consuming terminal. His counsel, if not always followed, was rarely ignored. Determined and indefatigable by nature, this counsel was often incisive and aggressive, yet no man could accept with greater equanimity the verdict of the majority of his co-directors, whatever that verdict might be. He had little patience with tardiness, his own engagements being punctiliously kept, alike with friend or foe—with clerk or magnate.

His keen intelligence—his nerve and iron will—were so subtly blended with a magnetic and impressive personality—with so buoyant an appreciation of humor—with so rare and genial a charm of social companionship that he won and retained to the limit of his three score years and ten, not only the admiration, confidence and respect, but also the affection of his co-workers in whatever station, and many an appreciative and grateful memory of him will long linger around 26 Broadway.

His unfailing and unbounded courage—which only death could quite subdue—was ever a veritable tonic to the wavering—a constant stimulant to all within the radius of its influence.

No adequate tribute can here be dedicated to the sacred endearments of his Church and home—nor to the many public and private benefactions and the endless chain of kindly and considerate words and deeds that punctuated and illuminated his long career. To voluminous biography must be assigned the labor and privilege of narrating his wonderful evolution, from the penniless boy of Fairhaven to the brilliant leader of vast and varied enterprises; a conspicuous Titan of modern achievement; an imperial and imperious gladiator of the industrial arena.

It seems eminently fitting that he should repose—at last—amid the cherished surroundings of his boyhood, and amid the people he loved so well.

"May he rest where the wand of the willow is waving,
And may grey-tinted mosses encircle his grave."

WILLIAM ROCKEFELLER.

It is remarkable that one American family bred in country life for over a century should produce in the same generation two brothers each destined, and in a sharply differentiated way, to become master-minds in the high finance of a continent. It was the case with the Rockefeller family which was settled at Richford, Tioga County, New York, in the late thirties and early forties of the last century. William Rockefeller, the second son, was born there on May 31, 1841, two years after John Davison, the eldest, and both had migrated with the family to Ohio many years before the birth of the oil industry which was to bring them fame and fortune. William went to the Owego (N. Y.) Academy for his first steps in learning, and later to the public schools of Cleveland, Ohio. His start in business, when he was seventeen, was as a bookkeeper to a prominent miller of Cleveland named Quinn, with whom he remained two years. Next he took a similar position with Hughes & Lester, a forwarding and commission house. After two years Lester retired and William entered the firm, which became Hughes & Rockefeller. It did a flourishing business, and during the following four years amassed profits that put young William in the modest category of a Cleveland capitalist, able at least to take advantage of opportunities around him. His firm dissolved in 1865, and the next step was memorable, namely, forming a co-partnership with his brother, John D., and Samuel Andrews under the title of William Rockefeller & Co. to conduct an oil refining business. They proceeded forthwith to build and equip the Standard Oil Works in Cleveland. Note the name! His brother and Mr. Andrews were already conducting the Excelsior refinery in the same town. Here, then, were the products of two establishments to be disposed of. New York offered the best market for surplus product and thither accordingly went the resourceful William Rockefeller in 1866. For this purpose he formed the firm of Rockefeller & Co. His ability as a merchant was demonstrated in the success of his marketing. The many refineries through the oil region and neighboring cities, in Pittsburg, Philadelphia, Cleveland and New York (mostly Brooklyn establishments) dealt as a rule through commission houses, jobbers and brokers. In New York William Rockefeller made his fight among these for the export trade. The entire petroleum business of New York was, of course, only a small fraction of what it is to-day, but it was infinitely more complicated in the carrying on. No larger container than the 50 gallon barrel was then known in commerce. The tank wagon, tank car and tank ocean steamer were far in the future. Dock room, warehouse room, lighters, repairing and refilling damaged barrels were necessary. To the providing of these Mr. Rockefeller addressed himself with surprising results. Other progress was organizing in Cleveland. In 1870 the three Rockefeller firms emerged as the Standard Oil Co. of Ohio, with $1,000,000 capital and William Rockefeller was named as Vice President. He was then in his thirtieth year. Business was growing. Combination of refineries had set in. The modest quarters at No. 2 Cedar Street no longer sufficed for the Eastern business. Accordingly it was moved, and the new corporation's sign was hung out at 140 Pearl. Here the really great beginnings of the Standard Oil export business were made—a business that under William Rockefeller's steady hand was to grow to the proportions of to-day, best perhaps indicated in the daily sailing of a great tank steamer laden with oil for European ports. The Erie Canal, the Erie Railroad and the New York Central in 1870 divided the carrying of the barreled Standard Oil. The export business grew by leaps and bounds. It was a spot cash business. Oil had to be paid for as soon as it was put on board. The financial talent of William Rockefeller herein found play, the new experience developing it amazingly. The warehousing, transfer and delivery of the oil required continually increased facilities. Competition was lively, but the time soon came when the greater New York oil refining interests followed their brethren of the West into the fold of the Standard Oil. The Pratts, the Bostwicks, the Devoes joined forces. The trade in case oil as well as barreled oil extended as petroleum production increased. In all this William Rockefeller displayed a master hand. Under his care money for any and all improvements—new plants, pipe lines, cars, steamers; what not—was always promptly found, always with increase of surplus and reserve. The Company moved to 44 Broadway where it paid rent for a time and then to its present quarters, the massive granite Standard Oil Building 26 Broadway, which is perhaps the one New York address of a private firm known all over the world—once, too, a hundred years earlier, the site of the law office of Alexander Hamilton. The Standard Oil Company of New York had been incorporated for carrying on the manufacture and sale of oil and oil products and William Rockefeller was elected President, a post he has filled to the present day. When the Standard Oil Trust was formed in 1882 he was one of the Trustees. When the now gigantic business was reorganized in 1899 with $100,000,000 capital, under the title of the Standard Oil Company of New Jersey, William Rockefeller was the first of its Vice Presidents. As a member of the Executive Committee of the Board his counsel on all points and his genius for monetary arrangement were alike sought continually. What was notable, although accepted without comment at the time, was that the ever increasing responsibilities of directing the handling of the enormous cash balances sat as lightly on his broad shoulders as had the financing of the modest establishment in Cedar Street. The provisions alone for banking the inflowing and outflowing sums required so intimate an acquaintance with the resources and management of banking institutions that Mr. Rockefeller became, as some assert, the leading bank expert of the United States and certainly among the top line of the country's financiers. His personal wealth was large. William Rockefeller's genius indeed allowed him to tread fearlessly in the maze of investment opportunities outside Standard Oil. His name was hailed with joy and placed upon the Board of Directors wherever his instinct for safe investment took him. If he accepted a directorship it meant an actual live interest in the concern which few similarly situated exhibit. A glance over the list of these outside interests as revealed in the financial publications is certainly astonishing.: National City Bank, Hanover National Bank, U. S. Trust Co., Anaconda Copper, Amalgamated Copper, United Metals Selling Co., director of Union Pacific Railroad; Chicago, Milwaukee and St. Paul; Lake Shore and Michigan Southern; New York Central & Hudson River; New York, New Haven & Hartford; Central New England; Delaware, Lackawanna & Western; Hartford & Connecticut Western; Harlem River and Portchester; New York & Harlem; Poughkeepsie Bridge Railway; the Consolidated Gas Co.; Mutual Gas Light Co.; Brooklyn Union Gas Co.; Carbide & Acetylene Co.—a vast array of diverse interests, surely. Of these the St. Paul road may be called his favorite, the making of the Chicago, Milwaukee and Puget Sound Extension—destined to be the great factor in the road's future—is in the largest degree the fruit of his efforts All these responsibilities, together with the great Standard Oil burden, he carries as efficiently to-day and with as little apparent effort as his lighter load of forty years ago.

Asked what was his most notable characteristic a friend replied his self-control. Never ruffled, never excited, even under determined efforts to excite him, he observes the same gentleness of bearing with young and old and high and low. All who know him speak of his modesty, his shrinking from notoriety. Of all the notable men of New York, he is, perhaps, the least known personally. In his youth and middle age the physical power suggested by his massive frame, square head and attractive, determined face with firm set jaws, blue, courageous eyes and strong mouth, bespoke the gladiator rather than the mild-mannered man of affairs he really was. With the proportions of the athlete he had a natural love of athletics, and this he indulged without stint when away from office cares. A love of the open has indeed been his from youth, and has led to his large holdings of forest land in the Adirondacks where he can lead the primitive life at will. In town one of the best dressed men, the holder of a box at the Metropolitan Opera House, a visitor to the theatres, in the country he becomes as to the manner born. He is a good shot, a fine driver of trotting horses. Many was the brush he and his brother John D. had over the roads of Westchester each behind his favorite pair. He is a lover and cultivator of flowers. One of the very first to recognize the merits of the Barbizon school he has made a collection of modern French masterpieces. Millet's "The Grafters," for instance, holds a place of honor beside his Rousseaus and Corots—and "The Grafters" is in no way inferior to the long exploited "Angelus."

Mr. Rockefeller married in his twenty-third year Miss Almira Geraldine Goodsell at Fairfield, Conn., and has two sons and two daughters, Emma, William G., Percy Avery and Ethel Geraldine, all now happily married. His fine estate on the Hudson between Tarrytown and Scarborough sees him most of his time. In town he has lived in the family mansion at Fifth Avenue and Fifty-fourth Street for thirty-five years. As a clubman he belongs to the Union League, Metropolitan and Gentlemen's Riding Clubs. So between his multifarious business interests and his many and varied activities outside, the life of William Rockefeller has been and is one of continual using of the faculties with which Heaven has lavishly endowed him.

HENRY MORRISON FLAGLER.

In those early days of the petroleum industry when the new Aladdin's lamp was rubbed and the genii called forth, there came Henry M. Flagler. He was assigned the duty of assisting in the conversion and dissemination of the earth's new treasure de signed to give light, to advance the pleasure and knowledge of mankind, and was splendidly fitted for the work. He became a member of the firm of Rockefeller, Andrews and Flagler, of Cleveland, Ohio, the foundation of the most wonderful corporation in the world, the Standard Oil Company. He brought to this task a brilliant business imagination that was capable of "building factories in the air," rather than castles, and in a new business, demanding sublime faith and confidence, he went forward to the achievement of his dreams. In his own person Mr. Flagler typifies that kindly spirit that has marked the Standard Oil apart from other great business machines, the antithesis of domineering, "steam roller" methods. From the headquarters of this great organization go no orders, but simple requests, or suggestions to be disposed of at discretion of the man on the scene of action, giving him the largest latitude of individual judgment. It is this humane treatment that has inspired the loyalty of the men in this huge organization, with a history of no strikes, or labor disturbances, but in which every employe is a responsible, active agent.

So in the vast personal affairs of Mr. Flagler on the East Coast of Florida, there is an army of men not merely loyal to the employer and his interests, but loving him as a business father. In this spirit they have wrought the transformation of the sub-tropical wilderness and builded the structures that are as permanent as time, bringing to the enterprises their individual genius and initiative, blending with the sound judgment of their chief. The Flagler improvements in East Florida have idealized nature in her pleasant moods and conquered her in her sternest aspects, creating a fairyland where nothing seems impossible. For the tourist there is a continuous round of pleasure with every beauty deprived of its concomitant annoyance, but to the analytical engineer, or man of affairs, this delightful whole is revealed as a monumental achievement of constructive genius, directed by artistic taste. Henry M. Flagler has woven his personality into the series of beautiful hotels and he has blended them into their fascinating surroundings. Of his work Edwin Lefevre wrote in "Everybody's Magazine:"

"Fate gave to Ponce de Leon for a ward the daughter of a companion who had died in his arms on the field of battle. On a visit to Spain, his last, he saw her. She was very beautiful and very young. Fame, wealth, power; Husks! Love, heaven. After awhile his ward consented to be his wife. But he, in his middle age, would be loved as only youth loves and is loved. Once more he sailed over the salt seas, ordered by the king on the old quests and by Eros on a new. The Caribs whom he subdued had often spoken of a magic land where was the Fountain of Perpetual Youth! A delectable vision came to him, and following its irresistible beckoning, he discovered on Easter Sunday—Pasquale, Florida in Spanish—March 27, 1513, the land he sought. In honor of the day and because it was a land green and beautiful, he called it Florida.

"He did not find youth. But, in seeking it, he grasped Immortality.

"Nearly four centuries later, from the gray north, a man named Flagler, a commercial discoverer, an industrial conquistador, past the age of Ponce de Leon, also went to Florida. It may be he sought the precious gold of the sunlight or the turquoise of the sky; perhaps merely a comfortable rocking chair on a hotel piazza. But he found what his brother conquistador missed. It did not gush from a fountain, but blossomed on the trees of his life's philosophy, which later bore marvellous fruit as you shall see. He found: his Second Youth, and, like Ponce de Leon, he also grasped Immortality.

"What he has done you may see for yourself; and the children of your children shall see still more clearly. The tramp of the marching years will not grind to dust his work, but make it the more solid—like the concrete of his viaducts and his buildings, which will grow harder, more like stone, with age. In no other place, in no other way, by no other man could the work have been done."

About 1877 Mr. Flagler went to Florida and saw its possibilities as a pleasure ground and realized its lack of accommodations. Then he decided to bring its possibilities to realization. The Ponce de Leon in St. Augustine was his hardest problem, to fit a thoroughly modern hotel into the environment of the oldest city in the United States, but he did it. The remainder was simply development of the lead. Next he saw the possibilities of East Florida for agriculture. He was a director in several great railroad corporations at the North, and no one was better qualified to realize the need of a railroad development for the benefit of the people who were to come in and settle up a new country. He could get no improvement by advice and suggestion, so he bought the railroad from Jacksonville to Daytona, 110 miles in length. After buying and extending it to Miami, he developed it into the means of helping thousands of poor men to help themselves to a comfortable livelihood, in a benign climate, by growing the products of an almost tropical region. When Mr. Flagler conceived the national and commercial importance of extending his road to Key West, he set about building it.

Mr. Flagler's investment in East Florida represents wonderful construction: permanence and beauty have been the considerations. The work will endure as long as the romantic fame of Ponce de Leon will survive. It has already conferred inestimable benefits upon mankind, but the best will be in centuries to come. Mr. Flagler, when he began these vast enterprises, could close his eyes and see a mental picture of the finished work, the comfortable hotels, the railroad trains in operation, the thousands of plantations, with their productions. Others are now seeing these things and in the years to come all may see them plainly. One of the oldest of his employes has said of him that: "He has the faculty of clear, logical reasoning and a perception so keen and quick that he unerringly detects a flaw anywhere at a glance. He is very careful and studies a thing thoroughly before he acts. Once he is convinced it can be done he goes ahead without regard to the time or profit. Fifty months or fifty years are all the same to him, so far as profits are concerned. And he is never impatient and never discouraged."

Mr. Flagler is remarkably self-contained and with habitual self-repression. He feels strongly, his associates know, but never gives expression to his feelings. This is partly inherited and partly the result of his early life. He was born near Canandaigua, New York, in 1830, the son of a Presbyterian clergyman. At the age of fourteen he felt that his support was a strain on the minister's meagre salary, and left home to make his own way. He went to Buffalo by canal boat, and to Sandusky, Ohio, by boat on the lake. He landed in the grain country at Bellevue, Ohio, where he worked long and hard. He went into the salt business at Saginaw, Michigan, when the excitement was strong there. Then he located in Cleveland, where his knowledge of grain growing became a factor in the commission business. There he met John D. Rockefeller, and when the latter left the produce commission business for oil refining, Mr. Flagler joined the enterprise. There he found himself. The constructive ability so well illustrated in his Florida projects was exerted in the oil enterprise; his love of permanence and his patience to wait for fruition of his plans were strong factors in the upbuilding of the Standard Oil Company. The men who founded that great commercial organization lived the simple, economical lives necessity had taught them, and put every dollar of their profits back into enlargement of the business. Mr. Flagler has been a director of the Chicago, Rock Island & Pacific Railroad, the Minnesota Iron Company, Duluth and Iron Range Railroad, Western Union Telegraph Company, International Bank Note Company, and Morton Trust Company, in addition to the two projects that have been his life work, and an investor in many others.

SAMUEL QUEEN BROWN.

With the death of Samuel Q. Brown on October 5, 1909, the petroleum industry lost one of its most distinguished and successful pioneers. Moreover, there departed a kindly gentleman, whose charm of personality had won him thousands of friends, many of whom had learned to lean upon his wise counsel in hours of perplexity. He was one man who had made the most of his opportunities, who had prospered amazingly, but who never forgot to acknowledge his indebtedness to a Divine Providence, who gave generously to the churches where he resided, not only to the Presbyterian, to which he belonged, but to all other denominations. He was a man who furthered every enterprise designed to secure the welfare of his neighbors and his fellow men.

Samuel Q. Brown was born in Pleasantville, Venango County, Pennsylvania, on September 19, 1835, two years after his parents had settled there, in what was known as the West. The family had previously resided in New York City, where Mr. John Brown had been a merchant. Being a man of strict religious sentiments, he believed the country would be a better place to bring up a family than the city. He and a number of others commissioned an agent to go West and select locations for them in Northwestern Pennsylvania. Early in 1833, leaving Mrs. Brown to follow with the household goods, and the stock of merchandise selected for the country store, via the Erie Canal, then the great highway to the West, Mr. Brown hastened forward by way of Harrisburg to prepare the home for the family. The agent, instead of locating his clients together in a little colony, as they desired, had procured widely separated tracts. That assigned to Mr. Brown was in the howling wilderness, several miles north of Titusville. When he found it he was so dissatisfied that he hurried on to Pleasantville, then an attractive small village, and secured a location there. When the family arrived the prospect was so discouraging they all decided to return to New York as soon as possible. That could not be until the stock of merchandise brought out could be disposed of. A part of the household goods were left packed for reshipment. However, the merchandise had to be sold on credit and before the collections could be made, all were so attached to the place and the sympathetic neighbors that they decided to remain. Thus Samuel Q. Brown was born and grew up in Pleasantville.

The subject of this sketch was not robust, physically, but he had a fine intellect. This may be the more readily appreciated from the fact that he matriculated and entered Allegheny College, Meadville, when thirteen years of age. He passed the freshman year with honors, but his health failed and he was unable to complete the course. He remained an invalid for several years, but finally recuperated, went to Pittsburg, took the course in Duff's Commercial College, and returned to Pleasantville to assist his father in the store, now grown to a business of some proportions. He was there in the flower of his young manhood when the news of Drake's wonderful well reached him. Opportunity needed to tap but lightly at his door. Forming a partnership with John L. Mitchell, his neighbor, one night he went racing across the Pithole Valley, down Cherry Run to Oil Creek, on his best horse, and secured leases on the John Buchanan and Archbald Buchanan farms at the mouth of Cherry Run. The firm was at once enlarged by taking into the partnership Hon. Henry R. Rouse, of Enterprise. Mr. Rouse had already taken an interest with W. H. Abbott and others at Titusville, which firm completed the second well to find oil. Brown and Mitchell kicked down a "spring pole" well, the third on Oil Creek, that pumped ten barrels a day from the first sand, but being drilled to the third sand later produced 300 barrels a day for a long period. After the tragic death of Mr. Rouse, the management of the property vested principally in Mr. Brown. When nearly a hundred wells had been drilled by themselves and sub-lessees, Mr. Brown put both farms into the Buchanan Farms Oil Company, with a capital stock of four million dollars, realizing one million dollars from his interest. He at once established a broker's office in Philadelphia, and the next year one in New York, where he dealt extensively in oil stocks, traveling by night from one city to the other, giving alternate days to each office.

While in the brokerage business, Mr. Brown obtained a charter for the Farmers' Railroad, along Oil Creek from Oil City to Shaffer. Owing to the opposition of Colonel Scott, this was obtained with difficulty, and originally for a horse railroad, only. After he had succeeded in getting it changed to steam power, Mr. Brown disposed of the charter to Bishop, Bissell and others, who constructed the Oil Creek Railroad. At about the same time Mr. Brown secured a charter for a pipe line, in 1862, from Tarr farm to Oil City, but it was impossible to obtain suitable pipe. A short line was built in 1863, but leakage at the joints was so excessive that the disastrous pond-freshet system was continued for a couple of years, but Mr. Brown had pointed the way for the ultimate triumph of pipe lines as soon as proper pipe was made. Along with his other activities at this time Mr. Brown, with his two brothers, opened a store at Oil City, which had not yet been named, the postoffice being known as Cornplanter. In 1865, Mr. Brown married Miss Lamb, of Pleasantville, whom he had known from childhood. In 1866 he became a partner in a large mercantile house in New York, continuing the Pleasantville store as a wholesale and retail branch. In 1867 he went to Nevada by way of Panama and San Francisco. Returning in March he contracted a cold, which resulted in severe hemorrhages from the lungs and his life was despaired of. Recovering partly, he traveled in the South during the following winter, deriving so much benefit that when oil was discovered near Pleasantville, he took an active part in the development of the territory, including several hundred acres of his own lands. He opened a bank in Pleasantville, in company with Mr. Mitchell, which was superseded later by the Pleasantville Banking Company, with Mr. Brown as President.

In 1872, following the agitation against the South Improvement Company, Samuel Q. Brown was elected a trustee of the Petroleum Producers' Agency, and later a member of the business committee of that organization. In 1877 he was an active operator in the Enterprise district, assisting at about the same time in organizing the Seaboard Pipe Line. In 1878 he was a leader in the organization of the Tide-Water Pipe Line Company, Limited. This company was organized November 23, 1878, and soon afterward began the construction of its line. It was a success from the start. In 1881 Mr. Brown moved to Philadelphia to take charge of the financial management of the Chester Oil Company, a Tide-Water refinery which was being built at Chester, Pa. In 1889 the line was extended to Bayonne, New Jersey, with headquarters in New York. He was a manager of that company from 1886 to his death and President from 1893 to 1908. He was elected President of the Tide Water Oil Company when it was organized in 1888 and continued in that office until May, 1908, when he was elected Chairman of the Board of Directors and remained so until his death. He was also a director of the Associated Producers' Company from 1894 to October, 1908, and was its President from 1903 to 1908. In all of these companies he was a strong factor in their success. His executive ability is shown by the phenomenal success of the business during the fifteen years he was the chief executive of the Tide Water companies. In his daily dealings with business affairs he was so just, kind and considerate, that he well merited the love and respect in which he was held by associates and employes. It is given to few men to be actively engaged in an industry for more than fifty years as was Samuel Q. Brown in the petroleum industry, and to a smaller number to pass from the scene of their labors enjoying the universal esteem of their fellows as he did.

Mr. Brown received in 1871 the honorary degree A. M. from Princeton University. He represented the petroleum interests on the Second Geological Survey Commission of the State of Pennsylvania. He was a Republican in politics and a member of the Union League Club, New York City, and various other clubs. The last twenty years of his life he lived in New York City where his widow and four children now reside.

HOME OF STANDARD OIL COMPANY, 26 BROADWAY, NEW YORK.

Page left intentionally blank

DR. M. C. EGBERT.

Dr. Milton Cooper Egbert has been identified with the petroleum industry since the beginning. He was at the Drake well when it was struck in August, 1859, and the next day had embarked in the business. He and his brother, Dr. A. G. Egbert, on that day purchased the Alexander Davidson farm on Oil Creek. This was the first farm ever bought for the purpose of producing oil, a fact which entitles Dr. Egbert to a place at the top of the list of petroleum pioneers. The farm, which was known as the Egbert & Hyde farm, is famous in oil history as one of the most profitable of the early period. It was in the center of activity during the wildly exciting times on Oil Creek. The best known wells on the Egbert & Hyde farm were "The Jersey," which made 400 barrels a day; "The Coquette," famed and erratic, which produced 600 barrels daily; and "The Maple Shade," which was a genuine thousand-barrel gusher and continued producing at a great rate for a long time. Development of the farm was begun almost immediately after its purchase, but its best days were in 1863, when the noted wells named were drilled into the "third sand."

This remarkable farm was in part responsible for the "boom" at Petroleum Centre, one of the liveliest oil towns in the world. It was separated from "the Centre" only by Oil Creek, and at the zenith of the glory of the wicked city it became necessary for Doctor Egbert to employ a deputized sheriff to keep the lawless element from overrunning his property.

Doctor Egbert was engaged in buying oil and shipping it to New York from 1867 to 1874, being associated in a partnership under the firm name of Egbert & Brown.

After the dissolution of the shipping partnership, Dr. Egbert continued as he had before, in the business of producing oil. He was active in many fields, including the great development in McKean county, Pennsylvania, the Bradford field. For several years he resided in Bradford and did business there. He was in West Virginia in the formative stage of that development and now has producing properties in Ohio. Thus it is seen that his activities cover the entire range of the Eastern oil fields. He was in at the beginning and is yet a factor in the most wonderful industrial creation in the span of human history.

The subject of this sketch was born in Mercer county, Pennsylvania, on May 18, 1838. Aside from the local schools, he was educated in Western Reserve Medical College, Cleveland, Ohio. After graduation he at once began the practice of his profession and was a successful physician when the oil business enticed him into a more exciting career. He was married in Rouseville, Venango county, Pennsylvania, in 1863, to Miss Emma Taft. He has two sons, Harry T. Egbert, of Oil City, and Victor E. Egbert, of Pittsburgh, Pa. Doctor Egbert's ancestry is traced to England, but the line is quite long in America. He has for some years resided in Pittsburg and has his business office in the Machesney building on Fourth avenue in that city.

acres in fee with 40 producing wells. Immediately after the shut-down in 1888, Mr. Carter began development, drilling 125 wells, some being dry, but on the whole it was a productive and profitable development. It is still producing in paying quantities, but not now owned by Mr. Carter. In addition to the development for oil, Mr. Carter established the Riverside Stock Farm on the property, and soon the broad and well watered acres were alive with horses, cattle, sheep and swine of the most approved breeds. Three splendid studs of horses there found home—French Percheron, English Clydesdale and Cleveland Bay, which, with a harem of sixty brood mares and their progeny, added both beauty and value to the farm. Three herds of pure blood cattle, Holstein Friesian, Jersey and English Shorthorn, a flock of imported Shropshire sheep, and a herd of Poland China hogs, gave variety and value to the rich soil of the Allegheny River flats. They also gave the surrounding country a start in economic farming by supplying the material for better grades, the object lesson of the successful big farm being of the utmost value to the community. Generations yet unborn will recognize the value and the blood of the stock introduced by John J. Carter in Forest County.

The timber on that farm Mr. Carter guarded as he did the hair of his head. After producing oil for twenty years, he sold the wells to the Standard Oil Company, and the forest and the fee to Warren parties, realizing handsomely from that great property.

In 1889 Mr. Carter associated himself with John Fertig, John L. McKinney and E. O. Emerson in the purchase and rebuilding of the Titusville Iron Works., and Mr. Carter was designated as a managing director, with the care and oversight of rebuilding and refitting the works, so as to put them on a substantial and ecomonic basis.

During the latter years of Mr. Carter's connection with the Titusville Iron Company, he instituted a profit-sharing propaganda, which he prides himself upon, and we believe with good grounds. In 1900 he proposed to the stockholders of the Company that the Company pay its employes the same dividend, paid the stockholders of record, based on the actual earnings of each man in the company's service, that is to say: if a man earned in the year 1899 $250 and the Company paid 10 per cent. dividend, that man's earned wages would be his capital, on which he was to receive 10 per cent. dividend, or $25, the same as the other stockholders. If a man earned $1,000 in the same year, he would get $100, and so with any other man, large or small, so that wage earners and capitalist were to share alike in the profits, according to the capital contributed.

The stockholders compromised with the proposition, and granted five per cent. to all wage workers on the basis above named, which was duly paid. This grant, by the stockholders, was generous and progressive and was highly appreciated by Mr. Carter and the employes of the Company.

In 1901-2 the same proposition was presented by Mr. Carter, and the same results obtained—five per cent. for each workman.

In 1903 Mr. Carter presented the same proposition to the stockholders ,and insisted that the same percentage of dividends paid the owners of the capital stock, should be paid to the wage earners, who, by their skill and labor had so ably contributed to the success and earning power of the Company. Mr Carter added: "This matter is now a fixed purpose of mine. I propose to present it regularly at each annual meeting, until it is adopted as a principle by the Titusville Iron Company."

The stockholders were not disposed to adopt the principle presented by Mr. Carter; and the project fell to the ground so far as the Titusville Iron Company was concerned, because of which Mr. Carter sold his stock, and the Company stopped paying to its employes the workingman's percentage of the net earnings of the Company.

In the winter of 1902-3, Mr. Carter began extensive purchases of oil territory in the Sistersville, West Virginia, field, until they amounted to more than $1,000,000 and his daily production exceeded 4,500 barrels.

On the first of May following he organized the Carter Oil Company and subscribed for the whole capital stock of $1,000,000, having previously sold to the Standard Oil Company 60 per cent. of his properties in the Sistersville field. In 1905 he sold the remainder of his stock in the Carter Oil Company to the Standard Oil Company and has since held the offices of President and General Manager of the Company, which has been a success economically, physically and financially. Perhaps no company in the same time has paid more handsome dividends than the Carter Oil Company. Wherever found the Carter properties are recognized by their snugness and preparedness to produce their quota of oil every day.

In 1907 the Standard Oil Company had Mr. Carter visit Japan to determine the oil productive qualities of that Empire. After remaining a year, drilling two of the deepest wells that have ever been drilled in Japan, he sold the Standard holdings there and came away satisfied with the work accomplished; and it is believed the Standard was equally well satisfied. In 1908 he was sent to California to look over that field and to determine its value as a producing factor. He took up large holdings in the Midway district, which have turned out most productive; and it is only fair to Mr. Carter to say: The Standard Oil Company is reaping handsome returns as the result of his la-bors, not only in California, but in every other field in which he has been engaged in its service.

Employes under Mr. Carter have always been treated generously and courteously. If any receives injury he is taken care of in the best manner, given the best medical aid at command, sent to hospital, if necessary, all at the expense of the Company. The man's family is paid full wages for a month and for the second one-half. If he is then unable to work his case is fully considered by Mr. Carter and he receives additional payment if it be needed.   When able to return, he is given a place, and he is treated with care and consideration.   This principle has been extended to all the companies in the Standard Oil Company and is practiced by each of them.   The high wages paid, and the care bestowed upon employes in every direction have been the causes that have made its men proud to be in the service of the Standard Oil Company.   The men who have worked for John J. Carter, or the Carter Oil Company, have always felt that both Mr. Carter and the Company were their friends.   Greater recognition than the high regard of one's employes cannot be bestowed upon any employer of labor.

At headquarters in Sistersville, the Carter Company has maintained a school where young men. of education and capacity—mental, physical and moral—could enter and pass through its four year course, receiving fair compensation from the first, with an appointment and advance at the close.   Many of these young men are now in positions of responsibility—of profit and trust—in various callings, and they look back on the school on the banks of the Ohio, as the starting place of their fortunes.   Each one of them has a kind word to say for the school and its founder.   As a business man Mr. Carter is active, prompt and progressive; as a public speaker he is earnest, forcible and convincing; as a citizen and neighbor, he is broad minded, courteous, liberal handed, and worthy of the highest consideration.

In July, 1866, Mr. Carter was married to Miss Emma, daughter of F. H. and Sarah Gibbs, at Nunda, Livingston County, New York.   Three children and five grandchildren live at this time to bless that union, the children being: Luke Berne Carter, who is Assistant General Manager of the Carter Oil Company under his father; Emma, the wife of Alex. D. Sharp, of Steubenville, Ohio; and Alice, who is the wife of Hugh Hern-don, Esq., of New York City—their home being at Pelham, N. Y.   Emma Gibbs Carter, Mr. Carter's wife, died at Titusville, February 6, 1902, respected and regretted.   Charles Gibbs Carter, the eldest born, died May 14, 1909, in Pittsburg, Pennsylvania, where he was a successful and leading lawyer at the bar of that city.

In 1908, Mr. Carter married Miss Alice, daughter of Joseph A. and Elizabeth Neill, of Titusville, Pa.   John J. Carter is an Irishman by birth, having first seen the light in the city of Westport, Ireland, June 16, 1842.   His father was a merchant who pros-pered and died, before the son had reached his third year.   A sister, older and married, took the boy to America—the land of freedom and fortune—where he became one of its defenders in war, a citizen of ability and of repute; as an earnest of which he is a Trustee of Bucknell University and of Allegheny College; a Fellow of the Geograph-ical Society of the United States; a member of the Duquesne Club of Pittsburg, Penn-sylvania; a member of the Army and Navy Club of New York; Vice President and one of the organizers of the Commercial Bank of Titusville; President of the Carter Oil Company; a member of the Grand Army of the Republic; a Fellow of the Loyal Legion of the United States; and the possessor of the Medal of Honor voted him by Congress, because his "conduct was particularly gallant" under the observation of the Division Commander at the battle of Antietam, Maryland.

GENERAL CHARLES MILLER.

Wherever machinery is operated there Galena lubricating oils are known. They lubricate ninety-eight per cent. of the railroad mileage in the United States and a large proportion of railways in South America, Europe and Asia, not to mention the thousands of other pieces of machinery whose work is made easier and whose life is prolonged by use of a perfect oil. General Charles Miller, inventor of the Galena process, and President for many years, now Chairman of the Board of the great manufacturing company that distributes the Galena products direct to consumers, is as widely and favorably known as his products. He has been an active factor in the petroleum industry since 1869 and in the life of the oil country since 1866. For more than forty years he has been a leader in the development of petroleum resources, a man of rare perception, striking executive ability and a progressive builder. He has traveled throughout the United States and Europe in connection with his business, always observant, alert alike to commercial opportunities and the life of the people in regions he has visited. He has ever been a student and is as well informed on the art and literature of the world as upon its industrial or commercial affairs. He is esteemed as the first citizen of Franklin, Pennsylvania, where he has made his home since 1866, and is interested in everything that contributes to its growth in material prosperity, or the civic betterment of the beautiful little city. He has recently promoted and constructed a new railroad line leading from Franklin to Central Pennsylvania—the Jamestown, Franklin and Clearfield—of which he is president. It is a part of the L. S. & M. S. System.

Charles Miller was born of Huguenot ancestry in Alsace, France, in 1843, and came with his parents to America in 1854. His father settled near Boston, Erie County, New York. When he was thirteen the boy clerked in the village store at thirty-five dollars a year and board. At seventeen he was clerking in Buffalo at one hundred and seventy-five dollars a year. In 1861 he enlisted in the National Guard of New York and in 1863 he was mustered into the service of the United States. In 1864 he purchased the store where he first worked, principally with borrowed capital, and embarked in business for himself. In 1866 he sold this store, formed a partnership with John Coon, of Buffalo, New York, removed to Franklin, Pennsylvania, and conducted a large dry goods store until 1869. In this latter year the firm purchased a refinery and a patent for the manufacture of lubricating oil. It closed out the dry goods business at a sacrifice and General Miller devoted his whole time to the new industry. In 1870 the refinery burned down, entailing very heavy loss on the firm, but the business was not abandoned or the head of the firm discouraged by this dire misfortune. With Henry B. Plumer as a new partner, the Dale Light Oil Works were purchased, the plant was remodeled for the different line of manufacture and the business pushed with greater energy than before. In 1873, Hon. Joseph C. Sibley, who had been a sales agent for the Galena in Chicago at the time of the great fire, perfected a signal oil superior in light, safety and cold test to any then in use and organized the Signal Oil Works, with the Galena company as partners. The two concerns have progressed side by side, each making many additions to meet their growing business. The three railroads that began using Galena oils in 1869 have used no other since, but they are traveling in larger company. It was a revelation to railroad managers to find an oil that would not evaporate in summer or freeze in winter and that would not heat in the journal box under ordinary conditions. These products have added one hundred per cent. to the speed, safety and smoothness of railroad operation and consequently to the pleasure of travel.

In 1878 the Standard Oil Company purchased the interests of Messrs. Coon, Plumer and Austin and the company was reorganized as the Galena Oil Works, Limited, with General Miller as President. It has since been incorporated on a broader basis as a joint stock company, including the Signal Oil Works, previously referred to. General Miller throughout remained President and manager of the business, until in December, 1910, he retired from the Presidency and became Chairman of the Board, his son-in-law, S. A. Mageath, being elected President. He is known personally to every railroad president in this country and equally well to thousands of railroad enginemen, meeting both on a common plane of humanity. He has traveled on the locomotive to supervise the lubrication and his mileage in the Pullman is exceeded by very few men not employed in the railroad service.

Despite this personal supervision of a business that is international in its proportions, the subject of this sketch has found time for other activities. He has devoted much time to the National Guard of Pennsylvania, rising by steady promotion, on merit, to the position of Major General, which post he held until retired on age. He was repeatedly elected President of the Northwestern Association of Pennsylvania of the

Grand Army of the Republic and has served as Commander of Mays Post, G. A. R., Franklin, and is now serving his eighteenth term. He was twice elected Mayor of Franklin and several times declined nomination to high political office because so engrossed in private business as to have no time for such honors. General Miller has felt that he served his community best by keeping his men employed at good wages and looking after the general welfare of this army of comfortable workmen. In addition to the oil works he has organized and financed several other industries with factories in Franklin, among them the General Manifold Company, the Keystone Carbon Company and the Pneumatic Tool Company. His sons are active in the management of these enterprises, which employ many persons in the lively little city. General Miller has been president of the First National Bank for the past ten years.

General Miller's chief personal interest is in his Bible class of eight hundred men, with a ladies' auxiliary of 200 members, being the largest Bible class in this country. The instruction is Scriptural, pointed, businesslike, free from bigotry or sectarianism. The teacher has never been absent when a journey of a thousand miles at the week end would bring him home by Sunday morning. He has been superintendent of the First Baptist Sunday School with over 1,900 members, continuously since 1874, as well as teacher of the Bible class and has given these institutions the same careful attention that has made his business a remarkable success. Nor has he been merely a Sunday Christian, as hundreds can testify, who have been recipients of his timely, kindly aid and counsel. Eternity alone will reveal all the good he has accomplished by his church work and numerous charities, but there are many who know the account is a large one.

In 1889, General Miller established a free night school for his employes and the youth of Franklin, which has since been maintained in growing usefulness. He furnished the spacious rooms, well equipped with furniture and appliances, and he regularly employs seven capable teachers to give the necessary instruction to the earnest pupils. This school has trained hundreds of young men for positions as bookkeepers, accountants, stenographers and clerks, beside advancing many others to higher knowledge and greater efficiency as mechanics. This school is the pride of its patron and of the city where he makes his home. It enjoys a reputation that extends much farther. The attendance is about two hundred.

The First Baptist Church, which General Miller assisted in organizing, has been an object of his especial care. He bore a large share of the cost of the handsome brick edifice, the lecture room and the parsonage. He and Honorable Joseph C. Sibley donated the massive pipe organ and have maintained the church choir, one of the best in the country. He assisted materially in the organization and maintenance of a branch of the church in the Third Ward of his city, and has been a liberal contributor to other denominations, both in Franklin and the surrounding country.

In the more than forty years since General Miller began the manufacture of lubricating oil, he has never had a strike among or trouble with his employes. He has treated his men as rational human beings, with bodies to nourish and souls to save. It has been his care to have them well housed, well paid, working under sanitary conditions. He has always been a friend to all who needed or sought his friendship, and has helped many into independent business by lending capital and friendly counsel. The Golden Rule has been observed in his relations with all men and particularly those who look to him for the employment that gives them sustenance. He has had in return faithful service that he believes has helped him to prosper. He is an Odd Fellow of high rank being Brigadier General on the staff of M. A. Raney, commanding Patriarchs Militant of the World. He is a thirty-second degree Mason. In short General Miller is a typical successful American, who has wrought his own fortune, is imbued with the spirit of patriotism and fellowship. He is a citizen of whom any community could be proud and any State glad to possess.

MARTIN MALONEY.

It is with some timidity that a writer undertakes a sketch of big hearted, generous Martin Maloney, lest he fail to portray his character on the one hand, or on the other shall offend the innate modesty of the subject. Mr. Maloney was born in Ballingarry, Ireland, November 11, 1848, and came to this country when seven years of age, endowed with abounding health and the energy characteristic of the sons of the Emerald Isle. The family located in Scranton, Pennsylvania. The boy attended the common school of that city until twelve years of age, when he went to work in the coal mines. At fourteen he began an apprenticeship as tinsmith, coppersmith, plumber and gas-fitter. He graduated later in the school of experience, the alma mater of so many successful Americans who accomplish things. Mr. Maloney started in business for himself August 5, 1868, when not quite twenty. He proved a hustler from the start. In 1874 he organized and built the Hyde Park Gas Plant in Scranton and had struck his gait. From that time it was forward march at a rapid pace with him.

In 1875, Mr. Maloney organized the Maloney Oil, Gas and Manufacturing Company. At this period he became acquainted with Mr. Henry H. Rogers, a man somewhat his senior, associated with Charles Pratt & Co., who became much interested in the young man's plans. Through the good offices of Mr. Rogers, Charles Pratt & Co. became associated with the corporation that was organized for the purpose of assisting in the development of the business of street lighting by the use of naphtha, then in its crude form and considered a dangerous by-product about an oil refinery. Mr. Maloney found it very difficult to obtain a satisfactory light on account of the crude condition of the naphtha and the imperfect mechanism of the burner, but he set about with accustomed vigor and determination to overcome these obstacles and developed a successful naphtha light system With the assistance of the Standard Oil Company, through Mr. Rogers and Mr. John D. Archbold, he was put in touch with William G. Warden, of the Atlantic Refining Company, which at about that time had absorbed the business of William L. Elkins. Through the co-operation of William L. Elkins, W. G. Warden, H. H. Rogers, George W. Elkins and other associates, he was able to effect the organization of the Penn Globe Gas Light Company and allied interests for the special purpose of developing this business, with the result that within ten years one hundred and thirty-seven towns and cities were under contract and lighted by this system, known as the Maloney Lighting System. The energy of the man who managed this undertaking can be appreciated.

At about this time, William G. Warden, on one of his visits to Europe, observed what was then known as the Aur light, now recognized as the Welsbach light, the parent of the incandescent principle of lighting. In the meantime the Penn Globe Gas Light Company, and the Maloney Oil, Gas and Manufacturing Company had enlarged the scope of their operations and became interested in the purchase and operation of gas plants. Then came the terrific shock to the gas interests of the country when Thomas A. Edison, Dr. Von Siemens, Hiram Maxim and other electricians succeeded in putting electric lighting on a commercial basis. The value of gas stocks was seriously affected in all parts of the world. But, Mr. Maloney and his associates were not frightened by these discoveries. They saw in it an opportunity and purchased the patents owned and controlled by T. S. C. Lowe. They at once proceeded to organize a larger and more comprehensive corporation for the purpose of taking up the gas interests, using the above mentioned corporations as the nucleus of the present United Gas Improvement Company, the founders of which were: Martin Maloney, William L. Elkins, William G. Warden, W. W. Gibbs, George W. Elkins, Thomas Dolan, P. A. B. Widener, Randall Morgan, Samuel T. Bodine and others. Mr. Maloney's connection with all of these companies continued until his retirement from active business a few years ago.

In addition to the companies mentioned, Mr. Maloney was connected with the management of gas, water, electric, power and other public utilities corporations too numerous to mention, in fact nearly all of the progressive organizations throughout the country for forty years. His career is so well known throughout the East as to make enumeration unnecessary.

This busy man of vast affairs found time for other matters. He was married in December, 1868, at Scranton, Pennsylvania, to Margaret A. Hewitson, seven children being born to the union, Margaret Maloney Ritchie and Helen Maloney Osborn, being the only two surviving. The faithful wife, Margaret, has been his friend and counselor and has assisted in his generous charities from the first. In recognition of his many good works, the great Pope Leo XIII, in 1902, created him a Papal marquis. In 1904, Pope Pius X conferred upon Mr. Maloney the title of Cameriere Segreto di Spada e di Cappa di S. Santita, making him a member of his household, in recognition of his many benefactions to the Catholic Church and other charities. Among these may be mentioned the beautiful Memorial Church of St. Catherine's, erected at the summer home of Mr. Maloney at Spring Lake, New Jersey, in memory of his deceased daughter, Catherine, and the erection of the Maloney Memorial Home for the Aged at Scranton, Pennsylvania, in memory of his father and mother. This latter institution is nonsectarian and domiciles more than one hundred inmates. We have before us the Scranton Republican of November 25, 1910, containing an account of the visit of Mr. and Mrs. Maloney to the Home on Thanksgiving Day, when the inmates testified their appreciation of his kindness, to which he modestly replied that he was merely the instrument of the actual creator of the institution in which Jew and Gentile are equal, recognizing no creed as necessary to shelter under the roof of the Maloney Home.

Mr. Maloney's business address is in Philadelphia. He is a member of the Union League and City Clubs of Philadelphia, of the Catholic Club of New York and Philadelphia, the Scranton City Club and the Scranton Country Club. But his favorite resort is his country home at Spring Lake, New Jersey, beautiful "Ballingarry." In this picturesque villa he has realized the dream of his youth and has named it for the ancestral home in Ireland, called by the early poets Innisfail, or the Island of Destiny. It is there that Mr. Maloney loves to entertain his friends and to plan how he may further help to bring sunshine into the lives of the unfortunates. He is of a deeply religious temperament.

CHARLES LOCKHART.

In the petroleum industry Charles Lockhart was a pioneer of pioneers. His first deal in oil was the purchase of three barrels in 1852, from Isaac Huff, who was a part owner in a salt well at Arnolds Station, Westmoreland County, Pa., that produced some oil. Disposing of this oil at a considerable profit, Mr. Lockhart conceived the idea that there was a good future for the oil business, and against the advice of Mr. McCully, the senior partner of the firm with which he was connected, he purchased a controlling interest in the salt well from which the oil was taken. From that time until his death, on January 26, 1905, he was an oil producer. Associated with him in his first oil venture was Mr. A. V. Kipp, who had charge of the property, as Mr. Lockhart remained with McCully & Co., and that partnership continued until dissolved by the death of Mr. Kipp in 1896.

After the discovery of oil on Oil Creek by Drake, Mr. Lockhart sent a representative to investigate and, the report being favorable, an organization was effected as Phillips, Frew & Co., Mr. Lockhart being a member of the firm. Land was leased and operations began at once on the Major Downing farm, now a part of Oil City where oil was struck in March, 1860, and 64 barrels were shipped by the steamboat Venango to Pittsburg, being the first oil in quantity to reach that market. The second producing venture of this firm was on the James Tarr farm, resulting in the famous Phillips No. 2, which astonished the world as the first great gusher. Its production for several weeks was at the rate of 4,000 barrels a day.

In May of 1860 Mr. Lockhart went to Europe with samples of crude and refined petroleum and was the first person to bring to the attention of commercial Europe this new product. The result was to start an export trade that has been of inestimable value to the producers of oil and to the commerce of this Nation. The same year Mr. Lockhart and William Frew began the building of a refinery at Brilliant station, near the site of the Pittsburg city water pumping station. This refinery was completed in 1861, and was a success from the start. It attained early to fame.

In 1862 Lockhart & Frew bought the producing interests of Phillips, Frew & Co., and with a new partner, William G. Warden, in 1865, established a commission business in Philadelphia. This firm, Warden, Frew & Co., built the Atlantic refinery in that city. When the Standard Oil Company, of Cleveland, became the nucleus of the great Standard Oil Company in 1874, all the refineries with which Mr. Lockhart was connected were merged into that corporation. He was identified with the Standard Oil Trust until its dissolution and afterward with all the corporations that went to make up the Standard interest. He was all the time an active producer as well as refiner and marketer of oil.

Mr. Lockhart had many other interests, investing in iron and glass manufacturing, timber in the south, mining in Colorado and other States, wheat farming in the Red River valley of the North, and shipping, being a stockholder in the International Navigation Company, operating the American and Red Star lines of steamships. He was President of the National Bank of Commerce, of Pittsburg, and connected with other financial institutions. But above all else he was oil producer, refiner and marketer.

The subject of this sketch had an interesting career before entering the petroleum business. He was born at Cairn Heads, near Whithorn, in Wigtownshire, Scotland, August 2, 1818. His father, John Lockhart, was the son of Charles Lockhart, of Ersock, a prosperous farmer and a prominent and influential man in his shire. His mother was Sarah Walker, daughter of James Walker, a linen manufacturer, of Sorbie a man of rare intellectual and business qualities, and to this ancestry Mr. Lockhart attributed much of his success. Early in 1836, he embarked with his parents for New York, and went direct to Pittsburg. Shortly afterward John Lockhart removed to a farm in Trumbull County, Ohio, but returned again to Pittsburg. The subject of this sketch did not accompany his parents to Ohio, but remained in Pittsburg, where he obtained employment with James McCully, where he continued for nineteen years, and in 1855 became a partner in the firm of James McCully & Co. Another partner was taken in at the same time, he being the late Major William Frew, a nephew of Mr. McCully. This partnership continued until 1865 when it was dissolved. The young men were then deep in the oil business.

Mr. Lockhart, in his private life, cherished the old friendships and was most sociable with the companions of his younger days, most of whom had been less fortunate. He never permitted the world to know of his benevolences, but it was understood by the few that he maintained a private pension list to aid less successful persons. His will was characteristic. He made no great bequests to charity, but gave the bulk of his fortune to his family, in whom he had the fullest confidence, and left to them the pleasant duty of keeping up his generous giving, having during his life acquainted them with all his desires. All in all Mr. Lockhart was one of Pittsburg's best citizens and one of the kindliest, as he was one of the most modest of men.

GEORGE HEARD.

George Heard, President of The Natural Gas Company of West Virginia, is descended from Protestant stock, his ancestors having come from the North of Ireland and settled in York and Lancaster Counties, Pennsylvania, before the Revolutionary War. Born in Crawford County, Pennsylvania, January 17, 1851, and having received his education at the State Normal School, Edinboro, and at the Erie Academy, Erie, Pennsylvania, Mr. Heard started in life in various employments connected with the production of oil. His earliest efforts were at Fagundas and Triumph Hill, Warren County, Pennsylvania, from 1871 until 1873. He then removed to Butler County, Pennsylvania, and three years later to Oil City, where he did a commission business on the Oil Exchange until 1883, first as Young & Heard, later on his own account, and then as Heard & Darr.

Mr. Heard was a member of the Committee of the Oil City Oil Exchange which devised the clearing house system for oil certificates and money. As early as 1883 this system was established and not long afterward the New York Stock Exchange adopted it for the clearance of money and stocks. During that year Mr. Heard joined the New York Petroleum Exchange, at that time located in the Mills Building, 18 Broadway. His operations on the New York Petroleum Exchange extended over a short period and in 1884 he removed to Pittsburgh, there joining the Pittsburgh Petroleum Exchange. He continued in the commission business until the Spring of 1886, when he turned his attention to the natural gas industry, in connection with The Natural Gas Company of West Virginia. For ten years he served as manager of the Company and in 1896 he was elected President, an office which he has since continuously held.

The Natural Gas Company of West Virginia was one of the first to engage in the business. It introduced gas into Wheeling, West Virginia, in September, 1886, and since then without interruption it has been supplying the residental and domestic demand in that city and its suburbs. The Company obtains its supply of gas for Wheeling from Washington and Greene Counties, Pennsylvania, and from Belmont County, Ohio.

In 1904 The Natural Gas Company of West Virginia began to operate for natural gas in Columbiana and Carroll Counties, Ohio, and it now supplies Salem, Lisbon, Sebring, Leetonia and other towns in those counties.

The late Captain J. J. Vandergrift and the late C. W. Batchelor, in conjunction with James I. Buchanan, Henry Fisher and others, organized the Company. The personnel of the Company at the beginning of the year 1911 was as follows: George Heard, President; Guy F. Batchelor, Secretary and Treasurer; Directors, John Pitcairn, S. H. Vandergrift, John J. Fisher, James I. Buchanan, James H. Lockhart, Clarence M. Brown, A. S. Hare, Guy F. Batchelor and George Heard.

The Natural Gas Company of West Virginia during its quarter century of actual existence has demonstrated the vitality of the natural gas industry. The Company is at this time delivering more gas than at any other like period during its existence.

On February 8th, 1882, Mr. Heard was married to Miss Margaret E. Neale, daughter of the late Charles T. Neale, of Pittsburgh and Kittanning. To them were born one daughter, Georgia Neale Heard, who is Mrs. Frank A. Hamilton, of Pittsburgh, and two sons, James Drayton Heard, who was graduated from Yale in the class of 1910, and Charles Clarke Heard, a student at Shadyside Academy, Pittsburgh.

CHARLES PRATT.

The late Charles Pratt, who died May 4, 1891, at his office, 26 Broadway, New York City, was born October 2, 1830, at Watertown, Mass. He was the son of Asa Pratt, who was of an old New England family coming from English stock. His education was very limited, being confined to the public schools of his native town and one year at Wilbraham Academy. After three years of apprenticeship at the machinery trade, he moved to New York and associated himself with the firm of Reynolds & DeVoe, manufacturers of paint and oils. He later became a partner and the firm name became Reynolds, DeVoe & Pratt. When crude oil was discovered Mr. Pratt had oil shipped by the barrel to the East River and started the Pratt Manufacturing Co. He built a large factory at Greenpoint, on Long Island, and the name of "Pratt's Astral Oil" became known as a trade mark all over the continent. After an interval of a few years, with the late Henry H. Rogers as junior partner, Mr. Pratt joined John D. Rockefeller in the first Standard Oil Company.

Perceiving the need of training young men to mechanical pursuits, in 1887 Mr. Pratt founded the Pratt Institute in Brooklyn. In has since become the model trade and industrial school from which the Carnegie Institute and other institutions of like character have taken their inspiration. The foundation of the Pratt Institute started the movement for trade classes in the public and in many private schools. The Pratt family is justly proud of this institution, of which Mr. Charles M. Pratt, the eldest son, is now President, as well as Vice President of the Standard Oil Company. The name of Charles Pratt is permanently enrolled in the annals of Brooklyn, by his gifts to the cause of education. He was deeply interested in the Adelphi Academy, a preparatory school for girls and boys, and after 1879 was President of the Board. Through his munificence the school building on Lafayette Avenue was increased in size and in 1886 he donated the means for erecting a handsome new building connected with the older part of the school. His gifts to the institution amounted to over $250,000. He also honored the memory of his father by establishing the Asa Pratt Free Reading Room in his native town. Mr. Pratt was a thoroughly domestic man, a Baptist and one of the founders of Emanuel Church, Brooklyn. He was also a liberal contributor toward many other charities, most of which have never come to the knowledge of the public.

The surviving children of the late Charles Pratt are: Charles M. Pratt, Frederic B. Pratt, Helen F. Dane, George D. Pratt, Herbert L. Pratt, John T. Pratt, and Harold I. Pratt.

BYRON DAVID BENSON.

The subject of this sketch was one of the giants in the petroleum industry of Pennsylvania and New York, taking an active part in the stirring times from 1865 to the latter part of the decade ending 1890. He died in the City of New York, February 8, 1888, although his home was in Titusville, Pennsylvania, he being at the time on business connected with the Tide Water Pipe Company, Limited. Mr. Benson was almost fifty-six years of age, having been born in the town of Fabius, Onondaga County, New York, on February 29, 1832. He was descended from John Benson, who came from Caversham, Oxfordshire, England, in 1638, and settled in Hull, Massachusetts.

Byron David Benson was, in the best sense, a self-made man. He was the eighth of the ten children of David and Jane (Sumner) Benson, New York farmers, and his only education was in the country school of the district. Before he was twenty-one years old he had engaged in the lumber business and was operating a saw mill at Brewerton, New York. During the War he was Sheriff of Onondaga County, and at the expiration of his term, in the Spring of 1865, he joined his friend and former associate, Major R. E. Hopkins, in a lumbering operation at Enterprise, Warren County, Pennsylvania. They both drifted naturally into the oil producing business and followed that industry for the remainder of their lives.

In 1874, Mr. Benson, with his partners, R. E. Hopkins and David McKelvey, leased from Dr. David Hostetter, of Pittsburgh, the Columbia Conduit Pipe Line, which had been built from the Butler County oil fields to Pittsburgh, but was bottled up at Sharpsburg by reason of not being allowed to cross the West Penn Railroad. The latter occupied the right of way of the old Pennsylvania Canal and under its franchise claimed dominion from the "center of the earth to the top of the sky." By carting the oil from the end of the line across the railroad, shipping it in boats, via the Allegheny and Ohio Rivers, to Parkersburg, West Virginia, and thence by rail to Baltimore, they made money for themselves and enabled Dr. Hostetter to sell his pipe line in 1876 at a large profit. Mr. Benson and his associates then organized the Seaboard Pipe Line and secured the complete right of way from Butler County to Baltimore, but were forced to abandon the project because of the failing production of the Butler district. In 1878 in connection with R. E. Hopkins, David McKelvey, Samuel Q. Brown and Josiah G. Benton, Mr. Benson organized the Tide Water Pipe Company, Limited, and in the following year the first of what are now known as "trunk" pipe lines, was built from Corryville, Pennsylvania, over the Allegheny Mountains to Williamsport, being extended a few years later to Tamanend, Penn'a, and then to Bayonne, New Jersey, the present terminus. To this enterprise, which prospered from the beginning, Mr. Benson devoted the remaining years of his life, being President of the Company from its organization until his death. He will always be ranked in the petroleum industry as one of the pathfinders.

Byron David Benson was married December 21, 1859, at Brewerton, New York, to Miss Minerva Stevens. Their three children are Robert D. Benson, William S. Benson and Mrs. Charles F. Emerson. The sons are carrying forward the work begun by the father.

DAVID McKELVY.

Since his retirement from active business, in 1892, David McKelvy, of Titusville, Pa., has lost none of his interest in the evolution of the oil industry. He was in the forefront of many exciting conflicts of dollars and finesse, brains and intrigue. The history of the Tide-Water Pipe Company, Limited, could not be written without crediting Mr. McKelvy with the highly important achievements of his own intellect and personality, at times when the fruits of well-earned success were menaced by unreasoning hostility and unfriendly competition. He was associated with the late Byron D. Benson and Major R. E. Hopkins in an alliance as loyal and enduring as the annals of co-partnership can exhibit. Each of these gentlemen was distinguished by peculiar abilities which, devoted to the common interest, lent remarkable strength to the combination. Mr. McKelvy was a business man of sagacity and experience, as were his partners, and he was also a lawyer of notable attainments.

The ancestors of David McKelvy were Scotch-Irish. He was born January 12, 1842, at Sugar Grove, Warren County, Pa., and received his early education in the public schools. He studied law at Warren, under the direction of Judge William D. Brown and Judge Glenni W. Scofield. In due time he was admitted to the bar and for a number of years he was engaged in general practice, in connection with these gentlemen. Officialdom had no attraction for him and in his subsequent career he would accept no public office. As a safe counselor and as a learned, brilliant advocate Mr. McKelvy was held in highest esteem. His attainments ripened during the years of his service as general counsel for the Tide-Water Companies.

At Enterprise, Pa., Mr. McKelvy, Mr. Byron D. Benson and Major R. E. Hopkins organized the Enterprise Oil and Lumber Company, the B. D. Benson Company and D. McKelvy & Company, the last named concern having its main office at Titusville, where soon these gentlemen made their homes.

The problem of establishing an independent outlet for the transportation of oil to the sea was one which at this time engaged many minds and engendered unbounded acrimony. Mr. David Hostetter, manufacturer of a patent medicine, who had acquired interests in oil, in 1874 conceived the idea of piping his product to Pittsburg. There connection was to be made with the Baltimore and Ohio Road. The line was completed in 1875 and turned over to Byron D. Benson, David McKelvy, R. E. Hopkins, William Brough and John M. Bonham, who operated it as the Columbia Conduit Company. These gentlemen withdrew when Dr. Hostetter sold to the Standard Oil Company. Mr. Benson, Mr. Hopkins and Mr. McKelvy then took up the project of a pipe line from the Butler field to Baltimore, Md. This project, known as the Seaboard Pipe Co., Limited, was abandoned chiefly in consequence of the opening of the Bradford field. The acquisition of a right of way, a delicate and difficult task, had fallen to Mr. McKelvy, who, in conjunction with General Herman Haupt, engineer for the Pennsylvania Railroad, succeeded in the face of apparently insuperable obstacles.

Messrs. Benson, McKelvy and Hopkins, as told elsewhere in this volume, then began the construction of the first trunk pipe line and organized the Tide-Water Pipe Company, Limited.

Mr. McKelvy never wavered in his belief in the feasibility of piping oil over the Allegheny Mountains to the Atlantic seaboard, a project which, during the constructive period, was regarded by many as superlatively impracticable. The task of designing and working out the pumping machinery was of vital importance. While the experience gained on the Columbia Conduit line proved of value, the fact remained that the Columbia was a four-inch line and the Tide-Water was to be a six-inch line and to cross the mountains. Mr. McKelvy applied himself to the intricate problems involved and with the co-operation of Mr. Holly, of the Holly Manufacturing Company, and of Mr. J. G. Benton, superintendent of the Tide-Water Pipe Company, arrived at the solutions which will long be deemed remarkable among the achievements of engineering.

Following the death of Byron D. Benson in 1888, Mr. McKelvy succeeded to the Presidency of the Tide-Water Companies. He served in that capacity and as general counsel, until 1892. In that year he suffered a severe illness which necessitated his retirement. The general offices of the Tide-Water Companies were then, as now, in New York City. Mr. McKelvy returned to his home in Titusville, where he now resides.

Mr. McKelvy was married June 20, 1872, to Miss Louise Wood, of Warren, Pa. They have two children, Charlotte, wife of Hon. George White, of Marietta, Ohio, and Robert, member of the Board of Managers of the Tide-Water Pipe Company, Limited.

WILLIAM H. LIBBY.

The subject of this sketch, William Herbert Libby, is of English descent. Ancestors of his mother landed in Massachusetts in 1620, and ancestors of his father landed in Maine about 1639.

Having emerged from school in possession of a bowing acquaintance with grammar and fractions, and after several years of clerical miscellany, Mr. Libby, in 1865, then in his twentieth year, began the petroleum business in New York, and in 1878 entered the service of the Standard Oil Company, devoting several years to the extension of its business in the various Oriental countries, and especially in the removal or modification of a series of obstacles imposed or threatened by Oriental Governments.

For about twenty subsequent years Mr. Libby was the accredited foreign representative of the Company, with official credentials authorizing his participation in all questions affecting its foreign commerce, and devoted these years to the investigations, negotiations, and constructive work incidental to industrial development.

It has been one of Mr. Libby's theories that arbitration and conciliation were the best guarantors of commercial progress, and that in business life the pen is more potent than the pitchfork.

Mr. Libby has been honored with the introductory autographs of ten succesive Secretaries of State, from William M. Evarts to John Hay, inclusive, and reviews with grateful appreciation the courtesy and consideration invariably extended him by the Department of State in Washington, and by the Diplomatic and Consular Representatives of the United States Government abroad, in the solution of many of the Company's world-wide problems.

As episodic of over 300,000 miles of travel, including several journeys around the world and sojourn in many of its European and Oriental capitals, Mr. Libby has been favored with the opportunity of meeting a great number of interesting personages fighting their battle of life in varied pathways.

A few years ago, with health seriously impaired, Mr. Libby welcomed the substitution of a home anchorage for nomadic activities, and at the age of 65 continues service in a semi-active advisory capacity, where he retains the keen interest of earlier days in whatever may concern the Company's welfare, in whatever may stimulate its esprit de corps, and especially in whatever may favorably influence its ever ramifying foreign affairs.

JAMES ANDREW MOFFETT.

A modest gentleman who has occupied a conspicuous position, is James A. Moffett, President of the Standard Oil Company of Indiana. This was the corporation that was made famous by the absurd imposition of a fine almost thirty times the amount of its capital stock, a judgment that was promptly reversed by the United States Circuit Court of Appeals sitting at Chicago. Mr. Moffett has won his way from the bottom and enjoys the respect and confidence of the business world to a remarkable degree, being a prime favorite with the large circle with whom he has had business dealings. His connection with the petroleum industry dates to its early days and his advancement to leadership was by hard, faithful work and close application. Like the other men of influence in Standard Oil affairs, he possesses intimate, practical knowledge of the various branches of the industry, gained by close contact.

James Andrew Moffett was born at Marlinton, Pocahontas County, West Virginia, on April 12, 1851, before that territory had separated itself, during the terrible civil strife, from the Old Dominion. His father was George B Moffett, a physician, who served as surgeon of the Forty-ninth Virginia Regiment, in General Robert E. Lee's Army. The father was of Scotch-Irish descent, his ancestors having been among the early settlers in Augusta County, Virginia, about 1725 to 1732. His mother was of English descent, but her ancestors settled in Botetourt County, Virginia, at about the same time that his father's people came to Augusta County. His maternal great-grandfather was George Skillern, a Colonel in the Provincial Army. Mr. Moffett followed farming at home until eighteen years of age. At that time he went to Parkersburg, West Virginia, where he entered the employ of J. N. Camden & Co., producers and refiners of petroleum. He gradually won promotion until he became Superintendent of the Camden Works. He next became Superintendent of the Pratt Manufacturing Company (successors to Charles Pratt & Co.), at New York. Later he was put upon the Manufacturing Committee of the Standard Oil Trust, advancing to Vice President of the Standard Oil Company of Indiana, then to be a Director of the Standard Oil Company of New Jersey. Again he advanced to become President of the Standard Oil Company of Indiana and Vice President of the Standard Oil Company of New Jersey.

Mr. Moffett took a most active part in solving the problems arising from the development of the Trenton Rock oil fields in Northwestern Ohio and Indiana and as the Vice President of the Standard Oil Company of Indiana was a factor in the building up of the refined and fuel oil trade of the great Northwest. His manufacturing experience was valuable in dealing with an oil containing new elements. The opening of those fields was an epoch in American petroleum history and the finding of a market for the product, one of the herculean tasks imposed upon the men who have directed that branch of the business. The success attending the efforts of Mr. Moffett is indicated by the appreciation shown by his business associates. He is thoroughly familiar with every detail of transportation and is the directing head of the wonderful pipe line system of the Standard, east of the Mississippi River, including nearly 10,000 miles of trunk lines and twice as many miles of pipe in the gathering systems of the various fields, with many millions of barrels capacity of iron and steel storage tanks.

Mr. Moffett has been chiefly connected with J. N. Camden & Co., Camden Consolidated Oil Company, Pratt Manufacturing Co. and the Standard Oil Company of Indiana. He is Vice President of the Standard Oil Company of New Jersey, President of the Standard Oil Company of Indiana, President of the Standard Oil Company of California, President of the National Transit Company, President of the Indiana Pipe Line Company, President of the Buckeye Pipe Line Company, President of the Eureka Pipe Line Company, President of the Cumberland Pipe Line Company, President of the Southern Pipe Line Company, President of the New York Transit Company, President of the Crescent Pipe Line Company, President of the Northern Pipe Line Company, and President of the South West Pennsylvania Pipe Line Company. He resides at No. 212 West Seventy-second Street, New York City, and is devoted to his family life.

Mr. Moffett is much engrossed in his business affairs and gives little time to social affairs, but he is an alert student of political matters at home and abroad.

MAJOR ROBERT EMMET HOPKINS.

The late Major Robert Emmet Hopkins was born at Pompey, N. Y., March 24, 1833. On May 9, 1901, he passed away at Tarrytown, N. Y.

An ancestor of Major Hopkins, John Hopkins,. who was born at Coventry, England, and died in Hartford, Conn., in 1654, was the founder of the family in this country. Indeed he was one of the founders of the city of Hartford. Hezekiah Hopkins, the father of Robert Emmet Hopkins, was born in Harwinton, Conn., and moved to Pompey, N. Y., in 1802.

After graduation from Pompey Academy, Robert Emmet Hopkins moved to Ohio and for a time taught school in that State, after which he returned to Pompey, also teaching there for a time. When twenty years of age he went to Brewerton on Oneida Lake, New York, and for several years engaged there in the lumber business, later entering the same business with Mr. Byron D. Benson, at Enterprise, Warren County, Pennsylvania.

In May, 1865, Mr. Hopkins moved to Titusville, Pa., to engage in the oil and lumber business. During an eventful and important quarter of a century Titusville was his home, and then the location of headquarters of the Tide Water Companies in New York caused him to remove to Tarrytown, N. Y.

On February 17, 1886, Major Hopkins was married to Miss Fanny Wayne Chambers. To this union one son was born, Robert Emmet Hopkins, Jr., in Titusville, March 25, 1888.

Before his removal to Titusville and before the second year of the War of the Rebellion, Robert Emmet Hopkins recruited a company of union volunteers for the 149th New York Infantry. Receiving a commission as Captain in that regiment he went to the front with his command and saw arduous and gallant service in the Army of the Potomac during the ensuing two years of the conflict. In 1863 he was captured by the Confederates during the bloody battle of Chancellorsville and was made a prisoner of war in Libby Prison, Richmond, Va. Two months later he was exchanged and returned to his regiment, of which he was in command during the winter of 1863-1864. Early in 1864 he was promoted to the rank of Major.

In Titusville, Major Hopkins, with his old partner at Enterprise, Byron D. Benson, and David McKelvy, formed a partnership under the title of D. McKelvy & Company which existed to a very recent date. The firm engaged in lumbering and in producing oil and was quite successful. Major Hopkins was one of the original trio whose energy and determination led to the building of the Tide Water Pipe Co., the pioneer of pipe lines which entirely changed the methods of transporting petroleum from regions where it was produced to the seaboard. This pipe line set an example to others which was speedily followed, until to-day there are in operation a series of pipe lines covering many thousands of miles. The career of Major Hopkins and the great success of the Tide Water Oil Company and of the Tide Water Pipe Line are inseparably connected. In another part of this volume will be found an account of the difficulties which confronted the three partners and which were overcome only by their sterling integrity and a degree of forethought which at the time seemed almost abnormal.

Major Hopkins was a member of the Loyal Legion and of the Union League; of the Founders and Patriots of America, the Quill Club, Ardsley Casino and others of less importance.

When he died, at the age of 68, Major Hopkins left a wide circle of friends to mourn his taking off. During his career he had been most helpful to many who were less successful and in fact his aid in many cases enabled others to succeed where otherwise they might have fallen in the warfare of competition.

JOHN WORTHINGTON.

An interesting figure in the petroleum industry is John Worthington, a confidential agent for the Standard Oil Company. His first connection with the business was in his capacity as civil and mining engineer for a furnace company. For thirty-eight years since he has been a student and investigator, with exceptional opportunities and has given the trade geological and scientific information of much value. He has visited many foreign oil fields and is one of the best informed men on the general subject of petroleum and natural gas.

Mr. Worthington was born in South Wales on March 14, 1848, and came to the United States with his parents when four years old. The elder Mr. Worthington was engaged with the Brady's Bend Iron Company and the family settled at Brady's Bend, Pa. After a course in the public schools, the subject of this sketch also entered the employ of the Iron Company, where he remained several years, the last two as civil and mining engineer. This was at the time when oil developments were making their way down the Allegheny River and the Iron Company became interested in the possibilities of its lands for oil purposes, the charcoal iron business being then a diminishing industry. Mr. Worthington was sent to Oil City in 1872 to run a line of levels from that place to Brady's Bend, taking in on the way every considerable oil development lying between. A little later the work was extended from Brady's Bend to the newly developed oil fields in Butler County. The result was to determine that the sand from which oil was being produced at Brady's Bend and on Armstrong Run—a famous field in that day—was eighty feet below the formation from which the Butler County wells procured their oil and that the latter were getting their product from the third sand of the Oil Creek region. In other words, Mr. Worthington made it plain that there was a fourth sand in that section of the country, and if this knowledge had been acted on then the famous fourth sand belt from Armstrong Run to Greece City would have been developed considerably before it was found by accident. This was done in the Tack & Moorehead well, which was deepened in the hope of finding better results than were obtained in the third sand.

To Mr. Worthington, then, belongs the credit of establishing the first accurate oil sand levels, which have come to be very important factors in oil field operations. In the fall of 1872 he resigned from the service of the Iron Company and became Superintendent of the Meclimans Farm Oil Company, operating in the fourth sand cross belt at Karns City, where he remained until the Company disposed of its holdings. He then engaged with the Parker's Landing Savings Bank and for four years was its Cashier, during the time when Parker was the center of the trade. In 1880, Mr. Worthington, on account of ill health, left the East and located in the San Juan country of Colorado, engaging in the mining business. He was elected the first Mayor of the new city of Ouray, Colorado, and served to the satisfaction of the citizens. After six years there he returned to the oil country and was in the brokerage business for eighteen months, then organizing, in connection with Frank Thomson, President of the Pennsylvania Railroad, the Nineveh Petroleum Company, of which he was manager. He was no believer in the theory that oil did not exist far below sea level, and his company located in the region where the oil bearing strata were deepest.

In June, 1889, the long experience and practical knowledge of Mr. Worthington, led to his selection as Superintendent of the newly organized South Penn Oil Company, which later took over the properties of the Nineveh Company, a post of considerable responsibility. Under his administration the company participated in the development of the great oil and gas resources of West Virginia, and was found always at the front, the largest single interest in that development. Later he was called higher and remains on the firing line. In addition to his oil interests, Mr. Worthington is a Director of the Union National Bank, one of the oldest and strongest of the financial institutions of Pittsburgh, Pennsylvania. He resides in the Schenley Park district in that city.

CALVIN N. PAYNE.

Among the early settlers of the seaboard colonies were members of the Payne family who left Albion's shores to help build up a New England. The parents of Calvin N. Payne, Nathaniel and Lucinda (Sill) Payne, moved from Saratoga County, N. Y., and made a new home in Warren, Pa. On May 25, 1844, Calvin N. Payne was born at Irvineton, Warren County.

When Sumter had been fired on and President Lincoln had issued his first call for troops, Nathaniel Payne raised a company and enlisted. He was soon afterward appointed Major of the 12th Pennsylvania Cavalry and left for the field of conflict. At that time Calvin N. Payne was but seventeen years of age, but his career of usefulness had already begun. In 1860 he had drilled for oil below Irvineton, on the opposite side of the river. At 217 feet he had found nothing and a few months later he took charge of drilling for Burtis Brothers on a well three miles from Youngsville, Warren County. The drilling was done by water power. This well is said to be the first well drilled by cable. For Burtis Brothers young Payne then went to Oil Creek, on the upper McIlheny farm to drill another well. It was the second location from the Fountain Well Number 2 (John Fertig) which was then flowing 400 barrels.

About this time, his father being on active duty with his command, Calvin N. Payne was called home to become head of the household and manager of the farm. He rented the farm, however, after several months had elapsed, and took charge of a commission house at Irvineton, engaging in the transportation of oil from the river to the railroad, and general freight from the railroad to the river.

In April, 1863, Calvin N. Payne became a railway brakeman, running between Erie and Warren. Less than a year later he was a conductor. He ran the first through train over the road after the Philadelphia and Erie termini had been connected at Ridgeway. His experience at railroading ended in March, 1865, when he contracted wth Dr. M. C. Egbert to drill a 1,000-foot well on top of a hill at Bull Run, at a time when oil was supposed to be confined to the valleys. A good flowing well was the result.

Mr. Payne continued his contracting business in the vicinity of Bull Run, meanwhile branching out as a producer, until 1873, when he removed to Butler and, in association with William Fleming, engaged in production on a large scale and with notable success. In 1879 the partners established themselves at Oil City and later at Titusville. Unfailing success rewarded their efforts.

From the year 1885 and during the quarter of a century which has elapsed before these lines are set to paper, Mr. Payne has devoted much of his time and a large measure of his great executive ability to the following companies:

From 1885 to 1889, as Vice President of the Pennsylvania Gas Company of Warren, Pa.; as President from 1889 to January 1, 1911; as President of the Columbia Gas, Light and Fuel Company of Meadville, Pa., until its absorption by the United Natural Gas Company; as Vice President of the Lawrence Natural Gas Company of Pittsburg from 1886 until the company was merged with the People's Natural Gas Company; as Vice President of the Mahoning Gas Fuel Company of Youngstown, O., from 1886 until its corporate identity was lost in the East Ohio Gas Company; as President, from 1886, of the Manufacturers Gas Company of Oil City, now merged with the United Natural Gas Company; as Vice President, from 1886, of the Meadville Fuel Gas Company until its merger with the Oil City Fuel Supply Company; from 1887 to 1905 as Vice President of the Northwestern Ohio Natural Gas Company of Toledo; as Vice President of the Northwestern Pennsylvania Natural Gas Company of Oil City, from 1886 until its merger into the Oil City Fuel Supply Company; as Vice President of the last named company, 1885 to 1907; as Vice President of the Salamanca Natural Gas Company, 1888 to 1908; as Director and General Manager of the United Natural Gas Company from its organization in 1886, as Vice President from 1888 to 1908; as Vice President of the Provincial Natural Gas and Fuel Company, of Ontario, Canada, from its organization in 1889 until 1909.

In 1889 Mr. Payne succeeded W. T. Scheide as General Manager of the National Transit Company and other pipe line interests. In 1902 he was elected Vice President, continuing also as General Manager until 1906, when William V. Miller became General Manager. As these lines go to press, Mr. Payne is still Vice President as well as Vice President of the Southwestern Pennsylvania Pipe Line Company, the Eureka Pipe Line Company of Pittsburgh, the Buckeye Pipe Line of Lima, O., The Indiana Pipe Line Company, Montpelier, Indiana, and the Cumberland Pipe Line Company of Somerset, Kentucky.

Mr. Payne at the present time is largely interested in manufacturing in Erie, Pa., having in 1888 organized with three other gentlemen, the Metric Metal Company at Beaver Falls. In 1891 an extensive plant was built at Erie and the business of manufacturing gas meters was removed to that city. In 1895 the Company was merged with the American Meter Company, the Erie plant being now known as its Metric Metal Works. It is one of the largest and most modern manufacturing plants in Pennsylvania and is under the management of Calvin N. Payne's eldest son, Frank H. Payne.

The Modern Tool Company, also organized by Mr. Payne in 1903, to manufacture high grade machine tools, is now one of the large and most successful plants of that city. Mr. Payne and Mr. Joseph Seep of Titusville are joint owners, Mr. Payne having been President since the organization.

Another large enterprise organized by Mr. Payne, is the Lone Star Gas Company of Texas, developing a large gas field in the northern part of that State and conveying gas through a 16-inch main 130 miles, supplying the cities of Fort Worth and Dallas.

In his pipe line activities, Mr. Payne was brought into intimate relations with Mr. Henry H. Rogers and acted as agent in some of Mr. Rogers' many charitable and public-spirited deeds, among them the erection of the Col. E. L. Drake memorial at Titusville, the gift of an endowment fund to the hospitals of Titusville and Oil City and the building of a nurses' home at Oil City.

Mr. Payne has been an active worker in the Presbyterian denomination as an Elder since he was 24 years old. On November 28, 1866, he married Miss Martha E. Dempsey, daughter of Francis Dempsey, an English army officer who came from Canada to Lockport, N. Y., and afterward settled at Erie. Pa. There are two sons and two daughters: Frank H. Payne, manufacturer, Erie Pa.; Mrs. J. M. Tate, Jr., of Sewickley, Pa.; Christy Payne, attorney for the Hope and Peoples Natural Gas Companies (Pittsburg), and connecting companies; Mrs. Florence Payne Byles, wife of Axtel J. Byles, a prominent attorney of Titusville, Pa.

JOHN WESLEY VAN DYKE.

Mr. John Wesley Van Dyke, Vice President of The Atlantic Refining Company, Philadelphia, is a descendant of William Van Dyke, who arrived in America about the year 1800, from Holland, and located in Franklin County, Pennsylvania, where he lived until the time of his death in 1865. William Randals Van Dyke, his son, was born in Mercersburg in 1821, and lived there until entering the Union Army in 1861. He died from wounds received at Drainesville, December 20, 1861. His son, the subject of this sketch, was born in 1850 at Mercersburg.

After receiving his early education at the Tuscarora Academy, Juniata County, Pennsylvania, John Wesley Van Dyke, at the age of eighteen, went to the Venango County, Pennsylvania, oil fields. For a short time he was employed as an oil well operative. Subsequently, he engaged in contract work, drilling oil wells and building oil well rigs. This led to the leasing of oil lands and producing oil on his own account in Venango and Butler Counties until 1873, when he entered the employ of the Standard Oil Company in their refinery at Long Island City, New York. For six years, Mr. Van Dyke remained in Long Island City, when he was sent to Brooklyn to take charge, as Superintendent, of the Kings County Oil Works. In this position he remained until after the discovery of the Ohio oil fields, and in 1886, he removed to Lima, Ohio, to become General Manager of the Solar Refining Company. He constructed and operated the Lima works and was thus brought into close contact with the Ohio oil business, especially the manufacturing processes, in the development of which he played an important part.

Mr. Van Dyke remained in Lima as Vice President and General Manager of the Solar Refining Company until the early part of 1903, when he removed to Philadelphia to become General Manager of The Atlantic Refining Company. Two years later he became Vice President of that Company, a position which he retains to-day and in which he exercises a potent influence in the refining industry.

Always alive to new mechanical designs, Mr. Van Dyke, from 1887 to 1892, gave much thought to the designing and perfecting of the apparatus which resulted in the commercial development of the Ohio oil fields. Subsequently he obtained patents for economizing waste heat from petroleum stills, as well as for two all steel tank cars. With the advent of heavy gravity crude oils from Texas and Kansas, he turned his attention to the development of apparatus and processes for their economical manufacture, and the processes and apparatus he developed in this work have superseded the former methods at all plants of the Standard Oil Company, where they are now being used under pending patents.

Mr. Van Dyke is a director of the Union Tank Line Company; of the Evansville & Southern Indiana Railway Company, and President of the Crystal Paper Company, Middletown, Ohio.

WESLEY HUNT TILFORD.

Wesley Hunt Tilford, who, at his death on March 2, 1909, was one of the Vice Presidents of the Standard Oil Company, left behind him a notable record of over thirty years in the service of the Company and of some years before that in a petroleum business with which his family was connected. In his time he had passed through all grades of the merchandising of petroleum, filling post after post with loyalty, credit and acumen. For nine years before his elevation to the Vice Presidency in 1908, he had filled the office of Treasurer of the Standard Oil Company, and from 1892 onward he had been a Director. Despite this long and prominent career, few outside the oil business knew him, so unobtrusive was he by nature. He was a man of few words but of great grasp of affairs, particularly strong in organizing qualities, and gifted with fine and accurate judgment. In addition he was a man of wide information and varied reading. He was courtly, kind-hearted and charitable. The great good fortune of the Standard Oil Company was the securing of the service of such a man. Ordinary qualities sharpened by business experience may carry a man safely through the details of an established business easily filling its place in the commercial economy; but to win and retain a leading place in a business ever growing, ever reaching out, ever conquering new worlds and gaining and holding new markets, called for qualities far beyond the ordinary, and it is the testimony of his associates that he always deserved his promotions. This is high praise from men themselves the peers of the giants of business in all ages and all climes.

Mr. Tilford was born in Lexington, Kentucky, on July 14, 1850. His boyhood was spent there. His father, John B. Tilford, had long been a banker in Lexington, but at the close of the sixties, he pulled up stakes, and came to New York, where he once more took up the banking business. Young Wesley went to Columbia College where he studied for a couple of years, but the call of business was too strong to allow him to wait for his bachelor's degree. His elder brother, John B. Tilford, Jr., had entered the field of oil, associating himself with Jabez A. Bostwick in the firm of Bostwick & Tilford. Attracted by the prospects of petroleum, Wesley gave up his college course, and entered as a clerk in the firm of his brother, then doing business in Pearl Street. When the firm dissolved the two brothers joined in a partnership of their own under the title of John B. Tilford Jr. & Co., which did well from the start and continued to prosper until, at the period of the Eastern oil amalgamations, a substantial offer from the Standard Oil Company induced them to cast their fortunes with that vigorous organization. As has been said, those were busy formative times in the oil business, and the new recruit proved his mettle by the splendid success of his visit to the Pacific slope in 1878. He there organized the oil trade in California, Oregon, Colorado and the surrounding States. On his return to the East he was welcomed to a high place in the home office, taking charge of the vast transportation problem with vigor and effectiveness. And so, strong in the esteem and confidence of all his co-workers, he continued to the end. He was a member of the New York Chamber of Commerce and belonged to the Metropolitan and Tuxedo Clubs.

HENRY M. TILFORD.

Henry M. Tilford resigned as a Director of the Standard Oil Company (New Jersey) on February 3, 1911, after long service with that corporation, in order that he might devote his time to more personal interests, of which he has many. He is of the well known Kentucky family of Tilfords and was born in the Blue Grass State in Lexington, June 14, 1856, migrating to New York to join an older brother in the oil business. The family is of English origin, but was among the pioneers of Kentucky, and fully identified with the land of Daniel Boone and the birth place of Abraham Lincoln.

Mr. Tilford was educated in a private school, after which he became a clerk with J. B. Tilford & Company, the senior partner of the firm being an older brother. Afterwards he engaged with the Empire Refining Company as a clerk. Later he removed to Baltimore to become manager of the Baltimore United Oil Company, of which he was later the Vice President. In 1887, Mr. Tilford returned to New York and became connected with the Sales Department of the Standard Oil Company. In course of time he became President of the Pacific Coast Oil Company, which later became the Standard Oil Company (California). Mr. Tilford was also President of the Continental Oil Company and of the Standard Oil Company (Ohio), and Vice President of the Standard Oil Company of New York, and was a director in a number of other corporations. He spent most of his life in the marketing and manufacturing branches of the petroleum industry, and is retiring before he reaches the threshold of old age.

Mr. Tilford was married in New York City, November 12, 1885, to Miss Isabelle W. Giles. They have three daughters, Isabelle, Katherine Hunt, and Annette Tilford. Mr. Tilford has been a quiet but generous giver to deserving objects of his charitable interest. He belongs to the Metropolitan Club, Union League Club, Riding Club, Tuxedo Club and the Southern Society of New York. He is unassuming in manner and enjoys a wide acquaintance in the business and social circles of the metropolis.

RICHARD CHARLES VEIT.

The subject of this sketch is the manager of the Marine Department of the Standard Oil Company, in itself a great organization, but only an integral fraction of the greatest commercial organization in the world. From office boy to stockholder and manager—it is a story typically American and always interesting. In this case it is particularly so, for the company with which he is associated is so colossal in its character that its products are carried on the backs of Syrian camels and Chinese coolies, are found in the camps and huts of Alaskan gold seekers and South American Indians, form some part of the packs of donkey trains crossing the mountains of Spain and Portugal, reach the region between the sources of the Nile and the Niger, invade the sand plains of Mongolia and the "Roof of the World" in the lofty Himalayas. And to Mr. Veit's department falls the task of starting the oil on its world journeys.

Richard Charles Veit is a native of New York City, where he was born on the seventeenth of November, 1855, the son of Charles A. and Ernestine (Morse) Veit. Receiving his educational preparation in the public schools of the city, at the age of thirteen he became an office boy in the employ of the Standard Oil Company, at a salary of three dollars a week. He has ever since been associated with that superbly systematized and managed company. But the enthusiastic and willing office boy of forty-five years ago is now one of the active factors in the guidance of the great commercial company that once, at least, received full value for its expenditure of three dollars a week.

Mr. Veit, in time, was given the management of the Standard Oil Company's immensely important and constantly growing Marine Department, and he took the keenest interest in building up a representative class of boats for the oil service in the United States and in New York Harbor, of which his Company may be justly proud. Under his management was developed the important factor of ocean towing—first the coastwise on the Atlantic, later towing from New York to San Francisco, and finally resulting in the construction of the British tank steamer, "Iroquois," and her consort barge, "Navahoe," for service between New York and London, the steamer and barge together carrying a cargo of 123,000 barrels of oil on each voyage, on practically the same transit time as ordinary tank steamers ,and materially reducing the cost of ocean transportation.

Mr. Veit has long been one of the substantial stockholders of the Standard. He is also financially interested in a number of other prosperous manufacturing corporations, including Charles L. Seabury & Co., Consolidated, and Gas Engine and Power Company. He is a staunch supporter of several of New York's philanthropic and other institutions, being Vice President of the J. Hood Wright Memorial Hospital and a patron of St. Mark's Hospital, the American Museum of Natural History and the New York Zoological Society, which has the Aquarium and Zoological Park under its management. He is a member of the American Society of Mechanical Engineers and of the New York Yacht Club, is Chairman of the Board of Trustees of the Atlantic Yacht Club, and is one of the Directors of the Lotus Club.

In 1880, Mr. Veit was wedded to Miss Mary K. Stobo, daughter of Alexander Stobo, of Weehawken, New Jersey. They have three sons, Russell Charles, Arthur Stobo and Kenneth Alden Veit.

Mr. Veit is one who believes the door of opportunity is open to every man. By his own energy, ambition, concentration and faithfulness he long since achieved success and attained the honorable reputation he holds to-day in the business world of the American metropolis and the Nation. Both success and reputation were won without the aid of powerful friends or relatives and are well deserved. His career is one that should lend hope and encouragement to the men of a younger generation, who have character and integrity as factors with which to achieve success.

WALTER C. TEAGLE.

Walter C. Teagle, the son of John and Amelia Belle (Clark) Teagle, was born May 1st, 1878, in the City of Cleveland, Ohio, which is also practically the birthplace of the Standard Oil Company. On both sides he is of thoroughly English ancestry.

Mr. Teagle's father was a member of the old firm of Schofield, Shurmer & Teagle, of Cleveland. His maternal grandfather, Maurice B. Clark, one of the pioneers of Cleveland, was the first partner of John D. Rockefeller, their earliest business association being in the grain trade. The business was later extended so as to include the oil trade, which was then in its infancy.

Mr. Teagle received a sound preparatory educational training and later matriculated at Cornell University. After completing his college course he entered upon an active business career, receiving his practical training with the above mentioned firm of Schofield, Shurmer & Teagle. During his connection with this firm he gained a thorough knowledge of the various details of the oil business and in 1900, when this firm, with others, was merged into the Republic Oil Company, he was elected Vice President of this Company. He remained the active manager of the Republic for about three years, when he accepted a position with the Standard Oil Company's Export Department.

The importance of this department is indicated by the fact that more than sixty per cent. of the Standard's refined products are disposed of in foreign countries, the field embracing the entire civilized world.

Mr. Teagle, upon joining the Export Department, was placed in charge of the marketing of the Standard's products in certain foreign countries and in the carrying out of this work the greater part of his time was spent abroad which brought him in close contact and made him familiar with the producing and marketing situation in all parts of the world, resulting in his eventually becoming the head of the Standard's Export Department. In recognition of his ability in successfully adjusting and disposing of the many perplexing situations which at various times confronted the Standard Oil Company in the administration of its foreign affairs, he was, on June 23rd, 1910, elected to membership in the Company's directorate.

Mr. Teagle's wife was the former Edith Castle Murray, of Cleveland, who died about three years ago. On April 26th, he married Miss Rowena Bayliss Lee, of Memphis, Tennessee.

Mr. Teagle is a strong advocate of life in the open air as a rejuvenator, spending at least a month each year hunting. He is a good sportsman, an excellent shot and derives as much pleasure from the anticipation of his annual outing with gun and dog as he does from its realization.

Mr. Teagle's travels, love of out-of-doors and extreme optimism have made him a man of broad mind, fine physique and pleasing personality.

CHARLES M. PRATT.

Charles Millard Pratt, Vice President of the Standard Oil Company of New Jersey, is the son of the late Charles and Lydia R. Pratt. He was born in Brooklyn, N. Y., November 2nd, 1855, and was graduated from the Adelphi Academy, in 1875, and from Amherst College four years later. He then engaged in business with his father in the Pratt Manufacturing Company, one of the first oil manufacturing plants in the East. His natural ability as a merchant and as a man of great executive force soon took him into the department of domestic sales. In 1891, upon the death of Charles Pratt, the management and conservation of the latter's varied interests devolved upon the son. For a number of years Charles M. Pratt was President of the Standard Oil Company of Kentucky; then he became Secretary of the Standard Oil Company of New Jersey, then Treasurer of that corporation and later Vice President.

Since the foundation of the Pratt Institute in 1887, the greatest civic achievement of his father, Charles M. Pratt watched its growth and now as President he never relaxes his efforts to further its aims. He has always been deeply interested in the welfare of his alma mater, Amherst, of which he is a trustee, and has presented to it a perfectly equipped gymnasium, known as the Pratt Gymnasium. He is also a Trustee of Vassar College, and has contributed largely to its work.

In 1884, Mr. Pratt was married to Miss Mary Seymour Morris, daughter of Ex-Governor Luzon B. Morris of New Haven, Conn. The children of this marriage were Morris Pratt, Theodore Pratt, Margaret R. Pratt, Katherine E. Pratt and Richardson Pratt.

The clubs in which Mr. Pratt holds membership are the Hamilton and Rembrandt Clubs of Brooklyn, the Nassau Country Club of Long Island, and, Alpha Phi Club of New York.

HERBERT LEE PRATT.

The subject of this sketch, Herbert Lee Pratt, is a son of Charles Pratt, known wherever petroleum is produced and in almost every place where its products are sold. He was born in the City of Brooklyn, November 21, 1871, and, with his interesting family, resides in that portion of Greater New York. His home is on Clinton Avenue, in the old center of wealth and culture in that Borough, an avenue that today is lined with some of the stateliest homes to be found in the metropolis.

Mr. Pratt was educated at Amherst College and after graduation, became a clerk in the Bergen Point Chemical Works. He next became assistant to the manager of the Standard Oil Company Pratt Works, and the Queens County Works, in Brooklyn. He is now manager of these factories and in addition of the Kings County and Long Island Works, with offices at 26 Broadway, New York. He is active in the affairs of the Standard Oil Company of New York and of Charles Pratt & Co. Outside the manufacturing business, Mr. Pratt is a director of the Peoples Trust Company, of Brooklyn, one of the strongest financial institutions in the Borough, maintaining, beside the central bank, three branches in different sections of the city. He is interested as an investor in many and various enterprises that tend to assist in the larger development of the city in which he resides, and gives to them careful attention.

Mr. Pratt is one of the directors of Pratt Institute, founded by his father, Charles Pratt, an institution that enables many young people in poor circumstances to obtain education and useful lines of instruction that would be otherwise unattainable. This institution is maintained by the Pratt family and is famed throughout the country for its beneficent advancement of struggling genius He is also interested in several other philanthropic and charitable foundations which the family has fostered, all of them constantly enlarging and extending their sphere of influence. Personally, he is an unassuming, hard working, democratic citizen, whose highest pleasure is to further the interests of his neighbors and the community of which he is a part.

Herbert Lee Pratt was married April 28, 1897, to Miss Florence Gibb, and the union has been blessed with five children, in the following order: Edith G. Pratt, Herbert L. Pratt, Jr., Harriet B. Pratt, Florence G. Pratt, and Frederic R. Pratt.

Mr. Pratt belongs to the Racquet and Tennis Club, the Alpha Delta Club, the Brooklyn Riding and Driving Club, the Hamilton Club, the Crescent Athletic Club and the Nassau Country Club. It may easily be inferred from this list that he is fond of sports and the outdoor life, and the inference is no mistake. He is of athletic contour and gives evidence of abounding vitality, including a great capacity for hard work.

FRANK Q. BARSTOW.

Frank Quarles Barstow, who at the time of his death, August 19, 1909, had been for over ten years a director of the Standard Oil Company, as well as an officer and director of many of its subsidiary companies, was closely identified with the history of petroleum almost from its beginning. He was, also, on the board of directors of various other industrial and commercial enterprises.

The Barstows came to America from the West Riding of Yorkshire in the "True-love," which set sail in 1635 for the coast of Massachusetts. Early in the last century descendants of the original colonists removed from New England to Ohio. Mr. Barstow's father was William A. Barstow, a successful miller in Wisconsin, who married Miss Maria Quarles, of Kenosha, formerly of Salem, Mass.

Frank Q. Barstow, born October 24, 1846, at Waukesha, Wis., was the eldest of four sons, all of whom were connected for many years with the Standard Oil Company. Incidentally, it is of interest to note that the father, William A. Barstow, was Governor of Wisconsin from 1854 to 1856, and also Colonel of the First Wisconsin Volunteer Cavalry during the Civil War.

Mr. Barstow received his early education in the schools of Waukesha and Madison, and at an academy in Sioux City. During two years of the Civil War, although not regularly enlisted, he attached himself to his father's regiment. After the conflict had ended, he spent two years on the plains with a Government survey. He then went to Cleveland, and engaged in various occupations. Eventually, he went into the oil business, operating under the name of Barstow, Darrow & Co., a refinery on the Run at Cleveland, which was afterwards purchased by the Standard Oil Company. In 1873, he entered the service of the latter company, buying barrel staves at first, and later following up the construction of works on the Run, and the building of tankcars, in the manufacture of which the company had but recently engaged. In 1877, he removed from Cleveland to Titusville, Pa., becoming First Vice President of the Acme Oil Company. It was there that he became associated with Mr. John D. Archbold, resulting in a close friendship of many years standing. In 1881, he removed with the offices of the Acme Company to New York City, where he occupied various positions along manufacturing and marketing lines with the Standard Oil Company, being elected one of their directors in June, 1899. He remained with this company until his death, a continuous service of thirty-six years.

Mr. Barstow went on various foreign missions for the company, the first being in 1892, when he looked over the ground in the Far East preparatory to the company opening up business in those countries. He visited South America on a similar mission, and, later, made several trips to Continental Europe, preliminary to establishing refineries abroad.

On October 8, 1873, Mr. Barstow married Miss Lois Catherine Buhrer, of Cleveland. They had two sons, William A. Barstow, and S. Buhrer Barstow. After coming to New York, Mr. Barstow and family resided in Brooklyn until 1884, when they removed to East Orange, N. J. He took pride in the development of the Oranges, and was one of the organizers of the Peoples Bank of East Orange; the Savings, Investment & Trust Company, and the East Orange Bank. He was a vestryman of Grace Church, Orange, and identified with various charities. His private benefactions were many and in keeping with the kindliness of his character.

HORACE P. CHAMBERLAIN.

Horace P. Chamberlain, General Manager of the Atlas Works of the Standard Oil Company, at Buffalo, N. Y., is of notable ancestry. When William of Normandy sailed from his native shores to win the crown of England, his personal staff included a nobleman whom he invested with the rank, the prestige and the responsibilities of Royal Chamberlain. As in so many historical instances, the office gave birth to the patronymic. At all events, the chamberlain of William the Conqueror was the founder of a family tree which throve in England and extended a branch, three hundred years ago, to the Colony of Massachusetts.

In 1638 Henry Chamberlain left Hingham, in the County of Norfolk, and with 132 of his neighbors he sailed on the good ship "Diligent." He was accompanied by his mother, wife and children. Arriving in due time in Massachusetts, Mr. Chamberlain and companions established a community to which they gave the name of Hingham, thus honoring their English home. There he spent the greater part of his life and in 1674 he died at Hull, Massachusetts.

Sylvester Chamberlain, the grandfather of Horace P. Chamberlain, was the first of the direct line to move westward. He located in Buffalo. His son, Hunting Sylvester Chamberlain, married Miss Betsy Maria Hyde, a daughter of Colonel James Hyde. It may be noted, in passing, that Colonel Hyde, to his other achievements, added that of inventing the first threshing machine. Hunting Sylvester Chamberlain and his wife had a number of children and one of them—Horace P. Chamberlain—is the subject of this sketch.

Born in Buffalo April 1, 1852, and educated in the public schools, Horace P. Chamberlain began his active business career in 1872 as a member of the Government engineering corps to which had been assigned the duty of surveying the Illinois River and its adjacent shores. In 1876 he went to Parker City and was employed as bookkeeper for the Union Pipe Line Company. The Union was subsequently sold to the Empire and later to the United Pipe Line Company. Meanwhile Mr. Chamberlain had been for a time at Petrolia, also as bookkeeper. In 1878 he removed to Olean and there served the United Pipe Line Company in the same capacity.

In June 1879, Horace P. Chamberlain was married, at Titusville, Pa., to Miss Frances Ann Archbold. The ceremony was performed in the home of John D. Archbold, the bride's brother. A few months later the young couple selected Titusville as the place of their abode and Mr. Chamberlain, leaving the service of the United Pipe Line Company, became associated with W. A. Archbold—also a brother of Mrs. Chamberlain—in the oil brokerage business at Titusville and Oil City. From 1882 to 1887 Mr. Chamberlain conducted his brokerage business alone. Then he became Assistant General Manager of the Standard Oil Company of New York, Atlas Works, at Buffalo. Three years later he was General Manager, a position which he has since then occupied continuously and with notable success.

In addition to nearly a quarter of a century's connection with the Atlas Works, Mr. Chamberlain has found time to devote a large measure of his energy and ability to the affairs of The Imperial Oil Company, Limited, of Canada, which was organized in 1897, with works at Sarnia, Ontario, and merchandising stations throughout the Dominion. At first he was General Manager of the Imperial. He is now President as well as General Manager, having attained the Presidency in 1908, as successor to the late Frank Q. Barstow.

In reaching out for new markets in foreign lands the Standard Oil Company, while introducing its illuminant, has metaphorically carried the torch of progress into many countries. In the ranks of the Company's employes were found able men well qualified to act as missionaries of commerce. Horace P. Chamberlain was of the number. He spent two years and a half—from December, 1904, to June, 1907—in establishing the Company's business in Roumania, in connection with the Romano-Americana. He has also visited Mexico and South America in forwarding the Company's interests.

Mr. Chamberlain and his family reside in Buffalo, on Jewett Avenue. There are two daughters and one son: Mrs. Helen Frances Chamberlain Cole, wife of Almeron Hyde Cole, a prominent attorney of New York City; Mrs. Ruth Chamberlain Magor, wife of Basil Magor, of Morristown, New Jersey, and John Archbold Chamberlain, who is Assistant to the General Manager of the Atlas Works.

ALFRED COTTON BEDFORD.

In Brooklyn, now a part of Greater New York, Alfred Cotton Bedford, Treasurer of the Standard Oil Company of New Jersey, was born November 5, 1864. His father, Alfred Bedford, is of English descent, while his mother traces her ancestry to Wales through old New England stock. The father, now retired, was for many years the representative in Europe of the American Waltham Watch Company. The subject of this sketch received his early education at the Adelphii College in his native city, afterward pursuing his studies abroad in England, Germany and Switzerland. He entered business life with the dry goods firm of E. S. Jaffray & Co., of New York, being employed there for nine months. He next entered the employ of the Bergenport Chemical Company, a subsidiary of the Standard Oil Company, on April 9, 1882.

Mr. Bedford remained in the manufacturing department of the Standard until January, 1907, when he was elected to the Board of Directors of the Standard Oil Company of New Jersey. He became Treasurer of this Company on January 20, 1910. While employed by the Standard Oil Company a large part of his time was divided and given to Charles Pratt & Co., a firm engaged in many large enterprises. As general manager of Charles Pratt & Co., Mr. Bedford represented them in many and various corporations, at one time being Director and Treasurer of the Long Island Railroad Company, Director and Secretary of the Ohio River Railroad Company, President of the Portland General Electric Company, of Portland, Oregon; President of Pratt & Lambert Varnish Co., President of the Self Winding Clock Company, Director in The Thrift and in many other industrial, electric lighting and railway companies, thereby acquiring a very general business training, with large and valuable commercial experience. He is one of the active young men of the Standard group, holding one of the most responsible positions in the Company and is widely known in the business world. He is a director in many of the subsidiary companies controlled by the Standard.

Despite the fact that Mr. Bedford has led a strenuous business life he has found time to devote to social life, his church and to philanthropic and charitable work. He has always been much interested in the work of the Young Men's Christian Association, being connected with the Y. M. C. A. of Brooklyn, N. Y. He has been especially interested in the educational work of the Pratt Institute of Brooklyn, being a member of its associate council, and in general educational effort designed for the benefit of those deprived of advantages. The Emanuel Baptist Church of Brooklyn, where he attends and is a member of the its board of trustees, always finds him to be an active promoter of religious enterprises and can depend upon his influence for success in its undertakings. He is especially interested in the charitable work of the Church, which has a wide field of usefulness.

Mr. Bedford is a member of the Lawyers' Club of New York, Hamilton Club and Twentieth Century Club of Brooklyn, N. Y.; the Duquesne Club of Pittsburg, Pa., and of the Nassau Country Club of Glen Cove, L. I. He is a frequent visitor in Pittsburg, where his Company has large interests.

On January 8, 1890, Alfred Cotton Bedford was married to Edith Kinsman Clarke of Brooklyn, N. Y., which union has been blessed by two sons, Alfred Clarke Bedford and Dean Bedford. Their home is a center of cultured society. Mr. Bedford is, personally, possessed of a genial disposition that endears him to his closest friends and business associates. He is happiest when giving assistance to those around him or making the task lighter for a friend.

EDWARD THOMAS BEDFORD.

It would have been difficult to foretell in the early sixties what the outcome of the oil industry, then in its infancy would be, or to prophecy that fifty years thence the Standard Oil Company would be one of the strongest organizations in this country and that its interests would extend almost over the entire world. Its rapid advancement and successful business career have been due in a large measure to the faithful efforts of the active and conservative business men who have always been at its head.

One of the most notable of these is Edward Thomas Bedford, who was born in that part of New York now known as Brooklyn, on February 19, 1849. He is the son of Frederick Thomas and Mary Ann Elizabeth (Pace) Bedford, who came from London, England, in 1848, and settled in Brooklyn. He attended the public schools of Brooklyn, where he early exhibited the intellectual powers which later ranked him among America's leading capitalists.

His first business experience was as a salesman for the firm of Charles Pratt & Company, dealers in oils. He was later connected with Robert Chesebrough, where he was largely responsible for the production and introduction of vaseline, a petroleum product, for the extensive sale of which this company is well known. He became a partner in Thompson & Bedford, Eastern selling agents of lubricating oil, and in 1893 became associated with the Standard Oil Company. In 1903 he was elected a director of the Company and became a member of its executive committee, which position he held until January 1, 1909, when he retired from active service, though still remaining in it as a director, his intention being to devote more of his time to the interests of the Corn Products Refining Company, of which he is President, and which has prospered under his management.

Mr. Bedford is also interested in the New York Glucose Company, the Self Winding Clock Company, the Colonial Oil Company, the Bedford Petroleum Company of France, the Title Guarantee and Trust Company, the Thompson-Starrett Company. Director in American Lloyds, Director in Matheson Lead Co., and a number of other thriving organizations, for it has been truly said that wherever Mr. Bedford's influence has been brought to bear upon the management of any concern, it never came to grief.

Aside from his remarkable career in the business world, Mr. Bedford is an expert horseman and breeder of some of the finest blooded stock in this country. It was on his farm at Greens Farms, Fairfield County, Conn., that the celebrated mare, Hamburg Belle, who holds the world's record of 2:01¼, was bred. Mr. Bedford, driving himself, holds the world's record for team to road wagon over a half mile track, of 2:12¼, also the race record to wagon of 2:08¼, which is the fastest mile so driven in which more than two horses competed.

His daughter, Miss Emily Bedford, like her father, a lover of fine horses, won a number of championships and blue ribbons in Madison Square Garden, Chicago, Philadelphia and Brooklyn, notably with Hildred and mate; with Donner & Blitzen, lady's pair, and Miss Ann, with which she won the championship at Philadelphia and Plainfield in the lady's saddle class. Patsy Palmer and Red Berry are also blue ribbon winners.

Mr. Bedford was married in December, 1871, to Miss Mary Ann Dingee, to which union five children have been born: Charles E., associated with the Standard Oil Company in its foreign and domestic marine oil department; Frederick T., Treasurer of the Corn Products Refining Company; Mary E., Emily H. and Gracie E.

FREDERICK HENRY BEDFORD.

Frederick Henry Bedford, prominent in the Thompson and Bedford Department of the Standard Oil Company of New York, was born July 25, 1854, in Brooklyn, N Y. His father and mother were born in London, England, but moved to Brooklyn, N. Y., in the fall of 1848. In 1861 they moved to Greens Farms, Conn., where Mr. Bedford received his education and led a farmer's life until he was about twenty-one years old. Later he engaged in the flour business and finally in the oil trade.

In addition to Mr. Bedford's connection with the Standard Oil Company of New York, he is a director of the Galena Signal Oil Company, of the Swan & Finch Company, the West Indies Oil Company, and President of the Standard Oil Company of Brazil.

The predilections of Mr. Bedford do not incline toward club life; nevertheless, he is a member of the Brooklyn Riding and Driving Club of Brooklyn, N Y., and of the Bridgeport Yacht Club of Bridgeport, Conn.

BENJAMIN FRANKLIN WARREN, C. E.

One of the constructive geniuses of the petroleum industry is Benjamin Franklin Warren, who did the engineering on the first great pipe line to the Atlantic Coast, that of the Tide-Water Pipe Company. His first connection with the oil business was as engineer in charge of the Middle Division of the Seaboard Pipe Line, proposed to be built between Bradys Bend, in Armstrong County, Pennsylvania, and Baltimore, Maryland. He was afterward given charge of the entire line, but it was never completed, a sudden decrease in production of the Butler and Clarion County oil fields rendering it useless. The project was abandoned in 1878, at which time the Tide-Water Pipe Company was organized by the same interests to transport crude oil from the rapidly rising Bradford oil field in McKean County. The line was first built from Rixford, in McKean County, to Williamsport, on the Susquehanna River, where connection was made with the Reading Railroad. Later it was extended to Bayonne, New Jersey. Mr. Warren was appointed manager of the Ocean Oil Company, a corporation owned by the Tide-Water Pipe Company, afterward (in 1889) merged into the Tide-Water Oil Company, and of which he remains a manager as well as Chief Engineer of the Tide-Water Pipe Company. Beside the Tide-Water oil interests he is connected with the Ulua Commercial Company, the Olancho Mineral Company and the Pontiac Mining Company, and has interests in several other going concerns.

Benjamin Franklin Warren was born in Philadelphia, Pennsylvania, on December 25, 1849, of good American stock. On the father's side his ancestry is traced back to the Warrens of Massachusetts, which family came from Richard Warren of the Mayflower, and his cousin, William Warren, who came to the colony about the same time. On the mother's side he is descended from Captain William Warner, who was a Captain in Oliver Cromwell's army and emigrated to America about 1658. Captain Warner settled at Philadelphia on the west side of the Schuylkill River, where he bought five hundred acres of land and named it Blockley, after the English town from which he came.

The subject of this sketch was educated in the schools of Philadelphia, passing from the Philadelphia High School to the University of Pennsylvania, where he was graduated. His first occupation was in sundry minor positions on a railroad. He was next attached to the United States Coast and Geodetic Survey, making a topographical survey of Pennsylvania. He was engaged in this work when appointed engineer of the Seaboard Pipe Line. He is a member of the Engineer's Club of Philadelphia, of the University of Pennsylvania Club in New York and of the Pennsylvania Society of New York.

Mr. Warren was married at Philadelphia, in 1883, to Miss Emma Frances Kinsey, of that city. They have no children living.

ROBERT DIX BENSON.

Among the younger leaders in the American petroleum industry is Robert D. Benson, President of the Tide Water Oil Company, next to the Standard Oil Company, the oldest and most successful of the great corporations engaged in the production, transportation, manufacture and marketing of petroleum. He is "to the manner born," having been familiar with the industry in which he is engaged, almost from infancy. Athough born in Brewerton, New York, May 14, 1861, his parents removed in 1865 to Titusville, Pennsylvania, the birthplace of the business of drilling for oil, and there he grew to young manhood. At the age of nineteen years he entered actively into the business and has devoted his life to the work.

Robert D. Benson is the oldest son of Byron D. Benson and Minerva (Stevens) Benson, late of Titusville, Pennsylvania. The ancestral line runs back to John Benson, of Caversham, Oxfordshire, England, who emigrated to America in 1638 and settled in Hull, Massachusetts, whence the succeeding generations migrated Westward into Central New York, where the subject of this sketch was born. His father was a well known and popular citizen of Onondaga County, New York, being elected sheriff of the county soon after the birth of Robert, a post of more than ordinary responsibility at that time, as the period was that of the great Civil War.

Robert D. Benson was educated in the public schools of Titusville and upon graduation, at the age of nineteen years, he entered the employ of the Tide Water Pipe Company, Limited, as secretary to his father, who was President of the Company. After one year in that position he went one year as a special student to the University of Pennsylvania, and in 1883 he became President of the Solar Oil Company, operating a small refinery located at Buffalo, New York. In 1888 he was elected manager of the Tide Water Pipe Company and a director of the Tide Water Oil Company. In 1896 he was elected Vice President of the Tide Water Oil Company and in 1908, upon the retirement of Samuel Q. Brown from active business, Mr. Benson was chosen President of the Tide Water Pipe Company and the Tide Water Oil Company.

The Tide Water Pipe Company, Limited, was organized by Byron D. Benson and associates in 1878, with a capital of $625,000. It was the first pipe line to compete with the railroads in carrying oil to the seaboard and demonstrated the superior economy of that means of transportation. Until 1888 it supplied refineries at Chester, Pennsylvania, and Bayonne, New Jersey, partly controlled by it and partly independent. In that year the Tide Water Oil Company was organized, capital $5,000,000, which acquired all of the refineries and consolidated the refining business at Bayonne. In 1908, when Robert D. Benson became President, the Tide Water Oil Company increased its capital to $24,000,000, and acquired control of the Tide Water Pipe Company, and the Associated Producers Company, an oil producing concern operating in the fields of Pennsylvania, Ohio, West Virginia and Illinois, and of the Okla Oil Company, operating in the fields of Oklahoma. In that year the Tide Water Pipe Company extended its pipe line from the original starting point in McKean County, Pennsylvania, to Crawford County, Illinois. The length of its trunk pipe line is now approximately eight hundred miles and the capacity of its refineries is about 300,000 barrels per month. The business of the Company is principally an export trade in case oil, shipped to South America and Oriental countries. The officers of the Tide Water Oil Company are: R. D. Benson, President; W. S. Benson, Vice President and Treasurer; Dickson Q. Brown, Vice President and Assistant Treasurer.

Mr. R. D. Benson resides in Passaic, New Jersey, where he has served in the City Council. He is a director in the Peoples Bank and the Trust, Guarantee Mortgage and Title Insurance Companies of that city and a director of the Muskogee Electric Traction Company and the Shawnee-Tecumseh Traction Company. He is also Vice President of the Associated Producers Company and the Okla Oil Company.

Mr. Benson was married on October 11, 1888, to Miss Harriet Granger and they have three children: Byron D. Benson, Robert Granger Benson, and Olive Benson. He belongs to the Union League Club, of New York, and the Yountakah Country Club of Passaic.

WILLIAM SUMNER BENSON.

Among the young leaders in business in New York is William S. Benson, second son of the late Byron D. Benson, former President of the Tide Water Oil Company. His principal interest is in the Tide Water oil group, but he is actively interested in many other business enterprises in various parts of the country, such as the Muskogee Electric Traction Company, the Shawnee-Tecumseh Traction Company, the North Jersey Rapid Transit Company, the Magnetic Iron Ore Company, the Platt and Washburn Refining Company, and others. He resides at Passaic, New Jersey, and is interested in the institutions of that suburb of the metropolis.

Mr. Benson was born in Brewerton, New York, February 21, 1864, the second son of Byron D. and Minerva Benson, his father being sheriff of Onondaga County at the time. The following year his parents moved to Pennsylvania, where his father engaged in the lumber business with Major R. E. Hopkins and David McKelvy. Soon afterward he engaged in the business of producing oil, his lumber trade being principally with the oil producers and oil town builders. That business he followed until his death in 1888, ten years after organizing the Tide Water Pipe Company, Limited, of which he was President. The subject of this sketch was educated in the public schools of Titusville, Pennsylvania, and the school of experience, which he entered at an early age. In August, 1883, he became secretary to the President of the Tide Water Pipe Company. October 26, 1903, he was appointed Assistant Treasurer of that Company, being also one of its managers or directors, and performing the duties of Secretary until June of that year. From 1888 until 1908 he was Secretary of the Tide Water Oil Company, organized in the former year with a capital of $5,000,000. He was also a Director of the Tide Water Oil Company during the same period. In 1908 he was elected Treasurer and Vice President of the Tide Water Oil Company and continues in that capacity, being also Treasurer and a manager of the Tide Water Pipe Company. He is a Director of the Associated Producers Company and of the Okla Oil Company, corporations of the Tide Water group.

The Tide Water Pipe Company, next to the Standard Oil Company, is the oldest and most successful of the great corporations engaged in the American petroleum industry. It was the first to lay a pipe line across the Allegheny Mountains from the Pennsylvania oil producing regions towards the seaboard to facilitate the export business, which, until recently, comprised more than one-half of the American petroleum trade. Through the Associated Producers Company, the Tide Water is a large producer of oil in the fields of Pennsylvania, West Virginia, Ohio and Illinois, and through the Okla Oil Company it is an active producer in the fields of Oklahoma. The Tide Water Pipe Company operates a trunk line of pipe from the fields in Crawford County, Illinois, to Bayonne, New Jersey, approximately 800 miles, and the refineries of the Tide Water Oil Company at Bayonne have a capacity of 300,000 barrels of oil per month. The greater part of the product is exported, principally as case oil to South American and Oriental ports. Mr. Benson has been familiar with the oil business since his boyhood and knows it in all its branches.

Mr. W. S. Benson was married at Titusville, Pennsylvania, to Miss Juliette Harton, on January 20, 1892. They have two daughters, Margaret H. Benson and Sarah Jane Benson. He is a member of the Union League Club, New York, the Yountakah Country Club, the Passaic Club and the Arcola Country Club.

DICKSON Q. BROWN.

Among the younger men who are influential factors in the petroleum industry is Dickson Q. Brown, Vice President of the Tide Water Oil Company and President of the Associated Producers and Okla Oil Companies. He is the son of the late Samuel Q. Brown, a pioneer petroleum producer, and was born at Pleasantville, Pennsylvania, April 2, 1873, in the midst of one of the notable oil developments of Venango County. He grew up in the model oil town, familiar with the processes of crude petroleum production almost as soon as he began attending the primary school, an experience which was of great value in his subsequent connection with the oil industry, which has been the work of his life.

After graduating from Phillips Exeter Academy, Mr. Brown entered Princeton University, taking the Bachelor of Arts degree in 1895, passing to the Massachusetts Institute of Technology, where he graduated, Bachelor of Science, in 1898. With this exceptional equipment he entered the refinery of the Tide Water Oil Company at Bayonne, N. J., where he worked for a year. He then spent some months in the oil producing fields with the Associated Producers Company, later becoming a student, for a year, in the Oil Research Laboratory of the Royal Technical School, Charlottenberg, Berlin, Germany. The young man was now fully prepared for a larger connection with the companies in which his father was deeply interested and he occupied various positions in the Tide Water group of companies, among the most profitable in the entire petroleum industry. He brought to this business the instinctive talent from youthful association with the producing fields and a technical training that is rare among the executive heads of oil companies. He is now Second Vice President of the Tide Water Oil Company, President of the Associated Producers Company and the Okla Oil Company, Secretary of the Tide Water Pipe Line Company, Limited, Vice President of the Tide Water Company of Massachusetts, etc. He is also identified with the Magnetic Iron Ore Company and other enterprises. His business address is at No. 11 Broadway, New York City.

Dickson Q. Brown is of Scotch-Irish lineage, his father, Samuel Q. Brown, and his mother, Nancy E. Lamb, being of the pioneer stock that settled Northwestern Pennsylvania and conquered the wilderness there. Pleasantville, where he was born, was one of the first villages established in that region, and was appropriately named. It is situated on a plateau, between the valleys of the Pithole Creeks, leveled and planed by the great glaciers of the ice age. From the beginning it has been peopled by educated, refined men and women whose impress has been put into its society, and whose influence has extended far beyond its boundaries. That it was an enterprising community may be inferred from the fact that its founders journeyed far into the wilderness to select the garden spot in which they located. Its citizens were interested in oil production on Oil Creek long before the development spread from Pithole into their own neighborhood, Mr. Brown's father being the first to appreciate the value of Drake's discovery.

Mr. Brown belongs to the Tiger Inn Club (Princeton), Sigma Chi Fraternity, University Club, Automobile Club of America, Princeton Club, Apawamis Club, Engineer's Club, American Society of Mechanical Engineers and other chiefly scientific and outdoor organizations. He has never been a candidate for political office, having no taste for such honors, but takes a lively interest in public affairs as a private citizen. He remains unmarried.

JESSE C. McDOWELL.

Jesse C. McDowell, President of the Dominion Natural Gas Co., was born in Summerhill Township, Crawford County, Pennsylvania, 1852, on the farm on which his Scotch-Irish ancestors settled originally, coming to that place from the Wyoming settlement late in the eighteenth century.

His early education, received in the common schools, was supplemented by academic studies in special preparation for the profession of land surveying and that of civil engineer. In the meantime he taught in the district schools for several terms. For a number of years he was engaged with his uncle, James McDowell, Jr., in land surveying and in the course of his duties gained wide acquaintance throughout Western Pennsylvania.

In 1881 Mr. McDowell began work in the Civil Engineering Department of the United Pipe Lines. A year later he was placed in charge of the construction of an eight-inch gas line from Wilcox, Pa., to Bradford, at that time the longest as well as the largest gas line undertaken. After its completion and extension to Olean, he was engaged for a year as pipe line gauger at Bradford on the west branch of Tuna Creek. He was made assistant superintendent of construction in 1883 and engaged in laying large pipe lines.

When the Thorn Creek excitement subsided Mr. McDowell became district foreman at Colegrove, McKean County, relinquishing that position two years later to engage in constructing the oil pipe line from the Lima, O., field to Chicago. He remained some time in the Illinois metropolis to procure franchises from the city for laying pipe lines to distribute oil to factories and other plants for fuel. After that he engaged in leasing, renting and purchasing property for the Ohio Oil Company in the Trenton Rock region of Ohio and Indiana, in 1892 going to Pittsburgh at the opening of the McDonald field. In this work he was acting as special agent of the National Transit Company. Shortly afterward Mr. McDowell was made superintendent of the Right of Way Department of that company and its affiliated companies. He resigned that position in 1889 to become Vice President and General Manager of the Philadelphia Company.

In 1901 Mr. McDowell was associated with Col. J. M. Guffey and others in the organization of the J. M. Guffey Petroleum Company and the Gulf Refining Company. He was Vice President and General Manager of both corporations and under his supervision was erected the great refinery at Port Arthur. While he was at the managerial helm a large fleet of oil steamers was purchased and equipped. These ships ply along the coast from Port Arthur to New York and intermediate points.

Turning his attention to natural gas, Mr. McDowell became interested in a combination of gas companies, which resulted in the birth of the Union Natural Gas Corporation. After serving for a time as Vice President and General Manager, Mr. McDowell joined with others in organizing the Kansas Natural Gas Company. He devoted four years of his life to that association.

For the past five years Mr. McDowell has been President of the Dominion Natural Gas Company. He is President of the International Petrol Company, a director of the Fayette County Gas Company and General Manager of the Tri-County Gas Company, all three corporations having headquarters in Pittsburgh. He is a member of the board of directors of the Columbia Gas and Electric Company, operating in Cleveland and Cincinnati, and of several other natural gas companies. He is a Natural Gas Consulting Engineer and served two terms as President of the Natural Gas Association of America. He is also a director of the American Union Trust Company of Kansas City and is interested in a number of financial institutions of Pittsburgh.

Aside from these activities Mr. McDowell is a farmer on a large scale. In Southern Texas, in the section known as the Gulf Coast Country, he has over sixteen thousand acres. He breeds Hereford cattle, produces rice and manufactures sugar—all on a large scale.

Mr. McDowell is a member of the Duquesne and Athletic Clubs of Pittsburgh and all in all he is one of that city's most active and successful men of affairs.

PHILIP RUPRECHT.

Philip Ruprecht, manager of the Standard Oil Company's foreign shipping system, who died suddenly on May 8, 1911, respected and loved by all assocates, was born in Marburg, Germany, in 1853. When he was but fifteen years of age he came to New York and began his business career as a clerk with the late Gustav Heye, under whom, in 1878, he entered the service of the Standard Oil Company at a time when the exporting of petroleum was done in wooden barrels. For twenty-one years Mr. Ruprecht saw continuous service in this department, the progress of which was inseparably connected with his own foresight and executive ability. In 1899, when Mr. Heye died, Mr. Ruprecht succeeded to the office which for the last twelve years he had filled greatly to his credit and that of the Standard Oil Company. He had charge of the chartering of all tonnage for the company's products and was the American agent of the various steamship lines plying between the United States, Europe and Asia, and carrying bulk petroleum in more than eighty large craft. The Anglo-American Oil Co., Limited, of London, alone had a fleet of over fifteen large four-masters and four steamers engaged in carrying case oil out to the Far East, returning with general cargo, under Mr. Ruprecht's management.

One of the Anglo-American Oil Co.'s bulk steamers completed in 1910, eight voyages between New York and England with a barge in tow transporting 1,000,000 barrels of petroleum.

The great prestige which the United States has gained in the eyes of the world as a commercial power has been brought about by a number of influences, one of the most potent of which has been the missionary work of the Standard Oil Company. It has dissipated darkness in benighted regions and relegated the grease pan and the tallow dip to the rear of the procession. It is universally conceded that Mr. Ruprecht's knowledge of the shipping affairs of the world has been a factor in the extension of the Standard Oil Co.'s foreign trade by cheap transportation of its products to all the faraway corners and islands of our globe.

Mr. Ruprecht was a member of the Produce, Maritime and Consolidated Exchanges, of the American Geographical Society, the American Museum of Natural History and a number of New York's German social and benevolent societies. He was a man of many virtues and of strong character, highly esteemed by his associates in the Standard Oil Company, all of whom sorrow in their loss, and by a large circle of personal and business friends in this country and abroad. He was the soul of honor in his wide dealings with men and left a record of which any man might be proud.

HON. MORTIMER F. ELLIOTT.

Honorable Mortimer F. Elliott, General Solicitor for the Standard Oil Company, who succeeded the late Samuel C. T. Dodd in 1905, was, like his predecessor, born in Pennsylvania, the territory that has furnished many of the legal giants of the country. The place of Mr. Elliott's birth was in Tioga County, one of the Northern tier in Pennsylvania, and, like so many successful professional and business men, he began life on the farm. After the ordinary course in the pubic schools he began the course at Alfred University, Allegany, New York, but did not complete it. He took up the study of law at Wellsboro, Tioga County, with the late Judge Wilson, and was admitted to practice about 1868. Mr. Elliott had the experience common to country lawyers of few clients in the beginning, but those who came to him remained with him, and so the practice grew, until it was noticed that at every term of court his name appeared as counsel on one side or the other of nearly every case. While the practice was developing he spent the time in deeper study of the law that stood him in good stead in the later years.

In 1878 the "boom" had begun in the Bradford oil field in McKean County, second from Tioga on the west. There were many new legal problems to solve and Mr. Elliott was drawn into the work in quite an accidental way. He had been employed by the County Commissioners of McKean County to assist the District Attorney of that county in the prosecution of a young lawyer, charged with murdering a girl. His work on that occasion attracted the attention of the McKean County Bar, particularly those new members who had come in with the oil development. He was engaged by G. A. Berry, Esq., of Bradford, to take charge of his cases involving oil properties. His quick grasp of the principles of oil production and other processes of the industry, as well as the relationship between leaseholders and owners of the fee was speedily appreciated. The illness of Attorney Berry terminated the first agreement, and Mr. Elliott made a similar arrangement with D. H. Jack, Esq., also of Bradford, a relationship that continued until he quit his general practice for the sole service of the Standard Oil Company. Mr. Elliott, once in the oil practice, soon had retainers from many prominent interests and appeared in some of the most important suits tried out in the Pennsylvania courts. Notable among these were Blair versus the Bradford Oil Company, Jayne versus Emery, and Sager versus the Anchor Oil Company. When these had been concluded, Mr. Elliott's standing had been fully established.

In 1882, Mr. Elliott was nominated by the Democratic State Convention of Pennsylvania for Congressman-at-Large, was elected and served his term at Washington, but in 1884 he refused a renomination and has not since accepted any political preferment. He was chosen counsel for the Union Oil Company, of Pennsylvania, upon the death of Hon. John Hall, who had long occupied the position, and remained with that corporation until it was sold to the South Penn Oil Company, and he was retained by the latter. In 1892 he removed his headquarters from Wellsboro to Oil City, Pennsylvania, to devote his whole time to the legal business of the Standard Oil Company. During the six years following he was conspicuous in the oil and gas litigation of Pennsylvania, West Virginia, Ohio, and Indiana. In 1898 he was summoned to New York, where he has since remained, his field of action broadening to include all of the oil producing sections of the United States.

As a trial lawyer, Mr. Elliott had few peers and his retirement from general practice was a loss to the Bar of his State. In the special oil and gas litigation, fortified with the Pennsylvania precedents and his wide knowledge of the principles involved he was generally successful in his cases in other States, where the same old questions came up to perplex the judges. The Pennsylvania decisions have been quite generally adopted by the courts of other States, involving oil and gas. Mr. Elliott's practice in the Federal Courts has been quite as brilliant as in the State tribunals, but his appearance as a pleader has been rare in recent years. He succeeded Mr. Dodd as General Solicitor of the Standard Oil Company in 1905, becoming counsel rather than advocate.

Mr. Elliott was a member of the Pennsylvania Constitutional Convention that drafted the Constitution of 1874. He was one of the youngest participants in the deliberations of that body, but proved himself well grounded in the fundamental principles of law and took high rank in the discussions. This experience was of value in his later practice, in establishing the relations of the petroleum and natural gas industries to the Constitution. He has ever been a student and ranks among the high authorities upon Constitutional and corporation law.

HENRY CLAY FOLGER, JR.

Henry C. Folger, Jr., secretary of the Standard Oil Company of New Jersey, director of the Tide Water Oil Company; director of the Tide Water Pipe Company; President of the Solar Refining Company of Lima, Ohio, and President of the Atlantic Refining Company of Philadelphia, was was born in New York City, June 18, 1857, son of Henry Clay Folger and Eliza J. (Clark) Folger. After the course in the public schools, he prepared for college at the Adelphi Academy. He entered Amherst College in 1875, graduating in 1879, B. A., receiving the degree A. M. afterward and that of LL. B. (cum laude) from Columbia University. He became a member of the Alpha Delta Phi Society, and was taken into the Phi Beta Kappa in his junior year. While in college he was especially interested in mathematical work and literature, being on the board of editors of the "Amherst Student." The literary taste he has carried especially into the study of Shakespeare, but ranging widely.

After graduation, Mr. Folger entered the employ of Charles Pratt, of oil fame, as a clerk. During the first years of his clerkship he studied law in the night course of the Columbia Law School, graduating with his degree at the end of the term. Meantime his natural ability as a mathematician led him into a systematic study of the yields and costs of petroleum and its products. This study qualified him in the middle eighties to take the secretaryship of the manufacturing board of the Standard Oil Company. In the early nineties he became associated with C. Vose in the management of the Standard Oil works on the East River and vicinity. In a few years he had so mastered the manufacturing problem that he was placed at the head of the manufacturing board of the great Company, a position he held until about three years ago, when he was elected a director of the Company. He might have been very successful in the law or in literature, but his first employment led him rapidly into the field of industrial efficiency and finance. He is a man of genial presence, cultivated mind and has a large circle of personal friends.

Mr. Folger is one of the most distinguished students of Shakespeare in the United States. He has probably the best library of Shakespeareiana in this country, comprising more than twenty thousand volumes, while he has written several monographs on the Bard of Avon. Mr. Folger is a mathematician of great natural aptitude and long cultivation, which makes a rare combination with literary tastes and exceptionl executive talent in business.

Mr. Folger was married in Elizabeth, New Jersey, in 1886, to Miss Emily C. Jordan. He is a member of the Grolier and Alpha Delta Phi Clubs and Nassau Country Club. His business address is at No. 26 Broadway, New York City.

ORVILLE T. WARING.

Among the great divisions of the oil business, none holds a more important place than that of the lubricating oils. To animal fats the task of oiling the machinery of the world had been devoted from time immemorial, with help here and there from the vegetable and whale oils, but it was not for long after petroleum had become the illuminant of the masses that the full adaptability of petroleum oils to every possible service in the wide range of reducing the friction of moving parts had become commonly known. Quite early in the history of petroleum, mineral lubricating oils were produced, but mainly of the heavier sort. Separate plants for manufacturing them on a small scale existed. After the naphthas and kerosene had been distilled from the crude, what remained—a black, viscid mass—at first seemed useless; yet in it were later found the lubricating oils, the petrolatum or vaseline series and the paraffine wax.

In 1878, Mr. Orville T. Waring, then a man of thirty-seven, who had been two years in the service of the Standard Oil Company after a dozen years of previous work in the oil business outside, was called in by his superiors, and asked what could be done to develop the trade in lubricating oils. Compared with the manufacture and merchandising of illuminating oils, petroleum lubricating oil had little or no standing in the volume of trade, so Mr. Waring's answer was that everything had to be done if there was to be any development. He was told to go to work, and accordingly took hold as Chairman of a Committee devoted to the end in view. It would be vain here to rehearse in detail the course and labors involved, which covered, firstly, the development through trained oil men and able chemists of variety in and standardization of the products and the cleansing of the oils from deleterious ingredients; secondly, the production in quantities to meet the demand that seemed instantly to rise for the new oils, and, thirdly, the marketing thereof. In ten years a practically new industry had been created. The list of lubricating oils had grown to a dozen grand divisions that ranged from the black oils for rough machinery through the cylinder, engine, spindle and neutral oils down to the finest oils for the most delicate operations, and back again through the greases and petrolates down to lubricants for ox-carts. These divisions comprised quite a hundred and fifty varieties. The automobile oils came later, and they comprise twenty different kinds. Out of the all but nothing figures of 1878 the figures in 1909 showed that the Standard Oil Company had in that year manufactured and marketed five and a half million barrels of lubricating oils of which over two and a quarter million barrels had been exported, and of paraffine wax, crude and refined, two hundred and twenty-three million pounds had been made, of which one hundred and sixty million pounds had been exported.

Mr. Waring was born in January, 1841, in Saratoga County, New York. His paternal ancestors were English and Dutch. He was educated in Troy, New York. He started in business life early as a commission merchant and manufacturer of petroleum products. On January 1, 1863, he went to Pittsburgh with the firm of Waring & Gregg, petroleum brokers. For two years he spent his time there and in the oil regions, attending to shipments and deliveries of crude oil between Oil Creek and Pittsburgh, by way of the Allegheny River. In 1865 he became a partner with the firm which had then become Waring & King, Mr. H. H. King having taken the place of Mr. Gregg. When, a little later, the concern located in Philadelphia and Baltimore, and did business under the name of Waring, King & Co., Mr. Waring went to Philadelphia to take charge of the growing Eastern business and became interested in different refining businesses. Disposing of the latter, Mr. Waring moved to New York in 1874, and in 1876 joined the forces of the Standard Oil Company with which he has remained to the present day. In January, 1911, his long and meritorious service was crowned by his election as Director of the Standard Oil Company of New Jersey.

Mr. Waring is President of the Plainfield Trust Company of Plainfield, N. J., the city in which he now makes his residence; Vice President of the Marsh Lumber Company, whose lands and mills are located in California; President of the Plainfield Riding and Driving Club; also President of the Hillside Cemetery Corporation; a Director in the Standard Oil Company of New Jersey; Vice President of the Rossendale-Reddaway Belting & Hose Company of Newark, N. J.; a Director in the Swan & Finch Company and the Chesebrough Manufacturing Company.

In 1886 Orville T. Waring married Miss Hester A. Griffith of Troy, N. Y. The union resulted in the birth of eight children. It may be said without flattery that Mr. Waring, in official and in private life holds the esteem and affection of as large and loyal a circle of friends in all parts of the country as any man in the oil industry.

MARTIN CAREY.

Martin Carey, Attorney of the Standard Oil Company, was reared in the oil fields of Pennsylvania, trained for the bar under the guidance of lawyers who first smoothed out entanglements in which the pioneers of petroleum production found themselves involved and established precedents which now are firmly-fixed fingerposts on the law's highway. Although a younger man by a generation than the late S. C. T. Dodd and Mortimer F. Elliott, who succeeded Mr. Dodd as general solicitor of the Standard Oil interests, Mr. Carey was often associated with them professionally, many years before he was tendered the position he now occupies.

Early in his career Mr. Carey closed his offices in Franklin and Oil City and removed to Buffalo. He engaged in general practice. In 1893 he associated himself in a law firm which has had a most distinguished history. In 1872 the firm was Bass and Bissell, composed of Lyman K. Bass and Wilson S. Bissell, who, twenty-one years later became Postmaster General in the second Cleveland administration. In 1874 Grover Cleveland joined the firm, which became Bass, Cleveland and Bissell. From 1876 to 1881 it was Cleveland and Bissell. Mr. Cleveland was elected Mayor of Buffalo, Governor of New York State and President of the United States and on his retirement did not return to Buffalo. His activity as a member of the bar of that city ceased, therefore, in 1881, when Bissell and Sicard succeeded Cleveland and Bissell. In 1893, as stated, Mr. Carey joined the legal alliance, which became Bissell, Sicard, Bissell and Carey. Four years later the firm of Bissell, Carey and Cooke succeeded. Mr. Bissell died in 1903.

In 1906 Martin Carey removed from Buffalo to New York City, to become attorney for the Standard Oil Company. There were many other safe counselors and brilliant advocates in the United States, but in this instance the position sought the man. Mr. Carey had a brilliant career at the bar of Venango County, Pennsylvania, before he removed to Buffalo, trying many important cases there and in the higher courts of his native State.

GEORGE CHESEBRO.

George Chesebro, Secretary and Comptroller of the National Transit Company, was born in the City of New York, July 20th, 1850. He is the son of Albert Chesebro, who was a resident of New York City for many years, although born in Stonington, Conn., in 1808. The elder Mr. Chesebro died in Jersey City in 1888. He was a lineal descendant of William Chesebro, who was born in England in 1594 and came to America in the ship Arabella, which sailed from Cowes, Isle of Wight, on March 30th, 1630. He took a prominent part in founding the Massachusetts Bay Colony and later spending a few years in Rehoboth, Mass., made his permanent home in Stonington, Conn.

The subject of this sketch was educated in the public schools of New York, and was graduated from the College of the City of New York. Soon afterward he entered the law office of Silas B. Brownell, in Wall Street, but after spending some time endeavoring to fit himself for the Bar he discovered that his tastes lay in the direction of commerce. He then abandoned his studies and entered the employ of S. B. Chittenden & Co., at one time a prominent mercantile firm in New York. Later he connected himself with the firm of A. T. Stewart & Company, spending a number of years as accountant in the woolen mills of that concern. When the firm discontinued the operation of their mill properties in June, 1883, George Chesebro accepted a position with the National Transit Company, at 44 Broadway, New York City. At that time Mr. John Bushnell was Secretary and Comptroller of the Company. Mr. Chesebro, after short service, was appointed Assistant Secretary and Assistant Comptroller and upon the resignation of Bushnell, in 1907, he was appointed to fill the vacancies caused by Mr. Bushnell's resignation from office in the various corporations with which the latter was then identified.

The Companies in which Mr. Chesebro then found himself an active factor are as follows, in the order of the dates of their incorporation:

	Incorporated.	Capital.
National Transit Company	1881	$25,455,200
South West Pennsylvania Pipe Lines	1886	3,500,000
The Buckeye Pipe Line Company	1886	10,000,000
Northern Pipe Line Company	1889	4,000,000
Southern Pipe Line Company	1890	10,000,000
The Eureka Pipe Line Company	1890	5,000,000
Indiana Pipe Line Company	1891	5,000,000
The Crescent Pipe Line Company	1891	3,000,000
New York Transit Company	1892	5,000,000
Cumberland Pipe Line Company, Inc	1901	1,000,000

The affairs of these Companies are now under the management of the following Board of Directors: James A. Moffett, as President; C. N. Payne, as Vice President; John D. Archbold, H. M. Flagler, Clement A. Griscom, A. C. Bedford, Walter Jennings, Walter C. Teagle, Joseph Seep, Robert S. Hampton, W. V. Miller, Charles H. Lay, Jr., H. M. Tilford, H. H. Rogers, H. S. Mustin.

In 1875, Miss Frances Augusta Amerman became the wife of George Chesebro. Their home is now at Belle Harbor, N. Y. There are three children, Mrs. Caspar A. Miller, residing in Foxburg, Pa.; Howard Irving, residing in Belle Harbor, N. Y.; George Chesebro, Jr., residing in Brooklyn, N. Y.

Mr. Chesebro is a member of the Graduates Club in the City of New York, Society of the Order of the Founders and Patriots of America, and Belle Harbor Yacht Club.

CLEMENT A. GRISCOM.

Clement A. Griscom, son of Dr. John D. Griscom, was born in Philadelphia on the 15th of March, 1841. His rudimentary education was received in public schools and after two years in the Central High School, he completed his studies at the Friends Academy.

The descendant of a family which has been identified with the history of Philadelphia since the seventeenth century, he inherited traits of character which enabled him to take rank among the prominent men of the city. His first occupation proved congenial and determined his future career. Upon leaving school at the age of sixteen, Mr. Griscom entered the old established shipping house of Peter Wright and Sons as clerk. He at once gave evidence of those traits, which at the early age of twenty-two, gained for him partnership in the business. Under his directing influence the firm began to purchase sailing ships for their trade and the profits increased immediately and largely. More vessels were purchased, the business grew to larger and larger dimensions and eventually Peter Wright and Sons became the agents of the old American Line, one of the prominent steamship lines of that time.

After this came the formation of the International Navigation Company (Red Star Line) accomplished through Mr. Griscom's negotiations directly with King Leopold, of Belgium, which company afterward absorbed the old American Line. Mr. Griscom was elected Vice President, May 13th, 1871, and President, January 4th, 1888, controlling and operating twenty-six ocean steamships, one of the largest fleets in the trade.

The old Inman Line was purchased by the Company in 1886 and subsequently it contracted for the steamships "New York" and "Paris," in which steamers he was the first to introduce twin screws for passenger service in the North Atlantic trade, and which were so subdivided as to render the ships absolutely unsinkable. Through Mr. Griscom's energy special Congressional legislation was secured which permitted these ships to sail under American registry, provided an equal amount of tonnage was built in the United States.

To comply with this provision, the contracts for the ocean liners, "St. Louis" and "St. Paul," were awarded to the William Cramp & Sons Ship & Engine Building Company, and the result proved that Mr. Griscom's confidence in the ability of the American ship-builders was not misplaced. In the Spanish war the United States Government secured the use of the Company's ships, including the "St. Louis," the "St. Paul," the "New York," which was temporarily known as the "Harvard," and the "Philadelphia," which, during her term of Government service, was called the "Yale." These vessels played an important part in the naval engagements, thus attaching to the boats an historic interest.

In 1902 the name of International Navigation Company was changed to International Mercantile Marine Company, the capital increased to acquire the fleets and businesses of the White Star Line, Atlantic Transport Line, Leyland Line and Dominion Line, Mr. Griscom being elected President, October 1st, 1902, which position he resigned in February, 1904, when he was elected Chairman of the Board of Directors.

In 1889 Mr. Griscom was a delegate to the International Marine Conference for revising the "Rules of the Road at Sea," twenty-eight nations being represented.

The Queen of Holland conferred the decoration of "Knight of the Order of Orange-Nassau" upon Mr. Griscom in recognition of the perfect discipline established upon the steamships of the International Navigation Company. The particular occasion which inspired Her Majesty to confer that decoration was the rescue by the crew of the American Line steamship "St. Louis" of the passengers and crew, consisting of 212 men, women and children, from the disabled Dutch Transatlantic steamship "Veendam" which sank shortly after the last boat-load had left the wreck. Mr Griscom has also received the Decoration of Chevalier of the Legion of Honor from the French Government.

Mr. Griscom was President of the Society of Naval Architects and Marine Engineers from its organization in 1893 to 1903, when he voluntarily retired and was made an Honorary Associate Member. He is also an Honorary Member of the British Institute of Naval Architects, an honor conferred on but three others at that time, the Grand Duke Constantine of Russia, Lord Kelvin of England and DeLome of France.

His position in the ocean steamship business, with its inter-continental traffic, does not occupy his whole time, a portion being devoted to railroad and banking interests.

Mr. Griscom was elected a Director of the Pennsylvania Railroad Company, September 24th, 1884, and appointed a member of the Road Committee, October 8th, 1884. From April 14th, 1881, to March 29th, 1892, he was President of the National Transit Company, of which he is still a Director.

CHARLES MELBOURNE HIGGINS.

Charles Melbourne Higgins, one of the prominent officers of the Standard Oil Company, is of English descent. He was born in Meadville, Crawford County, Pa.

Mr. Higgins' grandfather settled in Mercer County, Pennsylvania. His father put down one of the first oil wells in Pithole, Pennsylvania, and all his life he has been associated with the petroleum industry.

Mr. Higgins was educated in Meadville, Pa., and Cleveland, Ohio. Quite early in his career he entered the service of the Standard Oil Company of Ohio. His activities have ever since been devoted to that Company and to the Standard Oil Company of New York, as well as the Imperial Oil Company, Ltd.

In 1887 Mr. Higgins was married to Miss Mary Linda Caplinger, of Kentucky. Their son, Louis Severance Higgins, is a student at Harvard University.

Mr. Higgins is a member of the Ohio Society of New York and also of the Manhattan and City Clubs. His residence is No. 93 Riverside Drive, New York City.

JAMES SMITH.

Forty smoking acres of twisted iron and charred beams rising out of piles of brick and ashes, all still glowing with the fire that had burned over every square foot of it, was the sight that met the new manager of the Standard Oil refinery at Bayonne, N. J., on the morning of July 5, 1900. Over 500,000 barrels of oil had gone up in flame and smoke the day before and it was the wreck of tankage and pipe and pump that made the landscape of desolation that morning on the banks of the Kill von Kull. Here was a call for courage, for skill, for persistence and the magical power to manage men and get the utmost in sinew and service from them. Out of the chaos to bring order; out of destruction to reconstruct; such was the giant task laid that morning on the broad shoulders of James Smith. And he rose to it. A year later no one could have guessed at the horror and havoc wrought by the big fire. It was a memorable feat, and the stalwart James Smith deserved all the good words that came to him.

An excellent brain to plan and direct, a well-knit frame he had, but behind the physical man of forty-two years there were twenty-seven years of service in the oil business—and Standard Oil business all the time. It was in the railroad department of the Standard Oil works at Cleveland, Ohio, that James began his service with the Company as far back as 1873. He was then fifteen years old, fresh from graduation in St. John's Cathedral schools, under the special tutelage of Brother Thomas, a learned, wise and kindly teacher. The lad was worthy of better than the railroad afforded, and he quickly passed to office work at the cashier's desk, where the manager of the works soon singled him out from his fellows, and made James Smith his private secretary. The manager was Samuel Andrews, one of the early giants of the Standard Oil Company—and its first practical oil-man. It was with Samuel Andrews in fact that John D. Rockefeller entered the oil business in 1865 as his partner, and remained such until the formation of the Standard Oil Company of Ohio in 1870. James Smith could not have had an abler master. Thus it was that the young man learned the oil business in every practical detail, becoming, while still in the office of Mr. Andrews, assistant superintendent of the works, then one of the largest in the country. In time Samuel Andrews retired, and shortly afterwards—in 1880—James Smith, then twenty-two years old, was called to a wider field in New York.

He turned his back on Cleveland with regret. He had been born there on December 12, 1858, of honest Irish parents, who had settled in Cleveland the year before, his father hailing from Kilkenny and his mother from Wexford, Ireland. They were proud of their son. His success in New York consoled them, however, for losing him, for on arriving in the metropolis he had been appointed assistant manager of the great Bayonne refinery. He held the position from 1880 to 1885. At the latter date he was called to the office of the late A. M. McGregor, then at the head of the Manufacturing Department of the Standard Oil Company, controlling all the plants and refineries of the great company. Here once more he learned of a master, first as his private secretary and later as a subordinate manager. In 1896 when a re-organization of the department was made, Mr. Smith took a place in the company's council created for the purpose, and when the great fire of 1900 occurred with its loss of $1,500,000, James Smith, as above related, was sent from 26 Broadway as manager, to make good the enormous damage. From that time to 1908, he was at the head of the works, seeing the refinery rebuilt and extended, doubling its capacity to 45,500 barrels a day, and commanding an army of 6,000 men. For three years Mr. Smith held the higher position of Chief of the Manufacturing Department of the Company, an office of the gravest responsibility. He carried his years lightly and his energy, courage and unfailing good humor were an inspiration to all about him. It was a terrible shock to his associates when the man, in apparent good health, died suddenly of cerebral hemorrhage on May 15, 1911, at his post of duty. He will long be cherished in memory. He had never married. He had been an active member of the Engineers' Club, the New York Athletic Club, the Catholic Club, the Friendly Sons of St. Patrick, and of the Ohio Society.

WILLIAM LUKENS ELKINS.

(Deceased.)

The late William Lukens Elkins was born in Delaware County, Pennsylvania, May 2, 1832, and passed away in Philadelphia on November 7th, 1903. He was the son of George W. Elkins and Susanah Howell Elkins, original descendants of English Quakers.

He was educated in the public schools and began his business career at a very early age. After his father's death he obtained a position in a grocery store and after a number of years of active, conscientious service he became a member of the firm of Saybolt & Elkins, a firm which was engaged in the wholesale produce business.

Mr. Elkins was one of the pioneers in the petroleum industry. After a full investigation of the oil region of Pennsylvania he decided to go into the refining business and built his first refinery in what is now known as Fairmount Park, Philadelphia, in about 1865. In 1876 he sold one-half of his business to the Standard Oil Company, and in 1880 sold out his entire interest to it, and up to the time of his death was associated with that corporation, as a stockholder.

More than a quarter of a century ago Mr. Elkins turned his attention to steam and street railroads. He invested largely in traction companies and became active in their management, in New York, Philadelphia, Cincinnati, Chicago, Baltimore and Pittsburg. For years, and until his death, he was a director of the Pennsylvania Railroad and for several years was President of the Camden and Atlantic Railroad. then controlled by the Pennsylvania Railroad Company.

So varied were the activities of Mr. Elkins that he was a director of various banks and trust companies, including the Consolidation National Bank, Fourth Street National Bank and the Land Title and Trust Company, of Philadelphia.

In addition his capital was invested in various manufacturing enterprises, which were uniformly successful. For a number of years his building operations involved more than a thousand houses a year. His grasp upon industrial, financial and transportation enterprises, as well as all matters of civic concern, was never relaxed until the time of his death.

Mr. William L. Elkins was a member of the Masonic fraternity, the Union League. Art, Racquet, Huntington Valley, and the Country Clubs of Philadelphia. He was also a member of the New York Yacht Club, the Metropolitan Club of New York and the Chicago Club of Chicago.

In 1858 Mr. Elkins married Miss Louise Broomall, who died June 7, 1910. Surviving him are his children, George W. Elkins and Eleanor Elkins Widener. Two other children are deceased, William L. Elkins, Jr., died in 1902, and Ida A. Elkins Tyler died in 1904.

Perhaps among the great captains of industry no man exercised his ability and influence over a wider range of activity than did the late William L. Elkins. He was generous and unostentatious in his charity and took a great interest in questions of public welfare.

GEORGE W. ELKINS.

George W. Elkins, son of the late William L. Elkins, was born in Philadelphia, September 26, 1858, and educated in the public and private schools of that city.

When eighteen years of age, Mr. Elkins entered into the service of W. L. Elkins & Co. In 1880 he became Treasurer of the Elkins Manufacturing and Gas Company. In 1883 he became a member of the firm of M. Ehret, Jr. & Co.; later President of the Barrett Manufacturing Company, which succeeded Ehret & Company in the manufacture of coal tar products.

In 1904, George W. Elkins retired from business, although he is still active as an officer and director of various corporations, including the Barrett Manufacturing Company, American Coal Products Co., Crew Levick Oil Company, Vulcanite Portland Cement Co., United Lighting and Heating Co., Union Traction Co., Ohio Traction Co., the American Tobacco Co. and the Land Title and Trust Co.

In 1881 Mr. Elkins was married to Miss Stella E. McIntire, daughter of Colonel John K. McIntire, of Dayton, Ohio. He has four children—William M. Elkins, Stella E. Tyler, George W. Elkins, Jr., and Louise B. Sinkler, each of whom is married.

Although he is a member of the Corinthian Yacht, Art, Racquet, Union League, Philadelphia Country, Huntingdon Valley and the Philadelphia Cricket Clubs and an honorary member of Acacia Fraternity of Philadelphia, and of the Metropolitan and New York Yacht Clubs in New York, as well as a prominent Mason, Mr. Elkins devotes the major part of his time to the management and conservation of his large interests in the various financial and industrial companies mentioned.

CHARLES W. HARKNESS.

Charles W. Harkness, a Director of the Standard Oil Company, was born in Monroeville, Ohio, December 17, 1860. His father, Stephen V. Harkness, was born in New York State in 1818, the son of David Harkness, M. D. The mother of Charles W. Harkness was Anna M. Richardson, who was born in Ohio in 1837. The family strain is distinctly Scotch and English.

Stephen V. Harkness removed from Monroeville to Cleveland, Ohio, in 1867, and there became associated with John D. Rockefeller, William Rockefeller and H. M. Flagler in the oil business in a company which was afterward to become the Standard Oil Company.

Charles W. Harkness received his early education in Cleveland, and in 1883 was graduated from Yale. He began his business career in Cleveland as bookkeeper and clerk in his father's office, afterward becoming administrator and manager of his father's estate. In 1890 he moved to New York and became a resident of that city.

In 1896 Mr. Harkness and Miss Mary Warden, daughter of the late William G. Warden, of Philadelphia, were married. Mr. Warden was one of the most prominent figures, until the time of his death, in the petroleum industry, and was one of the most important factors in the Standard Oil Company.

In addition to his association with the Standard Oil Company as a director, Mr. Harkness is also a director of the Chicago, Milwaukee & St. Paul Railroad Company and a trustee of the New York Trust Company. He is a member of the Union Club of Cleveland and the University Club, Down-Town Association and Riding Club of New York and of the Morris County Golf Club of Morristown, New Jersey.

WILLIAM EDWARD BEMIS.

In 1640 Joseph Bemis, who had been born in England some twenty-one years before, arrived in Watertown, in what was then the proud old colony of Massachusetts. He established the American branch of a family which had long been distinguished on the other side of the water and the genealogical tree shows a line of men who have been and are prominent and successful in America.

William Edward Bemis was born August 12th, 1864, at Cleveland, Ohio. His father, George A. Bemis, was prominently connected with the insurance business in that city, a Mason of high standing, and a member of the Board of Education. He died in December, 1893.

After receiving an academic education in the city of his birth, William E. Bemis began his business career by entering, in 1882, the service of the Standard Oil Company. He organized the Statistical Department and later engaged in the Domestic Trade Merchandising as Eastern agent of the Standard Oil Company of Ohio.

Since 1902 Mr. Bemis has been interested in the foreign trade and particularly the development of the Company's business in the Far East. He has made numerous journeys to India, Burma, Java, Japan and China, as well as to European centers. He is a director of the Deutsch-Amerikanische Petroleum Gesellschaft of Hamburg, Germany; the Anglo-American Oil Company, Limited, of London; the Det Danske Petroleums Aktieselskab, of Copenhagen; the Raffinerie Francaise, and the West India Oil Company, New York.

Mr. Bemis resides at Larchmont, N. Y. He is a member of the Larchmont Yacht Club; of the Ohio Society of New York; the Camp-Fire Club of America; the Apawamus Golf Club, Rye, N. Y., and of the Caughnawana Hunting and Fishing Club, of Canada.

On May 13th, 1896, Mr. Bemis was married in Cleveland to Miss Frances Lavinia Ford. Mrs. Bemis accompanies her husband on his journeys over the globe.

Mr. Bemis is an ardent and enthusiastic sportsman. He finds his most congenial recreation in hunting big game and in fishing and has had many interesting experiences in remote parts of the world.

LAUREN J. DRAKE.

Lauren J. Drake was born January 29, 1842, in Concord, Erie County, New York. His parents, who had moved from Connecticut to the shores of Lake Erie, were of good old English stock. They sent their son to the district schools of Buffalo and to Springville Academy. After leaving school the young man was employed for a few years in a grocery establishment in Buffalo and there he acquired the basis of that knowledge of commercial conditions which proved of inestimable value later in his successful career.

When twenty-two years of age Mr. Drake went into the "oil country," as the Pennsylvania fields were called. For ten years succeeding he was a conductor on the Oil Creek Railroad. In 1875 he went to Keokuk, Iowa, where he established a bulk station for handling oil. He remained at Keokuk until 1885, when he removed to Omaha, Nebraska, to become general manager for the Consolidated Tank Lines Company. In this capacity he served until 1896 when he went to Chicago as general manager for the Standard Oil Company of all the business of the nine States which comprised the Standard Oil Company of Indiana.

In 1902 Mr. Drake was called to the main office of the Standard Oil Company, 26 Broadway, New York City. In February, 1911, he was elected to the directorate of the Standard Oil Company of New Jersey and of the Standard Oil Company of New York. He is also vice president and director of the Standard Oil Company of Indiana, and of the Galena Signal Oil Company. In March, 1911, Mr. Drake was elected to the presidency of the Standard Oil Company of Kentucky.

In 1863 Mr. Drake married Miss Mary J. Anthony, at Hamburg, N. Y. They have two sons and three daughters: Seth C. Drake, Louis G. Drake, Alice M. Drake, Lauren Jay Drake, Jr., and Clara Josephine Drake.

Mr. L. J. Drake is a member of the Union League Club of Chicago and of the Essex County Country Club. His residence is at East Orange, New Jersey.

FRED W. WELLER.

Fred W. Weller, President of the Standard Oil Company of Louisiana, was born in Cleveland, Ohio, June 12, 1865. He is the son of Joseph W. Weller and Robie J. (Wilbur) Weller.

When seventeen years of age Mr. Weller went to work for the Standard Oil Company, in his native city. Seven years later, in 1890, he was transferred to the Whiting Refinery, at Whiting, Indiana, to assist in the construction of the Company's plant at that point. He remained for two years at Whiting, as superintendent of the naphtha department.

In 1892 Mr. Weller was sent to France to superintend the construction of the refinery of Bedford et Cie at Rouen. He spent the ensuing two years abroad. In 1894 he returned to the United States and located at Parkersburg, W. Va., as General Superintendent of the Camden Refinery of the Standard Oil Company.

Mr. Weller removed in 1902 to Beaumont, Texas, to accept a position as Vice President and General Manager of the Security Oil Company. He directed the Company's affairs generally and supervised the building of its refinery, the laying of pipe lines, and other construction.

In 1906 Fred W. Weller removed to New York City to become Manager of the Bergenport Chemical Works of the Standard Oil Company and to assume managerial direction of the Bayway Refinery, which was constructed under his supervision. He was elected President of the Standard Oil Company of Louisiana in 1909. He is also a director of the Chesebrough Manufacturing Company.

HORACE A. HUTCHINS.

·Although Horace A. Hutchins has retired from active business pursuits, his activity in the petroleum industry, extending over forty years, has not been forgotten. He comes from English ancestry, who early settled in the American colonies. His paternal grandfather was born in Connecticut, from which State he emigrated in 1798 to the Western Reserve. Horace A .Hutchins was born January 19, 1838, in Warren, Ohio.

After securing a public school education, Mr. Hutchins entered upon his first occupation as clerk in a store in Cleveland, Ohio, and was so employed at the outbreak of the Civil War. He was appointed Paymaster in the Army, served throughout the war, and was brevetted Colonel by Secretary of War Stanton for meritorious services. When the war was over, Mr. Hutchins looked around for suitable business occupation.

At that time the refining of petroleum, at Cleveland, seemed to offer the best opportunities. Mr. Hutchins formed a partnership with Mr. George Westlake, of Cleveland, under the firm name of Westlake, Hutchins & Co. The enterprise proved a success from the start, so successful indeed, that the Standard Oil Company made overtures to absorb it, and in consequence Westlake, Hutchins & Co. sold out and Mr. Hutchins was invited to accept a position with the Standard Oil Company. He took charge of the domestic trade department, and held that position for thirty years, in the meantime investing the proceeds of his share of the Westlake, Hutchins & Co. sale in the stock of the Standard Oil Company. The result was a large increase in value and large dividends.

Mr. Hutchins was until his retirement a director in a large number of corporations. He is a member of the New York Yacht Club, the Union League and the New England and Ohio Societies of New York City. He has always been fond of horses and yachting. He has traveled extensively in Europe, and few men can lay claim to a more useful career or a larger circle of friends.

Mr. Hutchins married Miss Fannie Dodge, daughter of George C. Dodge, of Cleveland, Ohio, a well-known and highly respected business man of that city. Mrs. Hutchins passed away in 1889. Their son, Harley D. Hutchins, now manages his father's extensive interests. Their daughter, Mrs. Charles A. Work, died recently.

Mr. Hutchins started out in life at the bottom of the ladder, but, through his tact, perseverance and industry, he has accumulated a handsome fortune. He has always been loyal and true to his friends; is proud of his record as a good, square business man; and the biography of such a citizen is certainly worthy of a place in our gallery of distinguished Amricans.

CHARLES CLINTON BURKE.

Charles C. Burke has been identified with the petroleum industry since his boyhood, and it is doubtful whether there is any branch of the business to which he has not devoted his inventive powers and natural bent for investigation.

His ancestors came to America in the seventeenth century and settled in Massachusetts. He was born in Springfield, Windsor County, Vermont, and received his educational training at the Kimball Union Academy, Meriden, N. H. From Meriden, Mr. Burke went to Boston and began his business career there with a wholesale provision house.

After living in Boston about two years, he went to the Oil Regions, arriving at Titusville, Pa., in the early sixties. Crude petroleum was then being produced in great abundance. There were, however, few refineries in the country, and few men with practical knowledge of that branch of the business. In order to become proficient in it, he placed himself under the tuition of a well known chemist of the oil fields. After obtaining from him the general methods of refining, he supplemented this course of instruction by sending to Pittsburg for a German chemist whose services he utilized in the manufacture of various products from petroleum. Although he had not then attained his majority, Mr. Burke associated himself with others and secured a factory, which he reconstructed, and to which he added several stills and other improvements. Not long afterward this plant was totally destroyed by fire.

Not discouraged by this misfortune, Mr. Burke removed to Pittsburg and remained there several years as a refiner. In 1870 he established himself at New York, and became an owner in an oil refinery on Newtown Creek. This plant was operated successfully under his direct management until about 1883. In that year he was elected President of the Eagle Oil Company with works at Communipaw, N. J. His executive work in connection with the Eagle factory covered a period of two decades. During this time he served for several years as a director of the Standard Oil Company of New Jersey. He has originated several grades of lubricating oil which are celebrated for their excellent qualities, and has received letters patent for various valuable improvements in machinery.

Mr. Burke is a director of the Fulton Trust Company of New York, having been one of its founders. He is and has been for nearly twenty-five years a director of the Cheseborough Manufacturing Company (Consolidated) of New York. He has served as director, vice president and president of the New York Produce Exchange, and is also treasurer of the New England Society, and a member of the Union League Club of New York.

Mr. Burke has been married twice; in 1872 to Miss Elsie P. Ely, a daughter of the late Abner L. Ely, of New York, and in 1886 to Miss Elizabeth S. Cass, a daughter of General George W. Cass, formerly of Pittsburgh. Mr. Burke has several sons and daughters, and resides at Plainfield, New Jersey.

GEORGE B. GIFFORD.

George B. Gifford, manager of the Standard Oil Company's works at Bayonne, N. J., is the son of George Washington Gifford and Elizabeth Grant Gifford. His ancestry is English, his American progenitors having landed on the coast of Massachusetts in 1630. Plymouth was their first abode and afterward Little Compton, then a settlement in Rhode Island. Elihu Gifford, paternal great-grandfather of the subject of this sketch, was a captain in the Revolutionary army. Col. Gray, the maternal great-grand-father, served on the staff of General Washington during the campaigns in Massachusetts. Col. Gray was a descendant of Mary Chilton, the first woman to land at Plymouth from the Mayflower.

On January 15, 1861, George B. Gifford was born at Assonet, Massachusetts. He was a student through the various grades of the public schools at Fairhaven, Mass. When seventeen years of age he entered the service of Charles Pratt & Company, in their oil refinery at Brooklyn, N. Y., meanwhile taking a course in engineering at Cooper Union.

For twenty-five years Mr. Gifford was in the employ of Charles Pratt & Company. He started as a machine-shop boy, being promoted through various grades of increasing importance until, in 1893, he was appointed superintendent. He filled this position for ten years, becoming, in March, 1903, manager of the Eagle Works of the Standard Oil Company at Communipaw, N. J. Early in 1909 he was appointed to his present position as manager of the Company's works at Bayonne.

Essentially a business man, Mr. Gifford has had little time for recreation or club life. He is a member, nevertheless, of the Newark Bay Club, the Jersey City Club, and the New England Society of New York.

On November 1, 1883, Mr. Gifford married Miss Minnie M. Van Cott, of Brooklyn. The Van Cotts are descendants of one of the early Knickerbocker families. A son, George B. Gifford, Jr., is employed in the engineering department of the Bayonne Works.

PHILIP MARTIN SHANNON.

P. M. Shannon was born at Shannondale, Clarion County, Pa., and educated in the common schools of the vicinity. Before he had reached the age of fifteen he enlisted in the Sixty-second Pennsylvania Volunteers, commanded by Colonel Samuel Black, of Pittsburg. From 1862 to 1864 he served in the Army of the Potomac and participated in a number of hard-fought battles. In 1864, by reason of a gun-shot wound, he was honorably discharged from the army and returned to his home. For four years he was employed as a traveling salesman by a mercantile establishment of Pittsburgh. He went to New York and represented another establishment on the road for a year.

The attention of Mr. Shannon was called to the petroleum industry in the winter of 1869-70. In association with the late Richard Jennings, he first invested in the "Guerilla Well," at Parker's Landing. He was one of the pioneer operators in the once famous Millerstown field in 1871-72, where he cleaned up a neat little fortune. He was elected in 1873 Burgess of Millerstown and was an important factor in public affairs.

Mr. Shannon in 1876 was an active operator in the Bullion field and in 1880 he moved to the famous Bradford field, where he operated, as well as in the Allegany, N. Y., field on an extensive scale. In 1882 he drilled the "Shannon Mystery," in Forest County, Pa. He organized the firm of Melvin, Walker, Shannon & Co., which included J. M. Fuller and the Union Oil Company.

In 1885 Mr. Shannon was elected Mayor of Bradford. There was a rough population to deal with, but Mr. Shannon administered affairs so forcefully and wisely that this element was soon eliminated. Mr. Shannon removed to Pittsburgh in 1890, since which time his operations have been very extensive, covering large areas in Pennsylvania, Ohio and West Virginia. In association with C. P. Collins, R. J. Straight, of Bradford, Pa., and G. H. Strong, of Olean, N. Y., he invaded the Wyoming oil fields in 1890 with uninterrupted success.

In 1895 Mr. Shannon became President of the Pennsylvania Oil and Gas Co., a newly-organized corporation with a capital of $600,000. Extensive works were constructed at Casper, Wyoming, and there a large and prosperous business was founded by Mr. Shannon with the co-operation of his associates.

Although Mr Shannon has never sought political place he has filled at various times important offices of public trust. In 1890 he was urged to represent the counties of McKean, Warren and Venango in the National House of Representatives, but his business interests were so varied and extensive that he was constrained to forego the temptation.

Mr. Shannon for years has been prominent in Masonic circles. He is a thirty-second degree Mason and a past officer of the different lodges of the fraternity. He is a member of John S. Melvin Post, 141, G. A. R., and in consequence of his association with this organization of veterans he received his title of Colonel, although he was but a boy during his two years of active service in defence of his country.

In his varied career in the petroleum industry, few men have achieved more signal success than Mr. Shannon.

Always straightforward with his associates and conservative in his undertakings, Mr. Shannon enjoys a reputation which is synonymous with the highest degree of honor and intellectual vigor. After making his home in Pittsburgh for a number of years, Mr. Shannon, in 1909, removed to Buffalo, N. Y. He purchased the house at No. 1168 Delaware Avenue, in that city, in which the late lamented William McKinley made his last submission to the Divine will. That historic mansion is now Mr. Shannon's home.

LEWIS J. LEVICK.

Lewis J. Levick, President of the Crew Levick Company of Philadelphia, and Vice President of the Pennsylvania Paraffine Works, Titusville, Pennsylvania, is descended from English stock. In 1678, Richard Levick came from England and settled in Delaware, then a part of Pennsylvania. He was the founder of the family in this country. On both his father's and mother's side, Lewis J. Levick's ancestors were members of the Society of Friends and Mr. Levick himself is a birth-right member of that society. His father, Samuel J. Levick, was prominent in the ministry of the Friends.

After graduation from Haverford College, Pennsylvania, Lewis J. Levick was for a number of years associated in business with his father. In 1870 he became interested in marketing petroleum and its products with his uncle, J. Lewis Crew. The business had been established by J. Lewis Crew and his brother, Benjamin Crew, in 1862. Their refinery was located in Philadelphia at Twenty-second and Arch Streets, a neighborhood the character and appearance of which is now essentially changed.

In 1872, the firm became known as Crew, Moore & Levick, with the admittance of John W. Moore and was established at 113 Arch Street. This association was continued until 1885. In 1885, Mr. Moore died and the name was changed to Crew, Levick & Company and at that time the Seaboard Oil Refinery, located at South Chester, Pennsylvania, on the Delaware, was purchased. In 1889, Mr. Crew retired and the concern became a corporation under the name of Crew Levick Company. Lewis J. Levick, the subject of this sketch, became President; George W. Elkins, Vice President, and F. W. Hamnett, Treasurer.

In 1890, the Crew Levick Company purchased the Muir Oil Works and the Glade Oil Works, of Warren, Pennsylvania. Mr. William W. Muir had previously been interested in both of these works and at that time became the General Manager of the Crew Levick Company and still continues in that capacity. The Company also purchased, about the same time, considerable producing property and pipe lines located in the Tiona District, Pennsylvania.

As early as 1876, Lewis J. Levick, counter to the advice of his associates, decided that a great market was awaiting the products of the company in Europe and in that year, he made his first trip to England. His prescience in this matter has been amply vindicated, for the Company now enjoys an extremely large trade in lubricating oil specialties of its own manufacture and it has established agencies in almost every part of the world. Mr. Levick has visited Europe annually in connection with the Company's affairs during the last thirty-four years.

The capitalization of the Company is $750,000, and the personnel of its officers is as follows: President, Lewis J. Levick; Vice President, George W. Elkins; Treasurer, E. J. Hasse; Secretary, Michael Ehret; General Manager, William W. Muir.

In 1876, Mr. Levick was married to Miss Mary d'Invilliers. They have four children: Henry L. Levick, Mrs. Winthrop C. Neilson, Louise J. Levick and Suzanne Levick.

The interests of Mr. Levick are extensive and varied. He is a member of the Executive Committee of the Philadelphia Board of Trade, Director of the Chamber of Commerce, President of the Darby, Media & Chester Street Railway Company, Director of the United Lighting & Heating Company, Philadelphia, Director of the Righter Coal & Coke Company, West Virginia, and Director of the Providence Mills Manufacturing Company.

Mr. Levick has never held a strictly political office, but he has served as a member of the Civil Service Commission of Philadelphia, through two mayoralty administrations, under Mayors Ashbridge and Weaver.

He is a member of the following organizations: Union League of Philadelphia, the Society of Colonial Wars, Colonial Society of Pennsylvania, Historical Society of Pennsylvania, New Jersey Society, Academy of Fine Arts, Order of Runnymede, Philadelphia Country Club, Merion Cricket Club, Penn Club, Bachelors Barge Club, the City Parks Association, and others.

HENRY BRUCE BEATTY.

As it sometimes happens in the lives of successful men, the opportunity which suggested to Henry B. Beatty his future field of activity presented itself quite unexpectedly. It happened that while a young man in the oil business, he was attracted to a curiosity in the shape of a burning gas well at Slippery Rock, Butler County, Pennsylvania. While others looked upon this gas producer as an interesting freak of Nature, young Beatty saw its commercial possibilities, and urged his friends to organize with him a small natural gas company to pipe the gas to a nearby town and sell it as fuel to domestic consumers. This scheme was probably the first suggestion of a fuel gas company and was regarded as visionary, but it was the keystone of Mr. Beatty's career. Five years later natural gas was piped from another field to the Carnegie mills at Bessemer, and gave such results that the commercial use of gas became established, and a few years later it was piped to the homes and factories of Pittsburgh and other points in the gas belt.

Identifying himself financially with the Manufacturer's Gas Company of Pittsburgh in 1889, Mr. Beatty, in 1894, became an active and influential director of that corporation and through his personal force and thorough knowedge of the gas business was in 1896 made President. As a director he had been instrumental in introducing valuable improvements in the company's service, among others installing stations and machinery to pump gas from different fields, thus relieving the friction and immensely prolonging the life and earning power of gas property. From his acceptance of the Presidency, Mr. Beatty inaugurated a broad, successful policy of consolidation and handling of competing gas interests, accompanying it with improvements in office management and field work. Thus he built up the corporation to splendid proportions and earning power. The capital is now $21,000,000. It controls thirty-five subsidiary corporations, owns about a thousand gas and oil wells, operates through about twenty-five hundred miles of gas mains, holds under lease about a half million of proven oil and gas territory, with practically inexhaustible supplies of gas for the demands of the next fifty years or more, and connected with the great markets of Pittsburgh and surrounding towns in Ohio and West Virginia, by enormous mains, in some cases large parallel lines, insuring steady service to the public in case of accident on one line. Every department of this great corporation bears the personal impress of Mr. Beatty's individuality.

Mr. Beatty is still a comparatively young man, having been born August, 1857, in Mercer County, Pennsylvania. He comes of sturdy Scotch-Irish stock, his ancestors fleeing from Scotland to the north of Ireland during the persecution of the Covenanters. Subsequently his forefathers came to America where his great-grandfather, Ebenezer Beatty, served in the War of the Revolution under Washington, when but eighteen years of age. It is a distinction of this youthful patriot that his descendants have served in every American war since the Revolution to the present date. At the close of the War of the Revolution, during Washington's administration (1794), Ebenezer removed from Lancaster, Mifflin County, across the Alleghenies and settled in Butler County, where the old homestead still remains in the possession of his descendants. The son of Ebenezer, grandfather of H. B. Beatty, served throughout the War of 1812. The father of Henry Bruce Beatty was born in the old homestead. He taught school from 1845 to 1851, was a cattle broker until 1865, then merchant and oil producer. He was a man of strong character and high integrity. He married, in 1847, Agnes Braham, daughter of Samuel Braham.

Henry Bruce Beatty, after receiving careful schooling, associated himself with his father in the oil business at Rouseville. Later on he had further experience in the coal business with Strong & Gibson, where his pleasant personality and strong character won him a large circle of friends. In 1881 he moved to the Bradford Oil Field and became an active member of the Oil Exchange. Early in life Mr. Beatty read law, not with a view to practice, but to familiarize himself with fundamental principles in preparing for the responsibilities of business.

He has always been a lover of Nature and books, and has gathered about him in his beautiful East End home. Pittsburgh, as well as at his summer residence in Oakwood, Oil City, many choice and rare treasures. Like many other Pittsburgh men of affairs and wealth, he has taken leisure to indulge his fondness for art and literature, and through these strongly defined tastes, has found in home and society the needed relaxation and conservation of his business energy. In politics he is a Republican, in creed a Presbyterian, and to the support of these faiths, as well as to educational interests, he has been a liberal contributor. He married, in 1879, Miss May L. Strong, daughter of the well known capitalist, O. H. Strong. Mr. Beatty is a member of the Duquesne, the Union and Country Clubs of Pittsburgh and a prominent figure in Masonic circles.

THEODORE B. WESTGATE.

Before the creation of a Department of Commerce and Labor, prior to the passage of the "Hepburn rate bill," and before the enlargement of the powers of the Inter-State Commerce Commission, Theodore B. Westgate, of Titusville, grappled with the question of discrimination in freight rates. He belonged, as he still belongs, to the class of oil refiners generally designated as Independents who could not get their product to market without payment of freight rates high enough to stifle their attempts at competition with the Standard Oil Company. Study of the situation resulted in the acquisition by Mr. Westgate of facts which he has often placed before Courts and Commissions when questions of rebates have been under consideration. In a word, Theodore B. Westgate is the Apostle of a Fair Field and the unrelenting foe of destructive competition. His voice and his pen have been equally active in condemning what he terms the "crime of selling below cost." Neither foe nor friend in the business world has questioned Mr. Westgate's integrity, earnestness of purpose or his fighting ability. He has undergone cross-examination by some of the most eminent lawyers in the country without deviating from an insistence on his statistics or losing his imperturbability.

Theodore Beecher Westgate was born July 13, 1858, in Riceville, Crawford County, Pa. His father, Reuben B. Westgate, was of English descent; his mother, Huldah Ferry Westgate, of French extraction. After attending the public schools of Riceville, Theodore Westgate, when nineteen years of age, started his business career as clerk in a store. Two years later it was thought that his health was impaired and he went to Denver for recuperation. There he engaged in merchandising and was graduated from the Denver Business College. In 1882 he returned to Riceville and, with Arthur Westgate, an elder brother, engaged in the lumber business. He accepted, in 1886, a position as bookkeeper for the American Oil Works at Titusville. Five years after Mr. Westgate entered the service of the American Oil Works, he was admitted to partnership. For a number of years past he has been principal owner and the active managing head of the Company.

In 1899 Mr. Westgate went to Washington to appear before a committee of the Senate which was considering the regulation of combinations in restraint of trade. In 1906 he addressed the Eastern Official Classification Committee of railroad lines east of Chicago. One of the direct results of the deliberations of the committee was a reduction in freight rates ranging from eighteen to fifty per cent. In 1907 he was again called before a committee of the U. S. Senate, sitting at Cleveland Ohio, to investigate the rate question as it applied to the transportation of oil. In the same year he was called to testify before the Grand Jury at Jamestown, New York, and subsequently before the Federal Court at Rochester in trials which resulted in the imposition of fines on the Pennsylvania and the New York Central railway companies. Mr. Westgate's appearances before the Inter-State Commerce Commission have been numerous and on such occasions he has never failed to throw light on that phase of the oil business which has always been of absorbing interest to those connected in the remotest way with the industry. He has carefully studied the conditions of transportation and is considered an authority on freight rates.

Mr. Westgate was a Government witness in the Standard dissolution case and was called to Cleveland in March, 1908, where he gave in such testimony that much of it was considered of sufficient merit to be used in the brief of testimony before the Supreme Court of Missouri, when the case was argued, and he is pleased with the United State Supreme Court's decision, not because of the ruling for dissolution, but because his testimony is vindicated by that decision.

In 1892, when the Producers and Refiners Oil Company was formed, Mr. Westgate was one of the charter organizers. He was then elected a director and has served in that capacity until this writing. For the last ten years he has been Secretary and member of the board of managers. Mr. Westgate has been a director of the Pure Oil Company since its organization in 1894, as well as of the Pure Oil Pipe Line Company.

Mr. Westgate married Miss Lu Rouse in June, 1895. There are three children: Theodore H. Westgate, Florence June and Marian Alma Westgate. The Westgate home is at Titusville.

HARRY J. PARKER.

Harry J. Parker, President of The Parker and Edwards Oil Company, of Pittsburgh, Pennsylvania, was born December 26th, 1861, at Parkers Landing, Pa. His grandfather, the late Fullerton Parker, founded a steamboat landing at that point years before it was supposed that the community, which afterward took his name, would become celebrated in the annals of oil. The grandfather was also one of the organizers of the Parker and Karns City Railroad Company, and Exchange Bank of Parker,—being President of both organizations many years. Ephraim Parker—the father of Harry J. Parker—was of Irish descent; the mother, Margaret Phipps Parker, was descended from Scotch ancestry, being born at Kennerdell Mills, near Franklin, Pa.

After receiving his early education at the schools at Parkers Landing, Harry J. Parker attended the Chester Military Academy. His first occupation was that of ticket agent for the Parker and Karns City Railroad Company. From his early youth he has been an oil producer, having owned and operated a number of wells in the vicinity of his home as a boy since which time his operations have extended throughout lower Southwestern Pennsylvania, West Virginia, Ohio and Illinois. In 1903, he organized The Parker and Edwards Oil Company, which company has taken a prominent part in the oil producing business in late years. Since its organization, Mr. Parker has been its President, William C. Edwards its Vice President, and Edward A. Bream its Secretary and Treasurer. The Company has been successful, and is looked upon as one of the most substantial independent producing companies now in existence.

RICHMOND LEVERING.

Richmond Levering, President of the Indian Refining Company, is the son of the late Mortimer Levering, who was born at Philadelphia in 1849, and of Julia Henderson Levering, who was born two years later in Covington, Indiana. Mr. Levering's paternal ancestors came from England and settled in Philadelphia in 1685. His mother's family also came from England and in 1635 became Colonial pioneers in Massachusetts. At LaFayette, Indiana, June 15, 1881, Richmond Levering was born, and there he received his early education. After his graduation from Yale University with honors, Mr. Levering became manager of the California Asphaltum Sales Agency and a few years later President of the Arkansas Valley Oil-Gas Company. His start as an active factor in the oil refining business was made by building a small plant at Chicago in 1902 for running asphalt oil for special purposes. He was also engaged in selling fuel oil to several large concerns in Chicago. In 1903 a small refining plant was built in Jasper County, Indiana, but the crude oil production later giving out it was necessary to remove the plant to Georgetown, Ky.

The first plant of the Indian Asphalt Company at Georgetown, Ky., produced in 1905 simply gasoline, kerosene and fuel oil, with a capacity of 300 barrels daily. The capitalization was $400,000. The refinery was handling Kentucky crude oil. In 1906 the Company increased its capital to $1,000,000, and entered the Illinois oil fields, which were at that time just attracting public attention, and the capacity of the Georgetown plant was increased to 2,000 barrels daily. From this start Mr. Levering organized and became President of the Indian Refining Company and the investment of the Company now reaches sixteen million dollars.

The Company continued to purchase and develop oil property in Illinois in 1906-07. At this time another refinery was built at Lawrenceville, Illinois, with a daily capacity of 3,000 barrels and the Company increased its capital to $3,000,000. Further growth of the business necessitated the erection of a complete lubricating oil works at Georgetown and an increase in the capacity of that plant to 3,000 barrels daily.

In 1910, the Company purchased a refinery in New Orleans and increased the capacity of the refinery at Lawrenceville to 8,000 barrels daily. The Company also built another lubricating oil works. At the close of the year 1910, including the plants which the Company owns and operates under lease, the combined capacity is now 13,500 barrels daily. In addition to the oil refined by the Company, it purchases largely in this country and imports a large amount of gasoline. The business includes most of the large cities in America and recently it has spread into many foreign countries.

In 1905, Richmond Levering and Miss Laura Barnum were married at Mamaroneck, N. Y. Their children are Richmond Levering, Jr., and Walter Levering.

As well as one of the most prominent figures in present day oil history, Mr. Levering is one of the youngest. He is a member of the University Club of New York, Chicago Club, Chicago; University Club, Cincinnati; Queen City Club, Cincinnati; New York Yacht Club.

JULIUS W. COPMANN.

Julius W. Copmann, manager of the foreign department of the Indian Refining Company, is called the dean of a corps of diplomats who have established an immense traffic in oil in the remotest lands. In 1893 he went to the Far East to view the situation for the Standard Oil Company, traveling in Japan, China and India.

Upon the recommendation of Mr. Copmann, offices were opened in China and Japan, and the work of furnishing illumination to primitive communities far from any large center was inaugurated. The Far East to-day is flooded with light, transportation from the seaboard being accomplished by every known method, in accordance with the varying conditions.

Born in Holstein, then Holstein, Denmark, and now Holstein, Germany, on August 29th, 1853, young Copmann was sent by his parents to Hamburg, Germany, to be educated. His studies there were interrupted when he was seventeen years of age by reason of the fact that he crossed the ocean to make his future home in the United States.

The earliest business occupation of Mr. Copmann of real importance was when at the age of twenty-one he became a broker in empty barrels. He was confidential broker of the Tide Water Pipe Company until 1893. It was in this year that he made his first journey to the Far East. During the following fourteen years his headquarters were at Yokohama, Japan. He then retired from active business. It was not his intention to re-enter the world of petroleum, nor indeed to engage in any enterprise which would rob him of his well earned leisure, but negotiations were finally consummated which resulted in his taking charge of the foreign department of the Indian Refining Company on November 1st, 1910.

Mr. Copmann is widely known in many countries to those who are in any measure interested in petroleum and although of quiet and retiring tastes he is exceedingly popular and is called on frequently by his former colleagues in other companies authoritatively to settle disputed questions concerning foreign commercial conditions.

THE OIL WELL SUPPLY COMPANY.

It would be difficult to think of the petroleum industry without including this corporation, whose products are known and used around the world. It is the concern most frequently appealed to for drilling equipment to be shipped to strange places. Its complete oil well outfits are found in Australia, New Zealand, Borneo, Sumatra, China, Japan, India, Persia, Russia, Austria, Roumania, Egypt, South Africa and South America, as well as in every oil field of the United States from the Atlantic to the Pacific Ocean, in Canada at the North and Mexico at the South. Frequently the Oil Well Supply Company sends out American drilling crews to handle the American machinery and tools sent abroad. It manufactures and sells everything used in the drilling and operation of artesian wells for oil, gas and water; derricks and rigs of wood and steel; boilers, steam engines, gas engines, shackle powers, belts, clutches; drilling tools in all sizes and kinds, drive pipe, line pipe, casing, tubing, liners, steam pipe, gas pipe, and fittings; jacks, wrenches, elevators, cables and ropes of all sizes of steel and manila; pipe cutting tools, rig builders' tools, tank builders' and carpenters' tools; everything from a four ton "string" to a one-eighth inch bolt, and it carries a stock of these things in its hundreds of stores and branches in every oil field.

Although it first took the name of Oil Well Supply Company, Limited, in 1878, the business really extends back to almost the beginning of the oil industry. Mr. John Eaton, President of the Company, made his first visit to the oil regions in the fall of 1861, and is clearly the father of the oil well supply business. He made that first trip as a clerk for Joseph Nason & Co., of New York, to see what were the special needs of the new industry. In 1867, Mr. Eaton embarked in business on his own account with especial reference to the needs of the oil business. Two years later he, with Mr. E. H. Cole, formed the well known firm of Eaton & Cole, which later became the Eaton, Cole & Burnham Company, manufacturers of and dealers in oil well supplies. This business grew to great proportions and in 1878 the Oil Well Supply Company, Limited, was formed, to include this and several rival concerns, with Mr. John Eaton as President. The present corporation was organized in 1891 and the business has grown enormously. In lieu of the small factories, originally maintained in the East, huge manufacturing plants have been built at Oil City, Bradford, Oswego and Pittsburgh, and branches are maintained in every important oil center in the country.

The Oil Well Supply Company has branches and stores in twenty of the States and the first assurance that a new oil field has been established is the appearance there of the sign of this company. The field employes number about two thousand and they comprise an energetic army of business getters. To the upbuilding of this remarkable business Mr. John Eaton has devoted his life work. The esteem in which he is held by his army of employes in every field was recently betokened by the appearance in his office in Pittsburgh, on his birthday, of a beautiful oil painting by a famous artist, purchased by these field employes, who had to be limited in the amount of their voluntary contributions to the birthday present fund. The painting had been procured and was quietly hung without Mr. Eaton's knowledge until he arrived for the regular business of the day, where it greeted him as he approached his desk. Mr. Eaton has passed the allotted span of life, but is yet in the prime of vigorous manhood, looking forward with a keen eye and planning for the future. He is largely interested in oil production, both in the United States and Mexico.

The second officer of the Oil Well Supply Company is Mr. Louis C. Sands, Vice President, who has taken over many of the details of the extensive business. His is a typical "oil country" career, and in that fact also typically American. He was born at Greenport, Long Island, New York, and after finishing school he worked two years in a New York broker's office. He visited the oil region in 1881, was impressed with the possibilities of the business for a young man with technical training and decided to remain and make a thorough study of it in all its details. He got a job as tool dresser and worked on wells for four years. At the end of that time he engaged with the Oil Well Supply Company and has been there ever since. Mr. Sands is a modest man and if reciting his own history would probably let it end here. Truth, however, compels the statement that the Oil Well Supply Company found his services very valuable from the first. Mr. Sands made a specialty of new devices used in the business and of the foreign trade until executive duties attending the Vice Presidency, to which he had been elected, demanded practically all of his time. He continues a careful supervision of the foreign trade from the new viewpoint and makes frequent trips abroad in connection with the business. Mr. Sands has records and classified files of technical data pertaining to the production of petroleum with special reference to the drilling and equipping of wells, covering every known method and has accumulated one of the most complete libraries of petroleum literature, vieing with Mr. Eaton, who has himself been a valuable contributor to oil history.

JAMES H. BARR.

James H. Barr, President of the National Supply Company, began his business career at the age of sixteen in the office of Shaw, Kendall & Co., Toledo, Ohio. Although the firm no longer exists, the identity having been lost by corporate assimilation, Mr. Barr remained on throughout all the changes.

The parents of Mr. Barr were Scottish. They left the land of mist and heather and settled in Ontario, Canada. James H. Barr was born September, 1864, in Toronto. A few years after that event, the parents removed to Toledo, where the son enjoyed the advantages of a liberal education. In 1880 he entered the service of Shaw, Kendall & Co. as stated. When fourteen years had elapsed the National Supply Company was organized. The new corporation absorbed Shaw, Kendall & Co. and the Buckeye Supply Company. In 1896 James H. Barr became Secretary of the National Supply Company. His advancement to the Presidency followed in the ordinary sequence of events.

At the time of the publication of this volume Mr. Barr is President of the National Supply Company, the National Supply Company of Kansas, the Illinois National Supply Company, and the California National Supply Company.

The National Supply Company was organized for the purpose of furnishing oil well supplies to the fields of Pennsylvania, West Virginia, Ohio and Illinois. Its growth and expansion have been so great that the Company, or its subsidiaries, have since carried the business into Illinois, Kansas, Louisiana, Oklahoma, Texas, California and foreign countries. Offices and stores of the company are located throughout the oil regions of the States enumerated. The general offices and mammoth factory are at Toledo. Mr. Barr has headquarters in the Union Bank Building, Pittsburgh, in which city he resides.

JOSEPH I. C. CLARKE.

It was among the things unexpected when the Standard Oil Company, always credited with setting seals of secrecy on its springs of action, decided it needed some expert intermediary between it and the reading public,—not a newspaper, but a newspaper man. It did not lack for men well able to put into print what it wished to say, but they were all busy men fully employed with the work they had in hand,—the conduct of the great business of the Company. Someone experienced in dealing with the presentation of facts and opinions and knowing well the ways of publication, was desired, and the choice fell upon Mr. Joseph I. C. Clarke, for quite a quarter of a century well and favorably known as a journalist in New York. This was in April, 1906.

Mr. Clarke had not accepted the position without taking time to think it over. Much had been written about the Company. A lady with a facile pen, dipped in the corrosive ink of inherited antipathy, had not long before finished a History of the Company. A fiery publicist, hostile to society as it is, had written a book packed with hatred of all wealth and filled with venom against the Standard Oil. Congress and State Legislatures had investigated it. Lawsuits had been launched against it in goodly number. These had to be considered and something of the other side—the Company's side—examined before the arrangement was completed which began the Publicity Bureau of the Standard Oil Company.

It was not the desire of the Company to launch a campaign of argument against all that had been said in its despite, nor was it in Mr. Clarke's conception of his novel duties. The story of Standard Oil was thirty-six years old,—a most impressive story which awaited and still awaits a pen and brain to do it justice in detail as well as in the mass. Combination for entirely legitimate purpose, aggregation keeping pace with widened measures of economy, skill of the highest scientific kind in getting new products from the crude material, extension to meet broadened sources of supply and ever increasing demand, the organization of transit, manufacturing and marketing at home, and a tremendous, continuous campaign for markets abroad,—these were the main content of the story as Mr. Clarke saw it. What conflicts it had survived, what trials it had passed, what methods of its time it had outlived, were plainly not for his working attention. It was the greatest commercial institution in the country, in full working trim, with a gallant face to the future, at peace with its tens of thousands of workers, its hundreds of thousands of customers, and financially impregnable. As that live force it should find a voice wherever it was needed. On that simple basis the work was undertaken and has been carried forward,—to substitute fact for canard, to announce progress. A President of the United States, under ill advice and misinformation, wrote in a Message to Congress that much of a freely circulated Standard Oil pamphlet was untrue. One may not contradict a President but he had not long to wait to see every allegation in the pamphlet proved conclusively, and his utterance and his advisers discredited. It was the story of the illusory $29,000,000 fine told by the President of the Standard Oil Company of Indiana, with some newspaper extracts appended.

It is part of Mr. Clarke's duty to meet the press representatives and other inquirers who come to No. 26 Broadway, New York, in quest of news and information, and many and various are the questions about oil and the oil business and the persons conducting it now and in the past, he is expected to answer,—which calls for much patience and a cheerful aspect that must be natural to be lasting.

Mr. Clarke entered New York journalism in 1870, on the staff of the New York Herald, and during thirteen years succeeding, was reporter, correspondent, editorial writer, dramatic critic, literary editor, night editor and managing editor. In 1883 he became managing editor and part owner of the newly started Morning Journal, which post he occupied until 1895, retiring when John R. McLean, of Cincinnati, bought the majority stock of the paper. In 1898 he undertook the editorship of the New York Criterion, a literary weekly that is lovingly remembered by the elect, and remained with it two years. In January, 1903, he returned to the New York Herald as Sunday editor and filled the post for nearly three years, leaving the paper through a difference with Mr. James Gordon Bennett as to the propriety of the plays of a Sunday editor having any mention, good or bad, in his paper. For Mr. Clarke was a playwright also. The drama had long been his darling. He had published in book form in 1889, "Robert Emmet, a Tragedy of Irish History." He had written other plays meanwhile. Sir Henry Irving bought his version of "Don Quixote," in 1895. It was, however, "Heartsease," a collaboration with Charles Klein, for Henry Miller, that was the first to see the professional stage, in 1897. He subsequently did "Bonnie Prince Charlie," for Julia Marlowe, "Her Majesty," for Grace George, "The First Violin," for Richard Mansfield. "Lady Godiva," a play in verse, followed, with "The Prince of India," from

Lew Wallace's novel, and "Great Plumed Arrow," a monologue for Guy Bates Post. He made several translations also from the French and Italian.

Next to the drama and outside of journalism, Mr. Clarke has most loved poetry. In 1893 he published "Malmorda," a metrical romance, dealing with the Northmen's invasions of Ireland in the ninth century, and has contributed occasional poems to the magazines and newspapers. By one of those unexplained chances of composition, one poem of his, "The Fighting Race," bas attained apparently a lasting celebrity. It was printed in the New York Sun on March 17, 1898. a month after the blowing up of the Maine in Havana harbor, and pictured three Irishmen reading the list of the dead on the battleship, and finding many Irish names therein, thence passing on to the battle feats and apotheosis of the fighting Celt,—Kelly and Burke and Shea. Scarcely a week passes that it is not reprinted somewhere. Others of his poems, "The Soul of Nippon," "The Messenger from Marathon," "Bucky O'Neill," "The Fret of Father Carty," have had quite a vogue. His "Manhattan: an Ode," on the occasion of the Hudson-Fulton celebration, has been several times reprinted.

One of his leanings is toward mechanical invention, which led to a warm friendship with Thomas A. Edison, dating back to the days of Menlo Park when Edison was struggling to fame with the incandescent electric light. Mr. Clarke has just secured a patent for an airship of the helicopter type on a new principle.

Mr. Clarke is of Irish birth. He was born in Kingstown, Ireland, on July 31, 1846, the son of a barrister. He received his education in Ireland and London and in Paris. In 1863 he entered the English Civil Service, but, as he puts it, his views of the government of Ireland differed so totally with those of the Crown that he came perforce to America in 1868, settling in New York. In 1873 he married Miss Mary Agnes Cahill, and has two sons. William Joseph, born in 1876, now an assistant Corporation Counsel, and Harry Edward, born in 1884, and in business in New York.

Mr. Clarke has social activities and belongs to many societies. He is a Director of the American Dramatists' and Composers' Society, founded and was President of the National Art Theatre Society, fairly the forerunner of the New Theatre Organization. He has been President of the Friendly Sons of St. Patrick, the most influential of Irish organizations. His clubs are The Manhattan, The American Dramatists and the New York Press Club. He is President of the Tuinucu Sugar Co., which owns a plantation and sugar mill near Sancti Spiritus, Cuba. He has a country place, Rossallan Lodge, in Merriewold Park, Sullivan County, New York. In the old Creedmoor days he took up rifle shooting and won cups and medals. Now his outdoor pleasures are boating and the pursuit of the odd and the beautiful with a camera.

NICHOLS FIELD WILSON.

One of the most prominent among the notable personalities in the California oil fields is Nichols Field Wilson. His activities are by no means confined to petroleum, however, for his operations include real estate, banking and finance. He has handled over twenty million dollars' worth of land and securities and his business now is of such magnitude that he maintains offices in New York, San Francisco, Los Angeles, Seattle and London. He is president of the Lincoln Mortgage and Loan Company and of the London Petroleum Company; also a director of the Illinois Crude Oil Company and of the Yellow Stone Oil Company.

The parents of Mr. Wilson were both English Quakers, the branches of the family having been among the early settlers of South Carolina and West Virginia. Nichols Field Wilson was born in Concordia, Kansas, March 22, 1879. Thus it will be seen that, although he is now only thirty-two years of age, he has made remarkable success of every venture which he has undertaken. He attended the public schools of St. Joseph, Missouri, and when only fourteen years of age he became clerk to a firm of attorneys, enjoying at the same time four years of legal tuition. He was nineteen years old when the Spanish-American War called him, among so many other patriotic American boys, to the service of his country. He was a member of the Missouri militia and served under Major General S. B. M. Young, Commander of the Second Army Corps.

After peace was declared young Wilson again turned his attention to the law and for a year was employed in law offices in St. Louis. Then he removed to Los Angeles, California, since which time he has considered himself a Californian. He spends much of his time in New York and London, however, for the reason that his activities extend over the European Continent as well as over the United States.

Perhaps the latest of Mr. Wilson's accomplishments in the field of industrial organization was the formation of the California Consolidated Oil Company during September, 1910. The properties of the Company, which are exceedingly productive, are Mascot, Premier and Yellowstone in the Midway, Coalinga and Kern River districts. The average production is 150,000 barrels monthly.

The President of the Company is Rear Admiral Robley D. Evans, U. S. N., retired. Robert L. Dunn is secretary and Theo. P. Gilman is Treasurer. Mr. Wilson does not figure on the directorate, but his was the master hand which moulded the advent of the enterprise. Its success has amply justified his foresight and sagacity.

Mr Wilson is built physically on a massive plan and his face is as youthful as alert. He has always displayed great business sagacity and seems to possess that sort of executive ability which brings about desired ends through the conservation of time. What he has accomplished amounts to the usual life work of men twice his age, who are usually regarded as successful.

In 1899 Mr. Wilson married, at St. Joseph, Missouri, Miss Edith Brister. He is a member of the Olympic and Southern clubs of San Francisco.

HON. THOMAS W. PHILLIPS.

The subject of this sketch is truly representative of the petroleum industry. He engaged in the business of producing oil in the earliest years and has continued to this time. He has been active in every movement for the betterment of the industry and has been a foremost advocate of the interests of the oil producers at all times. He was born and reared on a farm and his dearest youthful ambition was to obtain a liberal education and become a preacher. Circumstances over which he had no control prevented him from realizing his desire to enter the pulpit, but he obtained an education not inferior to the course of the best college. He was licensed to preach and did so with success until an accident to his lungs, by being thrown from a buggy, compelled him to desist from public speaking.

Mr. Phillips made his advent into the oil business in 1861, less than two years after the striking of the Drake well, prospecting in his own county. In 1862 he went to Oil Creek where he purchased and shipped oil, secured oil lands and began drilling. In 1863 the firm of Phillips Brothers was formed, the brothers being, beginning with the eldest, I. N., J. T., C. M. and T. W. Phillips, and the firm became an active factor in the development of territory. It operated on Oil Creek and at Pithole, and later in the Clarion and Butler County fields. In 1873 the Jay Cook panic, in connection with a profound depression of the oil industry, due to an over production, so depreciated the value of the properties of the firm that it was embarrassed, with over a half million dollars of debt, but no property was sold adversely from it. Undaunted by misfortune the Phillips Brothers continued their operations as they might and in 1876 they were rewarded by the discovery of the Bullion pool in Venango County and profited largely from it. From that field they followed the trend down into Butler County to St. Joe and then to Thorn Creek. In 1884 they opened the famous Thorn Creek pool, with the Phillips well on the Bartley farm, that made as high as 4,000 barrels a day and maintained its output for weeks. By 1887 they had paid principal and interest of their debt. The same year Thomas W. Phillips purchased the interest of his brothers in the business and opened the Glade Run field in Butler County, one of the most profitable in the history of the business. In 1890 Mr. Phillips opened the Great Belt field, forming then the firm of T. W. Phillips Sons & Co., which took over his oil and gas properties and became an active operator in many sections. In 1896 the Phillips Gas Company was organized and in 1904, or shortly thereafter, the Home Gas Company of Butler, the Enterprise Natural Gas Company of Freeport, and the Citizens Fuel Company of Punxsutawney were bought, the name being changed to the T. W. Phillips Gas and Oil Company. Such is a brief outline of the business career of Mr. Phillips. His activities in other lines have been even more important.

During the Civil War a tax was laid on petroleum and Mr. Phillips took the lead in securing a modification and then a repeal by Congress. He was a warm friend of James A. Garfield and the latter visited the oil country with Mr. Phillips, and was a most important factor in having the onerous tax removed. When Garfield was a candidate for President in 1880, Mr. Phillips originated the campaign text book which

has been a feature of every National and many State campaigns since. When the Pennsylvania Legislature proposed to levy a tax on petroleum and on every drilling rig to secure revenues to pay the damages incurred by the railroad riots in 1877, Mr. Phillips was chosen to head the committee that went to Harrisburg to fight the imposition, which through his efforts, was defeated. Mr. Phillips was a leader in the Producers' Protective Association and in the "shut in" movement in 1888. He is connected with the companies that grew out of the Producers movement, the Producers Oil Company, the Producers and Refiners Company and the Pure Oil Company, being one of the trustees of the latter and a director in the United States Pipe Line.

Mr. Phillips' greatest public service was in connection with the Industrial Commission. He introduced the bill creating the Commission while a member of the Fifty-third Congress. He re-introduced it in the Fifty-fourth Congress and it passed during the closing hours of that Congress, but was not signed by President Cleveland. He induced Gen. Charles Grosvenor, of Ohio, to introduce it in the Fifty-fifth Congress and it was passed and became a law. The Commission consisted of five members of the Senate, five members of the House and nine other persons "who shall fairly represent the different industries and employments." President McKinley requested Mr. Phillips to accept a place on the Commission, which, after deliberation, he decided to do. In the organization of the Commission the Senate was complimented with the chairmanship which was given to Senator Kyle. Mr. Phillips was chosen vice chairman, presiding at most of its deliberations, and Representative Gardner second vice chairman. While the life of the Commission was originally to be two years, it was extended a year and a half to enable it to complete its very important work. The hearings will be well remembered, the report comprising nineteen volumes. There is no doubt this work caused the Congress to pass the Act creating the Department of Commerce and Labor and many of the subsequent laws regulating corporations. The Bureau of Corporations, in the Department of Commerce and Labor, was the direct outgrowth of Mr. Phillips' supplementary report, contained in the final report of the Industrial Commission.

Mr. Phillips is a member of the Christian Church, a trustee of Bethany College, Hiram College and of Drake University, and an active supporter of the Y. M. C. A. Fraternally, he is a Mason. His beautiful home in New Castle is one of the most comfortable in Western Pennsylvania.

JAMES McCLURG GUFFEY.

A work on oil and natural gas would not be complete without some account of Hon. James McClurg Guffey, who has opened more great oil and gas fields than any other, associated in many of his enterprises with John Galey, another pioneer. Mr Guffey made his acquaintance with the petroleum industry just prior to the Pithole furore, and he played his part in that remarkable development. When the "city" was in need of a government to keep the throng orderly, he was chosen borough clerk. That was in 1865. Prior to his coming to the Oil Region he had been in railroad offices in Louisville, Kentucky, and with the Adams Express Company at Nashville, Tennessee, having left the old home, where he was born, January 19, 1839, in Sewickley township, Westmoreland county, Pennsylvania, before he had reached the age of eighteen. After Pithole, Mr. Guffey took part in the stirring scenes about Shamburg, Petroleum Center and other portions of the Venango County development, until the trend of operations passed down the Allegheny River

In 1872 Mr. Guffey embarked in the oil well machinery and supply business in St. Petersburg, Clarion County. In 1873, in partnership with Smith Cook, he was operating in the Pickwick district, with a nice production. The producing firm of J. M. Guffey & Co. followed soon after. In 1876 he was a candidate for Congress in the old Twenty-fifty District of Pennsylvania, which included Clarion County. He was among the pioneer operators in the Bradford field of McKean County, where he was highly successful, and he took part in the hurly burly of Cherry Grove in 1882. At the close of that engagement he removed to Pittsburg and engaged in the natural gas business there in 1883. He has ever since made that city his home. He was interested in several of the pioneer gas companies that began supplying Pittsburg in 1884. In 1888 he developed the great gas field on the Grapeville anticlinal that created the famous glass town of Jeannette, and organized companies to pipe the product as far east as Johnstown, and west to Jeannette, Penn, Manor and Irwin.

Mr. Guffey took an active part in extending the oil and gas development southwest into Greene and Washington Counties, Pennsylvania, and into West Virginia, where he operated on a large scale. He and Mr. Galey were pioneers in the wonderful field at McDonald, Pennsylvania, where they had one well on the Matthews farm that produced 14,000 barrels in a day. That was in 1891-1892. In 1893 these enterprising pioneers began developing an oil and gas field in Southern Kansas, at Neodosha. Once the field was well under way they sold their interests to the Standard Oil Company, as pipe lines and refineries were necessary to its further development, and Mr. Guffey moved the scene of his operations to Corsicana, Texas, being again successful.

His next pioneer experiment was on Spindletop, near Beaumont, Texas, where he brought in the remarkable Lucas gusher, with a record of 65,000 barrels in one day. There he was compelled to organize a pipe line, refining and marketing concern to take care of his production, and this was done under the title of the J. M. Guffey Petroleum Company, capitalized at $15,000,000. This corporation was the basic organization of the Gulf Refining Company group, Mr. Guffey having withdrawn from control and ownership in the concerns several years ago.

The latest activities of this daring pioneer have been in coal properties. He owns a vast and valuable acreage of coal lands in West Virginia. He took out a charter some years ago for the Cheat River Railroad, but disposed of it before the road was built but the conception of the route is conceded to have been masterly.

In addition to his business activities, Mr. Guffey has been a prominent figure in the politics of his State and of the Nation. He is now Democratic National Committeeman for Pennsylvania, having been first elected to that position in 1896. For fifteen years he has been the foremost member of his party in the Keystone State. In the campaign of 1908, he opposed the nomination of William Jennings Bryan by the National Convention at Denver and that gentleman assisted in unseating him as National Committeeman by a forced proceeding. Mr. Guffey was, however, restored to that position by the next Pennsylvania Democratic State Convention, proving his popularity with the rank and file of the party. He was practically personally responsible for the election of W. H. Berry as State Treasurer on the Democratic ticket in Republican Pennsylvania.

Colonel Guffey as he is generally known, counts his staunch friends by the thousands. They are to be found in every region in America where oil and gas are produced and in many other places besides. He has large mining interests in the West and is invited into every project that looks good to any of his grateful friends. He has been a liberal contributor to many worthy objects and a pillar of strength in the erection and endowment of a number of Methodist Episcopal churches in Pennsylvania and other States. He is one of the leading citizens of Pittsburg and has been active and influential in its civic affairs. But above all else, he is identified with the tremendous development of the patroleum and natural gas industry throughout the country.

JAMES ISAAC BUCHANAN.

James Isaac Buchanan, who has been a factor in the development of the petroleum and natural gas industries, first became identified with them in 1877. He at that time became private secretary and business manager for the late Captain Jacob J. Vandergrift, an extensive oil operator at Oil City, Pa., one of the pioneers on Oil Creek, founder of the United Pipe Lines, the Imperial Refining Company, the Pennsylvania Tube Works, the Apollo Iron and Steel Company and the town of Vandergrift. Mr. Buchanan made friendships among those who follow the business. He has ever since been actively engaged in the production of oil and gas.

The subject of this sketch was born in Hamilton, Ontario, Canada, August 3, 1853, son of the late Hon. Isaac Buchanan, who, previous to the Confederation, was President of the Executive Council and Member of Parliament for Canada, and of the late Agnes (Jarvie) Buchanan. He is a grandson of the late Peter Buchanan, laird of Auchmar, Scotland. He was educated in Miss McIlwraith's private school in Hamilton, Ontario, and Dr. Tassie's Collegiate Institute, in Galt, Ontario. Mr. Buchanan began his business training in 1868, in a wholesale dry goods house in his native city. In 1870 he visited South Africa. He crossed the Continent from Capetown, by way of Pniel (now Kimberly diamond mines) to Durban, Port Natal, about 2,000 miles, in a Cape cart (two wheels) with a friend and two servants. The following year he returned to Canada and the business where he received his early training. Since then he has made several visits to Europe and traveled extensively in America. In January, 1877, he went to Oil City, Pa., and became a junior clerk in the Oil City Trust Company. Soon afterward he was chosen private secretary and business manager for Captain Vandergrift, an undoubted leader in the petroleum industry, removing with him to Pittsburg, Pa.

At the death of Captain Vandergrift, Mr. Buchanan became, under the provisions of the will, one of the trustees of the Vandergrift estate, managing the same with fidelity. He is now chiefly interested in the Pittsburg Terminal and Transfer Company, composed of forty large warehouses, of which he is President. He is President of the Pittsburg Trust Company, one of the strong financial institutions of the Steel City, and of the Terminal Trust Company of the same place. He is a director of the Keystone National Bank of Pittsburg, The Natural Gas Company of West Virginia, The Bush Oil Company, The Washington Oil Company, the Taylorstown Natural Gas Company, and the Manufacturers Light and Heat Company, and is widely known. He has twice made addresses before the Pennsylvania Bankers' Association and several times before Group 8 thereof, and various business and other organizations. He is a member of the Pittsburg Chamber of Commerce, Board of Trade and South Hills Board of Trade.

Although a busy man of large affairs, James Isaac Buchanan has not neglected the social side of life. He has been a Free Mason for over thirty-seven years and is Past Master of St. John's Lodge, No. 219, of Pittsburg. For twenty years, since 1890, he has been an active member of the Supreme Council of the Scottish Rite of the thirty-third degree, and, since 1897, Deputy for Pennsylvania. He is an honorary member of three other Supreme Councils and is also a member of the Royal Order of Scotland and the Royal Arch Chapter Council of Cryptic Masonry and the Knights Templar.

He is a member of the Pittsburg Art Society, of the Academy of Science and Art of Pittsburg, the Botanical Society of Western Pennsylvania, the American Association for the Advancement of Science, the American Geographical Society, the National Geographic Society, St. Andrew's Society of New York, St. Andrew's Society of Pennsylvania, the Duquesne Club, University Club, Union Club, Country Club, Pittsburg Athletic Association, all of Pittsburg, and the Caledon Mountain Trout Club of Ontario, and Railroad Club of New York. He was for eight years chairman of the Pittsburg Orchestra Committee of the Art Society, which promoted a higher standard of musical taste in Pittsburg, earning the commendation of the public by their energetic labors; and he was for three years President of the Athalia Daly Home for Self-Supporting Women, a memorial foundation established by the will of the late Dr. Daly.

Mr. Buchanan has been a member of the Presbyterian Church for forty years. For several years he was a trustee of the East Liberty Presbyterian Church and for the past fifteen years he has been an elder in that church. Some years ago he was President of the Presbyterian Union of Pittsburg. He was married July 11, 1901, in Pittsburg, to Eliza Macfarlane, daughter of Isaiah Graham Macfarlane and Margaret (McDowell) Macfarlane. They have no children, but their beautiful home at No. 330 South Negley Avenue, East End, Pittsburg, is the gathering place of many cultured people.

The esteem in which Mr. Buchanan was held by Capt. Vandergrift, after twenty-two years of close association, is reflected in Article XIV of his will as follows: "I also enjoin upon them (his children) that they bestow upon James I. Buchanan the same confidence, which I have always in my life reposed in him; as he has always been true and faithful to my interests, I feel assured he will be true and faithful to the interests of my children."

WILLIAM WALTER TARBELL.

The subject of this sketch is one of the younger men in the petroleum industry who are carrying forward the work of the pioneers. His father was a pioneer who contributed to the advancement of important details in the oil business, particularly to the storage of the product at the wells. The young man learned the elements of the petroleum business along with the alphabet and became familiar with its processes as he progressed through the grammar grades. Although he turned his attention elsewhere for an interval, he has been actively and continuously in the business since 1887, being now Treasurer of the Pure Oil Company, with offices in the Lafayette Building in Philadelphia.

Franklin S. Tarbell, the father, son of William Tarbell, who served throughout the War of 1812 and was given a Captaincy for notable bravery in the battle of Lundy's Lane, was born in Oxford, Chemung County, New York. His parents removed to Wattsburg, Erie County, Pennsylvania, in 1845, where he married Esther Ann McCullough, and resided until 1860. A few months after the Drake well was struck, he went to Rouseville to look over the new industry. He was so much impressed with the inefficiency of the vats used for storing oil at the wells and so convinced that he could improve upon the method, that he resolved to enter that business. The oil receptacles of that period were mainly square structures of logs, or planks, buried under ground, or rudely plastered with mud. The losses from leakage and the inconvenience of transferring the fluid to barrels were very great. Mr. Tarbell's first experiment in constructing a tank of staves, held tight by iron hoops, was a complete success. To meet the demand that followed its appearance he rapidly established tank shops at Rouseville, Petroleum Center, Pithole and Shamburg, where most of the wooden tanks used in the early oil fields were built. Mr. Tarbell, however, soon became interested in the production of oil, which business he followed in various parts of the Oil Regions to the time of his death in 1906. He was widely and favorably known among all who followed the industry in the Eastern fields.

W. W. Tarbell is the only living son of Franklin S. Tarbell and Esther A. Tarbell. He was born in Wattsburg, Erie County, Pa., on July 1, 1860, just four months before his parents removed to Rouseville, then the thriving metropolis of the lower Oil Creek Valley, an oil town that will ever be famed in petroleum history. His parents later removed to Titusville, the Queen City of the Oil Region, where he was educated in the public schools, graduating from the Titusville High School in 1876. In 1881 he graduated from Allegheny College, Meadville, Pennsylvania. He then read law and later spent four years, pioneering, in the West. Returning to the oil industry in 1887, Mr. Tarbell helped organize the Valley Oil Line, one of the first independent pipe lines to be constructed after the period of general pipe line consolidation of the preceding decade. This line transported oil from the Grand Valley field, in Warren County, to Titusville. About that time he became actively connected with the Petroleum Producers' Protective Association and has ever since been associated with the interests that grew out of that organization; with the Producers and Refiners Oil Company, Limited; with the United States Pipe Line Company, the first line to transport refined oil through pipes, and afterwards with the Pure Oil Company, of which he has been Treasurer since 1902.

The formation period of the producing, transporting, refining and marketing companies, comprising the Pure Oil group, was a strenuous one. Mr. Tarbell was in the thick of the fray, associated with such pioneers as Hon. Lewis Emery, of Bradford; Hon. Thomas W. Phillips, of New Castle; the late Hon. David Kirk, and the late Hon. J. W. Lee. The Pure Oil Company is now one of the influential factors in the petroleum industry, having producing properties in the important oil fields of Pennsylvania, Ohio, West Virginia, Illinois, Oklahoma and other States. It has a network of gathering pipe lines in the producing districts, and trunk pipe line from the fields to the Seaboard, refineries inland and on the coast; ocean going tank steamers, warehouses and marketing stations abroad. In fact it is engaged in every branch of the industry, from the production of the crude oil to the selling of the manufactured products in the export trade.

Mr. Tarbell has had no time for political work in recent years, but served in the City Councils of Titusville when a resident there. He takes the keen interest in public affairs of a good citizen and seeks no reward.

COLONEL E. V. D. SELDEN.

Edwin Van Deusen Selden is a well known refiner and producer of petroleum, being largely interested in the Crystal Oil Works at Oil City Pa. This business he owns in partnership with the Honorable James A. Fawcett, having established it in 1897. Since that time they have built it up into a very profitable enterprise, in the face of vigorous competition. Prior to the date mentioned he was in the petroleum brokerage business, having become a member of the Oil City Oil Exchange in 1878. He continued active therein during the most exciting years of the oil market and is yet President of the Exchange, as he has been for a number of years.

Colonel Selden's father was engaged in the manufacture of oil from coal at Kiskiminetas prior to Drake's discovery in 1859. His profitable business was then, like that of many other oil manufacturers, ruined by the advent of natural mineral oil in great quantities. The son, however, evened up the score by wresting fortune from the new natural oil that destroyed the manufacturing business of his father.

Edwin V. D. Selden was born in Lawrenceville (now a part of Pittsburgh), Allegheny County, Pa., on December 23, 1858, the son of George S. Selden, Esq., and grandson of George Selden, Esq., both lawyers of ability and distinction. He was educated in public and private schools in Meadville, Pa., and Philadelphia, Pa., and in the Episcopal Academy of Philadelphia. In 1876 he began the study of the law in the office of his father, which he continued until 1877, when he went to Parkers Landing, Pa., then a great oil center, to clerk for his brother. Mr. Selden was quick to master the details of the oil business and in 1878, he became a member of the Oil City Oil Exchange, where the oil market for the world was made. During twenty years, while trading in oil certificates was active, he was a well known figure on the floor, participating in some of the most exciting scenes ever witnessed in any commercial exchange. He was among the first of the petroleum brokers to realize that speculation in oil certificates was passing, and, in 1897, turned his attention to refining Pennsylvania oil, a venture whose very substantial success proved his sound judgment.

Beside being a prime mover in the Crystal Oil Works and President of the Oil City Oil Exchange, Mr. Selden is connected with the Citizens Banking Company of Oil City, where he resides. He is an active member of the Masonic fraternity, of the Pennsylvania Society of the Sons of the Revolution, of the Pennsylvania Society of the Founders and Patriots of America, of the Colonial Society of Pennsylvania, and member of the Ivy Club and of the Venango Club of Oil City; President of Venango Security Building & Loan Association; President of Home Savings & Loan Association. He was long active in the National Guard of Pennsylvania, having been First Lieutenant and Quartermaster, Sixteenth Regiment Infantry, N G. P., on the staff of Colonel Willis J. Hulings; was subsequently Colonel commanding the Twenty-first Regiment Infantry, N. G. P., 1898 to 1900. From 1900 to 1905 he was Lieutenant Colonel and Inspector of Rifle Practice for the Division, on the staff of Major General Charles Miller.

P. O. LAUGHNER.

P. O. Laughner, President of the Crescent Oil & Gas Company and of the Minnetonka Oil Company, Pittsburg, Pennsylvania, was born September 21, 1859, at Six Points, Butler County, Pa. His early education was received in the common schools of the county and was supplemented by a course in Edinboro State Normal School and in the Iron City Business College of Pittsburg. For six years he taught school and early in 1882 went to Oil City and became a member of the Oil Exchange. He was an active member until September, 1890, when, with his brother, E. E. Laughner, he engaged in the oil well supply business at Shannopin, Pa. The firm was known as Laughner Brothers and branch stores were opened at Coraopolis and McDonald, Pa.

For the last twenty years, Mr. Laughner has been a producer of oil, his operations extending through the various fields of Pennsylvania, West Virginia and Ohio.

The Minnetonka Oil Company opened the oil field at Cleveland, Oklahoma, and Mr. Laughner was largely interested in the Shire well in Crawford County, Illinois, which opened the Crawford County field. The Minnetonka Oil Company and the Crescent Oil & Gas Company have large holdings in the Crawford County field.

On his father's side, Mr. Laughner's ancestors are Dutch, on his mother's Scottish. He was married at Salem, Clarion County, Pa., on May 31, 1882, to Miss Emma C. Finley, daughter of the late William P. Finley. As a result of this union, three children survive, two sons, Aymer V., Chalmers C. and Gladys Marie Laughner.

Among the many oil men of present day prominence who have their homes in Pittsburg and control petroleum activities in distant fields, P. O. Laughner is one of the most active and highly respected. He is a member of the Union Club of Pittsburg, Pittsburg Athletic Association, the Pittsburg Board of Trade and the Pittsburg Press Club. He is a Mason of rank and an influential member of the Elks.

NOAH F. CLARK.

Known throughout the eastern oil fields, Noah F. Clark has been an active figure in the business for nearly forty years. His first connection with the industry was at Oil City. After two years' experience he became the purchasing agent at that point for Scofield, Shurmer and Teagle, well known refiners at Cleveland, Ohio. This he continued for five years and then became a producer. He was interested for a time with Munhall and Smithman. At the opening of the Bradford field he went into producing properties there. Later the firm of Clark & Foster took an active part in the developments in Warren County, Mr. Clark being the manager of the business. This firm opened the field in Elk County and was a prominent figure in the Kane field in McKean County. Mr. Clark was also a member of the Oil City Oil Exchange during its exciting years.

In 1889 Mr. Clark organized the South Penn Oil Company, which took over all the Clark & Foster interests in producing properties. He was Vice President and Manager. Afterward he was President of the Company for five years. During that time it operated extensively in West Virginia and Southwestern Pennsylvania as well as in the Elk and Warren County fields. He resigned his office and withdrew from the South Penn Company about 1901, and since that time has been engaged in the producing of oil and gas on his own account He has been connected with several other companies, of his own organization, making his headquarters in Pittsburg, although maintaining his residence in Philadelphia. Mr. Clark is producing oil and gas in West Virginia, Ohio and Pennsylvania, chiefly in Knox and Lincoln Counties, in Ohio, and in Marion and Lincoln Counties, in West Virginia.

Mr. Clark was born in Wiltshire, England, on February 23, 1854. His parents came to America and settled in Cleveland, Ohio, when he was fourteen years of age. He attended the public schools there until seventeen years of age, when he went to Oil City and engaged in the oil business. At nineteen he became purchasing agent for the Cleveland refinery, as stated. He was married in Oil City to Miss Rebecca Jack and to this union five children have been born, as follows: Arthur Clark, Victoria Clark, Eleanor Clark and Susan Clark. The family spends the summers at Chautauqua Lake, where Mr. Clark has maintained a pleasant cottage for many years.

Mr. Clark is an expert in oil and gas matters, and his success has proven his judgment. He has taken a vigorous part in the political affairs of the oil country and is widely known outside of the region, but has never sought public office. A man of fine physique and unusual strength he will be remembered by many of the old time producers and speculators for the practical jokes played upon them, never malicious but in the best of good humor. During the strenuous days of Warren and Forest County wildcatting and "mysteries" he took chances on "roughing it" with the field men occasionally and enjoyed it quite as much as any. He is thoroughly democratic in manner, meeting all men on the level.

Mr. Clark is a member of the Duquesne Club, the Fort Pitt Club and the Athletic Club, all of Pittsburg. He has offices in the Machesney building in Pittsburg and frequently visits the producing fields.

THEODORE N. BARNSDALL.

The subject of this sketch has been a conspicuous figure in the petroleum and natural gas industries of the United States. His father, William Barnsdall, a native of England, came to America when a young man and settled at Titusville, Pennsylvania, about 1835, where he married and where T. N. Barnsdall was born. The father was a pioneer oilman, he and the late Hon. Henry R. Rouse owning the first well drilled after the Drake well, the venture being located on the Parker farm, at Titusville. In connection with William H. Abbott, William Barnsdall built the first oil refinery in the Oil Region, on the same farm where the second oil well was drilled. He died in Titusville a few years ago at an advanced age, esteemed highly by all who knew him.

Theodore N. Barnsdall began his career as an oil producer at Titusville. Next he went into the Bradford field where he was very successful. He has operated in every oil field opened since then. He is a leading operator in Oklahoma, has large holdings in Pennsylvania, West Virginia, Ohio, Illinois and California. He is the largest single holder of territory in the prolific Osage Reservation. He is President of the Union Natural Gas Corporation; President of the Barnsdall Oil Company; President of the Pittsburg Oil and Gas Company; President of the Wildwood Oil Company; President of the Southern Oil Company; chairman of the Board of Directors of the Kansas Natural Gas Company. He is also largely interested in many other companies and partnerships, engaged in the petroleum and natural gas business.

Mr. Barnsdall resides in Pittsburg and is known wherever oil and gas are produced. He is widely known outside of the producing regions through the operations of his companies and he has traveled extensively in this country and abroad. In business he is aggressive and his physical and mental energy are unbounded. He is absolutely tireless.

EDWARD E. CROCKER.

Edward Edgar Crocker, son of Frederick and Mary Penfield Crocker, was born at Olean, New York, October 24, 1857. When he was five years of age his parents removed to Titusville and there he was educated in the public schools and was graduated from the Titusville High School.

When seventeen years of age Edward E. Crocker acquired his first experience in the oil industry. He started as a roustabout, became a pumper and driller and gained those practical experiences which enable him to say that there is little about the oil well that he has not done and does not understand.

He worked for his father, who was a producer at Bradford, and for several years divided his time between the Bradford, Pennsylvania, and the Allegany County, New York, oil fields. In January, 1886, he removed to Washington, Pa., to work there for McKinney Bros. A short time afterward he engaged with Col. J. M. Guffey, who was interested in the Southwest Natural Gas Company that supplied the coke region, acting in the capacity of superintendent. Mr. Crocker located at Connellsville and remained there in such employment for two years and a half. Then he connected himself with Amm & Company, and removed to Pittsburgh, his activities being divided between the fields of Beaver and Washington Counties. When Amm & Company sold out to the Forest Oil Company, a Standard Oil enterprise, Mr. Crocker was appointed local field superintendent, and eighteen months later he became Assistant General Superintendent, afterward General Superintendent of the Forest Oil Company, upon the death of Mr. Murat Compton.

In July, 1902, Mr. Crocker was transferred to the South Penn Oil Company and was made General Manager. Later, on the retirement of Mr. W. J. Young, he was made Vice President as well as General Manager, both of which offices he still holds.

The ancestry of Mr. Crocker is American. His father was one of the pioneers in the oil regions of Pensylvania and died in 1894 at the age of 84 years.

In March, 1885, Mr. Crocker married Miss Helen Cowles, daughter of Hon. Warren Cowles and Nancy M. Hayden Cowles. They have one son, Frederick S. Crocker, who is now in the oil fields following his father's footsteps in the acquisition of practical knowledge.

Mr. Crocker is a member of the Duquesne and Civic Clubs of Pittsburgh, of the Engineers' Society of Western Pennsylvania, the National Geographic Society and of the American Association for the Advancement of Science.

WESLEY S. GUFFEY.

Wesley S. Guffey is a petroleum pioneer, having made his start in the industry at Pithole, where he invested to good advantage, made some money, and acquired a fund of valuable experience. He has ever since been connected with the production of oil and gas in the various fields of Pennsylvania, West Virginia and Ohio. He has been one of the most successful men in the business and has amassed a comfortable fortune. Outside of oil and gas he has large investments in coal lands, mines and railroads. The firm of Guffey & Queen is one of the most widely known and Mr. Guffey is the senior member.

Wesley S. Guffey was born in Madison, Westmoreland County, Pennsylvania, on February 22, 1842. His parents were Pennsylvanians. He attended the old Sulphur Spring school and acquired the limited education it had to give him. Then he went to work, but did not neglect further study, as opportunity offered and is a very well-informed man of affairs. He has always taken a lively inteest in public questions and has been an influential factor in the affairs of his adopted home, Pittsburg. He has thrown his influence on the side of reform in that municipality and has made himself felt. He has never sought public office or preferment of any kind. In National politics he is a sturdy Democrat, but during the extra session of the Sixty-first Congress advocated retention of protection to petroleum and its products.

After following the oil development through many fields from 1865, Mr. Guffey located in Pittsburg in 1881 and has since made that city his home. He has built there a splendid dwelling where he keeps open bachelor house to his friends. Participating in the natural gas boom that swept over the region about Pittsburg between 1881 and 1900, he was generally successful in his ventures.

Mr. Guffey is a stockholder and director in several Pittsburg institutions, but his favorite investments have been in petroleum, natural gas and coal. With all of these he is thoroughly familiar in every detail. His judgment is rarely at fault and it is sought by many. He attends strictly to his business himself, being happiest in his office from which he directs the forces. Personally he is one of the most affable and agreeable of men. He counts his friends by legions in every part of the oil country and is most highly esteemed by all who know him.

Among his notable triumphs in the early days of the natural gas business were the development of the Grapeville field, the organization of the Cambria Natural Gas Company and other companies supplying gas to Western Pennsylvania towns. He operated in Greene County later with great success, and in West Virginia. The best of the Bristoria field fell to Guffey & Queen. In the famous McDonald gusher district Mr. Guffey was a fortunate bolder. He never wasted his time in market speculation, where so many oil producers lost what they made in the field. His forte has been the purchase and development of producing property.

FRANK M. LOWRY.

Frank M. Lowry, of Pittsburgh, Pa., is the son of the late Joseph Lowry, and of Eliza Lowry. His ancestral tree begins with good Irish stock.

On November 18th, 1856, Frank M. Lowry was born at Indiana, Pennsylvania. He was educated in the public schools and when twenty years of age he entered the oil industry, beginning as a pumper, serving as a tool dresser, driller and contractor and within a few years became an oil producer on a large scale. He turned his attention to pipe lines and built the Western Atlantic Pipe Lines, becoming General Manager. In this capacity he served for five years, when the company sold out its enterprise. Mr. Lowry then entered the service of the Standard Oil Company and remained in Pittsburgh over six years as Assistant General Manager of the Forest Oil Plant. He then organized the Tri-State Gas Company of Pittsburgh and became Vice President and General Manager. Five years later this company was merged with the Manufacturers Light and Heat Company and for a number of years Mr. Lowry was connected with that corporation, until he organized and started the Dominion Natural Gas Company, of which he is now Vice President and General Manager. He is also President of the Duquesne Oil Company of Pittsburgh, and a director of the Acme Glass Company, Steubenville, Ohio.

Mr. Lowry is master of the Harkaway Hunt Club; a member of the Duquesne, Pittsburgh Country, Pittsburgh Athletic and Allegheny Country Clubs.

The officers of the Dominion Natural Gas Company are: President, J. C. McDowell; Vice President and General Manager, Frank M. Lowry; Treasurer, D. Robertson; Secretary, A. J. Devlin.

JOHN G. JENNINGS

John G. Jennings was born at Brady's Bend, Armstrong County, Pennsylvania, July 28, 1864. He is the third son of the late Richard Jennings, Sr., who was one of the most prominent figures in the development of the Butler and Armstrong section of the Pennsylvania fields.

The early education of John G. Jennings was received in the district schools, then at the Chambersburg Academy, Chambersburg, Pa., supplemented by a course at Lafayette College, Easton, Pa., and completed by his graduation in 1884 from Princeton.

When but twenty years of age John G. Jennings embarked in the oil business. His first venture was in the Brush Creek pool in Allegheny County. Later Wildwood became the scene of his activities and in this field the young man was quite successful. He was an active operator in the development of Chartiers Township.

From McDonald the operations of Mr. Jennings and his associates extended in the Southern fields of West Virginia where extensive blocks of territory were acquired in the Sistersville field. When the Scio pool began to loom large as a factor in petroleum, Mr. Jennings was among the first on the ground. He and his associates were uniformly successful in their operations and Mr. Jennings was a prime mover in the organization of the Farmers & Producers National Bank, of which for a number of years he was President.

Mr. Jennings married Miss Katherine McCandless. They have three children: Charles McCandless Jennings, Richard Jennings and Katherine E. Jennings.

The firm of E. H. Jennings & Bros. Co., of which E. H. Jennings is President and John G. Jennings, Vice President, is the holding company of the Kanawha Oil Company, of which Mr. John G. Jennings is President, the Jennings Producing Company, Jennings Oil Company, Jennings Mines Company, and M. Murphy & Company, of which John G. Jennings is Vice President, and for the Delmar Oil Company, of which he is the General Manager. He is also President of the Columbia National Bank of Pittsburgh, as well as the General Manager of the Producers and Refiners Oil Company, Limited.

Mr. John G. Jennings is a member of the Duquesne Club, the Pittsburgh Country Club, and the Pittsburgh Athletic Club.

H. E. WORTHINGTON,

Mr H. E. Worthington, of Philadelphia, is President of the Union Petroleum Company, and has held that position since its organization. The Union Company owns and operates two refineries, besides which it exports illuminating and lubricating oils, naphtha, etc., in large quantities for all independent refiners, with whose interests the Company has always been closely identified. The refinery at Wellsville, New York, is acknowledged to be one of the most up-to-date in the oil regions.

At Marcus Hook, Philadelphia, the deep water station of the Company, every convenience exists for handling, exporting, importing and storing bulk cargoes of any size or description, transported by tank steamers or sailing vessels. In addition there are facilities for barrel cargoes, and a new plant has been completed for the manufacture and filling of cans and cases. This is of large capacity and is the only independent casing plant in Philadelphia. Shipments are made from there to all parts of the world.

The company has also a finely equipped station in Philadelphia, adjacent to the steamship wharves and railroads, where lubricating oils of every description are handled.

M. L. BENEDUM—J. C. TREES.

Among the most successful of the younger oil producers are Michael Lake Benedum and Joseph Clifton Trees. Both were born in the same year, ten years after Drake's success on Oil Creek, but they have carried the work of development into distant fields. They have operated as the Benedum—Trees Oil Co., the J. C. Trees Oil Co. and under other company names and are still so operating. The J. C. Trees Oil Company opened the wonderful field at Caddo Lake in Lousiana, late in 1909, with a well that produced about 2,500 barrels daily for many months. This property they sold to the Standard Oil Company, near the close of 1910 for several million dollars, after taking out of it probabl a million barrels of oil. They are the principal holders in the Arkansas Natural Gas Company, now laying pipe from the Caddo Lake region to cities in the North, including Little Rock and possibly St. Louis.

Michael L. Benedum was born in Bridgeport, West Virginia, July 16, 1869, his father being a merchant in the town. He first engaged in the milling business, but when he had saved a little money joined his employer in an oil venture. It proved a dry hole. He soon afterward joined the engineering corps of the South Penn Oil Company and was then transferred to the leasing department, being promoted until he was assistant superintendent in West Virginia. In 1898 he started for himself and met remarkable success, first at Belmont, W. Va., and then in the deep field in Wetzel County. He sold a block of leases with wells to the Standard Oil Company in 1902 for $500,000. Since then he has been joined with Mr. Trees in the producing business.

Joseph Clifton Trees was born November 10, 1869, son of Isaac T. and Lucy (Johnson) Trees. He attended the public school at New Texas, Allegheny County, until fourteen years of age. Then began the struggle for further education. Working summers he attended Normal School at Indiana in winter and later, drilling on oil wells in summer he attended the Western University of Pennsylvania until he was graduated. This was in 1895 and he at once engaged with the Woodland Oil Company hunting up leases in West Virginia. In the fall of the same year he joined W. M. Graham, of Pittsburg, in an oil well which proved dry. The next spring he embarked in the business for himself and has ever since been remarkably successful.

THEODORE E. TACK.

Theodore E. Tack, of New York, President of the American Oil Development Company, Pittsburfi, Pa., has been actively engaged in the petroleum industry for nearly half a century. His brothers, Augustus H. and Frank Tack—both have joined the silent majority—were associated with him during the greater part of the period.

The founder of the American branch of the family, John Christopher Tack, came to this country from Germany soon after the American colonies had attained their independence. John Tack, his son, married Miss Sarah Dunn, who was born in the United States of Irish parentage. Their son, the subject of this sketch, was born January 6, 1837, at Philadelphia. After attending school in the Quaker City until he was fifteen years of age, Theodore Tack obtained employment with Thomas Allibone & Co., merchants in cotton and Southern produce. Meanwhile he attended school at night. Five years afterward, during the panic of 1857, Mr. Tack entered the service of Sharpless Brothers, then and until recent years, one of the largest dry goods concerns in the country. He was still with that concern when, in the winter of 1862-63, the Volunteer forces of Pennsylvania prepared to defend the State from the invasion of the Confederate Army under General Lee. Theodore E. Tack was a member of Starr's battery which was attached to the First Regiment of Infantry, National Guard State of Pennsylvania. He served throughout the period of his enlistment and until the enemy had been driven from the Commonwealth.

Late in 1863 Theodore E. Tack, in association with Augustus H. Tack, established in Pittsburg the first oil brokerage house between Philadelphia and Pittsburg. A few years later they were joined by their brother, Frank Tack, upon his return from three years' service in the army under General Thomas. Later they engaged also in the production of oil in Pennsylvania and West Virginia, and were also associated with the Citizens Oil Refining Company of Pittsburg. The brothers in 1873 went to Parkers Landing and from there went to Titusville. While achieving results as producers they operated also on the oil exchange at Oil City. From 1878 to 1880 the Tack brothers turned their attention to the Bullion field and organized the McCalmont Oil Company. In 1900, David Kirk's interest in the corporation, having been acquired by the Tacks, the McCalmont was merged into the American Oil Development Company. Theodore E. Tack has twice been President of that Company, his present term having begun in 1909. Theodore A. Tack, of Philadelphia, son of the late Augustus H. Tack, is Vice President; Harry L. Tack, son of the late Frank Tack, is General Manager at Pittsburg, and Willis H. Siegfried, also of Pittsburg, is Secretary.

Theodore E. Tack was married at Pittsburg, November 25th, 1868, to Miss Mary A. Cosgrave, daughter of John S. Cosgrave, a prominent merchant who was a member of the firm of Bageley, Cosgrave & Company. Of the twelve children born to this union seven are living: Mrs. Mary Tack Farley, Augustus Vincent Tack, Mrs. Richard Gwinn, Madame Julia Tack, a religious of the Order of the Sacred Heart; Mrs. Allan A. Ryan, Theodore E. Tack, Jr., and Frank L. Tack. Theodore E. Tack and his family have made their home in New York City since 1883.

AUGUSTUS H. TACK AND FRANK TACK.

The late Augustus H. Tack was one of a triumvirate of brothers whose interests were common and safeguarded by enduring fraternal loyalty. For thirty years this tripartite alliance continued, until broken, January 10, 1893, by the death of Augustus H. Tack. The surviving brothers, Theodore E. Tack and Frank Tack, carried on their joint enterprises during the succeeding seventeen years until, on February 26, 1910. occurred the death of Frank Tack.

Born in Philadelphia, Pennsylvania, October 18, 1834, Augustus H. Tack spent his boyhood in that city and there received a practical and useful education. When eighteen years of age he began his business career in a minor capacity in the service of C. J. Fell & Brother, wholesale dealers in spices. After eleven years with that firm, Mr. Tack, in 1863, joined his brother, Theodore E. Tack, in the oil brokerage business, under the style of Tack Brothers. Later they engaged in producing and Augustus H. Tack was the "field man" of the firm and when the Tacks organized the McCalmont Oil Company he served the Company in the same important capacity.

In 1864 Augustus H. Tack was married to Miss Adele Lehman, of Neufchatel, Switzerland. Mrs. Tack has also passed beyond. They are survived by a son and daughter, Theodore A. Tack, attorney, Vice President of the American Oil Development Company, and Adele G. Tack. Mr. and Miss Tack are residing in Philadelphia.

Frank Tack, youngest of the three Tack brothers, was born at Philadelphia, March 7, 1839. His first employment was in the office of Charles Rhodes, a conveyancer. Four years had been spent with the title-deeds and parchments when an event occurred which was destined to change the avocations and environments of many thousands of Americans—the outbreak of the rebellion. Young Frank Tack enlisted in the Anderson Cavalry. Early in the conflict he was in several important engagements. Late in 1861 he was assigned to the headquarters of General George H. Thomas, commander of what was then designated in colloquial parlance as the Army of the West.

When peace had been restored Frank Tack joined his brothers, Augustus H. and Theodore E. Tack in the oil brokerage business and in the production of oil in Pennsylvania and West Virginia. Some years after the formation by the brothers of the McCalmont Oil Company Frank Tack became treasurer of the corporation. After the McCalmont had been merged into the American Oil Development Company, Mr. Tack was elected treasurer, an office which he filled until the day of his death, February 26, 1910.

In 1873 Frank Tack was married to Miss Mary L. Sweetser, daughter of Henry F. Sweetser, of Titusville, Pa. Their son, Harry S. Tack, general manager of the American Oil Development Company, lives in Sewickley, Pa. Their daughter, Mrs. Philip Norvell, also lives in Sewickley with her mother.

L. A. MEYRAN.

Louis Albert Meyran, Vice President and Treasurer of The Manufacturers Light & Heat Company, Pittsburgh, Pennsylvania, near which center he was born, June 23rd, 1859, is an important figure in manufacturing and financial circles. His father, the late Charles Meyran, a native of Germany, organized in 1885, The Manufacturers Gas Company to convey gas from wells in Washington County to Pittsburgh. Fourteen years later the name of the Company was changed to The Manufacturers Light & Heat Company, additional gas properties were taken over, and, in 1903, the capital was increased to $25,-000,000 authorized; about $21,-500,000 issued and quite a number of other smaller companies were merged with it, so that to-day it is one of the largest natural gas companies in the country, supplying natural gas for fuel, light and heat to fully seventy-five thousand consumers, which included many mills and factories in Western Pennsylvania, West Virginia and Ohio. In addition, the Company has an oil production of about 450 barrels per day.

From the early days of the corporation, L. A. Meyran has been interested in its development and during the last few years he has devoted the greater portion of his time to its affairs.

After receiving a classic education at the Western University of Pennsylvania, Mr. Meyran studied for three years at the leading college of Hanover, Germany. He was graduated in 1878 with honors. Returning to the United States, for a few years he engaged in Chicago in the iron and steel brokerage business. In 1882, with others, he interested himself in building the plant of the Canonsburg Iron Company, Limited, at Canonsburg, Pa. This Company afterwards became the Canonsburg Iron and Steel Company and Mr. Meyran was made Secretary and Treasurer. The plant was sold in 1899.

In 1902, Mr. Meyran became interested in the Parkersburg Iron and Steel Company at Parkersburg, West Virginia, with which he has been identified in various official capacities.

When in Canonsburg, he was chiefly instrumental in drilling the first well near that city, to supply gas to the works with which he was connected, and he has been an important factor in the development of oil and gas in other districts.

Mr. Meyran is Vice President of the Germania Savings Bank, organized by his father in 1870, now one of the leading financial institutions of Pittsburgh. He is a member of the Engineers' Society of Western Pennsylvania, and of the Technical Society of Pittsburgh.

In 1885, L. A. Meyran and Miss Marie Herrosee were married. One son, Carl P. Meyran, is emulating his father's active and successful career.

THE NATIONAL SUPPLY COMPANY.

The National Supply Company, with main offices at Toledo, Ohio, and Pittsburg, Penn'a, is one of the largest companies in the oil and gas well supply business in the United States. The National Supply Company was organized in 1894, with a few stores in West Virginia and Pennsylvania. It absorbed the firm of Bayne, Wilson & Pratt, which was one of the pioneers in the oil well supply business in the original oil fields of Pennsylvania. This firm had made a great record in selling the Farrar & Trefts machinery, etc., and was noted for its hustle and progressiveness. It is still well known among the old operators from Pennsylvania. Messrs. Wilson and Pratt both continued with the new company, the former becoming President of it a few years later.

In 1896 The National Supply Company combined with the Buckeye Supply Company of Toledo, which Company had several stores in Northwestern Ohio and Indiana. From these small beginnings The National Supply Company has grown in fourteen years until it now serves every known oil and gas field in America, and through its export office in Pittsburg many of the larger fields in other parts of the world. There are at present about seventy branch stores operated by the various subsidiary companies of The National Supply Company of West Virginia; the National Supply Company of Ohio serves Pennsylvania, West Virginia, Ohio and Indiana; The National Supply Company of Kansas operates in Oklahoma, Texas and Louisiana; The California National Supply Company in California, and The National Supply Company, Ltd., in Canada. These branch stores are all amply stocked with all kinds of machinery, tubular goods, and supplies, in fact everything needed in drilling, equipping and operating an oil or gas well.

Here may be found the various specialties which have made The National Supply Company well known throughout the oil country, as the Farrar & Treft's boilers, which have been the recognized standard in the oil country for about thirty-five years, not only in the United States but abroad; the National Tube Company's casing, tubing, line and drive pipe, Texas special rotary pipe, and California Diamond B. X. casing; the "Roebling" wire sand, casing, and tubing lines, and drilling cables; "Columbian" Manila drilling cables; "Superior" gas engines; "Ajax" steam engines, and the "National" special California tubular boilers, and the "National" special Texas boilers.

The main factory is located at Toledo, Ohio, and has grown from a small affair to a plant covering a large area, employing half a thousand men and manufacturing a varied line of oil country supplies and the National Portable Drilling Rigs.

The National Supply Company has been one of the few companies to recognize the need of, and institute at convenient points, branch stores, where the operator and producer can obtain their supplies from stock, and avoid the long delays occasioned by shipments direct from the factory. It was the first company to offer to the oil country trade wrought steel pipe in place of wrought iron. This departure was a very revolutionary one, as wrought iron pipe was considered by the oil men as an absolute necessity. It required only a few years, however, to convert the operators, and to-day wrought steel pipe is very generally used as casing, tubing and line pipe.

The National Supply Company is again in the van in offering to the trade the National Portable drilling rigs. For some time there has been a growing demand for something to replace the old standard derrick. The greatly increased cost of lumber has made the standard derrick a very expensive item in the cost of drilling. The machine on wheels was designed, and is now used for shallow drilling, but cannot replace the derrick, as it is not substantial enough for drilling over 2,000 feet. Neither is the bull wheel on a machine large enough to accommodate a cable long enough to drill to such a depth. The National portable rigs are designed to replace the standard derrick. They are set firmly on the ground, built strongly and substantially with a steel frame and a reinforced wooden mast; have bull wheels large enough to hold long cables, and will handle the heaviest tools and casing. In addition, they can be dismantled and removed in a very short time. The cost of the rig can be saved on three or four wells. There are several hundred of these rigs now in use, and the No. 2, or heavy rig, is drilling wells to depths of 2,300 to 2,500 feet in the deep gas fields of West Virginia as quickly as a standard derrick, and handling strings of casing weighing over 30,000 pounds. This record cannot be equaled by any other portable rig or machine.

The officers of the National Supply Company are: William Hardee, President; Wm. C. Hillman, First Vice President; James H. Barr, Second Vice President; Charles H. Clapp, Secretary and Treasurer; Rolland J. Free, Assistant Secretary and Treasurer.

THE PEOPLES NATURAL GAS COMPANY.

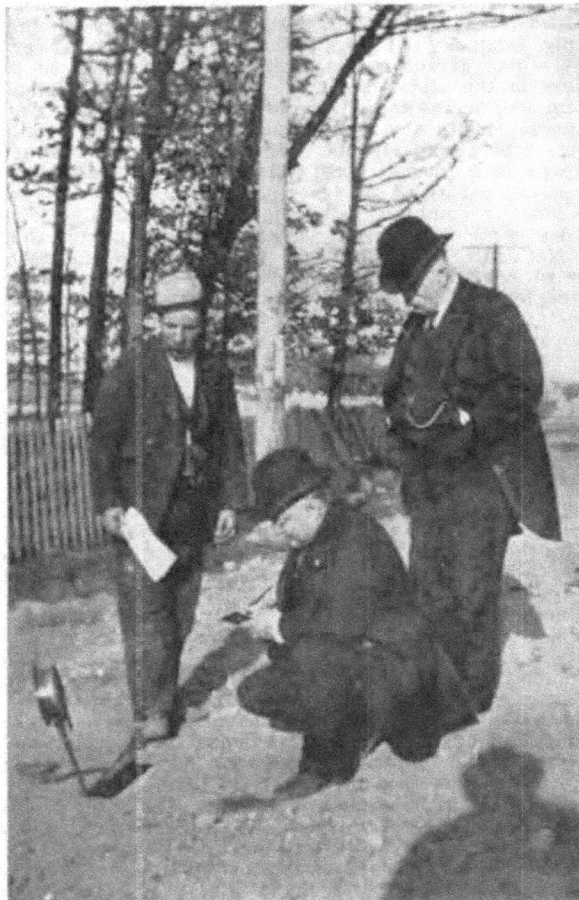

TESTING FIRST LARGE GAS LINE LAID WITH RUBBER JOINT.

One of the important inventions in connection with the transportation of natural gas is the rubber joint, which enabled the companies to take gas a long distance in large quantities. With the old style collar they could not have put together a line larger than 10-inch and made a good job of it. The illustration shows the late E. Strong, S. R. Dresser and a foreman in the act of testing the first large gas line laid with the rubber joint.

The Peoples Natural Gas Company was incorporated in Pennsylvania June 26, 1885. The original incorporators were Edward O. Emerson, J. N. Pew, Theodore Johnson, Robert C. Pew and R. S. Duffield of Pittsburgh, and J. S. Robinson of Allegheny, Pennsylvania. The original capital stock authorized was $200,000, which was, soon after the incorporation of the company, increased to $1,000,000.

The Company forced its way into Pittsburgh over private property and against severe opposition, both political and competitive. After two cases which were carried to the Supreme Court of Pennsylvania, the Company's right to enter the streets of Pittsburgh generally was made secure.

In the year 1890 the field pressure of gas declined rapidly, and the supply of gas to Pittsburgh began to fail. Many engineers, among them Mr. George Westinghouse, and the officers of the Philadelphia Company as well as Mr. J. N. Pew, then President of The Peoples Natural Gas Company, considered the question of supplementing the output of the wells by various devices such as building of large storage tanks, increasing the size of pipe lines, etc. To Mr. J. N. Pew belongs the credit of conceiving the idea of handling natural gas by means of pumps. He experimented in a small way in Wilkinsburg, and his theories being justified by the experiment, he ordered from the Hall Steam Pump Company the first commercial gas compressing station. This station was located in Murraysville field and delivered gas to Pittsburgh. Other stations were added from time to time in the Armstrong County field, all of steam engine type until 1905, when a large steam plant was erected at Brave in Greene County, for the compression of gas produced in Pennsylvania and forwarded to Pittsburgh. In 1902, Mr. J. N. Pew experimented with gas engines, but was not successful in the use of them; in 1907 a gas engine plant was installed in Clarion County, and gradually gas engines are replacing the smaller steam engine plants in Armstrong and Westmoreland Counties.

The Peoples Natural Gas Company has extended its business, and has taken in the following cities in addition to Pittsburgh and Wilkinsburg: Fayette City, Belle Vernon, Monessen, and other small towns along the Monongahela River; Greensburg, Latrobe, Turtle Creek and other towns and boroughs along the main line of the Pennsylvania Railroad. The present authorized capital stock of the Company is $11,100,000.

The present officers of the Company are: A. C. Bedford, President; J. W. R. Crawford and J. G. Pew, Vice Presidents; Christy Payne, Secretary; Thos. Nicoll, Treasurer; George H. Jones, Comptroller.

HOPE NATURAL GAS COMPANY.

Hope Natural Gas Company was incorporated in West Virginia, August 1, 1898; principal offices of the company at Oil City, Pa.

It was originally incorporated to produce and transport natural gas from Marshall County, West Virginia, for sale to the East Ohio Gas Company. On January 21, 1904, the principal office of the Company was changed from Oil City to Pittsburgh, Pa., and the plan of the Company was enlarged so as to include the production of gas throughout the State of West Virginia, and the marketing of gas in the following West Virginia cities: Parkersburg, Sistersville, Williamstown, St. Marys, Waverly, Murphytown, Smithville, Burnt House, Petroleum, Friendly, Paden City, Eureka, Belmont, Lima, Mannington, Metz, Glovers Gap, Wadestown, Littleton, Uniontown, Wileyville, Wolf Sum-

VIEW OF 18-INCH GAS LINE TESTED TO 775 POUNDS TO SQUARE INCH.

SHOWING 16 FEET OF HEAVY 18-INCH PIPE TORN BY PRESSURE TEST FOR 1,000 POUNDS.

mit, St. Joseph, Colliers, Smithfield, Wallace, Brown, Rinehart, Churchville, Pine Grove, Jacksonburg, Hastings, Fairview, Wise and Clarington, as well as for Akron and Cleveland, Ohio, Pittsburgh, Penn'a, and other cities. Its capital stock has been increased from time to time until the amount now authorized is $15,000,000. It has a number of small gas engine pumping stations at different points in West Virginia, with its main station at Hastings, where it operates a plant of half steam and half gas engine type.

The present officers of the Company are: A. C. Bedford, President; J. W. R. Crawford, Vice President; J. G. Pew, Vice President and Manager; Christy Payne, Secretary; George H. Jones, Comptroller; W. Y. Cartwright, General Superintendent; John B. Tonkin, Treasurer.

THE GULF REFINING COMPANY.

The Gulf Refining Company, incorporated under the laws of the State of Texas, with principal offices at Pittsburgh, Pennsylvania, was organized in 1901, immediately after the great Lucas gusher on Spindle Top announced the discovery of the Texas Oil Fields. Within a month after the bringing in of this well the Gulf Refining Company had already purchased a tract of over four hundred acres of ground upon which to build storage tanks and a refinery, near Port Arthur, Texas. During the month of February, 1901, the first pipe lines were laid, at the rate of over a mile a day, and work was immediately started on plans for a refinery. In the same month the construction of steel storage tanks was commenced and for over a year hundreds of men were employed in their erection.

As soon as the first storage tank was completed an experimental refinery was constructed. This experimental plant was utilized for some time in determining the various purposes for which Texas oil could be advantageously used. Later the experimental plant was dismantled and a refinery, with a capacity of 7,500 barrels per day, was erected, on the water front, near Port Arthur.

PLANT PORT ARTHUR TEXAS

PLANT OF THE GULF REFINING

The history of this plant, which is the largest independent oil refinery in the United States, is one of continued development. The capacity of the plant has been increased from 7,500 barrels per day, in the beginning, to 30,000 barrels per day. The plant covers approximately 500 acres of ground. It includes 92 stills of all kinds, having an aggregate capacity of 71,000 barrels; 11 agitators for treating oils, of an aggregate capacity of 21,000 barrels; 175 working and storage tanks of an aggregate capacity of 2,250,000 barrels; besides cooper shops, barrel houses, case and can factories, plants for making and restoring sulphuric acid, boiler shops, machine shops, pipe shops, carpenter shops, car repair shops; also store building, bakehouse, boarding house and 46 dwellings for the use of its employes.

The refinery is running Oklahoma, Caddo and Texas crude and employs over 500 men.

Upon the decline of the Texas oil fields, the Gulf Pipe Line Company was organized for the purpose of constructing a pipe line from the refinery at Port Arthur to the Glenn Pool, Oklahoma, a distance of 450 miles. The capacity of the main line which was originally 14,000 barrels per day, has been increased by additional pumping stations and loops to a present capacity of 22,000 barrels per day.

The route of the line is mostly an air line. The work of pipe laying was started February 13, 1907, and was completed August 13, 1907, exactly six months later. The first oil was pumped from Watkins Station in the Glenn Pool August 15, 1907.

The country traversed presented a number of difficult and peculiar engineering problems. A spur of the Ozark Mountains, 1,200 feet high, had to be crossed, and for miles through this section there was no soil, the ditch being blasted into solid rock. The rainiest winter for years caused serious inconvenience, and numerous shallow, prairie streams delayed the construction until enough pipe lengths could be screwed together on the near shore, a windlass rigged up on the far shore and the jointed sections pulled across. Streams like the Neches River and Sulphur Creek were spread over bottoms miles wide.

The directness of the course adopted required the hauling of practically all of the pipe, from railroad unloading stations, for distances in some cases as much as thirty-five miles, and in many instances the heavy sections of pipe, weighing 600 pounds each, had to be carried long distances on the shoulders of the laborers, owing to the roughness of the country traversed.

More than 1,500 laborers were employed in the work, divided into ten gangs. A

COMPANY AT PORT ARTHUR, TEXAS.

schedule of more than two miles per day was figured out, and so accurate was the rate of progress, as estimated in advance, that when the gaps were closed it was found that the different gangs had finished their work no more than four days apart on the average.

The main distributing stations of the Gulf Refining Company are located at Boston, New York, Philadelphia, Pittsburgh, Tampa, Atlanta, New Orleans and Houston. Throughout the South local distributing stations are quite generally established, principally in the States of Texas, Louisiana, Mississippi, Alabama, Georgia, South Carolina, Florida, Tennessee and Arkansas.

The company owns and operates, through one of its allied corporations, 693 tank cars. Through another allied company it operates a fleet consisting of eleven ocean going vessels with an aggregate carrying capacity of 242,000 barrels, the most prominent of which is the SS. Oklahoma, the largest tank steamer ever built in the United States, having a cargo capacity of 61,000 barrels. In point of size, this steamer ranks among the largest in the oil carrying trade in the world and is 1,800 tons larger than the next American built oil steamer. This fleet is supplemented by eleven bulk oil barges for river and inland water deliveries.

In addition to the refinery products marketed at home, the Gulf Refining Company has built up a very large export trade. During the year 1909 the export business of the Company aggregated over 2,000,000 barrels.

The Gulf Refining Company manufactures three grades of illuminating oil, known as Radium, Lusterlite and Sunburst. These oils are of superior quality and are made to meet the legal fire tests of the home and foreign markets. The illuminating oils sold under the brands above mentioned also give excellent satisfaction in oil stoves and heaters.

The Company manufactures four grades of naphtha, or gasoline, as follows

Stove Gasoline, for domestic use in stoves; also used largely by cleaners, manufacturers of rubber goods, etc.

Motor Gasoline, an excellent article for automobiles, having given satisfaction wherever used.

Painters Naphtha, used largely by painters, varnish makers, oil-cloth manufacturers, etc.

Peerless Engine Naphtha, which is used throughout the country by many automobile owners, and on account of its volatile nature and superior qualities is now being extensively used by some of the most prominent automobile maufacturers for testing their machines in the factory.

This Company also manufactures a variety of cylinder, steam engine, gas engine, dynamo and machine oils, together with a line of lubricants especially adapted for automobile use; the popularity of these oils is due largely to their high viscosity, low cold test and freedom from carbon; also asphaltum oil, used for fluxing and other purposes, and asphalt of various grades, used for roofing, roofing papers and street paving.

The Gulf Refining Company is the largest producer, with the exception of the Standard Oil Company, of Gas Oil, supplying some of the largest plants in the United States and Europe. The Company also has a large and growing Fuel Oil trade, supplying many of the important railroad systems in the Southwest; also many manufacturers in Texas, Florida and the Mississippi Valley. For eight years past this Company has furnished a large percentage of the Liquid Fuel used by the British Admiralty in the war vessels of that Nation.

Through other allied companies, the Gulf Refining Company controls a large area of producing territory in Oklahoma, Texas and Louisiana, thus assuring a sufficient and uninterrupted supply of crude oil for its refinery and fuel oil business.

The Company has recently erected for its own use an extensive office building at Beaumont, Texas, and maintains offices at Boston, New York, Philadelphia, Pittsburgh, Atlanta, Houston and New Orleans, as also an European office in Paris, France.

The present officers of the Gulf Refining Company are, W. L. Mellon, Chairman of the Board; Geo. S. Davison, President; George H. Taber, General Manager of Manufacturing; G. R. Nutty, General Manager of Sales; R. B. Mellon, Treasurer, and W. J. Guthrie, Secretary. The general offices of the Company are all located at Pittsburgh, Pa. Mr. F. C. Proctor, of Beaumont, Texas, is General Counsel.

THE PHILADELPHIA COMPANY.

A large part of the natural gas, electric light for illumination and power, illuminating gas and street railway service of Pittsburgh and the surrounding territory in Allegheny County, Pennsylvania, is furnished by the Philadelphia Company, of Pittsburgh, and its various subsidiary corporations. This Company began its operations as a distributor of natural gas, October 1, 1884, and its growth was so rapid that within a few years it was supplying natural gas to mills and residences in Pittsburgh, Allegheny and other adjacent cities and towns. The supply at first was obtained in fields adjacent to the consuming district but with the growth of the Company new territory in other States was sought and pipe lines ample for all needs of the Company's great consuming district were laid to distant counties and other States.

The business of the Company was confined to natural gas distribution until February, 1899, when the scope of its operations was broadened by the purchase of the Allegheny County Light Company, which furnished a large part of the electric current to domestic consumers in Allegheny County; the Chartiers Valley Natural Gas Company, the Pittsburgh Consolidated Gas Company, which supplies Pittsburgh and adjacent territory with artificial gas for illuminating purposes; and the United Traction Company, which operated street railway lines in Pittsburgh and Allegheny. In January, 1902, additional street railway properties in Allegheny County were acquired, giving the Company a very comprehensive system, reaching all important sections of the county. In 1905, the Beaver Valley Traction Company, operating street railway lines in the Beaver Valley and in the Ohio River Valley, was purchased.

In its natural gas operations the Philadelphia Company controls approximately 1,000 producing oil and natural gas wells, about 3,000 miles of pipe lines reaching important adjacent fields and the most populous consuming centers, and it supplies nearly thirty-eight billion cubic feet of natural gas annually to over 110,000 consumers in its territory. In twenty-four years to March 31, 1911,, the Philadelphia Company expended for gas and oil wells, transportation pipe lines outside of the City of Pittsburgh, pumping stations, telephone lines and tools, $18,684,000, no part of which was charged to its capital account.

The directors and officers of the Philadelphia Company are: James H. Reed, James D. Callery, H. J. Bowdoin, George E. McCague, Edwin W. Smith, Patrick Calhoun, B. S. Guinness, Russell H. Boggs, George E. Tener and M. H. Furlaud. President, James H. Reed; vice President, James D. Callery; Secretary, W. B. Carson; Assistant Secretary, J. L. Foster; Treasurer, C. J. Braun, Jr.; Assistant Treasurer, J. W. Murray; Auditor, C. S. Mitchell; General Manager, Joseph F. Guffey; General Superintendent, W. L. McCloy; General Purchasing Agent, J. H. Reed, Jr.; General Contracting Agent, S. B. Stewart; Land Agent, John Gates, Jr.

The same officers are in charge of the Consolidated Gas Company, which supplies Pittsburgh with illuminating gas.

The Pittsburgh Railways Company operates 600 miles of street and interurban electric railway lines in Allegheny, Washington and Westmoreland Counties, and the lines of the Allegheny County Light Company, furnishing electric current for light and power, extend to every populous section of Allegheny County.

UNION NATURAL GAS CORPORATION.

The Union Natural Gas Corporation, Farmers Bank Building, Pittsburgh, Pa., was incorporated in May, 1902. It supplies natural gas to about 95,000 domestic and manufacturing consumers through its underlying companies in Central and Northern Ohio and in Northwestern Pennsylvania. Its sources of supply are in Ohio and West Virginia and in McKean and Elk Counties, Pennsylvania.

OFFICERS AND DIRECTORS FOR YEAR 1911.

DIRECTORS.

T. N. Barnsdall,	H. McSweeney,	P. W. Lupher,
G. T. Braden,	Jos. Seep,	W. W. Splane,
E. P. Whitcomb,	W. A. Shaw,	Harry W. Davis.

OFFICERS.

T. N. Barnsdall..President
E. P. Whitcomb................................Vice President and General Manager
W. R. Hadley...Secretary and Treasurer
Geo. R. Prink.....................................Assistant Secretary and Treasurer

EXECUTIVE BOARD.

T. N. Barnsdall,	E. P. Whitcomb	G. T. Braden

THE FEDERAL OIL AND GAS COMPANY.

The Federal Oil and Gas Company was organized in January, 1909, under a Delaware charter, with an authorized capital of $1,000,000. The company was organized for the purpose of purchasing and operating producing oil properties.

Immediately after its organization it took over one of the Barnsdall properties, commonly known as the Whitcomb holdings, near Nowata, Oklahoma, consisting of some four thousand acres, upon which there were one hundred and five producing wells. To this property was soon added that of the Dawson Oil Company, located in the same vicinity. By successive purchases lots Nos. 39 and 194 of the Osage Reservation, together with the properties of the Cherokee Development Company, the Georgie Bella Oil Company and the Coody Oil Company, have been acquired. Through these, with other minor purchases, together with the development of the property already owned, the company is now in the possession of leaseholds to the amount of some twelve thousand acres, upon which there are two hundred and seventeen producing oil and gas wells, together with three hundred and fifty acres of land in fee through which the company derives the royalty from fifty-five wells.

The original officers of the company were C. G. Kiskaddon, President; Alex. Campbell, Vice President; E. W. Moore, Treasurer, and Perry A. Shanor, Secretary. These officers still retain their respective positions with the exception of Alex. Campbell, who has been succeeded by W. A. Chase of Nowata, Oklahoma. The directorate of the company consists of the following gentlemen:

Hon. J. K. Tener, President First National Bank, Charleroi, Pa.
W. J. Gilmore, President W. J. Gilmore Drug Co., Pittsburgh, Pa.
W. McK. Smith, Banker and Oil Producer, Washington, Pa.
Hon. J. M. Galbraith, Judge, Fiftieth District, Butler, Pa.
Gordon Montgomery, Publisher, Pittsburgh, Pa.
C. G. Kiskaddon, Attorney-at-Law, Pittsburgh, Pa.
W. A. Chase, President Producers State Bank, and Oil Producer, Nowata, Okla.
Elmer W. Moore, Attorney-at-Law, Pittsburgh, Pa.
Theodore Hoffman, Oil Producer, Pittsburgh, Pa.
R. F. Whitmer, President, Wm. Whitmer & Sons, Philadelphia Pa.
Theo. F. Meyer, President Meyer Bros. Drug Co., St. Louis, Mo.
E. Harry Porter, United States Marshal, Beaver Falls, Pa.
Perry A. Shanor, Secretary, Federal Oil & Gas Co., Pittsburgh, Pa.
W. F. P. Lofland, Dover, Delaware.

The general offices of the company are located in the Frick Building Annex, Pittsburgh, Pa. The company also maintains offices at Bartlesville and Muskogee, Oklahoma.

INDEX

GENERAL.

BIOGRAPHICAL.

COMPANIES.

www.ingramcontent.com/pod-product-compliance
Lightning Source LLC
Chambersburg PA
CBHW081143270326
41930CB00014B/3024